The Lobster Coast

The Lobster Coast

REBELS, RUSTICATORS, AND THE STRUGGLE FOR A FORGOTTEN FRONTIER

Colin Woodard

VIKING

VIKING
Published by the Penguin Group
Penguin Group (USA) Inc., 375 Hudson Street,
New York, New York 10014, U.S.A.
Penguin Books Ltd, 80 Strand,
London WC2R 0RL, England
Penguin Books Australia Ltd, 250 Camberwell Road, Camberwell,
Victoria 3124, Australia
Penguin Books Canada Ltd, 10 Alcorn Avenue,
Toronto, Ontario, Canada M4V 3B2
Penguin Books India (P) Ltd, 11 Community Centre, Panchsheel Park,
New Delhi–110 017, India
Penguin Books (N.Z.) Ltd, Cnr Rosedale and Airborne Roads, Albany,
Auckland, New Zealand
Penguin Books (South Africa) (Pty) Ltd, 24 Sturdee Avenue,
Rosebank, Johannesburg 2196, South Africa

Penguin Books Ltd, Registered Offices: 80 Strand, London WC2R 0RL, England

First published in 2004 by Viking Penguin, a member of Penguin Group (USA) Inc.

1 3 5 7 9 10 8 6 4 2

Maps drawn by Jojo Gragasin, Logan Design Group LLC

LIBRARY OF CONGRESS CATALOGING IN PUBLICATION DATA
Woodard, Colin, date.
The Lobster Coast : rebels, rusticators, and the struggle for a forgotten frontier / Colin Woodard.
p.   cm.
Includes index.
ISBN 0-670-03324-3
1. Atlantic Coast (Me.)—History. 2. Frontier and pioneer life—Maine—Atlantic
Coast. 3. Atlantic Coast (Me.)—Social life and customs. 4. Atlantic Coast (Me.)—
Biography. 5. Maine—History. 6. Frontier and pioneer life—Maine. 7. Maine—
Social life and customs. 8. Maine—Biography. I. Title.
F27.A75W66 2004
974.1'044—dc22   2004041496

This book is printed on acid-free paper. ∞

Printed in the United States of America
Set in Electra
Designed by Francesca Belanger

For my grandfather,
Weston Neal Andersen
He chose Maine.

Acknowledgments

The Lobster Coast is largely a work of synthesis and as such owes a great deal to the work of hundreds of chroniclers and archivists, historians and journalists, naturalists and biologists, archeologists, genealogists, and art historians, letter writers and purveyors of oral tradition. I have cited these in the comprehensive references published in the back of this volume; those wishing to read further on the various topics and issues raised in this book will also find a short list of recommended titles. Readers should be aware that I have altered some of the quotes from seventeenth- and early eighteenth-century sources to reflect modern standards of punctuation and, in rare cases, spelling, to ensure that they are comprehensible to contemporary readers.

I am extremely grateful to all the people who took the time to share their opinions, wisdom, or expertise with me. While I haven't named all of them here, most appear within these pages. Thanks to each and every one; I couldn't have written this book without them.

Several people went above and beyond the call of duty to help me along the way. On Monhegan, Tralice Bracy contributed enormously to my understanding of island life and directed me to some outstanding archival sources. Barbara Rumsey of the Boothbay Region Historical Society pointed me toward several fascinating research avenues; her *Colonial Boothbay* also helped focus my attention on the coast's Scotch-Irish heritage. I also am indebted to novelist Sanford Phippen of Hancock for helping this Waterville-born writer better understand the nuances of life Downeast. A special thanks also to Bob Steneck of the University of Maine's Darling Marine Center for taking an entire day out of his schedule to show me around the bottom of the sea, as well as to lobstermen Zoe Zanidakis, John Murdock, David Norton, Harvey Crowley, and Jennifer Elderkin for helping me learn what goes into catching lobsters from the surface.

The Lobster Coast also benefited from the advice and suggestions of experts in a variety of fields: Carl Wilson of the Maine Department of Marine Resources, James Acheson of the University of Maine at Orono, David Platt at the Island Institute, and William Barry at the Maine Historical Society Library, which became my second home during much of this past winter. George Irvine, Wendy Bellion, Samuel Loewenberg, Larry Plummer, and Julie Lehrman all took the time to read earlier drafts of these chapters and offered invaluable advice and criticism; many thanks. Any shortcomings that remain are, of course, my own.

I am also grateful for the support and assistance of librarians and staff at the Portland Room of the Portland Public Library, the research library at the Maine Historical Society, the Maine Folklife Center at the University of Maine in Orono, the Monhegan Historical and Cultural Museum, the Wiscasset Public Library, the Library of Congress in Washington, D.C., and the Oliveira Memorial Library at the University of Texas–Brownsville, which helped keep this project alive during a difficult period on the U.S.-Mexico border.

I am continually thankful for the support and advice of my agent, Jill Grinberg, and for the thoughtful suggestions and editorial guidance provided by my editors at Viking, Rick Kot and Hilary Redmon. I also remain grateful to editor William Frucht, whose enthusiasm for my first book, *Ocean's End*, made the rest of this possible.

Finally, heartfelt thanks to my parents, for edits, for encouragement, for everything.

Portland, Maine
December 2003

Contents

Maps appear on pages x–xi, 31, 55, 59, 93, 95, 121, 127

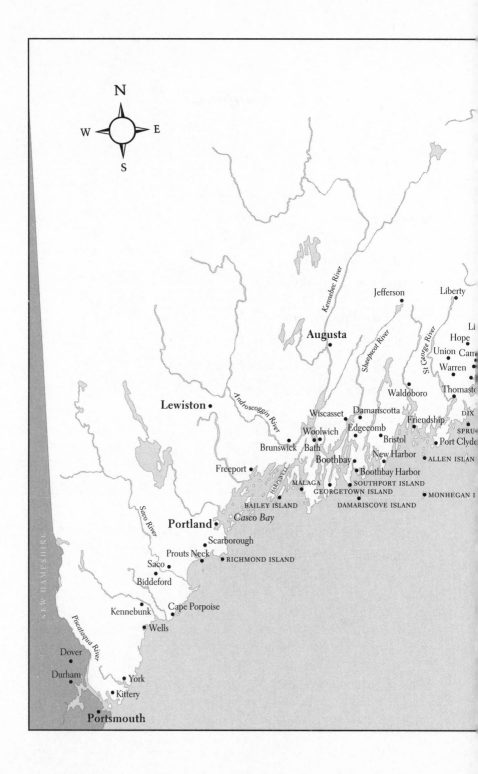

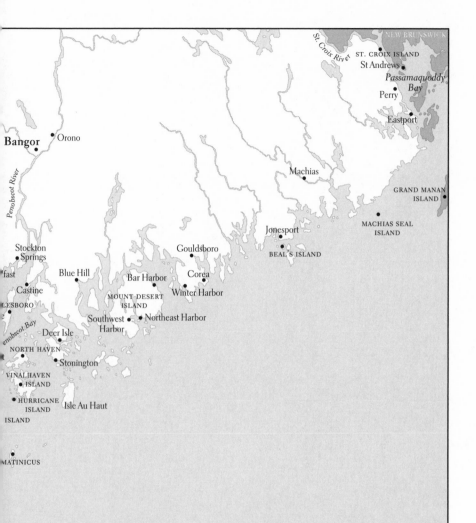

St. Croix River

NEW BRUNSWICK

ST. CROIX ISLAND

St Andrews

Passamaquoddy
Bay

Perry

Eastport

Bangor

Orono

Penobscot River

Machias

GRAND MANAN
ISLAND

Jonesport

MACHIAS SEAL
ISLAND

Stockton
Springs

Gouldsboro

BEAL'S ISLAND

fast

Blue Hill

Bar Harbor

Corea

Castine

MOUNT DESERT
ISLAND

Winter Harbor

LESBORO

Southwest
Harbor

Northeast Harbor

enobscot Bay

Deer Isle

NORTH HAVEN

Stonington

VINALHAVEN
ISLAND

HURRICANE
ISLAND

Isle Au Haut

ISLAND

MATINICUS

THE COAST OF MAINE

0   10   20   30

MILES

PART ONE

The Island

Monhegan

In winter the *Laura B.*, the mail boat to Monhegan Island, is usually fairly empty. A handful of islanders gather in the small aft cabin, warming themselves by the tiny black stove, while their groceries and shopping bags chill on the deck alongside rows of propane tanks and other large island-bound parcels. Mailbags rest in the starboard cubbyhole, protected from the elements, which can be extremely assertive during the fourteen-mile crossing from the mainland. From November to April, the *Laura B.* is the only link to the mainland for Monhegan's sixty year-round residents, making the round-trip journey from the tiny fishing town of Port Clyde only three times a week.

But on this last day of November, the *Laura B.* is packed with people. There are nearly as many people on board as live on the island this time of year, most of them mainlanders on their way out to help friends and family prepare for the most important day of Monhegan's year. Tomorrow, December 1, is Trap Day, the day Monhegan's lobstermen begin their unique, winter-only lobster season.

At a time of year when most of Maine's seven thousand lobstermen have hauled up their traps and brought their boats around to secure winter anchorages, Monhegan's fourteen lobstermen are getting ready to set their traps for the first time since spring. Once the fishermen have set their traps, they'll continue fishing through the dead of winter, braving ferocious weather and subzero temperatures that often leave their twenty-eight- to forty-foot boats encased in frozen spray. The lobstermen can handle this with the help of a sternman or two, but on Trap Day they need all the help they can get moving their heavy traps down to the town wharf. There are only twenty aging, beat-up pickups on the island, but each lobsterman needs to get a gang of six hundred traps, weighted metal cages weighing forty to fifty pounds apiece, out of their backyard, down the hill, and stacked up on the town wharf where they can be loaded onto the lobster boat. It can't be done much beforehand because the island's 8,400 traps can't fit on the granite wharf. Even if they did fit, they'd make offloading the *Laura B.* next to impossible. So, just before Trap Day, the entire village and dozens of mainlanders turn out to move the traps in the maritime equivalent of a barn-raising ceremony.

I'm on my way out to help Zoe Zanidakis, the island's only female lobster boat captain and onetime proprietor of the Monhegan House, one of the island's three summer inns. But there's a problem. About two months ago, Zoe quit answering her phone. She stopped picking up her cell phone and left e-mail and answering machine messages unreturned. It was as if Zoe had dropped off the face of the earth. After failing to track her down through several mutual acquaintances—nobody seemed to know where she was—I decided to board *Laura B.* as planned and track her down on the island. After all, no Monhegan lobsterman would ever miss Trap Day, least of all a ninth-generation islander like Zoe. Monhegan lobstermen make or break their season in the first few weeks of December, harvesting lobsters in an area that has not been fished in six months. But Trap Day has a ritualistic importance that transcends dollars and cents. "It's like cleaning the slate," one islander explained to me. "We all come together to get the boats ready and any of the crap and hard feelings that have accumulated in the community are wiped away." As we pass Allen Island and begin the final, seven-mile open ocean crossing, I'm certain Zoe is out there on the gray, humplike shape looming on the horizon.

It's a mild day for Maine in early winter—forty-five degrees and almost sunny, with still air and gently swelling seas—so many of the passengers spread out on deck, lounging amid the luggage, propane, and building supplies. I join them, and halfway up the port rail I find Billy Payne, who runs one of the island's two small stores. Billy, tanned from a vacation in South Carolina, tells me Zoe is nowhere to be found. "They say she's in a movie out in Hollywood," he says, breaking into an understated smile. "But nobody seems to know for sure."

The *Laura B.* lolls along, unperturbed by the swells. She's nearly sixty years old, and her wooden hull is only sixty-five feet long, but she was built for tougher chores than the Monhegan mail run: running soldiers and ammunition around Pacific bases during the Second World War. Slowly, steadily, Monhegan grows before us, its features becoming more detailed with each passing minute. First the rocky cliffs emerge from their forested crown. Then the forest reveals its inner anatomy of pine, spruce, and fir trees, straight and tall on the island's interior, stunted or dead along the exposed headlands. Guillemots and other cold-loving seabirds flutter over the primeval scene.

At first only one or two houses are apparent, poking out from the forest like lost children, along with the lighthouse tower, which sticks up from its hilltop like a ship's funnel. But as we round the island's northern tip and head down the western shore, the village slowly reveals itself. A cluster of wood-shingled houses, fish houses, and boat sheds stand on the gentle hillsides facing the shore. There are two hundred all told, but as we approach the harbor it's clear that most of the buildings are boarded up for the winter.

We slip past the nasty ledges guarding the north entrance and into the harbor, or what passes for one. Monhegan, a sausage-shaped island two miles long and three-quarters of a mile wide, doesn't have a single deepwater cove or inlet in which one can protect so much as a skiff. All it has is Manana, a small grass-covered hump of rock that protrudes from the sea alongside Monhegan like a whale calf cuddling next to its mother. Monhegan's lobster boats are moored in the narrow passage between the two islands, an anchorage as uncomfortable as it is beautiful. The four-hundred-yard-wide passage is well protected by the tall islands on either side, and the ledges at the narrow north entrance afford reasonable cover from northeasterly winds. But the harbor is completely open to the south, and in a southwesterly storm the seas race through the harbor unimpeded. During particularly fierce winter storms, waves have crashed through low-lying parts of the village, but the lobster boats themselves ride the tempests out on their heavy moorings.

We enter the harbor and come alongside the town's heavy granite wharf. Stacks of lobster traps are already growing at the base of the wharf, and one of the town's aging pickups is driving down the dirt road, piled high with more traps to be unloaded. But as we tie up and begin collecting our bags from their pile on the foredeck, the first thing I notice is the camera crew.

The three-man crew has set up a tripod-mounted camera and a big pole-mounted mike right on the edge of the wharf to film the mail boat's arrival. The height of the tide is such that the camera is pointed right in our faces, and a couple of people pause to stare at it as we head down the gangway. "Just move along," one of the cameramen barks, waving us along with a gloved hand. "Pretend we're not here." I try but just up the hill from the wharf I encounter a giant boom crane, poised to capture Trap Day action on the wharf. As I stand, gaping, the pickup pulls alongside me.

I drop my bags and start stacking lobster traps.

A burly, red-faced man in a flannel shirt has climbed to the top of the truckload of traps, stacked six-high in the same inverted ziggurat pattern farmers use for hay bales, which makes sense since the traps are approximately the same size and weight as a large hay bale. He passes traps down to the four of us on the ground and we carry them, in turn, to the growing stack on the wharf belonging to that particular fisherman. It's not hard to tell which traps go with which stack. Each lobsterman has already rigged his traps, and every second or third trap has a buoy and a coil of rope inside. The distinctive main buoys are painted in the unique color pattern of their owner, in this case white with an orange top and matching orange and white spindle. Later, when the traps are deployed and the buoys are floating on the surface, there will be no confusion as to whose traps are whose. It quickly becomes evident to me that the traps with the buoys in them are much heavier than the others. These "headers" are the first to be hauled up in the strings of two or three traps used on the island. Often these are more heavily weighted than the other traps in their string, serving as the anchor for the other traps they are attached to, called "tailers."

The truck is empty, and the four people who came down with it jump in the back and start riding up the hill for another load. We haven't yet spoken a word apart from "got it" or "over there." Another truck rolls in, loaded with traps containing fluorescent pink buoys topped with a black ring. The scene repeats itself. By the time the *Laura B.*'s crew has finished hoisting the heavy cargo onto the wharf with the boat's gantry crane, truckloads of traps are already waiting to be piled up in her landing zone. After an hour or so, the same trucks begin reappearing with fresh loads of traps. The men and women in the respective crews start acknowledging my existence the second or third time around. We shake our introductions with gloved hands. One couple is from Port Clyde and attended Georges Valley High School at the same time I was at a track and basketball rival a few hours to the northwest. Another guy turns out to be from Boothbay and knows my father. As we stack traps I ask if anyone's seen Zoe. I get all sorts of answers.

"Out to help Zoe? Haven't seen her since October," a taciturn sternman tells me. "They say she's doing stunt work out in California." A middle-aged resident assures me she's acting in her own movie and that that's why the film crew is here, sleeping in Zoe's house at the top of the hill. "No, no, no," a third islander asserts. "She's in Australia with that actor Russell Crowe." After hearing variations of these and other stories throughout the day, I feel like I've stepped into a novel cowritten by the ghosts of Franz Kafka and the Brontë sisters.

After a teal and white truck comes down to the wharf for the third time, the driver introduces himself. He turns out to be my host, John Murdock, a lobsterman in his mid-forties who also runs one of two year-round bed and breakfasts on the island. "Colin!" John laughs. "Was wondering where you were. Welcome to Monhegan! When we get this unloaded, toss your bags in and we'll show you your room." Fifteen minutes later I'm in the back, bouncing up the hill with a couple of John's friends.

We pass the imposing Island Inn, its windows boarded up for the winter and a film crew on the lawn, round a corner at the crossroads, and pull up in front of John's rambling house. John's wife, Winnie, shows me to my room, where I dump my bags and change footwear before heading around back to where John's traps have been stacked all summer, waiting for this day. A second stack belongs to his nineteen-year-old son, Ben, who has his own friends out on the island helping. But Ben has been distracted by a problem with his boat's engine, and most of his six hundred traps are still sitting in the backyard. Half of John's stack has already been moved down to the wharf.

By early evening, the wharf is stacked so high with traps that no more can be safely added. A narrow passage to the wharf's boat ramp passes between the fifteen-foot-high towers of green-, black-, or yellow-coated metal traps. A few boats come alongside and take on twenty or thirty traps for the first run, scheduled for the following morning. After that, the wharf grows quiet as most islanders turn in early in preparation for the manic day ahead.

⌒⌒⌒

The next morning I awaken to the news that Trap Day, like so many Maine winter events, has been postponed by Mother Nature. It had been blowing at thirty miles an hour from the southwest for much of the night. It was quiet now, but the wind had driven a heavy swell into the unprotected mouth of the harbor that would make loading traps from the wharf more difficult than it was worth. Monhegan's lobstermen, who make all-important decisions collectively down at the Stanley fish house, had decided to hold off for a few hours. They were meeting again at eleven to decide if they would go out in the afternoon.

It's an unseasonably warm fifty-five degrees, and the road down to the wharf is turning muddy, with pools of water accumulating in the ruts left by the town's little fleet of trucks. All that warm air hanging over the forty-degree water has created another hazard. A pea soup fog is flowing slowly over the village, whose clapboard houses drift in and out of the gray mist. Despite the towering piles of traps, I can't see the wharf until I'm almost standing on it. Inside the traps, the fluorescent paint on the buoys glows as it refracts in the swirling fog. I walk through the narrow canyon between the traps and peer out to sea. I see only two of the fourteen lobster boats in the harbor, their sterns piled high with traps. Manana, just two hundred yards away, is completely invisible, though the foghorn on her far side cries out plaintively from time to time. Big swells crash into the wharf's granite blocks every few seconds, and their splash sizzles on the ocean surface like bacon in a frying pan.

There's no breakfast place on Monhegan this time of year, but there's fresh coffee down at Billy Payne's store. Billy isn't there when I come in, but he's left a pad of receipts on the counter for patrons to fill out. Some have weighted theirs down with little piles of change and banknotes. Rita White, an elderly lady who once managed not to visit the mainland for seven years, is playing solitaire at one of the store's little booths, and a couple of lobstermen are shooting the shit by the coffee thermoses. Somebody's collie is napping on the floor. I greet people good morning, which seems to take everyone but the dog aback, as if they have gotten out of practice since the summer people went away. Rita sizes me up at a glance. As is often the case in Maine, I'm not sure if I've passed inspection, but she nods assent to my sitting opposite her to drink my coffee.

The lobstermen are speculating on the result of the upcoming fish house meeting, and there's general agreement that the swells won't die down before nightfall. Problem is, tomorrow is Sunday, and a few of the captains observe the Lord's day of rest. Traditionally, Monheganers don't start their season until everyone is ready. If somebody has engine trouble or a sick relative ashore, fishing is postponed until they can start too. But a number of years back, the fishermen by the coffee thermoses recall, the majority decided to start the season on a Sunday, and some of the older fishermen watched them leave from the beach. "Didn't do relations much good on the harbor for a time," one recalls.

As if on cue, pastor Ted Hoskins comes into the store. Hoskins, middle aged with a white sea captain's beard, is the minister of the Maine Sea Coast Missionary Society, a century-old organization that provides social services to Maine's fourteen year-round island communities, none of which have a resident cleric. The Harvard-educated son of Isle au Haut's summer minister, Hoskins usually makes the rounds to his far-flung flock on the *Sunbeam V*. He conducts weddings and funerals or just talks to islanders who, by midwinter, are getting tired of talking with one another. This weekend, however, Hoskins is on Monhegan to bless the fleet. So is fishing on Sunday taboo? I ask. "Oh, gosh, it depends on who you talk to." Hoskins laughs. "Some think it brings bad luck. But of course there are all sorts of things that fishermen say can bring bad luck." There's wearing blue clothing on the boat, some say, or carrying black bags. Others say you should never whistle (it calls the wind) or say the word "pig," which apparently dooms one's boat, as does setting down a hatch cover upside down. "Rest assured," one of the lobstermen by the thermoses pipes up, "if we go out, then the next time something breaks they'll say it was because we set out on Sunday, no matter how long from now that is." Everyone has a laugh about that.

The talk turns inevitably to lobstering and, before too long, to Zoe Zanidakis's mysterious absence. One lobsterman asserts that Zoe is definitely in California, working on her own movie. The film crew here on the island, he maintains, were probably part of the production and, in any case, were quickly making themselves unpopular. They should have had the common sense not to film on the dock as the *Laura B.* came in, he asserts, or to put their boom crane "in the way" on the hillside. A female fisherman—they don't like the term "fisherwoman"— chimes in that none of it surprises her. "Zoe's always wanted to be famous, she just needs to decide what she wants to be famous for," she says, arms akimbo over her rubber overalls. "I mean, Linda Greenlaw [of *The Hungry Ocean* and *The Perfect Storm* fame] was famous for being a fisherman. Zoe seems to be trying to be famous by *not* fishing."

On my way back from the store, the film crew appears out of the fog in front of me, right in the middle of the road, camera trained on my approach. "Keep coming! Keep coming!" the cameraman directs me, imperiously waving his hand. I ignore them as ordered, passing by their position without a glance. "Great," he says, still looking through his view finder in the opposite direction. "Call your agent," he quips, his back to me, as he jabs a thumbs-up in my direction with his free hand. The next time I look over my shoulder the crew has vanished in the mists, as if they had been but an apparition.

At midday, the island is still wrapped in fog, awaiting word from the Stanleys' fish house.

Built in the 1780s, more than 170 years after the first Europeans began fishing from here, the fish house is believed to be the oldest structure on Monhegan. Island fishermen have gathered to make important decisions here for a century or more, partly because of its convenient location. The little two-story structure perches on Fish Beach, one of two one-hundred-yard-long stretches of sand on the harbor, where the lobstermen land their skiffs and drag them ashore after a day of fishing. (Nearby "Swim Beach," which is protected from the strong tidal currents running through the harbor, is reserved for summer recreation.) But the real reason that the harbor's informal legislature meets here, rather than at some adjacent fish house, is probably be-cause the Stanley clan has owned it for generations. And for much of the last century, it is said, the Stanleys' word was practically law on the island.

Stanleys were living in Maine long before the American Revolution, and have been on Monhegan since 1883, when William Stanley came here to man the island's lighthouse. He bought the fish house in 1899, and passed it on to his son, Will, a master carpenter who built many of the homes in the village. William's grandson Dwight, how-ever, embraced lobstering, and by the 1940s had such influence over island affairs that he became known as the "king of Monhegan," a title occasionally ascribed to his son, Sherman M., who retired in the mid-1990s and now winters in Florida. The time of kings may be over, but Sherman's son Shermie Stanley, who serves as harbormaster, is still re-garded as the informal leader of the fishing community. Someday Shermie's son Dwight may take over at the fish house, becoming the sixth generation of Stanleys to do so.

The lobstermen now gathering at Monhegan's fish house effec-tively determine when, how, and by whom the ocean bottom for two miles around the island is lobstered. Until very recently, anybody hold-ing a Maine lobster fishing license was eligible to fish anywhere in Maine waters under Maine law. But in reality, each lobstering commu-nity controlled and defended its own bit of territory or "lobster bottom" from would-be interlopers. These traditional methods have proved remarkably effective at conserving the state's lobsters, virtually the only important commercial fish species that has not been fished into near-oblivion.

Monhegan, whose residents are particularly dependent on lobster-ing, has a long history of careful, long-term conservation. In 1907, the fish house took the unusual step of asking the legislature to ban lobster fishing within two miles of the island from July to December, initiat-ing the island's unusual winter-only fishery. In Dwight's day, the fish house mobilized to free undersized lobsters from the traps. Doug and Harry Odom, proprietors of the island store at the time, compelled one of their unwilling fellow lobstermen to comply by threatening not to sell him anything. In 1974, when Sherman Stanley and his brother

Alfred led the harbor, the island's lobstermen voluntarily imposed a six-hundred-trap limit on themselves when most mainland lobstermen fished twice as many. These conservation measures have kept Monhegan's lobster bottom unusually productive.

Things don't always go smoothly out on the water, however. From time to time, lobstermen from adjacent harbors get into disputes over where one's territory should begin and the other's end. A growing harbor occasionally tries to bully a shrinking one into ceding territory. Sometimes an aggressive fisherman or two will decide to fish wherever they want to, and woe to anyone who tries to stop them. First, warnings are left: a note left in an interloper's trap, a knot tied around the buoy. After that, things may escalate into full-scale lobster war. Traps are cut—sometimes hundreds of them in a single day. Sometimes shots are fired, and boats are rammed or sabotaged. It can, in the words of one lobsterman, get "really ugly, really fast."

A few years back, things were getting really ugly in the waters around Monhegan. In the fall of 1995, the mainland town of Friendship, sixteen miles to the northwest, the island's chief rival, launched a full-scale incursion into Monhegan's traditional territory. Much of this territory was not recognized under the 1907 state law, and Friendship, with a winter population nearly twenty times larger than Monhegan's, had been "pushing the line" especially hard since the late 1970s, when bigger, safer boats made it easier to tend traps this far from home. The invasion triggered a vicious lobster war. Traps were cut and, near the end of the season, vandals sank John Murdock's *Sea Hag* while she sat at her mooring in Port Clyde, causing $13,000 in damage. "When they came out here and boats started getting damaged and guns were being toted around, I thought: this is wrong and somebody in the state ought to know about it and ought to help us," recalls Doug Boynton, one of Monhegan's leading lobstermen. "We were pushed to the point where we felt if we didn't do something, we would lose our lobster bottom, and that would be the end of the winter community out here."

Things went from bad to worse. As tempers flared, Department of Marine Resources commissioner Robin Alden tried to negotiate a compromise, but it fell apart after a single season. The dispute had laid bare the gap between the laws of the state and the laws of the fisher-men. In the fall of 1997, Karl Pitcher and five other Friendship lob-stermen decided to use the state's laws to crack open Monhegan's waters once and for all. Using a loophole in the state's lobster regula-tions, the Friendship lobstermen attempted to register as legal mem-bers of Monhegan's winter-only fishing fleet, even though they kept their boats in Friendship. If the move went forward, it would have rep-resented a 50 percent increase in the number of lobstermen in the Monhegan Island Conservation Zone, more than enough to reduce each islander to a starvation-sized piece of the pie. Or, as Shermie Stanley put it at the time: "If ten more people come into your cran-berry bog, there's not going to be that many cranberries for you."

That's when Monhegan's lobstermen met at the fish house and de-cided to fight the law with the law. Rather than setting their traps in the winter of 1997, they bundled their families into their boats and took their case directly to the Maine state legislature in Augusta. If the laws weren't changed to keep nonislanders out of Monhegan waters, Doug Boynton told anyone who would listen, it would undermine the traditional territories system that had served the lobster industry so well. Harbors that hadn't managed their resource well, he told re-porters, shouldn't be allowed "to uproot as a posse and raid another area." John Murdock's family camped out in Augusta for much of the winter. His younger son, Kyle, age eight, proved one of the most effec-tive lobbyists, engaging senators in the elevators and paging for mem-bers of the house. "They basically just moved in," recalls Senator Marge Kilkelly of Wiscasset, who championed the islanders' cause. "Their absolute commitment to their way of life and the fact that the legislature literally controlled whether or not they survived really made an impression. At a point when we're losing many of the people in small island communities, here was a chance to help one that had done an incredibly good job of taking care of themselves for a long time."

The effort paid off. In February 1998, the legislature passed a law effectively closing Monhegan's grounds to nonislanders by a stagger-ing margin: 29 to 1 in the Senate and 132 to 14 in the House. On Feb-ruary 27, the islanders piled into the House gallery to watch Governor

Angus King sign the unprecedented law. "Maine has a long history of recognizing tradition," King said. The legislation, the governor proclaimed, was "nothing new" but rather "a recognition by the Legislature and the governor of something that's been the law for nearly 100 years."

In the three years since, the island's lobstermen say things have been going well. Tension with Friendship has been reduced, but they fear that's only because the lobstermen there are embroiled in some internal dispute of their own. "There's probably just a changing of the guard there now," John Murdock says with a chuckle. "Pretty soon the next generation of Monhegan-haters will come along, because they've been raised that way by their family members who hold them up on the shores of Friendship saying, 'See that island out there? It will all be ours someday!' "

But for now, the island remains in Monhegan hands, and at midday, word comes down from the fish house: given the swell and fog, Monhegan will start its season at 6:30 the following morning.

I get up at six the next morning and walk down to the dock. It is still night, but the skies have cleared. The moon, nearly full, casts shadows from the village houses and dances on the gently undulating ocean. There isn't another soul on the wharf, but the lobstermen are already out on their boats, turning on lights, squaring away gear, and moving out to "the line" at the harbor entrance. There they hover, bathed in moonlight, while Ted Hoskins reads the blessing of the fleet over the marine radio. I've heard that Shermie used to blow his whistle and the fleet would charge out cowboy-style, all hoots and hollers. But when the lobster boat's diesel engines fire up at 6:30, only a few whoops and yee-haws echo across the harbor. Then, red and green running lights twinkling on the water, the boats tear out of the harbor, disappearing around the back of Monhegan and Manana.

Over the next hour, the wharf changes from a tranquil observation post to a hive of frenzied activity. The whole town has turned out to get the traps down to the dock, onto the boats, and down to the lobster bottom. Trucks trundle up and down the hill with new traps to replenish the great stacks. Boats, sometimes two or three at a time, come up to the dock, and people begin scrambling like pit crews to get them under way. We form bucket brigades, passing traps down from trucks, across the wharf, and down to the lobstermen on the boats below, who stack them in astonishing piles that overhang the aft rail and extend all the way to the cockpit housing. We move countless bait tubs filled with crushed ice and bags of stinky five- to six-inch-long herring. All the while, little Kyle Murdock is issuing orders as he marches across the tops of the trap stacks in his green rubber boots.

In the early afternoon, people start arriving at the wharf with food for everyone. In between unloading trucks and loading boats, we munch on apples and muffins, fill our cups with coffee from the thermoses, and down slices of hot pizza from the North End Market. While snacking I learn that the film crew has managed to piss off the wrong people and has been told in no uncertain terms that they are not to film on the dock today. Apparently the cameraman got right in the face of some of the lobstermen while they were working on their engine. This was the sort of thing the crew might have been welcome to do had their social standing been higher. A gregarious photographer from Portland's Salt Institute for Documentary Studies, clearly in seventh heaven amid the traps, gained permission to shoot people up close. But under the circumstances, the film crew got a shot of an enraged fisherman, eyes bulging, screaming, "Get your fucking camera out of here and don't come back!" They had retreated up the hill to their boom and were trying to capture some of the action from there. In Maine, a bad attitude can get you a long way in the wrong direction.

By four o'clock the sun is setting and the stacks of traps are vanishing like snowbanks in springtime. Doug Boynton is the first to finish, his crew marching off the *Alice B.* and up the hill like mock heroes. "Out of the way," someone jokes. Doug tells me it's been the smoothest Trap Day he's ever seen. An hour later it's nearly dark, but the temperature still hovers at fifty degrees with a clear navy sky and flat calm. We load the thirty traps onto *Sea Hag* and John Murdock invites me to hop onboard for the last set.

We head out of the harbor through the north passage. It's that magical twilight time when the fading sky transforms the ocean into a mesmerizing silver-blue kaleidoscope. The bow wave appears almost fluorescent as we power out beyond Manana. Holden Nelson, the new owner of the Monhegan House, helps out by impaling the bags of herring on the long, skewerlike baiting needles used to bait the traps. When John reaches the spot where he wants to deploy the first traps, he throttles us down to a near-stop. Chris, John's sternman, goes back and forth to the stern a couple of times, placing a header, then a footer trap on the starboard rail. Chris flips the doors of the header out and, as we drift forward, throws the buoy and rope out into the water. Holden slips bait into each of the traps, and John ties them together with a type of nylon rope that floats, preventing it from hanging up on the bottom. At John's signal, Chris tosses the header overboard. John guns *Sea Hag* forward, balancing the tailer on the rail with his spare hand. A few seconds later, the rope linking it to the sinking header trap has played out and John shoves the tailer overboard. A few moments later he slows again and the crew repeats the process. For John, spacing is everything. "I want to be able to haul a trap, take the lobster out, bait it, set it back, and as I'm going out and all the ropes are rushing overboard then, within seconds, I'm onto the next one and hauling that in," he explains. "No need to be looking all over the place for your next buoy, especially on rough days when they get harder to find, or when you get older and your eyesight gets a little worse."

When the last tailer drops overboard we turn back toward the north end of Manana. A gannet, a great white coldwater seabird, soars over the boat, checking us out. In a lifetime in Maine, I've never seen one on our coast, but John says that out here he sees them all the time in the winter. The bird does a little loop and soars off to the southeast and into the fading sky.

Back in the harbor, as Holden and Chris begin cleaning up, John glances over the moorings, taking attendance. Every lobsterman is accounted for, their boats hanging off their respective moorings and their skiffs rowing toward or already pulled up on the beach in the shadow of the fish house.

Only one mooring lies conspicuously empty, the one with *Equinox* painted across its top, the one belonging to Zoe Zanidakis.

I'd met Zoe on Monhegan several months earlier, at the height of the summer tourist season. I was researching this book, and a number of acquaintances suggested I speak with her while on Monhegan. In a state where the ties between land and families remain strong, Zoe had rock-solid Monhegan credentials. Her mother's family, the Bracketts, had been on the island for more than a century and had run the Monhegan House for more than seventy years. Zoe, a single mom, grew up on the island, attended its white clapboard one-room school, and raised her son, Ron, here. Like most islanders, she had one foot in the fishery, and one in the summer tourist trade. She'd been lobstering for twelve years, building her way up from an old thirty-foot gasoline-powered lobster boat to the *Equinox*, a fast, forty-foot Young Brothers diesel. For many summers she'd run the family's inn and restaurant, but the previous winter she'd sold it to Holden and started taking fishing parties out on *Equinox*, which was specially rigged for the purpose. Now she was promoting a novelty calendar, "The Lobsterwomen of Maine," in which she was featured as Miss March. "Come on out," she said. "I'll take you fishing."

The day before our appointed meeting, I caught one of the boats out to Monhegan. In summer, there are plenty to choose from: six round-trip boats a day running to the island from Boothbay, Port Clyde, and New Harbor. The *Hardy*, a double-decked excursion boat out of New Harbor, was packed with day-trippers, eager to hike out to the hundred-foot-high cliffs on the back side of the island. The crossing was balmy, almost serene. At the dock, the island's trucks were waiting to transfer luggage of short-term guests like myself to the Island Inn, Monhegan House, or Trailing Yew. The infirm could catch a ride in the truck's cab, but everyone else just walked up the hill and down the dirt roads to their given lodgings. The two hundred or so cottages in the village were open for the season, flower boxes hung from the windows, occupants seated in Adirondack chairs on the porches or the fresh green grass on the lawn. In the half-mile walk to Monhegan House, I passed three painters working at their easels capturing, respectively, the grassy hump of Manana, lilies planted along the base of a summer porch, and the weather-beaten profile of an old fish house, recently converted to summer lodgings. I passed a cadaverous-looking

Englishman near the entrance to the island's tiny post office and was sure I'd met him before; I later learned this was Eric Clapton, whose elegant sailing yacht *Blue Guitar* was moored among the lobster boats, the Union Jack ensign hanging from the sternpost. When I reached Monhegan House, my luggage was waiting for me on the porch steps. I carried it in to the reception desk, where Holden Nelson said hello, told me how to get to my room, and promised to check me in later. People came and went through the swinging screen doors, some pausing by the stone fireplace to peek at today's *New York Times*, which had arrived from the *Hardy* with my luggage. The restaurant—one of two on the island—was gearing up for lunch service, while future patrons passed the time on the rocking chairs out on the porch, watching people walk past on the main road. A truck went by maybe once or twice an hour and traffic noise consisted of conversation and the quiet padding of people's feet.

In summer, the village seemed crowded. Indeed, the resident population quadruples to around 240 in summer, twice that if hotel guests are added to the tally. In the early afternoon, when the waves of day-trippers reach their crescendo, there can be as many as 1,500 people on the island, enough to tax the tiny community's water supplies and trash collecting abilities. In the height of summer, many residents feel overwhelmed by the tourist onslaught. When some of the boat companies added extra boat trips a few years back, Billy Payne closed his store early and posted a sign on the door protesting the island's "population explosion." But others say it's not the sheer numbers that trigger resentment; it's the minority of short-term visitors who can't seem to grasp that they've arrived in a real, living island community. A few think they are coming to a resort like Newport or Nantucket, and arrive at the dock with golf clubs and tennis racquets (there are no facilities for either) or evening wear or high-heeled shoes (which don't mix well with either the dirt roads or the rustic ethos of the established summer community). But the most dull-witted think they're visiting a theme park like Colonial Williamsburg or Disneyland. Monheganers have awakened to find day-trippers wandering around their kitchens and living rooms and have apprehended them picking flowers in the backyard. "Where is the T-shirt shop?" one such person asked me that summer, and stood agape and confused at the notion that there wasn't such an establishment in the village. In fact, I informed her, apart from Billy Payne's store, the North End Market, and Black Duck— Barbara Hitchcock and Pam Rollinger's tiny gift shop—there was no shopping on Monhegan at all. She looked at me in horror and, after a long pause to gather her wits asked, desperation in her voice: "Well, why do people come *here* then?"

The answer, of course, lay all around her. We stood in the center of one of the great anomalies of early-twenty-first-century American life: an ancient, self-governing village, essentially classless and car-less, whose homes, sheds, and footpaths appear to have thrust themselves out of the wild and arrestingly beautiful landscape. There's a deep sense of rootedness on Monhegan unusual in our young, frenetic nation, a sense of knowing where you are, who you are, and where lies the critical fulcrum that balances what is individually possible with what is communally desirable. And it is certainly one of the few places in the world where the scions of great moneyed families are socially and politically outranked by persons who earn their living stuffing rotten herring in nylon bags in an effort to ensnare large bottom-feeding bugs. It is, despite its many problems and challenges, an embodiment of Thomas Jefferson's utopian vision for this country: an egalitarian republic of small, self-sufficient producers, where democracy is practiced directly by the citizens, and aristocratic privilege is unrecognized or unknown. It's an anachronism, to be sure, something better suited to a tiny community on a remote island than to, say, New York City. But being immersed in it pulls at something deep within our civic being, a hint of a simpler, perhaps nobler world that might have been, but can never be again.

But it was Monhegan's staggering beauty that first attracted outside visitors. As elsewhere on the Maine coast, painters were the first to discover this island's arresting scenery, and over the years many of the major figures of American painting have been drawn here. Stroll around Monhegan and you find yourself walking through one painting after another. There are the fish houses Robert Henri captured on a stormy day in 1903. Nearby Fish Beach is the setting for George Bellows's *Cleaning Fish* (1913), Eric Hudson's *An Island Harbor* (1926), and Samuel Triscott's late afternoon *Fish Houses and Beach* (c. 1910). From the hillside, on a cloudy, snowy winter's day, there's the vista of cottages and Manana that Andrew Winter painted in 1944. Nearby, the great bronze bell that Jamie Wyeth immortalized in *Bronze Age* stands near the lighthouse, though when he painted it in 1967 it was perched on Manana's grassy southern bluff looking out over the open ocean. Follow the footpath that snakes along the cliffs toward the back side of the island and you'll pass a rounded granite promontory littered with the crushed shells of crabs dropped by the seagulls who captured them; it's the setting for Jamie's *Gull Rock*. Farther up the shore you'll reach the bold cliffs and headlands that have been painted by Henri and Kent, George Bellows and Edward Hopper, Jamie, Andrew, and N. C. Wyeth. Their paintings attracted other painters and, ultimately, cottagers of all sorts searching for a pastoral setting to while away the summer months.

It's a scenario that was repeated in communities all along the coast of Maine in the late nineteenth and early twentieth centuries. Artists discovered beautiful places and, in painting them, put them on the maps consulted by the East Coast's summering classes. What Henri and Kent did for little Monhegan in the early twentieth century, Thomas Cole and Frederick Church did for mountainous Mount Desert Island in the mid-nineteenth. Fitz Hugh Lane discovered the gentle beauty of Penobscot Bay's outports and islands—lighthouses perched on rocky points beneath gentle hills. Hopper made the lighthouse at Seguin Island into a subconscious national icon, while Winslow Homer did the same for the rocks of Prout's Neck, near Portland.

Many of those who saw these paintings wanted to see the places they depicted. Most were wealthy, some shockingly so. In the mid-nineteenth century, they started coming to the Maine coast, staying in boardinghouses and, shortly thereafter, the new resort hotels that sprang up all the way from the sandy beaches of southern Maine to the stark mountains of Mount Desert. These pioneering "summer people" liked what they found. America was in the midst of the Industrial Age, its cities noisy, polluted, and swelling with immigrants with strange customs, languages, and religions. In coastal Maine, comfortable city dwellers saw a simpler time, when New England was still rural, agrarian, and Protestant. Here they could "rusticate," recharging their batteries amid this dreamy world of the recent past, where noble, simple Yankee folk went about their lives, in harmony with their surroundings, God, and one another. And so the "Maine Myth" was born: a story of a stalwart, self-sufficient place that has somehow dodged the excesses that plague the rest of the country and retained the more connected, humane life that characterized the lost Golden Age of the early American republic. Maine, the state tourism board would later declare, was the way life should be.

The reality was somewhat different. Like other parts of New England, Maine's few industrial towns were attracting large numbers of immigrants—Irish and French, Italians and Finns, Ukrainians and Jews. But the summer folk rarely saw these places, most of which were located well inland to harness the power of the state's many rivers. They came instead to the southern beaches or the tiny outports of Maine's central and eastern coast, places that have defined Maine for outsiders since the days of John Smith. And along this coast, the population was surprisingly homogenous; most inhabitants were descended from their community's original seventeenth- and eighteenth-century English and Scotch-Irish settlers. If a summer person visited a Barters or Beal's Island, he or she could count on meeting members of the Barter or Beal clan there. There were Pendletons on Pendleton Point, Dyers on Dyers Neck, and McFarlands on McFarland Shore. Certain families had been on this coast long enough, undisturbed by major immigrations, to have developed an almost European conviction that there was a blood-and-soil link between the people and the land. They were, in large part, Protestant, though the Puritans' old Congregational Church had never had a monopoly on power here as it had for more than a century elsewhere in New England. Though there were plenty of echoes of New England's Puritan past in the design of the town greens and old meeting houses, there was much that didn't jibe with classic Yankeedom. Even the dispersed settlement patterns upon the land and the names of the oldest towns were patterned after places in the English West Country, as opposed to the Puritan strongholds of East Anglia.

But the greatest misconception—one that remains today—is that the coast's people lived in an elevated state of preindustrial simplicity. Few of Maine's summer residents of the late nineteenth century were aware that the coast's economy, once vital, had recently undergone a thorough and devastating collapse. Maine wasn't preindustrial; it had just been deindustrialized.

A few decades earlier, Maine ice, granite, lumber, salt cod, and foodstuffs filled the docks of the United States' Atlantic ports, themselves clogged with Maine-built sailing ships. But those goods had been displaced by refrigerators and cement, by fresh fish caught by Gloucester steamships and cheap lumber and foodstuffs moved from the Midwest by the nation's railroads. Practically overnight, all of Maine's industries collapsed. As a result, the coast was losing population. The wild meadows and weather-beaten farmhouses the summer people found so picturesque had been abandoned by their owners, thousands of whom had moved to Ohio in hopes of a better life. With the offshore fishing industry in decline, residents of many coastal towns tried to build an industry around the only resource they had left: the summer people themselves.

Coastal Maine's unusual geography contributed to its rise to economic prominence and its collapse into backwater. The coast is only 293 miles long from Kittery, in the far south, to Eastport, the easternmost town in the United States. But the shoreline is so jagged and convoluted that, stretched out, it would span 4,568 miles, more than that of the rest of the East Coast combined. When the shorelines of the coast's 4,617 islands are included, this figure jumps to more than 7,000 miles, a distance greater than that between Boston and Tokyo. North–south rivers, bays, and inlets carve the mainland into a series of peninsulas, which resemble the coast's islands in that they are isolated by land, but easily accessed by sea.

In the eighteenth and early nineteenth century, when much of America's commerce moved north to south along the eastern seaboard in the holds of sailing vessels, this ragged shoreline was an enormous asset. There were countless deepwater anchorages in the inlets, rivers, bays, and islands, many located adjacent to the oak, pine, and pitch needed to construct wooden ships. Productive fisheries bred able seamen, and granite, ice, and other goods could often be loaded directly

onto ships from the places where they were extracted. But when commerce shifted onto east–west railroads, the coast's diffuse population
and frequent river crossings discouraged rail development, as did its
geographic position, perched north and east of the rest of the nation.
After the Civil War, the state fell into a malaise so profound that, in
many places, it has yet to recover. As late as the 1970s, Maine's people
were the poorest in the nation when incomes were adjusted for the
cost of living. It's an economic tragedy that has shaped generations of
Mainers, adding a layer of bitterness and irony to what was already
there.

From the start, living in Maine was a serious undertaking. The
early settlers had to contend with the rigors of life on this first frontier:
a short growing season, a long, bitter winter, rocky soils and strong
ocean tides. While Europeans had been living in Maine for more than
a decade by the time *Mayflower* arrived in Plymouth, settlement here
was stunted by nearly a century of warfare with the coast's true natives,
the Wabanaki Indians. There were times in the seventeenth century
when the settlers had no real rulers at all and had to make do entirely
on their own. Surviving here required competence, self-sufficiency,
and a willingness to assist and cooperate with one's neighbors. And
while many survived, cobbling together a living by a combination of
farming, fishing, hunting, and woodcutting, there were few great fortunes to be made. While indentured servants manned the estates of
the Virginia and Maryland aristocracy, the Maine coast was an almost
classless society in which any person in good standing with his neighbors could expect equal respect and treatment from anyone else. To a
surprising extent, this remains the case today, especially in the few
nooks and hollows that outsiders have yet to discover.

As a group, native Mainers have a reputation for being skeptical of
outsiders. While most visitors have a wonderful time here and return
again and again, many also report bewildering encounters with locals
in which they feel they were treated like trespassers, even invaders.
Here they have run afoul of Maine's peculiar historical experience.
For English Maine began as the feudal preserve of a wayward English
knight and, out of the wreckage of his plans, wound up being annexed
by Massachusetts to become a colony of a colony. Like that of many

colonial people, this experience was a mixed, but ultimately negative one. The Boston elite ruled the "District of Maine" in their own interests, employing graft, corruption, and cronyism to hatch multimillion-acre land speculation schemes on the Maine coast. This prompted eighty years of armed resistance by the people living on these lands, who were determined not to lose their freehold land to the emerging New England aristocracy. This rebellion helped end Massachusetts's formal overrule in 1820, but much of the state remains in Boston's economic orbit. Even today, Mainers can be pridefully defiant of any perceived attempt by an outsider to "lord over them." This can be as simple as a flashy visitor behaving obnoxiously at a restaurant or as serious as a newcomer trying to take control of the annual town meeting, where community residents still vote on every line in the budget by a direct show of hands.

For example, a few years back, the credit card giant MBNA set up shop on the central coast, and company executives sought to generate local goodwill by donating money to worthy causes. As part of this campaign, company executives decided they wanted to support the tiny libraries of Maine's fourteen surviving island communities. But the executives, accustomed to thinking big and moving fast, quickly ran afoul of Maine pride. Their plan was to jump in their over-the-top luxury helicopter, fly out and "evaluate conditions" at each island library and then decide what they wanted to do to help them. Stefan Pakulski of the Rockland-based Island Institute cautioned the executives against this approach; islanders associate sudden helicopter landings with emergencies and, besides, one doesn't impress Maine islanders by flashing conspicuous wealth in their faces. The executives were flummoxed, but agreed to a compromise: they would instead take *Affinity*, the company's opulent seventy-foot yacht, with its uniformed crew and tasteful Hinckley-built picnic boat. Pakulski's growing concern turned to dread when, one Sunday morning, one of the MBNA guys called him to say: "We're taking a helicopter out to Matinicus this afternoon, do you want to come along?"

Matinicus, eighteen miles east of Monhegan, is the remotest and toughest of Maine's island communities, a craggy rock, two miles across, located so far out to sea that its fifty-one residents have no scheduled boat service and must get their mail flown in by small aircraft. On a coast populated by no-nonsense people, Matinicus has a reputation for not tolerating any nonsense. So it was with a sinking sense of doom that Pakulski found himself hurtling toward the island's tiny grass-and-gravel strip in the leather-lined interior of the MBNA chopper. Soon they were landing, without permission, on the island's private airstrip, where the updraft of the helicopter's rotors drove chunks of gravel toward the two tiny island-owned planes which, Pakulski later learned, had fragile fabric skins. The pilot shut off the engine and, as the rotors slowly spun to a halt, Pakulski and the MBNA party stepped out of the helicopter. A woman had been standing beside a station wagon, watching the landing; presumably, she was their ride to the schoolhouse meeting the MBNA guys had apparently set up at the last minute. But as they approached, the woman jumped into the car and drove away. "There was nobody around, nobody there at all," Pakulski recalls. "They're all suit-and-tie, looking pretty good, and we're standing alone on this dirt road and nobody knows exactly where to go." After an uncomfortable spell in which no welcoming party materialized, the group began walking into the village. "There's no cars, no people, not a sound, and as we start to go by houses I started having this feeling like we were being watched, that there were people behind the curtains looking at us, this strange group of aliens." When they finally found the school, the station wagon was sitting there in the parking lot. Ultimately, the meeting went forward, but in the end Matinicus was the only island community that decided they did not want MBNA's money. Perhaps they'd looked their gift horse in the mouth and found it lacking.

On the second morning of my summer visit to Monhegan, I wandered down to the dock. Zoe pulled up at the ramp a few minutes later in *Equinox*, her long, broad, sky-blue lobster boat. "Hop on board," she said to me and another guest, a vacationing schoolteacher with an insatiable penchant for fishing. "Let's see if we can catch a foolish codfish or two." A few minutes later we were speeding out of the harbor's wide southern entrance and into the afternoon sun.

    Zoe had her boat outfitted for summer fishing charters. The work deck seemed bare without the tools of the trade: spare lobster traps and buoys, plastic tubs filled with squishy herring, and the big metal water tank in which lobsters are stored after capture. Instead, Zoe had tucked away a dozen fishing poles and lifejackets and, under the semienclosed wheelhouse, a basket of snacks and a cooler of refreshments. The boat was surprisingly comfortable, not least because Zoe had designed it with summer charters in mind, expanding the wheelhouse and adding places where extra passengers could sit. *Equinox*, like so many other things on the coast, was designed to toil through the winter and host visitors in Tourist Season.

Monhegan has been receiving summer visitors since the late nineteenth century. In those days Zoe's great-great-grandfather, George A. Brackett, pursued herring and mackerel in his steam-powered seiner *Novelty* in the spring and fall and set hooks out for cod and other groundfish in the winter. But in the summer, *Novelty* became a party boat for summer guests, with Brackett at the helm, "playing up the role of salty Down Easter to the hilt," according to one historian. It was his daughter, Zoe's great-grandmother Elva Brackett, who bought the Monhegan House in 1927, throwing the family into the center of the island's burgeoning tourist industry. Zoe grew up working in the hotel, and seemed hard-wired to be an accommodating host: friendly, fun, generous with her time and patient with the incompetence of her guests, as I learned when I managed to tangle my fishing reel on the very first deployment.

She also clearly loved Monhegan and its lifestyle. She spent most of her childhood on the island, an experience she says offers an incredible degree of freedom. "You hang out with more adults growing up out here and form a certain independence as a young child," she explained. "You leave the house in the morning, can see your parents for lunch or whatever, but you're on your own in a certain sense. I mean, you have guidance—I heard everything that Ron was into no matter what! But when school was out I was hardly ever at home—I was out on the beach or in the water or out in the woods rooting around somewhere." So it came as a shock when, at thirteen, she went to live with her father in New Jersey. "In city life there's nowhere to go," she recalled. "I felt trapped almost, confined like a wild animal in a zoo or something. I remember that very, very well." She came back to Maine for high school, but that meant living on the mainland, because Monhegan doesn't have one of its own. Like many islanders she ended up at Maine Central Institute, a boarding school in the farming country of central Maine which, while pastoral, still didn't feel like home. Before she could drive, Zoe rode her bicycle the eleven hours to Port Clyde when school was in recess. "To go from cows and chicken coops to the smell of the ocean was so welcoming. I'd be pedaling faster and faster, saying to myself, 'Get me there, get me there, get me there.'"

A few years later, Zoe was back on the island, divorced, with a young child. "Never went to college," she says regretfully, "but my mother always said I went to the College of Hard Knocks." There was little to do in winter. So, like a lot of people, she tried her hand at lobstering, serving as a sternman for Don Cundy. Some take to it, some don't, but Zoe fell in love with it. "There was the freedom—being on the ocean, dealing with the environment, which is harsh at times, but you adapt. It really made me feel alive, like I was really doing something that made sense." With support of friends, family, and established lobstermen like Cundy and Sherman Stanley, Zoe worked her way into the fishery, building herself into a successful, aggressive lobsterman. "I can't believe I have a fifteen-year-old son and have spent twelve years fishing. It seems like only yesterday."

I peered out the cabin windows. Along most Maine shores, brightly colored lobster buoys carpeted the water this time of year so thickly in some places that, if they were stepping-stones, one could easily walk across whole rivers and bays. Out here there was not a single buoy to be seen, and the ocean looked strangely empty without them. But as we passed beneath the great cliffs on the back side of the island, Zoe thought she saw something in the water. It turned out to be a small white toggle buoy, still attached to a worn-looking line that descended into the forest green water. The islanders lose a number of lobster traps during Monhegan's frequent winter storms, but some of them turn up weeks or months later. This string of traps had lost its main buoy—the line was frayed—but its subsidiary toggle buoy had kept it afloat but unnoticed, at the foot of Black Head, one of the back side's dramatic cliff-lined headlands. Zoe snagged the toggle with her boat hook and pulled the line into the boat. We'd unexpectedly had the chance to haul a lobster trap, albeit one that had been on the bottom not for several days, but for several months.

Zoe ran the line through the block or pulley that hung over *Equinox*'s starboard side and down to the boat's powered hauler, a specially designed wheel that does the once backbreaking work of pulling the heavy traps up from the bottom. A few minutes later, the trap broke the surface, covered in growth and dented a bit in one corner from a storm-driven tumble across the bottom. It turned out to be the only trap attached to the buoy, a "single" rather than a "double" or "triple." Once the trap was hanging from the starboard pulley, Zoe swung it onto the starboard rail and had a look at a plastic tag bearing the owner's license number. Most licenses have four- or even five-digit numbers, but this one read, simply, "1A," indicating the first license ever issued by the state of Maine. The trap belonged, then, to Shermie Stanley, who inherited his license from his great-grandfather, Charles Murphy, and might well pass it on to his son, Dwight. I was starting to understand why Shermie planned to name his new boat *Legacy*.

The trap had been on the bottom for months, so I was surprised to find two large lobsters waiting patiently in the back chamber of the trap, healthy apart from a patina of green algae growing on their shells. Zoe tossed the lobsters back into the water and brought the trap onboard. (Later in the day we would leave the $60 trap on the dock for Shermie to pick up.) Zoe spun *Equinox* around to the east and, backs to the island, we headed off into the wide, welcoming ocean.

Fifteen minutes later, Zoe slowed the engine to idle and tossed out an anchor. We were in open water, two miles from Monhegan and at least ten miles from anything else, but the anchor hit bottom only twenty feet down. "Allen Shoal," Zoe said good-naturedly, handing each of us a pole. "I usually have good luck here."

We dropped our lines in, leaving the reels open until we felt the heavy metal lure hit the bottom. Then we began "jigging," jerking the lure up off the bottom every second or two in the hopes of attracting the attention of a hungry cod. It's the technique used by the first European fishing parties who came here four centuries ago, except that in those days there were no rods, reels, or lures. Fishermen simply lowered baited hooks, hauling up monstrous four- and five-foot-long cod, hand over hand, one after another, until men or bait were exhausted. But times had changed. The three of us jigged for more than an hour, with only three fish to show for it. Two of them were little pollock who became impaled by their bellies when they passed over our bouncing hooks; they were doomed, so Zoe tossed them in a bucket for her cat. The other fish was a pathetic six-inch baby cod, a tiny miniature of the cod of lore, which weighed as much as 150 pounds. Zoe gently took the hook out of its mouth and set it back in the water where, after a shake of surprise, it vanished into the deep. Apart from the eviscerated pollock, we wound up returning to the island empty-handed.

Such a poor outing would have been unthinkable to any previous generation of fishermen. The first Europeans to visit these waters were shocked by the quality and quantity of the fish they caught almost every time they threw a hook in the water. There were nine-hundred-pound halibut and shoals of codfish the size and weight of a grown man. One early English expedition was so "pestered" by codfish in the Gulf of Maine that they reported being "forced to throw numbers of them overboard again." Captain John Smith described the region as "the strangest fish pond I ever saw" and noted that the Wabanaki Indians "compare their store in the sea to the hairs of their heads."

America originated in the pursuit of these fish. Encouraged by the accounts of early reconnaissance parties, French and English merchant adventurers set out to explore, colonize, and conquer the fishing grounds of the Gulf of Maine, a semienclosed sea stretching from Cape Cod to Nova Scotia, bounded on the north by Maine's rocky shores. It quickly became clear that the area that is now Maine had the most productive waters and the greatest supply of snug harbors, so it was here that European merchants built their first permanent, year-round outposts in what would later be called New England. English fishermen from the western ports of Devon, Dorset, Somerset, and Cornwall had been living at Monhegan, Damariscove, Southport, and other Maine islands for the better part of a decade by the time the Pilgrims landed at Plymouth Rock. When the Pilgrims were starving in the winter of 1622, it was Maine fishermen who saved them with a boatload of cod. Soon thereafter, the Pilgrims kept their colony alive

by coming to Maine to fish themselves. Later, the Puritans of Massachusetts Bay relied on cod fishing to finance the expansion of their
tiny colony, which through accident of history eclipsed, overwhelmed,
and eventually annexed its neighbors in Maine. For New England was
first ruled not from Boston or Plymouth, but from York, Maine, a tiny
fishing hamlet that English authorities declared to be the region's first
chartered city and seat of its governor and Anglican bishop. But it is
the winners who write history, and, through a series of strange and
largely forgotten events, New England came to be led not by West
Country nobles, loyal to the English church and crown, but by a
group of religious fanatics hostile to both.

But after helping to found New England, Maine's fisheries faded
in importance for a time. Most of the people who emigrated to Maine
in the colonial period were farmers, not fishermen. They came to
Maine, America's first frontier, in search of freehold land unavailable
in their hometowns back in England, Northern Ireland, Massachusetts,
or southern New England. There they would begin a long struggle for
local control of the land and sea that, in some respects, continues to
this day.

Maine's tradition of local control has deep roots. Some communities, like Friendship and Monhegan, look at one another with suspicion. In others, being "from away" can mean having been born in a
nearby town as well as New York or New Jersey. During an interview
with Mary Brewer, longtime editor of the *Boothbay Register*, I asked if
she had been born and raised in Boothbay. She began to nod yes, but
caught herself short, smile falling from her face. "I was raised here,"
she said sheepishly, "but I was born up to Miles," the hospital in
Damariscotta, ten miles to the north. I hope they don't hold that
against you, I joked, but Brewer, who'd lived in Boothbay all her life,
answered in all seriousness: "Oh, no, they know me by now."

Despite these extremely local allegiances, the towns and villages of
the Maine coast fall into three distinct regions, each defined by a
shared history, environment, and settlement pattern. There is a wide
variety of opinion as to where one region ends and the other begins.
But for clarity, I've settled on some specific definitions based on shared
history, which will be used throughout this book.

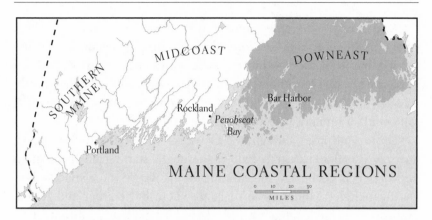

MAINE COASTAL REGIONS

Southern Maine, which extends from the New Hampshire border to just north of Portland, is by far the wealthiest, most densely populated part of the coast. It's the least characteristic region, with low, sandy shores, few islands and peninsulas, and long, deep historical and cultural ties to Massachusetts. It's the oldest part of the coast, the part with the oldest continuously inhabited towns, and the only section that remained populated throughout the horrid English-Indian wars of the late seventeenth and early eighteenth centuries. Maine's very oldest families trace their roots back to the early settlers of southern Maine towns like York, Kittery, Scarborough, and Wells, many of whom came from the English West Country. Today, however, it is often looked upon by other Mainers as "not really Maine," occasionally as an appendage of the corrupted, foolish societies to the south.

The Midcoast stretches to the western shores of Penobscot Bay and includes Monhegan, the Boothbay region, Pemaquid, Rockland, Camden, and Belfast. Rocky, island-strewn, it has long been the heart of the coast, site of the first fishing stations and of England's first full-fledged New England colony. But the tragic Indian wars cleansed the land of Europeans and set back their settlement plans by more than a century. Its reconquest was spearheaded by Scotch-Irish immigrants, many of whom were recruited by land speculators for their tenacious, warlike reputations. Later, these same families would lead eighty years of violent resistance to the land speculators themselves, an action that helped prompt Maine's secession from Massachusetts in 1820.

The often-used Maine moniker "Downeast" is a sailing term that refers to direction, not location. The prevailing winds on the Maine coast blow from the southwest in the warm months, so ships from Boston were able to run downwind as they sailed along Maine's north-easterly-trending coast. Thus they were said to be going "Downeast," a concept that remains with us to this day.

For our purposes, though, the Downeast coast refers to the rugged, sparsely populated eastern half of the coast, starting on the eastern shores of Penobscot Bay and running all the way to the Canadian border. It includes Mount Desert Island, where Bar Harbor and Acadia National Park are located, plus Machias, Jonesport, and Eastport. This was the last region to be settled by British subjects because it belonged to France until 1763. France never established much more than a garrison here, in large part because the region's colder climate, ferocious tides, and thin, glacially scoured soil made such undertakings difficult. The task of settlement fell to a great wave of land-hungry English and Scotch-Irish settlers who moved here from other parts of Maine and New England in the last decades of the eighteenth century. It was this movement that pushed Maine to the forefront of the American fishing industry in the first half of the nineteenth century. Most Downeast people discovered they couldn't survive by farming, and turned to the sea out of necessity. There they rediscovered the Gulf of Maine's incredible bounty, and helped establish the maritime way of life on the coast. But the Downeast coast's harsh conditions and remote location have always minimized both settlement and economic activity, and the region remains the poorest, least developed part of the Maine seaboard.

❧

Today New England's storied fishing grounds have been largely closed for lack of fish. Between 1980 and 2002, the region's haddock catch fell by 70 percent, halibut by 86 percent, and cod by 75 percent. Virtually every major commercial fish species—yellowtail flounder, red-fish, cusk, and hake—is in crisis, its numbers so depleted that state and federal authorities have imposed draconian restrictions on fishing. As traditional species collapsed, fishermen turned to creatures once derided as "trash fish"—dogfish, silver hake, even sea urchins and baby eels—only to see their numbers crash as well. Lobster alone has bucked the trend.

The fisheries disaster has undermined the Maine coast's working waterfronts and the way of life for thousands of families. From York to Bar Harbor and beyond, processing plants, fish piers, and boatyards have been replaced by waterfront hotels, condominiums, and yacht marinas. In the past, inshore fishermen might seine herring in the spring, trap lobsters in the summer, set hooks for cod and haddock in the fall, and man shrimp boats in the winter. Some years the mackerel runs would be strong, in others, menhaden. But now only lobster remains and most everybody is in it. The number of fishermen on the coast who rely on lobstering for the majority of their income has more than doubled over the past thirty years. Now the humble lobster carries an entire culture on the back of its armored shell.

Sherman M. Stanley has fished for most everything out of Monhegan at one time or another. He trapped lobsters hereabouts for nearly fifty winters, took parties jigging for cod and pollock in summer, and in other seasons did everything from mackerel seining to setting long lines of hooks for cod, pollock, and other groundfish. He says what's happened to the fish in his lifetime is a tragedy.

"When I first took charter parties in the 1950s and 1960s I could go to Allen Shoal and just load the boat up with fish," Stanley says, seated at a stool in his workshop and running his fingers through his trim white beard. "In spring I'd catch great big pollock from anywhere from twelve to twenty-five and thirty-five pounds. Codfish, Jesus Christ, I'd catch them all summer long and it would get to the point where we'd unhook them and let them go because the people would have all they wanted and I had five or six or seven hundred pounds set aside for the three hotels!

"Now it's a hell of a job to go catching fish, and in many cases it's the fishermen themselves who've ruined it," he says. "There's no reason at all that the finfish should ever have become depleted so badly except for waste. My friend Leslie Davis, he was an older man, and in the war years he went fishing out of Portland in a dragger. And he said they would run through windrows of [dead] fish. If [the dragger crews] were fishing for redfish they wouldn't keep pollock, cod, or haddock; it went right through the scuppers. He said they'd run through them for miles before they'd find redfish. I just hate to see stuff wasted like that."

The "draggers," large vessels that drag weighted trawl nets along the bottom to scoop up the fish that live there, are far more efficient at catching fish than smaller boats tending strings of baited hooks. But the technology carried the seeds of its own destruction. Unlike hook or trap fishing, trawl nets scooped up and killed virtually everything in their path, including baby fish and various bottom plants and animals that provided food or shelter to commercial fish species. "In the seventies the draggers used to stop by here in the spring to sell us bait," Sherman's son Shermie recalls. "We'd buy ten or twelve fish totes full of undersized flounders—I mean there were several hundred of them in one of these [laundry-basket-sized] things and they were killing them by the thousands each day. Codfish, haddock, they were killing everything and 'cause they were afraid that they'd lose one fish they would fish everything out and then sort it out on the deck, sell what they could for lobster bait and throw the other stuff over the side. That really put a hurt on the fish inshore." Shermie is visibly angry when he talks about this, in part because the resulting collapse took away a large part of his annual income, which he earned by setting long strings of baited hooks for cod and haddock. "Draggers killed them, but they made us suffer for it."

The draggermen have suffered too. Most have lost their boats, and many of those who hang on discourage their children from entering the fishing business. One thing is for certain: If and when the fish finally recover, draggermen will not be back to business as usual. Fishing technology is so good that fishermen are now perfectly capable of wiping out even the most prolific creatures. To have a healthy fishery in the long term will mean adopting techniques and technologies that are sustainable, which is what Maine lobstermen have been doing all along. At stake is more than just the health of an industry; it is the way of life of one of our nation's most distinctive and emblematic cultures.

During and after college, I lived for several years in Hungary, a fascinating country coping with the sudden collapse of the Soviet empire.

Many things about Hungary were quite different from my native Maine, but one aspect was immediately familiar. Hungarians, by and large, looked on resident foreigners with healthy suspicion. Who did we think we were, they asked, with our fancy clothes and plastic money, buying up goods and property, eating in restaurants that were, by local standards, outrageously expensive? Where did we get off, we arrogant Western folk, telling Hungarians how to run their businesses, fix their economy, reform their political institutions, and create meals with green vegetables instead of great cupfuls of tasty pork lard? "This is Hungary," people would often assert by word, gesture, or attitude, "and we Hungarians are in charge here, so don't you get any funny ideas about running the place." Many of my non-Hungarian friends still live in Budapest and most are not only fluent in Hungarian, they are married to Hungarians and sending their Hungarian-speaking children off to Hungarian schools. But they stay with the knowledge that they will always be foreigners, that they will never, ever be accepted as Hungarians, no matter how long they live there. Perhaps their children will be accepted, and certainly their grandchildren will be, should they stay on. Because, after all, almost every Hungarian you meet has a German or Romanian or Serbian or Slovak or Russian grandparent or great-grandparent back there somewhere. In the end, European nationhood isn't about race, it's about shared culture, values, and a powerful sense of covenant between people and the land.

When I was growing up in the 1970s and 1980s, Maine had a very similar ideology, one that, while diminished, still holds sway on much of the coast. In this way of thinking, one does not become a Mainer simply by moving here, establishing residency, and getting a driver's license. Nor can one call oneself a "native" simply because one was born and raised in the state. There's an old saying here: "Just because the cat has her kittens in the oven, it don't make them biscuits." Multigenerational family ties matter. I was born and raised in Maine and, even when I did not live here, have always considered myself a Mainer. But I'm not a "real" native because my father and maternal grandparents came here "from away" as young adults. If the native Mainer is a home-grown North American nationality, then people like myself are the first-generation immigrants, oven-born, but not verifiably biscuits. In Maine's more ornery quarters, newcomers are sometimes regarded not

as potential Mainers, but as foreign colonists, folks imbued with different values, tastes, and ideas from those practiced here. And, as those
"from away" are often perceived to have more money, education, and
political connections than their "native" neighbors, these colonists are
often suspected of wishing to "take over" the town and remake it in the
image of someplace else. One might regard all this as the reactionary
paranoia of an isolated, unworldly people—except that this is exactly
what has happened in many towns up and down the coast. As elsewhere in the world, the old is vanishing, and the new looks, sounds,
and smells an awful lot like an exclusive suburban subdivision.

‿‿‿

Despite being inhabited, on and off, since 1610, Monhegan has escaped many of the problems and divisions that affect the mainland.
The islanders—natives and nonnatives, summer and winter residents
alike—share a fierce commitment to upholding the island's wild landscape and the living, working character of its single village. They don't
want to end up like Nantucket, a leading fishing port that is now little
more than an island playground for the stupendously wealthy. Monhegan, through a combination of geography, wisdom, and dumb luck,
has maintained a sort of idealized vision of coastal Maine: a place
whose people, regardless of origin, appreciate and defend land and
culture against those who would remake it in the image one of Anywhere, USA's more upscale neighborhoods.

Consensus building is far easier here because there is no strong divide between natives and nonnatives. Whereas many Maine harbors
are dominated by people with multigenerational ties to the fishery,
most of Monhegan's fourteen active lobstermen are the children of
summer people. Dave Boegel, Matt Weber, and Lucas Chioffi all
summered on the island. Danny and John Murdock first came as
small children after their grandparents acquired a summer cottage in
the village. For Doug Boynton, whose father was a foreign service officer, the family's Monhegan cottage was the only U.S. home he'd ever
known until he moved into his first college dormitory. "I've still never
lived anyplace else in this country." He laughs. "Sometime I really
ought to visit America though." Now his brother also lives here, and
Boynton and Murdock children have made up nearly half the popula-

tion of the island school. The lines between summer and winter families have blurred and faded away into irrelevance. "There isn't the ethic that you have to have been born here or lived here for so many generations to be accepted," says Doug's brother, Bill, who managed the town's stripped-down government for many years. "I don't think it's because people are more enlightened, it's just the reality of living out here."

Unlike most coastal communities, Monhegan has been inoculated against sprawl and overdevelopment. Three-quarters of the island is protected by the Monhegan Associates, a land trust established in 1954 through the joint efforts of Sherman M. Stanley and cottager Ted Edison, son of the famous inventor. Edison foresaw a time when cottages, hotels, perhaps even golf courses and country clubs might spread all the way to the clifftops of Black Head and was willing to donate his own land to preserve the island's natural beauty and village character. "I figured the island can only support so much," Stanley recalls. "It seemed to me that it would probably be a lot better off not to have any large developments and condos and such out on the back side, 'cause people like to have a place to go and sit on a rock and paint or 'fugitate' or whatever they needed to do. Maybe I'm wrong, but I think we went the right way."

That decision has kept most of the island undeveloped, which has helped keep the community from outstripping its limited water supply or from introducing expensive novelties like police, fire stations, and paved roads. But in recent years it has also created a winter housing crunch, as more and more of the village's finite properties have been sold to wealthy summer residents. The winter population has been slipping for more than a decade, largely because young people are priced out of the housing market. Islanders agree that the lack of affordable housing is now the biggest threat to island life.

But the older generation has stepped in to help. Doug and Harry Odom, bachelor brothers who ran the island store for more than three decades and hauled traps until they were both in their late seventies, have sold several properties to young fishing families for a fraction of what the market would have borne. "We look at Boothbay as a good example of a place that's full of new people who own all the good spots and all that," says Harry, now in his late eighties and living with his brother in the mainland village of Damariscotta. "If you took these lots that we sold to [fishermen] and you had all summer people there then there'd be nobody to take care of the island in wintertime. That would be a mess."

Robert and Tralice Bracy were among their beneficiaries. Robert had been lobstering for several years and wanted to stay on the island, but the couple, who hail from Port Clyde and Thomaston on the mainland shore, found that island land was priced out of their reach. "If you're starting out as a young fisherman, you already have a huge investment in your boat and traps; and if you're investing in property as well, it's definitely a hard go," says Tralice, now curator of the Monhegan Museum, which is housed in the lightkeeper's house overlooking the village. Then the Odoms made them an incredible offer: the sale of a house lot near Burnt Head priced at a tiny fraction of what the market would bear. "It was a huge gift on Doug and Harry's part," says Tralice, whose new home was built for less than what a neighboring house lot recently sold for.

For his part, Harry Odom believes that, thanks to the land trust, Monhegan's unique community will persevere. "People'd love ta' buy places there on that wilderness land and on all those trails that are out there, but the [land trust] prevents that," he says. "Fifty years from now, I don't think it's going to change too much. It's nice to have it that way."

On the mainland, however, change is occurring at a staggering rate. With growth rates two to three times the state average, the counties of Southern and Midcoast Maine are losing their sense of place, rapidly transforming from a rural landscape of farms, woodlots, and working waterfronts to a sprawling suburban region of strip malls, subdivisions, and waterfront condominiums. Greater Portland had the worst sprawl in the northeastern United States in 2001, and the ninth worst in the nation. Statistics show that the majority of this growth is due to newcomers moving into the state. (In the year 2000, one in ten residents of most Southern and Midcoast Maine communities had been living in the state for less than five years; today there are few communities where nonnatives do not outnumber natives.) Coastal Maine, long considered a place apart, is succumbing to the forces of homogenization spreading from a once-distant megalopolis. It's an experience shared by people across the continent and around the world, as distinct cultures vanish, unnoticed, like the plants and animals of Amazonia.

Take the Boothbay region, for example. Boothbay, Boothbay Harbor, and Southport Island sit together at the end of a fourteen-mile-long peninsula at the heart of Midcoast Maine. Its many snug harbors and sheltered waterways put it on European maps very early on; Southport and other nearby islands were the sites of some of the first fishing stations, most predating the *Mayflower* voyage. Because of the persistent Wabanaki Indian resistance, the peninsula wasn't successfully settled until about 1730, when a tenacious band of Scotch-Irish settlers moved in and refused to yield. These borderlanders, descendants of the lowland Scots of *Braveheart* fame, gave the region a distinctive flavor that persisted right up to the last decades of the twentieth century. Look at a list of the first generation of Scotch-Irish and English settlers and most of the family names are immediately recognizable. In some cases, people with the same name still occupy land promised to them by an agent of the English crown in the early 1730s. More often, however, native families sold the last of their land a generation or two ago. The cost of buying or owning waterfront property has exploded in recent decades; locally generated incomes have not.

Barbara Rumsey, director of the Boothbay Region Historical Society, has long been concerned about the cultural transformation of the peninsula. It's not that new people are bad. People have been summering on the peninsula for 150 years and, as on Monhegan, many have stayed on, blended in, and minted new "native" families. Rumsey herself came as a child in 1952, attended local schools, and never left. But today's newcomers are different from those of the past. "The old summer people, the 'rusticators,' came here because they wanted to go blueberrying," she recalls. "Now people are moving here because it fills their lifestyle needs. They're attracted by the Y, the golf course, and the hospitals and they're totally oblivious to the cultural context they've arrived in. They don't even bother to learn to pronounce the 'Boothbay' correctly." It's said as one word, with the emphasis on "Booth," but some newcomers persist in putting the emphasis on "Bay," years after moving to the area. This amazes Rumsey, who recently started correcting some people on this point. "I guess I'm trying to give them the chance to integrate in the smallest of ways," she says, "to at least pay lip service to what already exists."

These attitudes are important because it's the newcomers who will shape the region's culture in the coming century. Curious as to whether the rate of cultural change was truly accelerating, Rumsey turned to the property tax rolls of Boothbay, the largest of the region's three towns. She counted the number of dwellings in various years between 1900 and 1999, then carefully determined if each was owned by a newcomer or native, which she defined as one who was born in the region or married to someone who was. The results were stark. In 1900, two-thirds of Boothbay's dwellings were in native hands. In 1950 that figure had fallen to about half, and in 1999 only one-quarter of the town's homes were owned by natives. Boothbay, a town where roots were long and deep, had become a community of transplants.

⁓

James Stevens, who passed away in July 2002, had particularly deep roots to this part of the coast. Sitting at the dining room table in his old Boothbay farmhouse some months before he died, he calmly related his children's ancestry, tallying the generations with his long fingers, painting the history of the Midcoast with his words. His wife, Evelyn, is descended from Stephen Larrabee, who moved to the shores of Casco Bay, near what is now Portland, in the first half of the 1600s, and was ambushed and killed on one of the bay's islands in the bloody Anglo-Indian conflict known as King Philip's War. His family traces its roots back to Massachusetts Puritans and the first wave of Ulster-born Scots who came to Maine in 1720. Stevenses were living on Georgetown Island, six miles east of James's farmhouse, when King George III ruled the Midcoast and Downeast Maine still belonged to Louis XV of France. James's great-great-great-grandfather Thomas Stevens owned a third of the revolutionary privateer *Black Prince*, which was lost in a 1779 naval engagement at Castine. Later generations served in the militia during the War of 1812 when eastern Maine was occupied by the British. After the Civil War, when summer people discovered the Maine coast, James's maternal grandfather ran summer hotels at Popham Beach, site of the first ill-fated English colony in New England.

James Stevens was born at Popham Beach in 1916, but at age four moved twelve miles up the coast, where his father became a cofounder of the Goudy & Stevens shipyard. Stevens grew up in the yard, playing around in the wood chips or putting plugs in the bungholes of the fishing and passenger vessels as they rested on the shipways. He worked in shipyards for much of his life, building minesweepers for the Navy during World War II, elegant yachts for the Mellons and Rockefellers in the 1960s, and state-of-the-art steel fishing trawlers for Rockland fleet owner Frank O'Hara in the 1980s. Along the way he launched a large flotilla of descendants: eight children, twenty-four grandchildren, and, by the summer of 2002, twenty-two great-grandchildren.

He has also watched the region transform, as newcomers arrived in ever-larger waves, each less interested in the region's character than the one previous. "There's been more change in this region since 1945 than there was from the American Revolution to the start of World War Two," he says. "Used to be that the same people lived in their grandfathers' homes and things like that. I'd go the grocery store and see a clerk and would have memories of their grandparents and things like that. I mean, you felt a warmth to the people you met every day. But now there's no feeling at all. For a local person like myself, you've got a whole population that acts and thinks and feels differently than you do." Even the character of the summer people has changed, as the family cottages have given way to time-share condominiums. The newcomers, he said, had "brought devastation to people like myself."

He looked out across the fields to the Damariscotta River, blue and inviting in the early summer sun. "It's very beautiful when you stop to think about it," he said of the farm he's lived on since 1955. "When I bought it you didn't think of things like that; you just took the shore for granted," he said with a smile. "Surprising the way things work out."

"I can't take it with me," he added after a pause, "but I'd like to keep it for as long as I'm alive."

While out on Monhegan that summer, soaking in the scenery made famous by Henri, Kent, Bellows, Hopper, and the Wyeths, it occurred to me that I'd never seen the rocky shorelines that Winslow Homer painted near his studio at Prout's Neck, a few miles from my Portland home. So one bright, frigid January morning I drove down to the little summer colony, perched on a little evergreen-covered point jutting out from the Scarborough marshes. I drove down the point's one road, past boarded-up summer cottages buried in snow, armed with a map marked with the location of the relevant stretch of shore. I was almost there when I rounded a corner and braked to a stop.

The road was barred by a gate with an electronic passkey reader. A great sign read:

WINSLOW HOMER ROAD
POSITIVELY NO PASSING
PRIVATE WAY
For Residents and Their
Guests Only

I should have known. Mainstream American attitudes toward shoreline access probably came to these southern Maine latitudes decades ago. Still, it was winter, and the place was pretty much abandoned. I put the car in park and started consulting my map, looking for a likely way to approach the shore. But, as I was contemplating a march over a nearby snowbank, a police cruiser pulled up behind me and flashed his headlamps. *Move on*, they said. He tailgated me right off Prout's Neck.

Homer, I decided, would have to wait.

For Bruce Reed, shoreline access isn't a matter of recreation or cultural heritage, it's essential for him to feed his family.

Bruce is a wormer and, like hundreds of other Mainers, makes his living digging bloodworms out of the oozy gray mudflats at low tide with a handheld hoe. Sport fishermen love to bait their hooks with bloodworms, which can grow to be over two feet long, with four tiny fangs and translucent bodies that reveal their blood-red body fluids. Worm diggers used to be the poor cousins of clammers, who dig in the same flats but with a different type of hoe and under far tighter regulations. Lobstermen traditionally looked down on the diggers as not quite fishermen, and draggermen looked down on all of them. But these days the draggermen are lobstering, the clammers are suffering from a shortage of clams, and bloodworms are big business. "Used to be in the state, more or less, but in the past couple of years there's been a big overseas market," Bruce explains as we drive through his hometown of Wiscasset, an old shipping town on the Sheepscot River near the base of the Boothbay peninsula. "Ship 'em to Europe, Spain, and so forth. That's where the most of the orders are from now. I don't know if there's bloodworms over there or not, but they seem to want ours." Demand has boosted the price—Bruce can sometimes get twenty cents for a single squirming worm—but I wonder if it's high enough given what diggers go through to capture these invertebrates.

We're on our way to dig some worms right this moment, in fact. In the back of the pickup, Bruce has a couple sets of thigh-high rubber wading boots, three different types of digging hoes (for various mud conditions), and an assortment of white plastic buckets to store the catch. I'm fortunate in that this is an extremely easy dig. It will be low tide in early afternoon, so there's no need to get up at an ungodly hour or stay up past one. It's a beautiful summer day, warm with clear skies and a light refreshing breeze, so no need to bundle up against winter storms. Best of all, we're just driving a few miles down Westport Island, a long, bridge-linked bolt of land that makes up the eastern shore of the lower Sheepscot River. Turns out bloodworms move around a great deal, so when the worms abandon the Midcoast, Bruce and his fellow wormers often pile into a pickup and drive all the way to far eastern Washington County three or four hours away. There the tide falls twenty feet or more twice a day, exposing the bottom of entire bays as far as the eye can see. The diggers will work two tides, napping in between, pile into the car, and drive back to Wiscasset. There they would sell their worms, head home for a shower and a bite to eat, and pile into the car to do it all over again. When the worms are on the Midcoast, the flats of Wiscasset, Boothbay, and Westport echo with Downeast Maine accents as the migration is reversed. I'm getting tired just thinking about this, and we haven't started digging yet.

After winding along Route 144 for a while, we pull onto a dirt driveway and down to the shore. We park on the edge of the turn-around because it's not Bruce's driveway. In fact, he doesn't even know the people that well, but says he waves on his way down to the water and they wave back. We pull on the waders, grab hoes and pails, and march through the woods to the shores of a slowly emptying cove. "Got it about right," Bruce says, surveying the tide's progress. Digging is all about timing. When the moon starts pulling the water out of the coves, a digger wants to be right there working the flat as it scrolls out from under the sea. That way, when the rarely exposed, rarely dug area finally appears, the digger is already there and can work it until the water starts forcing him back to shore, which is where he wants to be at the end anyway. Bruce leading the way, we march out onto the flats.

Our boots sink into the mud up to our ankles and sometimes nearly to our knees. Each step requires pulling one's foot out of the ooze, which clings like wet cement and only releases with a vacuum-sealed pop. By the time we're far enough out to start digging, there's a long trail of marks behind us, each a testament to a hard-fought battle to step out of the mud. I'm pretty much winded when Bruce bends forward and starts swinging his hoe, turning over the mud, and snatching bloodworms at a steady, determined pace. I start parallel to him and, despite his patient coaching, am repeatedly outsmarted by the wily worms. Bloodworms don't like to be exposed to the air, and a digger has to move fast to catch them before they bore away into the deep. They do this at an incredible pace, literally corkscrewing through the grainy ooze. Bruce intercepts most of them before they can get away; I do not. After a half hour I've discovered a number of never-before-used muscles, none of them very powerful, but Bruce is still chopping away, his progress marked in even patterns expanding across the flats. As we get farther from shore, he points out the telltale marks of a recent dig. Somebody's been here recently, and may have dug out the supply. Bruce hopes they didn't time the tide right and, another half hour later, he's relieved to see the marks don't make it to the deeper areas. He continues digging for another hour and a half, his hoe chopping down with the steady regularity of a southern chain gang.

As the sun gets lower in the sky, the cove is bathed in a magical gold glow, and the sea begins reclaiming the bottom. Bruce decides it's time to call it a day, and we loll through the mud to the rocky shore. We get the buckets out and start counting worms. Bruce has several hundred and pronounces it a decent day. I've managed to get a couple dozen. I have to talk him out of paying me for my worms, worth a fraction of what Bruce might have dug up if he weren't stopping to show me the ropes. At the end we have a large bucketful of worms, the envy of trout fishermen from Bigelow Stream to the French Alps. We clean up, march up to the truck, and head off to the dealer.

Though he's built for digging—short, compact, and wide-shouldered—Bruce's back is hurting. It's been hurting more and more each time he digs, in fact. Few clammers or wormers continue digging past age fifty, but Bruce is only in his mid-thirties. A car accident seems to have caused some lasting stress that's irritated by the work, and Bruce knows his digging time is limited. "I gotta get out of digging and the sooner the better, 'cause the more I dig, the more it's going to hurt." He shakes his head. "People love digging because you're independent. You don't have a boss. You can go out when you want to go, and people love that part," he explains. His father was a digger and Bruce has been doing it since he was thirteen. "If I'd known back then what I know now then I would have definitely been doing something else. But when you're young you don't think about later on. It's all right, I guess, if you have a spouse who works and has got good insurance, but my wife doesn't work and for me and the kids insurance is really expensive." He'd like to start his own business and get out of digging before his back gets any worse.

Then there's the matter of shoreline access. Maine law allows people to cross unposted private property, and in the past access to the flats was virtually a given. "Twenty years ago nobody cared, 'cause everyone knew the diggers and wouldn't think twice about you crossing their land to the flats," he says. "Now, though, it's a different matter." In addition to their lack of curiosity about Maine's traditions, people arriving from other parts of the country often have a very narrow view of private property rights. In recent years, just about every digger has found themselves shut out of a flat that their family had been digging for generations. The land changes hands from locals to newcomers, and the latter tend to get frightened when they discover burly, flannel-shirted strangers marching through their woods with nasty-looking metal implements slung over their shoulders. Diggers are frequently confronted by NO TRESPASSING signs or even sheriff's deputies responding to the panicked calls of a new homeowner.

A couple of years ago Bruce and his brothers followed the worms to

Islesboro, a ten-mile-long island in the middle of Penobscot Bay, three hours by car and ferry from Wiscasset. Bruce went to an area he'd dug in the past, parked the car on an unposted dirt road, and walked down to the flat to check for worms. There weren't any, so Bruce hiked back up to the truck. "So there I was, getting my boots and stuff off and a vehicle pulls up right in front of me, blocking me off," he recalls, a pained look in his eyes. "And this guy and lady are in the truck saying, 'There's no parking here and you're not allowed to cross here and I'm calling the town constable and having you arrested' and going on and on. Finally I said, 'Look, what do you guys think, anyway?! You rich people own this land and you won't even let us people who are trying to make a living get to the flats. All we want to do is just go there and make a living,' I says. 'I clean up after myself, don't make any messes, won't hurt your property any.' And she just kept running on at me, but finally let me go." He was shaking his head at this point, clearly upset by it all. "Well, the next day my brothers were getting ready to take the ferry and the lady comes up to them, thinking it was me, and says she's sorry. They said she apologized and was very nice and that they had a good conversation. She probably thought about it after I left. I mean, I wasn't nasty to the lady or anything, I just wanted to make my point across."

Not everyone thinks it over, however, and clammers and diggers are finding they have to invest in boats to ensure access to the flats. Bruce says some of the younger diggers haven't helped the cause, littering or laying rubber on property they visit. But most are respectful, he says, and are still running out of places to go. In Boothbay, James Stevens was one of the last large property owners to welcome diggers. It remains to be seen if future owners will follow his lead.

⌢⌣⌢

The winter of 2001–2002 was a difficult one for Monhegan's lobstermen. There were plenty of lobsters, and the winter was unusually mild and comfortable. But the September 11th terror attacks had turned the lobster market upside down. When John Murdock brought his first bumper load of lobsters into Port Clyde the buyer there told him he could offer no price. This had never happened before, which, as Winnie Murdock put it, made things "pretty scary." Later in the season, a warden caught one of the younger lobstermen with a bunch of under-sized lobsters, a major transgression of both Maine law and Monhegan ethics, which reportedly triggered some chilly divisions in the fish house. All in all, the season was one most Monhegan lobstermen will be happy to forget.

But nobody will forget Zoe Zanidakis's exploits that year. On the day after Christmas, she returned to the island as mysteriously as she'd left, deeply tanned and having lost a surprising amount of weight. The next morning she set traps in heavy weather, and continued through January, still offering no coherent explanation as to where she'd been.

Then, in early February, the cat came out of the bag.

Zoe was a contestant on the new season of *Survivor*, the CBS reality television series, one of nine chosen from some fifty thousand applicants. While we were moving traps on Monhegan, Zoe, her fellow contestants, and a large production crew were "shipwrecked" on a remote island in the Marquesas in the South Pacific. Under the show's rules, she would be disqualified if she said anything to anyone about her true whereabouts before the show aired.

Ratings for the series must have gone off the charts in Midcoast Maine that winter. People gathered in bars, restaurants, and living rooms to watch Zoe struggle with the elements, fellow contestants, and the artificial challenges thrown at them by *Survivor's* producers. They shared in the drama when Rob, a construction worker from Boston, called Zoe a liar, an accusation that the *Lincoln County News* suggested might make him fit for lobster bait. Each week the contestants met in a faux Polynesian meetinghouse — tiki torches blazing — and voted one of their members off the show. A few weeks in, Zoe, who may have intimidated the others with her considerable survival skills, was voted off the island and back to her own.

"I remember sitting there on the boat after hauling, before the show had aired," she says. "I'd just been on this amazing whirlwind and now I was back and it was all still and crystal clear out there on the water. I remember thinking, 'What the hell am I doing?' "

Then she just sat there, looking out at the ocean horizon, thinking about her island until the sun had set and the twenty-first century faded into the deepening night.

PART TWO

Proprietors

TWO

Dawnland

In the early morning hours of May 18, 1605, a lookout on a small English ship sighted the cliffs of Monhegan.

The twenty-nine men aboard the *Archangel* were desperate to make landfall. They had been at sea for nine weeks and were out of fresh water and firewood. Four days earlier they'd nearly wrecked their vessel on the shifting sand shoals off Nantucket. Then, for three days and nights, a powerful southwesterly gale drove their vessel north and east up into a little-known and poorly charted region.

And now, finally, they were again in sight of land: a high, rugged island, a forest of oak, fir, and spruce bounded by rocky cliffs and ledges. By daylight the island could be seen by a lookout more than twenty miles away, but it wasn't on the captain's sea charts. Only a handful of navigators had ever come this way and, if any had seen Monhegan, they'd failed to locate it properly.

Gale-force winds blew the crests off the advancing waves in stinging white streams, straining the *Archangel*'s rigging and rendering the decks wet and treacherous. After several days without heat or warm meals, the crew was cold, wet, and exhausted.

They sailed alongside Manana, its humplike shape covered in knobbly pine and crowned with great hardwood and spruce trees, through which the winds howled. Huge waves thundered against the shore, throwing spray high in all directions. But soon the *Archangel* made the northern end of Manana and turned into flatter seas. A few minutes later, the ship dropped anchor off Monhegan's northern shore, sheltered behind the island's massive bulk. "It appeared a meane high land . . . an island of some six miles in compass," ship's chronicler James Rosier wrote, "but I hope the most fortunate ever yet discovered."

The *Archangel's* captain, George Waymouth of Devon, England, was on a reconnaissance mission. Most other European expeditions to the Northwest Atlantic seaboard had been seeking in vain for a quick shipping passage to the Spice Islands of southern Asia.* Other expeditions experimented in trade with the natives of these shores and had returned with reports of bountiful fish, furs, and sassafras, a plant that was in great demand in England because it was thought to cure syphilis.

But the *Archangel* had crossed the Atlantic as part of a much longer-term project: the planting of a full-fledged colony on North American shores. Waymouth was to scout for an appropriate site for this colony, which would be the centerpiece of a year-round English presence in the New World. There had been no English settlements on the North American mainland since the mysterious disappearance of the Roanoke colony in 1587. To avoid a repeat of Roanoke, Waymouth was commissioned to gather information on the geography, natural resources, and native inhabitants of the area around his chosen site. In the hold he had goods to trade with the natives, an unassembled pinnace for inshore exploration, hooks, nets, and salt for the capture and curing of fish, and dogs and firearms to repel attackers.

The expedition's principal patron, Henry Wriothesley, the Earl of Southampton, was passionate about the New World and a consummate risk taker. At thirty-one, Southampton had already invested considerable sums of money in three other expeditions, including a failed attempt to set up a permanent trading post on the island of Cuttyhunk, not far from Nantucket. He'd been imprisoned twice: once for carrying on an affair with one of Queen Elizabeth's ladies-in-waiting, a second time for his part in a failed attempt to storm the palace and arrest Elizabeth's favorite advisers. Southampton was also the primary supporter of William Shakespeare. Some academics believe that Shakespeare and Southampton were lovers, and that the Bard's penultimate play, *The Tempest*, took place on a fictionalized Cuttyhunk Island.

*Waymouth himself had commanded just such a mission to Labrador and the Canadian Arctic in 1602, but confronted with iceberg-choked channels, his crew had rebelled and forced him home.

Southampton and other proponents of New World colonization feared that if England didn't act quickly, its American claims would be pushed aside by its European competitors. Theoretically, England claimed much of the American coast as its own—from northern Florida to northern Nova Scotia. The problem was, France, the Netherlands, and Portugal had overlapping claims to much of the same land. The French, in particular, were already trying to colonize the Maine coast. While Waymouth was preparing the *Archangel* for its mission in the winter of 1604, a party of French colonists were literally freezing to death on the tiny island of St. Croix in the river of the same name, located just inside Maine's present boundary. Unprepared for eastern Maine's subarctic climate, a third of the French party died, and in the summer of 1605 the survivors relocated to Port Royal (now Annapolis Royal) on the southern shore of the Bay of Fundy. The impending struggle between England and France for control of the Gulf of Maine region would bedevil the lives of Maine residents for 150 years.

So Southampton convinced his brother-in-law, Thomas Arundell, and English chief justice Sir John Popham to join him in financing a fact-finding mission to the eastern seaboard of North America. Waymouth, who'd been studying architecture and mathematics since his return from Labrador, was hired to command the mission. While his party sailed down the River Thames, the three investors returned to their London homes to await *Archangel*'s return.

Within hours of dropping anchor, the men aboard the *Archangel* witnessed the Gulf of Maine's incredible bounty.

Captain Waymouth led a landing party ashore in search of wood and water. Walking along the Monhegan shoreline adjacent to its impenetrable forest, the party found freshwater springs trickling down the cliffside and plenty of windfallen trees. They found "much fowle of divers kinds" nesting on the rocky shore, wild berries, and, most significant, "places where fire had beene made." Somebody already frequented the island they had just discovered.

While the landing party filled the boat with firewood, the men aboard the ship decided to try their hand at fishing. Each baited a hook attached to a handline and dropped it over the side. By the time

Rosier and Waymouth returned from shore, the men had caught more than thirty enormous cod and haddock, enough to feed the crew for several days. This, Rosier wrote, "gave us a taste of the great plenty of fish we found afterward wheresoever we went upon the coast."

Indeed, throughout their month-long stay on the Maine coast the Waymouth party found marine resources the likes of which they'd never seen. A few days later, Waymouth sent the ship's boat out into Muscongus Bay, where "in small time with two or three hooks" the men aboard caught enough cod, haddock, and skates to feed the crew of twenty-nine for three days. That very evening they set a small fishing net near the shore of Allen Island and hauled up a net filled with rock-fish, flounder, lumpfish, and "thirty very good and great lobsters." On their return voyage, boatswain Thomas King tossed a hook over the side while the *Archangel* was becalmed in shallow water less than thirty leagues from shore. Rosier saw King immediately haul up "an exceedingly great and well-fed cod."

> Then there were cast out 3 or 4 more [hooks], and the fish was so plentifull and so great, as when our Captain would have set saile [to continue toward England], we all desired him to suffer them to take fish a while, because we were so delighted to see them catch so great fish, so fast as the hooke came down: some with playing with the hooke they tooke by the backe, and one of the Mates with two hookes at a lead at five draughts together hauled up tenne fishes; all were generally very great, some measured five foot long, and three foot about.

Throughout the expedition the party "generally observed, that all the fish of what kinde soever we tooke, weere well fed, fat and sweet in taste."

Other explorers were also taken with the size and quality of the Gulf of Maine's fish stocks, which they compared favorably with the Grand Banks of Newfoundland, then the greatest fishery in the west-ern world. A member of Bartholomew Gosnold's 1602 expedition to Cuttyhunk, John Brereton, reported great stocks off Cape Cod. "We had pestered our ship so with Cod fish, that we through numbers of

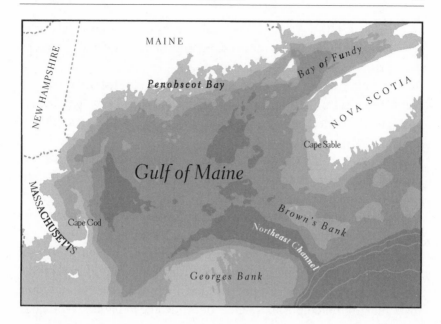

them overboord againe; and surely, I am persuaded that in [the spring] there is upon this coast, better fishing, and is as great plentie, as in Newfoundland." (Only later was it learned that the best cod fishing in the area was actually not in spring or summer, but in the dead of winter.) Martin Pring, casting hooks in Penobscot Bay in 1603, found "excellent fishing for cod . . . better then [in] Newfoundland" and with excellent beaches for drying the catch. James Davies was similarly delighted with the summer fishing in the region. "We found fyshe abundance so large and great as I never saw the lyke cods before [and] nether [did] any man in our shipe."

The English had discovered living resources that would attract, shape, and sustain the communities of the coast of Maine for the next four centuries. Early explorers were flabbergasted by the largesse of the Gulf of Maine, a semienclosed sea stretching from Cape Cod to Nova Scotia. They saw great pods of whales, acres of thrashing tuna, vast schools of salmon, herring, and mackerel, clouds of puffins and terns, shoals of mussels and oysters, vast mudflats infested with fat clams, cod and haddock biting at the hook, and enormous lobsters foraging in the rockweed. The waters off England and France seemed barren by comparison.

Few places in the world's oceans are as suited to sustaining marine life as the Gulf of Maine. By a wonderful accident of geography, geology, and climate, the Gulf was a fertile oasis in a world ocean that is, ecologically speaking, largely desert.

From the sandy shoals of Nantucket to the massive tidal flats at the head of the Minas Basin, the Gulf of Maine measures 450 miles. Its coastline is ragged, particularly along the rocky shores between Portland, Maine, and St. John, New Brunswick, where deep bays and estuaries reach five, ten, twenty miles inland between long peninsulas and many thousands of islands dot the coast. If stretched into a straight line, the Gulf's shoreline would run for 7,500 miles, and several thousand miles farther if island shores were included. All that coastline makes for an incredible abundance of prime ocean habitat, with large quantities of rocky, complex seafloor located near enough to the surface to get life-sustaining light.

Waymouth had no way of knowing any of this. His charts probably depicted the Gulf as a humble embayment of the Atlantic dotted with a dozen islands and completely open to the wider ocean to the south. He had no idea that he had sailed into a separate sea, an oceanographically distinct chamber of the Atlantic Ocean not unlike the Baltic or the Mediterranean. Even if he could have looked at a modern map, Waymouth would have seen what appears to be a large bay yawning wide open to the south. But surface maps are deceiving. There is a southern boundary to the Gulf of Maine, one that Waymouth passed over without ever realizing it was there.

Hidden just ten to one hundred feet beneath the waves at the entrance to the Gulf are two enormous submerged islands, Georges Bank and Brown's Bank. These banks separate the Gulf from the surrounding ocean, deflecting and containing various ocean currents, shaping the flow of the tides, and providing hundreds of square miles of additional sunny bottom habitat for plants and animals. Two relatively narrow channels provide the only deepwater connections into the Gulf. The largest of these, the Northeast Channel, the riverbed of an ancient glacial river, is only twenty-two miles wide.

Entering the Gulf of Maine from the Atlantic, Waymouth would have noticed the water change from bright blue to deep green. He did not know that this change in color was due to the profusion of microscopic plants floating in the Gulf's sunlit surface waters. It was the presence of these single-celled plants that supported the incredible bounty of marine life Waymouth encountered on his trip.

In the oceans, as on land, almost all life begins with plants, which capture and store energy from the sun through photosynthesis. Grazing animals survive by eating these plants, and are in turn eaten by carnivorous animals, which might be eaten by larger ones. Plants, with a few recently discovered exceptions, are the source of life's energy.

The Gulf of Maine is a haven for the microscopic plants on which fish, lobsters, and other marine animals ultimately depend. More than sixty rivers annually drain some 250 billion gallons of fresh, nutrient-laden water into the Gulf, fertilizing the sea. The world's most powerful tides sweep through the Gulf, stirring the water and keeping nutrients suspended in the lighted surface waters where the plants can live. The tides also benefit marine life by creating unusually vast expanses of salt marshes, estuaries, clam flats, mussel banks, rockweed and seagrass meadows which serve as nurseries and feeding grounds for many Atlantic creatures. With ample food and habitat—and in the absence of overwhelming fishing pressure—marine life abounded in the Gulf of Maine.

Waymouth's party also noticed the seabirds nesting in noisy multitudes on the shores of Monhegan, Manana, and surrounding islets. It was the height of breeding season, and the air was filled with a cacophony of cries and flapping wings. There were swooping gulls, diving cormorants, and rustling little bright-beaked puffins. There were clusters of soaring gannets and nimble terns, and great rafts of eider ducks. Elegant, goose-sized flightless birds shot through the water, catching fish in their long beaks and waddling ashore to trade places with their mates at the nest. Waymouth, Rosier and other seventeenth-century Europeans called these birds "penguins," a term which later, after the discovery of Antarctica, was applied to their southern cousins there; scientists later called these birds great auks.

The early explorers also saw rivers and streams darkened by the passage of countless waves of shad, alewives, and salmon. Four-hundred-pound sturgeon climbed up the major rivers, laden with caviar. Whales were commonplace along the coast. So were shoe-sized oysters, which formed sprawling banks in briny waters from Massachusetts Bay to the rivers of Midcoast Maine. Lobsters weighing twenty pounds or more could be simply gaffed in shallow water from an open boat or collected by hand while wading along the shore.

But the explorers were most impressed by the incredible quantity of commercially valuable cod, haddock, and halibut they found on shallow banks throughout the Gulf. Cod, especially, was a product that could be easily cured and shipped back to Europe for sale to the hungry masses there. With control of these cod-choked waters, Waymouth knew, great fortunes could be made.

Waymouth was a seasoned captain, and it didn't take him long to learn what many mariners have since discovered: Monhegan is a lousy anchorage. Powerful tides from the St. George River swept through the area, testing the hold of *Archangel*'s anchors, which might well have been clinging to little more than kelp and seaweed on the rocky bottom off the island's northeast shore. All night long the southwesterly gale would have funneled between Monhegan and Manana, driving seas through the passage to batter and roll *Archangel*'s small, tubby hull. After what was probably an uncomfortable night's sleep, Waymouth's men set off toward the mainland, stretched before them to the north.

Archangel raced downwind, driven by the storm and seas across six miles of open water and into the wide channel between densely forested Allen and Burnt islands. The crew began sounding for the bottom with lead weights attached to a line and found deep water within sight of the waves crashing over mid-channel ledges. Again, fearful of being wrecked, Waymouth kept the ship in open water while his mate, Thomas Cam, took the ship's boat out in search of a safe harbor. Fortunately, Cam didn't have to sail far in the angry seas. Right behind Allen Island's north end, Cam discovered a sheltered, deepwater harbor formed by Allen and two smaller islands. "We all with great joy praised God for his unspeakable goodnesse, who had from so apparent danger delivered us and directed us upon this day into so secure a Harbour," Rosier wrote.

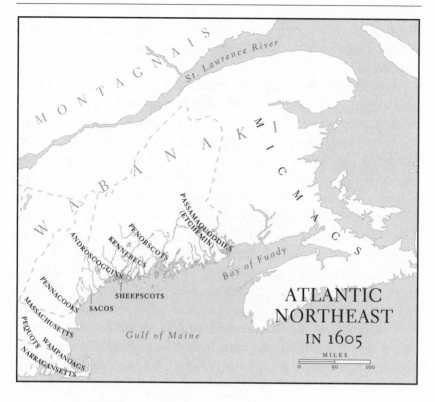

Here they rested for the better part of two weeks. The men dug wells ashore and cut lumber to replenish the ship's store of spare spars, yardarms, and storage barrels. The carpenter and cooper set to work assembling the pinnace, a large boat for exploring the coast which had been shipped in pieces in the cargo hold. Some set out fishing, while others dug a test plot and seeded it with garden seeds to test the quality of the soil. Rosier led a party of fourteen men armed with guns and pikes on marches around Allen and Burnt islands, finding forests of spruce, white birch, beech, and maple, but no people. However, near the anchorage were the remains of a campfire about which were scattered "very great egg shelles bigger than goose eggs, fish bones, and, as we judged, the bones of some beast." Somebody had recently been on Allen Island to feast on great auks.

On May 30, Waymouth and thirteen crew climbed in the newly completed pinnace and set off to explore the mainland coast. James

Rosier and fourteen men were left behind to tend to the ship, securely moored between Allen and Benner islands. Seven hours later, they had company.

It was late afternoon when the watchman spied three birch-bark canoes entering the harbor. They carried some two dozen men and women, average in size, with long dark hair, which some of the men had tied in large knots behind their heads. Their bodies were painted with black soot, their faces smeared with black, blue, or red pigments. The newcomers paddled their canoes to the nearest of the islands and quickly built a fire on the shore. They stood about the crackling hearth in their long beaver and deerskin mantles and dressed deer leggings, beholding the strange vessel and its pale, strangely dressed occupants.

Rosier's men beckoned them with their hands and hats. Three of the newcomers climbed into one of the canoes and paddled it out alongside the *Archangel*. The leader spoke out to them "very loud[ly] and very boldly" in Algonquin, declarative at first, but ending in what were clearly questions. Rosier could not understand him, but the man punctuated his queries by pointing his paddle toward the open sea.

The English and the Central Wabanaki, "the people of the dawn," had been introduced.

⌒⌒⌒⌒

By the time of Waymouth's voyage, the shores of the Gulf of Maine were thickly settled as far east as the Penobscot River. The Wabanaki tribes, the natives of Maine and the Maritimes, numbered perhaps twenty thousand, while another sixty thousand Algonquin-speaking Indians lived in the remainder of New England. European explorers hadn't found a "virgin wilderness," but rather an ancient, developed land of crop fields and gardens, villages and managed woodland deer parks. Samuel de Champlain, sailing down the coast that very summer, wrote that "there is a great deal of land cleared up and planted with Indian corn." Sailing along the coast in 1614, John Smith counted forty villages between Cape Cod and Penobscot Bay and "many Iles" planted with mulberries and cornfields. "The sea Coast as you pass shows you all along large Corne fields," he reported.

The Gulf had been claimed and occupied for a very long time, probably since the day it was created. Geologically speaking, the Gulf of Maine is extremely young. At the height of the last ice age, sixteen thousand years ago, the entire region was under a mile-thick sheet of ice. The advancing ice scoured the landscape of northern New England, and its crushing weight formed hundreds of depressions in the bedrock that would later become lakes and ponds. Much of the debris was plowed up in the front of the ice sheet and carried far to the south. This ice sheet began to retreat as temperatures rose some twelve thousand years ago. Much of the glacial debris—billions of tons of sand and gravel torn from the mountains, valleys, and plains of Maine and beyond—was left behind, much like the dirty little mounds left behind after the melting of the snowbanks made by passing plows, but on a much larger scale. These deposits are still with us today in the form of Martha's Vineyard, Nantucket, Long Island, and Cape Cod.

As the ice retreated, a newly sculpted landscape slowly scrolled out from beneath the glaciers. Huge icebergs calved into the Atlantic, slowly exposing the Northeast Channel, an icy passage between two great capes of dry land, now Georges and Brown's banks. Then appeared the central basin of the Gulf, crushed and scoured by the weight of the ice sheets, followed by the well-scraped shores of what are now northern New England and the Canadian Maritimes. In Maine, huge streams of water poured from the melting glaciers, forming powerful north–south rivers: swollen versions of the Androscoggin, Kennebec, Penobscot, and St. Croix. Retreating glaciers carved valleys between north–south ridges, shaping the ragged topography of today's coastline. As the melt continued millennium after millennium, the world's seas steadily rose.

Humans were living in the region even as the ice melted some ten thousand years ago. Maine, newly emerged from the ice, was then tundra, a stark landscape of sedges, grasses, and dwarf pines not unlike Arctic regions today. This vegetation drew caribou herds, and Paleo-Indian hunting parties followed. At this stage, the Gulf itself offered little sustenance. Georges Bank was high and dry, a large cape that blocked most water flow to the North Atlantic. Tides were very small, and the infant Gulf was shallow and unproductive.

Indian cultures evolved with the local ecology. Over the millennia, tundra gave way to white pine forests, white pine to birch, maple, oak, and other hardwoods. Mastodons and caribou gave way to moose and white-tailed deer, rabbit, raccoon, and beaver. Salmon, trout, and other fish made their way into glacier-sculpted rivers, streams, and lakes. People learned to hunt, trap, fish, preserve, and prepare these creatures. The glaciers melted on.

But four thousand years ago, the rising seas finally surged over Georges and Brown's banks, and the Gulf's mighty tides began, stirring the garden of life beneath the waves. Cold ocean currents flowed in through the Northeast Passage, and the Gulf of Maine flickered to life for the first time. Blooms of microscopic plants fed great swarms of tiny copepods and arthropods, which soon attracted schooling fish and baleen whales. Shellfish larvae found purchase in mudflats, rocky shores, or sunlit sea bottom. Seals, seabirds, and predatory fish discovered these new breeding and fishing grounds—as did the region's Indians.

The Wabanaki and their neighbors possessed this resource-rich region, but they had no concept of private land ownership. Instead, the right to use the natural resources in a designated stretch of land or sea was held collectively by a clan or tribe. Among the Wabanaki such clans consisted of anywhere from fifty to one thousand people, groups of kin united under a tribal leader on a voluntary basis. The territorial boundaries between these clans were well known and typically encompassed the drainage basin of a particular river or stream. These territories were held in common by all the people and could not be alienated without the tribe's approval. Intrusion by another clan—to poach deer for instance—was a serious offense and possible grounds for war.

The Wabanaki used their commons sustainably, striking a balance with nature by shifting their settlements and diets on a seasonal basis. East of the Kennebec—home of the Sheepscot, Penobscot, Passamaquoddy, Micmac, and other Wabanaki tribes—the harsh climate largely precluded agriculture and clans lived from hunting, gathering, and, most of all, fishing. The French Jesuit missionary Pierre Biard, who lived among the Eastern Wabanaki from 1611 to 1614, described their annual cycle:

> Their food is whatever they can get from the chase and from fishing; for they do not till the soil at all. . . . In the month of February

and until the middle of March is the great hunt for beavers, otters, moose, bears . . . and for the [deer]. . . . In the middle of March, fish begin to spawn, and to come up from the sea into certain streams, often so abundantly that everything swarms with them. . . . From the month of May up to the middle of September they are free from all anxiety about their food, for the cod are upon the coast and all kinds of fish and shellfish. [After this time, they] withdraw from the sea, beyond the reach of the tide, to the little rivers where the eels spawn, of which they lay in a supply. . . . In October and November comes the second hunt for [moose] and beavers; and then in December . . . comes [the tom cod] which spawn under the ice . . . [and] the turtles bear little ones.

West of the Kennebec, warmer temperatures had allowed western Wabanaki, Massachuset, and Wampanoag Indians to adopt agriculture. They planted corn, squash, beans, vegetables, and tobacco in extensive village gardens, which were often the property of the cultivators for the duration of the growing season. Clans also created woodland pastures for deer and moose by setting controlled fires that cleared the underbrush and encouraged the growth of plants favored by these animals.

But across the region, Indians depended on the living bounty of the Gulf of Maine. During pupping season, Wabanaki hunted harbor and gray seals and adorned their homes and bodies with their soft hides, rubbing seal oil into their skin and hair. In summer some tribes would set out in canoes and hunt whales with harpoons and bow and arrow. In tidal coves and bays, Wabanaki men captured fish in weirs, corrals of wooden stakes into which fish swim at high tide, but are unable to escape when the ocean retreats. They also fished with hooks, throw-nets, and spears. They traveled to the farthest offshore islands to hunt seabirds. Great feasts were held beside oyster banks and clam-infested mudflats, where huge quantities of shellfish were also smoked or dried and stored away for winter. In the process, they left staggering shell heaps behind; a single heap of shucked oyster shells in Damariscotta covered an area of more than sixty acres to a depth of nearly thirty feet. Lobsters were collected by hand along the shore and eaten with relish; surplus lobsters were either preserved or cut up for use as bait for bass or cod. Wabanaki culture and the Gulf of Maine region had evolved together, and for thousands of years Maine's natives enjoyed the benefits of a perpetually renewable resource.

The Wabanaki called their country Ketakamigwa, "the big land on the seacoast." They believed they had lived in Ketakamigwa since time began, which, in a sense, was true. According to myth, they were created by Gluskap, an immortal hero who used his powers to improve and transform the world. Gluskap confronted selfish creatures that trampled on the well-being of others and taught that power should only be used for socially constructive purposes. Gluskap is said to have left the Wabanaki just prior to the arrival of the first European explorers, leaving them to face their greatest challenge alone.

The Indians and the *Archangel* crew brought very different experiences and assumptions to their first encounter in Allen Island's tiny harbor.

The Indians, a fishing party of Sheepscots from Pemaquid, were part of a small Midcoast confederacy of villages called Mawooshen. They had never encountered Europeans themselves, but they had known of their existence for several generations and were already familiar with many of the trade goods the strangers carried to the New World.

For many centuries, Wabanaki had participated in an informal long-range trading network, bartering furs and other products with neighboring tribes in exchange for items they could not produce themselves or that could be profitably resold to a third party. Sheepscots, Penobscots, and Micmacs supplied Saco and Massachuset Indians with fine furs and moose skin moccasins in exchange for surplus agricultural produce. From the Narragansets of Rhode Island they obtained stone pipes and wampum, the finely crafted blue and white quahog shell beads that served as a sort of regional currency. Some goods were traded and retraded over incredible distances. From A.D. 900 to 1500, Wabanaki gathered to trade at a great seasonal village in Naskeag at the confluence of Penobscot and Blue Hill bays. When the site was excavated in the late twentieth century, archeologists found a huge number of foreign artifacts. There were stone tools and arrow points traded from the Great Lakes, Pennsylvania, northern Vermont, and central Nova Scotia. Archeologists identified more than thirty tools made from a type of stone found only in northern Labrador and used widely by Dorset Eskimos there. Most incredible was what they found alongside the Dorset tools: a silver Norse penny minted in the late eleventh century and buried at Naskeag since around 1200. Norsemen from Leif Eriksson's Greenland colony traveled far into the Canadian Arctic and traded with Dorset and Thule Eskimos; Norse objects have been found in Dorset and Thule sites from Hudson's Bay to Ellesmere Island. By the time Europeans arrived in what is now Canada, Indian and Eskimo traders had for centuries been trading goods over hundreds, even thousands of miles.

In 1497 John Cabot, an Italian navigator in service to England's Henry VIII, discovered Newfoundland and its fantastic cod fishing banks. A decade later, dozens of French, Basque, and Portuguese fishing vessels were crossing the Atlantic every year to catch cod in the Gulf of St. Lawrence. Many fishing crews must have encountered the Micmac and Montagnais Indians who lived on the eastern shores of modern Quebec and the Canadian Maritimes. Somebody got the clever idea of trading surplus tools or clothing or trinkets for the Indians' fur clothing, which could fetch a handsome price in Europe. The Indians, who hadn't learned the art of metalworking, were happy to trade furs for steel knives, copper cookware, iron hatchets, and manufactured beads and clothing. By the time French explorer Jacques Cartier officially discovered mainland Quebec in 1534, this transatlantic fur trade was already at high pitch. Cartier was frightened by his first encounter with Wabanaki Micmacs. Two fleets of forty or more canoes surrounded his boat, yelling loudly and shaking furs on the end of sticks to signal their desire to trade. Cartier, overwhelmed and fearful for his safety, tried unsuccessfully to escape from the persistent Micmacs, and had to fire the ship's cannons to scare them away. The next day the French crew encountered a smaller group of Micmacs shaking beaver and deer pelts in the air, and a profitable traffic took place. The Micmacs literally traded the clothes off their backs in return for "knives and other cutlery, and a red cap to give their chief."

Substantial quantities of European goods made their way to Maine long before the Europeans themselves. Bartholomew Gosnold's 1602 expedition encountered New England natives who possessed "a great store of copper, some very redde, and some of a paler colour." In 1603, Martin Pring's men reported that western Wabanaki living near the Saco River wore "plates of Brasse a foot long and a half a foot broad" on their chests. The Pemaquids who confronted Waymouth's party at Allen Island had a few iron arrowheads of their own.

Some of these goods had been acquired directly through overland trade with the Montagnais Indians, who maintained an important trading center at Tadoussac on the north shore of the St. Lawrence in what is now Quebec. English explorer John Walker traveled up the Penobscot in 1580 and stole from an unattended building a cache of three hundred dried moose hides probably intended for this thriving wholesale trade. When Champlain first visited Tadoussac in 1603 he met some Maine Wabanaki, possibly Sheepscots, who were trading furs with Montagnais middlemen. Certainly by 1606, groups of Sheepscots frequently made the fifty-day overland journey to Tadoussac to trade furs for European goods.

By the time *Archangel* reached Maine in 1605, Micmac middlemen dominated the trade between New England Indians and European ship captains in the Gulf of St. Lawrence. Gosnold's 1602 expedition to the Gulf of Maine was approached by "a Biscay shallop with sails and oars" manned by eight Micmacs. The leader wore "a Wastecoate of blacke worke, a paire of Breeches, cloth stockings, shooes, hat, and band" and another Indian drew a map of the coast for the stunned Englishmen "and could name Placentia," a fishing area in southeastern Newfoundland much frequented by French vessels. These Indians "spoke divers Christian words," probably of French or Basque origin. European sailors often saw Micmac merchants sailing along in lightweight shallops, but the Micmacs also skillfully operated vessels that had two masts, were as long as forty feet, and weighed twelve tons. They ranged as far south as Massachusetts Bay, and one of their leaders, Messamouet, had visited France, where he had been a houseguest of the mayor of Bayonne.

Traders also related information about the Europeans; unfortunately European crews hadn't always behaved themselves. Cartier himself soured trade relations with the Montagnais when he kidnapped their eccentric chief, five other adults, and four children and carried them off to France. Some European fishing crews in the Gulf of St. Lawrence may have been involved in theft, rape, and kidnapping. They'd also started to decimate populations of great auks, guillemots, and other seabirds the Indians depended on. Maine Indians, with their regular contacts with Micmac and Montagnais, were probably better apprised of the unpredictable behavior of the "ship people" than their neighbors to the south.

Such intelligence may explain the cool reception the Italian navigator Giovanni da Verrazano received in 1524, though he was the first European visitor to the Maine coast. Though he was warmly welcomed by Narragansets and Wampanoags on the southern New England coast, on his arrival in southern Maine, Verrazano found the western Wabanaki to be "of such crudity and evil manners, so barbarous, that despite all signs we could make, we could never converse with them." Verrazano landed his men ashore and marched them around, tromping through the Wabanakis' homes and generally making a nuisance of themselves. The Indians, shadowing the trespassers through the woods, made a great deal of noise and shot arrows at the intruders. They consented to trade, but only when they were perched on top of a sheer cliff with the Europeans floating in a tiny boat beneath them; the goods were traded in a basket hauled up and down the cliff with a long rope. When the Indians completed the transaction they "made all the signs of scorn and shame that any brute creature would make, such as showing their bare buttocks and laughing immoderately." Verrazano named the coast *Terra Onde di Mala Gente*, "the Land of the Bad People."

Nor was this the extent of European misbehavior. A year after Verrazano "discovered" the New England coast, Portuguese explorer Estevan Gomez seized fifty-eight Indians from either Maine or Rhode Island and tried to sell them into slavery in Spain. In 1603, Martin Pring's crew terrorized friendly Wampanoag Indians with their dogs. "When we wanted to be rid of the Savages company wee would let loose the Mastiffs and suddenly with out-cryes they would flee away," Pring recounted. As his men prepared to depart, the Indians encouraged them by setting the surrounding woods on fire. On the other

hand, just months before Waymouth's arrival, Champlain had established friendly trading relations with the Penobscots, members of the
very same confederation as the Sheepscots.

So, standing by their beachside fire in May 1605, the Sheepscots
probably had mixed feelings about the interlopers. They knew one
had to be on guard for European treachery: newcomers often behaved
in a rude and grasping manner. But if cordial relations could be established, the tribe knew they could gain direct access to valuable goods,
cutting out the Montagnais and Micmac middlemen. The Indians
probably approached the *Archangel* with guarded optimism.

George Waymouth arrived with preconceptions of his own, drawn
from the recent English experience in Ireland. While Waymouth was
growing up, England was engaged in its first overseas imperial conquest: the subjugation of the Irish in eastern Ulster and southwestern
Munster. This campaign, conducted between 1565 and 1576, was carried out with unusual brutality. English forces burned captured villages and crop fields and relocated their owners to reservations. Women
and children were put to the sword in order to "kill the menne of
warre by famine." Two hundred people were massacred in a single day
while attending a Christmas Day feast. By the end of the campaign,
Munster had become a wasteland. "Out of every corner of the woods
and glens [the Irish] came creeping forth on their hands, for their legs
would not bear them," recalled Edmund Spenser, the English writer
and poet, who lived in Munster after the war. "They looked anatomies
of death; they spake like ghosts crying out of their graves. They did eat
of the dead . . . and if they found a plot of watercresses or shamrocks
there they flocked as to a feast for the time. [But] in short space there
were none almost left and a most populous and plentiful country suddenly left void of man and beast."

The leaders of these ventures, many of whom were from the English West Country, were among the leading figures in the subsequent
exploration and colonization of America: Sir Walter Raleigh, Martin
Frobisher, and Sir Richard Grenville. Some were among the closest
confidants of Waymouth's patrons. The first Earl of Essex, Walter Dev-

ereux, the man who led the Christmas feast massacre and the execution of all six hundred Scots inhabitants of the isle of Rathlin, was the father of one of the Earl of Southampton's closest friends, Robert Devereux. Just six years before the *Archangel*'s departure, Southampton and Robert had gone to Ireland together to restore order to the province. Sir Humphrey Gilbert, who would play a central role in the colonization of Maine, had served as military governor of Munster and ordered war against "manne, woman, and childe" to terrorize the Irish. He ordered that the paths to his encampment be lined with the heads of recently slain Irish "so that none could come into his tente for any cause [without first] passing through a lane of heddes," according to his chronicler. "It did bring greate terrour to the people when thei sawe the heddes of their dedde fathers, brothers, children, kinsfolke, and friends, lye on the grounds before their faces, as thei came to speak to the said collonell."

The English claimed that their brutal conquest was justified because the Irish were "savage" and "barbaric," a "wicked and faythless peopoll" who preferred to "live like beastes, voide of lawe and all good order . . . more uncivill, more uncleanly, more barbarous and more brutish in their customs and demanures then in any other part of the world that is known." The English felt they were bringing civilization to the Irish much as the ancient Romans had brought civilization to conquered Britons.

The Irish were considered "savages" because their society failed to conform to a number of English cultural practices. Instead of orderly agricultural villages answerable to feudal lords, the Irish had a fluid pastoral society based on cattle herding. Many husbandmen moved seasonally with their herds, a life the English equated with that of Tatar nomads who "neither possessed any grounds, nor had any seats or houses to dwell in, but wandered through the wilderness and desert places driving their flocks and herds before them." Irish marriages were insufficiently rigid, allowing for easy dissolution and for unions between close relatives that the English regarded as incestuous. Finally, the Irish, while Christian, observed many pre-Christian rituals and traditions that the English considered pagan.

North American Indian society shared many of these "barbaric" traits. Here were strangely clothed people who migrated about their territories, spoke in strange languages, had little shame in their nakedness and no knowledge of Christianity. One of the sailors on Bartholomew Gosnold's 1602 voyage to the Gulf of Maine, Gabriel Archer, thought the Micmacs' sealskin breeches resembled "Irish Dimmie trousers." The following year, Martin Pring found Wampanoags wearing "Beares skinne like an Irish mantle over one shoulder." In his published accounts Pring referred to the Indians as "savages," and rumor had it that they even spoke a Gaelic language, some obscure dialect of Welsh. Other early-seventeenth-century Englishmen saw similarities between Indian and Irish clothing, houses, footpaths, sleeping arrangements, and hairstyles. English explorers immediately concluded that they had encountered another wild race that needed to be "civilized."

The Sheepscot man in the canoe finished his greeting oration and stood in his canoe, staring up at the newcomers with an expression that was difficult for them to read. The officers decided they'd just been asked to leave, but Rosier, the ship's cape merchant, would have none of that. He pulled out an iron knife for the Indians to see and, like a good salesman, demonstrated its use by cutting sticks. He demonstrated the use of a comb and a looking glass. Multiple samples of each were displayed for the Indians, who paddled alongside the ship for a better look. Then Rosier started showing off the contents of his box of trade goods. Knives were handed down to the Sheepscots as presents, as were looking glasses and tobacco pipes, brass bracelets and rings, and peacock feathers, which the pleased Indians put in their hair. The ice now broken, the Indians paddled ashore and were soon replaced by a second party of four Indians to whom the English gave similar gifts. The cycle was repeated until nightfall, until all the Sheepscot men had, in turn, come out to the ship. (The women, Rosier noted, remained safely ashore.) "When I signed unto them they should goe sleepe," Rosier recalled, "they understood presently, and pointed that at the shore, right agains our ship they would stay all night: as they did."

At dawn, three of the Sheepscots were back and this time were en-

ticed to come aboard. The English took them belowdecks and presented them with a meal of salt pork, barreled cod, dried peas, and
ship's biscuits. They enjoyed the peas and biscuits immensely, but declined the meat and fish until they were stewed over the fire. They
marveled at the construction of the cook's iron cooking pot and metal
storage containers, and a soldier's metal helmet and firearms. The English demonstrated the use of one of the guns, the report of which
scared the Indians, who promptly fell flat on the floor. They were also
afraid of the ship's dogs—probably mastiffs—which Rosier had tied up
to put the Sheepscots at ease. Through elaborate hand signals, Rosier
and the Indian party's leader agreed to return at midday to trade furs
for knives, which the Sheepscots clearly valued. With that settled, the
Indian fishing party departed for the mainland.

A few hours later, Waymouth returned with his boat party, and
there was considerable rejoicing. Waymouth had discovered "a great
river"—in reality the modest St. George—but had returned to fortify
the boat with tall sidings to protect against possible arrow attack. Waymouth delighted in Rosier's account of his contact with the Indians
and "of the kinde civility we found in a people, where we little expected any spark of humanity."

At the appointed hour, twenty-eight Sheepscots arrived in four
canoes bearing skins and furs, and went straight to the island shore.
Again, a single canoe was sent to reconnoiter the *Archangel*, this carrying two of the Indians who'd been aboard the ship and a newcomer,
who was clearly in command of the party. The leader, probably the
sagamore or headman of the Pemaquid village, scrutinized the English ship and crew. The English beckoned their former guests to
come aboard, but the sagamore would not allow it. After a time he
signed that he was going ashore and would return shortly. It started to
rain. The Indians' fire was extinguished. It was impossible to conduct
trade in the downpour. After an hour, the same three Indians returned
and, this time, agreed to climb aboard and come to the Englishmen's
fire. The Indians were drenched and so the crew gave them some of
their own clothes to wrap themselves in. The captain gave the sagamore one of his own shirts, a necklet, and a "great knife." The others
each received a knife, a comb, and a looking glass. The use of the
looking glass was demonstrated, the Indians laughed in amusement.

Huddled around the fire, the group shared food and drink. The Indians tasted, but wouldn't drink, their crude brandy. But they "liked well" the beer, asked for seconds of sugar candy and raisins, and again showed a mysterious fondness for the ship's biscuits. The three men set aside some of each food to share with their company ashore. Rosier says they treated the Sheepscots "with as great kindness as we could devise" because "we found the land a place answerable to the intent of our discovery . . . fit for any nation to inhabit."

All the next morning Rosier traded with the Sheepscots on the island shore. The Indians presented a skin, in return for which Rosier offered objects from his trade box, driving a hard bargain for mere "trifles." For goods worth four to five shillings, Rosier acquired "40 good beaver skins" and a pile of otter, marten, and other furs which would fetch a small fortune in Europe. With trading complete, a large number of the Indians joined the English aboard the ship, eating by the ship's fire, and were "very merrie and bold, in regard to our kinde usage of them." At dusk the captain took two of the Indians with him to a nearby beach and impressed them by catching a large number of fish with a large seine net. Waymouth gave most of the fish to the Indians on the shore, where Rosier was busily learning some Algonquin vocabulary. The Englishman pointed to an object, asked its name, and recorded the answer on paper, an exercise the Indians took great interest in: "they would of themselves fetch fishes and fruit bushes and stand by me to see me write their names." Waymouth tried to impress them with a bit of "magic." He produced a lodestone, a magnetic rock carried by all ships to remagnetize the compass, and used it to make a knife spin and to lift a stitching needle with his sword. "This we did to cause them to imagine some great power in us," Rosier wrote, "and for that to love and fear us."

That night the captain had two Indians over for supper in his cabin, where they "behaved themselvs very civilly" and did not "eat or drinke more than seemed to content nature." At the end of the meal "they desired peas to carry a shore to their women, which we gladly gave them, with fish and bread, and lent them pewter dishes, which they carefully brought againe." The English were invited ashore, where they sat on deerskins and smoked strong, sweet-tasting tobacco by the fire. The women, who previously had hidden in the woods, stood behind the circle of men, and were judged "well favoured in proportion of countenance" despite being short, "fat," and blackened with animal oils, sun, and body paint. With them were two eighteen-month-old boys, "very fat and of good countenances, which they love tenderly," to whom the English gave chains and bracelets.

At the end of the evening, the two Indians who had come to dinner were invited to sleep aboard the *Archangel*, but their companions demanded that one of the crewmen stay with them in exchange. Waymouth sent Owen Griffin, "one of the two [crewmen] we were to leave in the Country if we had thought it needfull or convenient." Griffin, a Welshman, had probably been selected because his Welsh language skills were expected to be helpful in learning the language of the "savages." The Indians slept on an old sail aboard the *Archangel*, while Griffin went ashore and witnessed a Wabanaki religious dance:

> One among them (the eldest of the company as he judged) riseth right up, the rest sitting still, and sodainely cryed, Bowh, waugh; then the women fall downe and lye up on the ground and the men altogether answering the same, fall a stamping round about with both feete as hard as they can, making the ground shake, with sundry loud outcries and change of voyce and sound; many take the fire stickes and thrust them into the earth, and then rest silent a while, of a sudden beginning as before, they looke round about, as though they expected the coming of something (as hee veerily supposed) and continue stamping till the younger sort fetch from the shore stones of which every man take one, and first beate upon them with the fire sticks, then with the stones beate the ground with all their strength, and in this sort . . . they continued about two hours.

During one of the pauses, the ship's watch out in the harbor could be heard singing and the Indians asked Griffin to sing as well. He did, "looking and lifting up his hands to heaven" as he sang. The Indians were confused, and with gestures asked the Welshman if he worshiped the moon. No. The sun? No. What then? Griffin, frustrated, lifted his hands to the heavens again. The Indians looked about in the sky, trying to figure out what star he pointed to, and laughed to one another.

Following another day of easy relations, the Sheepscots urged the English to follow them to the mainland where they had furs and tobacco to trade, perhaps for the much-loved biscuits. Waymouth agreed, loaded half the crew into the pinnace, and set out with the Indians. But on approaching the mainland shore, Waymouth feared savage treachery and insisted on again exchanging pawns. A young Indian was left with Waymouth, while the eminently expendable Owen Griffin was sent ashore to check things out. Griffin was safely returned, but reported an assembly of 283 Indians with bows, dogs, and "wolves which they keepe tame at command." The Indians claimed the furs were at the head of "a little nook of a river," but Waymouth feared a trap. The English decided the Sheepscots were of "the ranke of other salvages." Waymouth turned his boat around and rowed, unmolested, back to Allen Island.

At ten the next morning, the Indians returned: six men in two canoes. Two Indians happily came aboard to visit, but the other four stayed in their canoes. They were all pleased when Rosier gave them a metal pot full of peas and biscuits. The bashful foursome took theirs ashore to eat, but one came back to return the metal pot and was talked into joining the others warming by the fire belowdecks. Meanwhile, Rosier loaded the pinnace with seven or eight crewmen, a box of trade goods, and a platter of peas, and rowed ashore. One of the Indians ran off into the woods before Rosier got ashore. The others, hankering for more peas, welcomed the English to the fireside. Suddenly the English were on them, grabbing them by the hair and fighting them into the pinnace. On the *Archangel* they were stowed below with the others, their canoes and belongings.

The crew spent the next three days loading supplies. On June 8 they weighed anchor and sailed up into the St. George River. Meanwhile, the sixth Indian hid in the woods, was likely picked up by a passing Indian fishing and fowling party, and spread word of the kidnapping far and wide. Even Champlain, sailing down the coast two weeks later, learned of it. At the mouth of the Kennebec, Chief Anas-

sou told him an English crew "had killed five savages of this river, under cover of friendship." The entire Mawooshen confederacy, which
stretched 150 miles from Mount Desert Island to the Saco River, was
in an uproar.

The *Archangel* spent the next week exploring the St. George River,
which Waymouth thought an ideal location for a colony. Rosier
equated it favorably with the Thames: not only did the St. George offer
miles of sheltered, deepwater anchorages, it had "as much diversitie of
good commodities as any reasonable man can wish for present habitation and planting."

After surveying this tract of Mawooshen, Waymouth sailed down
the river and off into the rising sun.

THREE

The First Frontier

When the *Archangel* returned to England on July 18, 1605, Sir Ferdinando Gorges may well have watched her anchor from the great fort looming over Plymouth harbor. At thirty-nine, Gorges was the military governor of Plymouth, a war hero charged with protecting that West Country harbor from enemy warships. He was a self-made noble, a commoner whom Queen Elizabeth had knighted for his service to Protestants in Europe's ongoing wars of religion. He had distinguished himself on the battlefields of France and the Low Countries, and despite his youth, the queen trusted him with Plymouth Fortress, her first line of defense against any future Spanish Armadas.

But the young knight had greater aspirations than running a fortress. Gorges wanted to join the great landed aristocracy and become a noble in the medieval sense: the master of a hereditary domain of rambling estates, tenant farmers, and subordinate towns. But times had changed. In England, the Middle Ages had come to a close, and Gorges was too young to have fought in the Irish wars in which several West Country nobles carved out their own earldoms. By this time, Plymouth was becoming one of the principal ports in the exploration of America; as explorers and fishing vessels came and went beneath the walls of Plymouth Fortress, Gorges's dreams followed them over the western horizon. He would spend the rest of his life—and much of his fortune—trying to make his dream a reality on the rocky shores of Maine.

Waymouth, upon his arrival, gave Gorges three of the Indians he'd kidnapped from Allen Island. The reasons for this gift are not entirely clear. Gorges may have been one of the expedition's sponsors; he was in any case a close friend of a sponsor, Chief Justice John Popham.

Whatever the reason for the gift, Skidwarres, Mannido, and Sassaco-moit spent the next three years with Gorges at the Plymouth fort.

Gorges was enchanted with his three captives and their descriptions of Mawooshen, their richly endowed coastal homeland. He spent enormous time and energy on them, teaching them English and collecting intelligence from them on the conditions in coastal Maine. As he listened, Gorges developed an elaborate plan to build a medieval domain for himself in the lands of his Indian guests.

There were some hurdles to overcome, however. First and foremost was the fact that the Indians' land had been claimed decades before by the English crown, sight unseen, along with much of the rest of northeastern America. (In fact, the French king claimed much of this same land as well, which may have also come as a surprise to Gorges's captives.) Would-be colonizers needed King James's official authorization to occupy or conquer "His" lands. And in the early seventeenth century, such authorization came in the form of a royal charter, a feudal instrument granting a specific lord the right to conquer, possess, and govern new territories in the king's name. Royal charters were very much a medieval arrangement. The overseas domains they authorized were not part of the English realm, thus not subject to its laws and Parliament. Rather, the chartered lord was a vassal to the king, and ruled not a colony, but a private estate, complete with its inhabitants.

To secure such a charter from the king, Gorges formed an alliance with Chief Justice Popham, a "huge, heavie, ugly man" who had received the other two Sheepscot Indians that George Waymouth had kidnapped. Popham had also been beguiled by the stories his Indian captives told about their home country, and was happy to join Gorges's scheme. Like Gorges, Popham was a West Country native, but he had the all-important political connections within the court of King James in London. Thus enfranchised by Popham, Gorges enlisted the help of several other West Country dons, including Sir Humphrey Gilbert, the brutal veteran of the Irish war. But when they went to London to plead their case to the king, they faced competition: a rival clique of London-based notables led by Southampton himself. They both must have made good arguments, because when James finally issued his royal charter in April of 1606, he divided the North American coast between the two factions, each of which had created a stockholding company to finance the effort. Southampton's group—the London Company—had permission to colonize south of the Potomac River, while Popham and Gorges's Plymouth Company had the right to set up a domain north of Long Island. Either company could settle in the middle ground—a stretch of mid-Atlantic seaboard claimed by the Dutch—but were prohibited from settling within one hundred miles of each other. At the stroke of a pen, King James had sanctioned the expropriation of millions of acres of real estate and the subjugation of its inhabitants, who numbered in excess of 100,000.

Things went badly for the Plymouth Company from the start. Fund-raising was a failure, and their first colonization attempt a disaster. In August of 1606, Gorges dispatched his protégé, Henry Challons, and two of Gorges's Indian captives to set up a colony near Pemaquid, followed a month later by a supply ship commanded by Martin Pring. Challons got lost, blundered into the Caribbean, and was captured by the Spanish. Meanwhile, Pring arrived at Monhegan and waited for Challons in vain before exploring the area with the help of his guide, Nahanada, one of Popham's captive Indians. Pring determined that the mouth of the Kennebec would make a better settlement site than that of the St. George, but he had no authority to settle. He released Nahanada and returned to England.

Had the expedition succeeded, the first permanent English settlement in America would have been in Maine, rather than Virginia. But in December, the better-financed London Company dispatched ships to the mouth of the Chesapeake, where they founded Jamestown. Virginia would develop as the private preserve of a powerful corporation, creating a model for the British East India Company's operations in India, in which Southampton was also invested.

Undeterred, Gorges and Popham invested heavily in a second attempt. This was a more serious and expensive undertaking involving two ships carrying 124 people, trade goods, twelve cannon, the captive Indian Skidwarres, Sir Humphrey Gilbert's son Raleigh, and the leader of the expedition, George Popham, a nephew of the chief justice. Gorges and Popham's plan called for the construction of a trading fort, not unlike those that would soon be constructed in India. The "Indians"—whether North American or South Asian—would bring local products to the fort and, eventually, would submit to the Company as its vassals. Resultant fortunes could be reinvested in further ventures. Their ships departed in the summer of 1607, arriving off the Maine coast in early August.

It became painfully and immediately clear to the expedition that the Mawooshen Wabanakis were not going to cooperate. Shortly after their landfall at Allen Island, the hotheaded young Gilbert ordered Skidwarres and a dozen men into the ship's boat and, although it was midnight, ordered the kidnapped Indian to lead him to Pemaquid village. There they discovered nearly one hundred men, women, and children led by none other than Nahanada, who'd shared years of captivity with Skidwarres in England. On seeing the English the Indians let out "a howlinge" and surrounded them with bows and arrows at the ready. But they were spared amid the joyful reunion of the two Indians. A couple of days later, Gilbert and the young Popham sailed their ships over to the Indian village and were greeted by "Nahanada with all his Indians with their bows and arrows in their hands," who told them not to come ashore. The English talked Nahanada into meeting with them, but after an hour or two Skidwarres and the Indians "suddenly withdew themselves from us into the woods and lefte us."

Sharing even less respect for Maine's climate than they had for its native inhabitants, the colonists constructed their trading fort on a completely exposed head at the mouth of the Kennebec, even though there were plenty of protected, deepwater coves just upriver. At low tide their harbor became a mudflat and their homes were constantly buffeted by powerful winter storms. (Jane Stevens, the woman whose home now stands on the site of the fort, calls it "the coldest site south of Greenland.") The colonists' clothes were thin, their houses flimsy, and they would have had scant harvests from gardens laid out in late September. To make matters worse, the colony's leaders were at one another's throats. George Popham, "an honest man, but ould, and of an unwieldy body," was getting pushed around by Raleigh Gilbert, whom Gorges described as a man of "loose life, prompte to sensuality [with] little zeal in Religion . . . head-stronge and of small judgement and experience." By early December the colony was deeply divided, with one faction fraternizing with the Indians, the other becoming hostile to them.

Despite the appeal of direct access to European goods, the Wabanaki did their best to let the colony fail. From the fragmentary accounts that survive, Skidwarres and Nahanada kept contact to a minimum, while Gilbert managed to offend other area bands with his aggressive negotiating style. George Popham grew sick and died in midwinter. Four years later, Indians from a nearby Kennebec band told a Jesuit missionary that Popham had been honest and trustworthy, but that they had put him to death through magic because they feared the English settlement. Popham's death only made matters worse: under Gilbert the English "beat, maltreated, and misused [the Kennebecs] without restraint." Consequently, the Indians, "anxious about the present, and dreading still greater evils in the future determined, as the saying is, to kill the whelp ere its teeth and claws became stronger."

What happened through the remainder of the winter remains mysterious. Most of the colonists' diaries and reports were lost in later decades, save for those of the original colony ship, which left Maine in early October. Historians have pieced together fragmentary evidence— the records of a subsequent lawsuit, Wabanaki chieftains' later comments to French explorers, and Gorges's writings and letters—which suggests that tensions between the English and the Kennebecs erupted into open conflict. Samuel Purchas, a London editor who had read many of the lost diaries, wrote in 1614 that a fight broke out between Indians and settlers inside the colonists' fort, resulting in an explosion that destroyed the supply house and killed several Kennebecs. A number of the colonists died during the winter, due to fighting, accidents, hunger, and disease. Suffice it to say that when the supply ship arrived in the spring of 1608, the surviving colonists resolved to leave with it. (Even Gilbert, who wasn't one to give up a fight, had news that his brother was dead, making him the inheritor of the vast family fortune, and so returned to England.) Those who couldn't fit aboard the supply ship sailed back to England in the thirty-ton pinnace *Virginia*, a ship they had built themselves the previous fall.

The first attempt to colonize Maine had failed miserably. "All of our former hopes," Gorges later wrote, "were frozen to death."

Fishing, not feudalism, allowed the English to first settle in North America. There wasn't much choice in the matter. The French, who got along handsomely with the Wabanaki and Montagnais Indians, had the fur trade pretty well tied up. English settlers at the Kennebec and Jamestown had learned the hard way that farming, mining, and lumbering wouldn't support a community placed in an unfamiliar land, thousands of miles from home, that was owned and occupied by displeased natives. Fishing could, however, and there were few better places to fish than the Gulf of Maine.

Lobsters were everywhere. On their way to the Kennebec, Raleigh Gilbert's men caught fifty lobsters "of great bignesse" by simply rowing a boat over shallow water and gaffing the unsuspecting lobsters with a boat hook as they were spotted along the bottom. But there was no way to transport them back to the markets of Europe. Lobsters begin to putrefy almost immediately after death, they can't be salted or dried, and nobody yet knew how to keep them alive for more than a few days. Lobsters were good for a fresh snack, but useless for trans-Atlantic commerce.*

Cod, on the other hand, was nearly perfect. Properly dried and salted, codfish would keep for many months. It was relatively light and easy to transport and, since salt cod was a cheap source of animal protein, there was insatiable demand for it in the markets of Europe. Haddock, halibut, herring, and other fish could be preserved, but none were as profitable as cod. For the next two and a half centuries it was the fish to catch.

Since the early 1500s, English, French, and Basque fishermen had been making fortunes from cod caught in the waters of Newfoundland and the Gulf of St. Lawrence. In the seventeenth century, Gulf of Maine cod would sustain not only the early settlers of Maine, but those of Jamestown, New Plymouth, and Massachusetts Bay. Had the Gulf of Maine not been such ideal habitat for the Atlantic cod, Virginians, Pilgrims, and Puritans would surely have starved to death, and Maine's first successful European settlers would not have come at all.

*Early-seventeenth-century English crews were familiar with the European lobster, and were aware that these animals could be eaten.

The Gulf of Maine cod fishery emerged quietly from the failures of the early English colonies. The collapse of the Plymouth Company's colony on the Kennebec was a massive financial disaster for its shareholders. Ferdinando Gorges, convinced that Maine was "over-cold" and thus not inhabitable, spent the next few years sulking in his Plymouth fortress. When John Popham died in 1607, his heir, Francis Popham, tried to recover some of his late father's losses by sending an annual fishing expedition to Monhegan. His crew caught cod in the surrounding waters, then took them ashore on Monhegan to split, dry, and salt them for the return trip. In 1610 they were joined by fishing vessels from Jamestown. The Virginia colony, like its northern counterpart, had destroyed any possibility of profitable trade with the Indians through abusive behavior. The Virginians knew even less about farming and fishing than Gilbert and Popham's men, and only 67 of 105 colonists survived the first winter. Sick and starving, the survivors came to Maine to fish not for profit, but merely to have something to eat.

It was Jamestown's first leader, Captain John Smith—of Pocahontas fame—who really put the Gulf of Maine fishery on the map. In 1614 Smith led an expedition from England to the Gulf of Maine, where he intended to hunt whales and mine for gold and copper. He set up shop at Monhegan, already the center of European activity in the region. His crew built crude quarters on the island, planted gardens, and assembled their boats. Three fishing crews were operating in the area that spring: Francis Popham's as well as two French ships. Despite considerable effort, Smith couldn't find precious metals in the area, nor manage to kill the swift fin whales feeding there. Instead he followed Popham's example and sent most of his men out in boats to fish for cod. Despite the fact that the best time for fishing had already passed, Smith's thirty-seven fishermen caught and cured nearly fifty thousand large cod, realizing a massive profit on their return to Europe.

Smith was in love with the coast of Maine. "Of all the foure parts of the world that I have seene not inhabited," he wrote, "I would rather live here than any where." He named the region "New England" and, in a widely read pamphlet, advocated the creation of a network of fishing and fur trading stations along its coast. Spain might have its gold mines, but England could have its own mines in the Gulf of Maine, a body of water laced with "silvered streams" of valuable fish. The land, he wrote, "is great enough to make many Kingdomes and Countries, were it all inhabited."

On his return to England, Smith called on Gorges. The charismatic explorer mesmerized the dreamy knight with his grand vision of a "New England" built on the backs of fishermen-farmers. Gorges sold the idea to the other shareholders of the Plymouth Company, which named Smith the official "Admiral of New England." The Company dispatched Smith with two ships and seventeen colonists to set up a permanent outpost on Monhegan, but they never made it. Smith's ship was dismasted in a violent storm just 350 miles from port and was forced to return to Plymouth. Smith sailed again in a smaller vessel, but was promptly captured by a French pirate. He managed to get back to England in 1616 and got Gorges to support a third colonization attempt, this one equipped with three ships. But Smith was cursed: a southwesterly gale kept the ships bottled up in Plymouth harbor for three months, at which point the investors backed out. Smith continued to tirelessly promote New England, but he'd lost favor with Gorges, who looked to other lieutenants to help fulfill his vision of a feudal Maine.

But while Gorges set to work on yet another grandiose colonization scheme, English fishermen inspired by Smith's accounts were quietly constructing New England's first permanent European settlements. Though often forgotten, the colonization of New England began in much the same way as that of Newfoundland: an accidental by-product of the pursuit of fish. In 1615, four ships sailed from the West Country to catch fish around Monhegan. Eight to ten ships made the crossing in 1616, and six years later, thirty-seven. Even Gorges purchased a fishing vessel and used it to reconnoiter his domain "under color of fishing" to cover the costs.

Many of the fishing crews were veterans of the hundred-year-old Newfoundland fishery, which hundreds of English vessels participated in each year. As in Newfoundland, fishermen required extensive drying beaches ashore, where they built wooden stages to cure the split cod and presses for squeezing valuable oil from cod livers. As in Newfoundland, there was extensive competition for prime beaches, which

were parceled out on a first-come, first-serve basis at the beginning of
each fishing season. Competing boat crews would risk life and limb in
mad races to claim the best spots. Captains soon saw the advantage
leaving a caretaker or two behind at the end of the season to hold
down the beach; protect stores from winter storm damage or Indians;
and prepare stages, buildings, and gear for the coming season. Captain
Christopher Levett, one of Gorges's business partners, calculated that
a fifty-man crew could double their profits by leaving a year-round
fishing party on their station; the men would catch more fish, allowing
the ship to focus on transporting the catch to market. When the fish
weren't biting, the men might plant crops and tend to livestock, reducing the need for supplies, or earn extra profits by fur trading with
Indians.

We don't know exactly where and when the first permanent fishing
stations were established, but several were in operation prior to 1620,
when the Pilgrims arrived in the *Mayflower*. Monhegan, the fishing
hub of New England, was home to a substantial year-round fishing and
trading station by 1619, when it first appears in the scant documentary
evidence that has survived. Other early stations included Pemaquid,
Cape Newagen (on the tip of Southport Island), and Damariscove, a
small offshore island seventeen miles west of Monhegan with a snug
harbor and freshwater pond. When the wayward Pilgrims were facing
starvation in the spring of 1622, they dispatched a boat to Damariscove
to beg for supplies. There they found a bustling harbor and a fortified
station surrounded by a ten-foot-high spruce palisade and armed with
a cannon and "ten good dogs." Thirteen men manned the station year-
round "at the cost of Sir Fedinando Gorges," fishing the surrounding
waters through the winter with two shallops, and in spring the harbor
was clogged with ships. Fortunately for the Pilgrims, the fishermen
were generous, filling their shallop with the cod that ensured the survival of New Plymouth. Even so, the date of the *Mayflower*'s arrival at
Plymouth Rock would become part of American historical mythology,
while the date of the Damariscove station's foundation would be lost
and forgotten.

Life at an early-seventeenth-century fishing station was difficult,
dangerous, and lonely. In the Gulf of Maine, the best cod fishing was

in the dead of winter, and the men were sent to sea whenever the weather permitted. They fished from shallops, small open boats with a small sail, which carried three or four men. The shallops could not sail into the wind, meaning the men often had to row against an icy blow in one direction or another. They wore heavy canvas clothing which would have stiffened on the coldest days, when the boat began icing up. At the intended fishing grounds, each dropped a weighted handline over the side, with a hook at the end baited with whatever was handy: bits of lobsters or crabs, herring or mackerel, or chunks of seabirds (particularly the flightless great auks, which were easily caught, killed, and salted for bait). The cod bit quickly in those days and a good fisherman would catch 350 to 400 in a day, according to Nicolas Denys, an early-seventeenth-century French fish trader who wrote a comprehensive account of the fishery. Fishing was exhausting work. Cod put up little fight, but they weighed over one hundred pounds apiece and were at the end of forty to two hundred feet of coarse, dripping lines that had to be hauled in hand over hand from the gunwales of the pitching boat. A fisherman then removed the hook from the flopping cod and cut its tongue out, sticking it on a pointed iron nearby to keep track of how much of the boat's catch was his. If short on bait, he could slit open a few cod and either scavenge some undigested shellfish or simply "cover their hook entirely with the entrails of the Cod, in a mass as large as the two fists." Cod were not picky eaters. At the end of the day the fishermen would land their catch ashore where a member of their crew had spent the day cleaning, salting, and drying the previous day's catch. They would eat their supper, some so exhausted that they would fall asleep at the table. Others collapsed into tiny wooden bunks in a communal sleeping room, not unlike that aboard a ship.

"If they did this every day they would not be able to stand it," noted one observer. Fortunately for the fishermen, there were plenty of days when the weather was so terrible that fishing was impossible, and weeks of the year when the cod stopped biting. But even on fish-free days there was endless work to be done. Barrels, stages, boats, and buildings needed to be either built or repaired. Lumber and firewood had to be cut and carried to the station—a journey that grew longer with each passing year as the forests were cut back. Animals—chickens, goats, pigs, and sheep—had to be taken care of and, in summer, gardens tilled, planted, and tended. When the weather was right, thousands of dressed salt cod were laid out on the stages to dry, then carried in if it threatened to rain. Sundays were the only true day of rest.

One had to be tough and practical-minded to engage in this sort of work. The men were contracted for tours of duty that could last three years or more. They were posted in tiny company-owned stations thousands of miles from home, without women, church, or community. They faced death by drowning, exposure, sickness, Indian ambush, or French raiders. Not surprisingly, the job attracted a rough and rowdy crowd. The vast majority of station personnel were seamen from boisterous West Country ports. At the end of their terms, many returned to their homes in Cornwall, Devon, Dorset, and Somerset. Others stayed, mingled with the daughters of later settlers, and formed one of the first kernels of the old Maine settler stock.

These were not the stern, sober, Calvinist ideologues who would soon settle in Massachusetts. Indeed, even the Pilgrim party that came begging for fish at Damariscove may have been a bit shocked by the behavior of these grizzled salts. A subsequent visitor to the island, John Josselyn, described the arrival of a "walking tavern," a merchant ship laden with wine, brandy, rum, and tobacco. The merchant came ashore, giving each fisherman "a taste, or two, which so charms them" that they could not be persuaded to go to sea "for two or three days, nay sometimes a whole week, till they are wearied with drinking." At the end of the year, some men found they had drunk away their share of the station's profits. Once courts were established, islanders faced charges of drunkenness, assault, swearing, and cheating or mistreating Indians.

In 1618 and 1619, Gorges's fishing agents reported that the Indians of New England had been nearly wiped out by a terrible plague. European crews and station personnel had unknowingly transported Eurasian pathogens to the New World—hepatitis, smallpox, cholera, measles, whooping cough, and bubonic plague—for which the Indians had no resistance. Richard Vines, who spent the winter of 1616 at Biddeford Pool, reported that area Indians had been stricken with "a pestilential putrid fever" that had no cure. Over the next four years, more than three-quarters of the Wabanaki died, including entire villages in coastal areas close to European outposts. Sailing down the coast in 1619, Thomas Dermer found Indian lands "not long since populous, now totally void" and small groups of survivors covered in plague sores. Another English visitor recalled that the Indians "died on heapes as they lay in their houses and the living that were able to shift for themselves would runne away & let them die. . . . And the bones and skulls upon . . . their habitations made such a spectacle that as I traveled in that Forrest . . . it seemed to mee a new Golgotha."*

This "Great Dying" completely altered the social and political landscape of the region. Before the 1616–19 plagues, Gorges had little hope of ever realizing his vision of a vast feudal domain in New England, at least not one populated by Englishmen. The Indians of New England were numerous and had proved capable of repelling English colonization attempts on several occasions. If the plague hadn't struck, the English conquest of the New World might have resembled that of India or China, where a small cadre of English officials ruled a foreign population through the use of native intermediaries. The plagues opened the door to a full-scale colonization attempt of the sort some of Gorges's colleagues had prosecuted in Ireland. The land, Gorges wrote, "was left a desert, without any to disturb or oppose our free and peaceable possession thereof."

In 1620, Gorges unveiled an ambitious new plan to King James. To secure the "planting, ruling, and governing of New England," the king was asked to replace the Plymouth Company with a new, more powerful entity called the Council of New England. Through this new body, Gorges intended to impose English rule over a domain stretching from the St. Lawrence River to Philadelphia and, theoretically, from

Golgotha is the Aramaic name for Calvary, outside Jerusalem, the site of Christ's execution.

sea to sea. Gorges outlined for his king a wonderfully anachronistic strategy. Two-thirds of all the land in this vast realm would be divided between Gorges and thirty-nine other patentees, giving each noble his own county. The patentee list was a veritable Who's Who of royalist aristocrats and included some of the most powerful nobles and gentlemen in England. The extent and quality of their respective counties would correspond to their feudal rank and standing. These men would act as personal sovereigns, subdividing their new counties into baronies and hundreds, manors and lordships, and presiding over local courts. The Council of New England would appoint the governor and had the power to overrule local assemblies. Merchants would be carefully regulated and harnessed to the will of the nobility through guilds and other medieval institutions. Anyone wishing to fish or trade within New England would have to obtain an expensive permit from the Council. Subpatents would also take medieval forms: rather than being granted land outright, a potential settler would have to pay his lords an annual rent and would need his permission to move away. The inhabitants of Gorges's New England would be tenants, not private landowners.

King James was currently being frustrated in his efforts to establish an absolute monarchy by reform-minded middle-class Calvinists who called themselves "Puritans." They wished to purify the Church of England—and commercial activities—by freeing them from lingering medieval forms. But the "new" England proposed by Gorges would be ruled by men loyal to the crown, good Anglicans with respect for tradition, royal prerogative, and approved commercial, political, and religious practice. Coastal Maine would be the center of power of a royalist North America. Delighted, James gave Gorges everything he asked.

The Council of New England's problems started almost immediately. The Council's strategy hinged on the assumption that it could fill its treasury by extorting fees and taxes from the fishing and fur trading companies plying the Gulf of Maine. Companies wishing to operate in New England would have to surrender to the Council 10 percent of their initial capitalization and 1 percent of all exported goods, and were required to deliver five chickens and a pair of pigs, calves, and "tame rabbits" to Monhegan with every outgoing ship. But the merchants and fishermen of the West Country and Virginia refused to comply. The Virginians appealed to the king's council and received an exemption for its fishermen. The merchants, for their part, flagrantly ignored the Council's monopolies. Lacking a navy or other means to enforce their rule, the Council found itself without operating funds.

As commercial tithes failed to materialize, the Council's members tried raising capital by selling patents for their only real asset: land. But Gorges and his partners did a terrible job screening their applicants, an oversight that doomed Gorges's plans for a royalist New England.

The Council granted its first patent to a group of "merchant adventurers" led by one Thomas Weston, a London ironmonger with a tongue of gold. If Gorges had looked into Weston's background he would have learned that Weston was an unscrupulous lout who had already been hauled before the Privy Council for smuggling Dutch cloth into England. Weston's business proposal was even more outrageous. He represented a small group of Protestant radicals—the famous Pilgrims—refugees from Gorges's beloved Anglican Church. Weston had just illegally dumped a shipload of these radicals right in the middle of the Council's New World domain. He had cheated, deceived, and manipulated the gullible Pilgrims into settling in the Massachusetts wilderness instead of taking up a Dutch invitation to join their thriving trading station on Manhattan Island. The Pilgrims, who had no money, few supplies, and little farming or fishing experience, had survived their first winter at New Plymouth by plundering Indian granaries and foraging for shellfish at low tide. They had fled to Holland a decade earlier to escape the very king, church, and country Gorges championed. They were exactly the sort of people the Council didn't want showing up in New England. But Weston proposed that his "merchant adventurers" be given a patent to the area around Plymouth, where their starving hirelings were expected to build a lucrative fishing and fur trading settlement. The land would later be subdivided among the Pilgrims, who would pay annual rents to the Council.

Gorges was completely taken in by Weston's sweet-talk. Not only did the Council approve Weston's scheme, it apparently granted Weston his own patent for a second settlement at the lower end of Massachusetts Bay. This scheme was even more addled than the first.

Weston planned to round up sixty single Anglican men from the taverns of London and settle them to fish and trade at Wessagusset (now Weymouth, Massachusetts). Rather than question this scheme, Gorges, as governor of New England, issued Weston a license to purchase and transport a load of cannon to his new colony, where the vagabond promised to erect a great fortress. Instead, Weston sold the cannon for personal gain. He recruited his London barflies, a group one of his colleagues deemed "not fitt for an honest man's company" and described by Weston himself as "rude fellows." They partied heavily with local Indians, quickly consumed all their provisions, and were soon selling their blankets, clothing, and labor to the "savages" in exchange "for a capfull of corne." Others took to stealing from the Indians and Pilgrims alike. The Pilgrims, led by the Miles Standish of Thanksgiving fame, finally hatched a plot to rid themselves of these ruffians. Standish and a group of soldiers marched into the pathetic settlement and, over the protests of everyone there,* lured a group of Indians into the palisade to trade and promptly slaughtered them. Wessagusset was no longer a safe place to live. Weston's men dispersed, many settling on Massachusetts Bay and the southern Maine coast, further contributing to the rowdy, lawless atmosphere there.

Another early grantee was Gorges's son, Robert, New England's first deputy governor. In 1623, Robert was sent to govern New England with the help of an admiral to enforce the fisheries monopoly, an Anglican chaplain to preside over the churches, and a retinue of gentlemen, servants, and colonists. But Robert Gorges was as pretentious and impractical as his father. He'd been personally granted the entire north shore of Massachusetts Bay, but landed instead at the ruins of Wessagusset, probably because he didn't want the bother of building houses. He attempted to arrest Weston at New Plymouth for stealing his father's cannons, but was talked out of it by the Pilgrims' governor. His admiral was too weak to stop interloping fishermen, while his priest spent his time composing, in Latin, a fanciful epic poem about New England. Robert, "not finding the state of things

---

*When Standish arrived, one of Weston's men told him: "We fear not the Indians, but live with them and suffer them to lodge with us, not having sword or gun, or needing the same."

here to answer his quality and condition," returned home after a few weeks, leaving the Pilgrims and the scattered residents of New England to their own devices.

But the most disastrous patent was that issued to the Massachusetts Bay Company, a group of two knights and four gentlemen proposing to colonize an abandoned fishing station on Cape Ann. The Earl of Warwick, Robert Rich, an influential member of the Council, championed the application, convincing Gorges not to block it. It's not clear if Gorges was aware that the Massachusetts Bay Company's shareholders were ninety of England's more radical Puritans. Nor is it clear if the Council ever voted on the patent. The Earl of Warwick, now emerging as a Puritan leader himself, absconded with the Council's official seal and may have simply granted the patent on his own. More impressively, Warwick somehow got the new king, Charles I, to upgrade this bogus patent to a royal charter. The Puritans, who dominated the English Parliament, were King Charles's archenemies. As soon as he came to the throne in 1625, Anglican authorities had embarked on a wholesale campaign to purge Puritan influence from the church. Two days before granting the Massachusetts charter, Charles angrily dissolved Parliament and stepped up persecution of Puritan leaders. His plan may have been to drive the reformists out of the country and into the New England wilderness where, he thought, they could do little harm.

The Puritans had another trick up their sleeve. When writing their charter, they purposefully neglected to mention where the Company's governing board would meet. The king likely presumed the board would meet in England, where he could keep a watchful eye over its deliberations and imprison anyone who got out of hand. But the Puritans took the charter and all powers of government with them to the shores of the Gulf of Maine. They intended to govern themselves.

With horror, Gorges heard rumors of a Puritan plan for a mass exodus to his overseas realm. As the dispute between the king and the Puritan-dominated Parliament escalated toward civil war, the wealthy, well-connected politicos of the Massachusetts Bay Company prepared to move not hundreds, not thousands, but tens of thousands of hardline Puritans to "Royalist" New England. Gorges knew all his dreams would come to naught if loyal settlements weren't quickly established to contain this dangerous contagion. He concentrated his effort on his personal fief between the Piscataqua and Kennebec rivers, which he called the "Province of Maine."

⌒﹏﹏﹏

At the dawn of the Puritan Migration, in 1630, there were probably fewer than seven hundred Englishmen scattered across New England, including the three hundred Pilgrims at New Plymouth. Gorges had invested all his money and a quarter century of his life in New England and had little to show for it. But that would change. Gorges married his fourth wife in 1629, replenishing his coffers in the bargain. Realizing the immense threat Massachusetts Bay presented, he turned the Council into a patent mill. Between 1629 and 1631 the Council issued more than three times as many patents as had been issued in the nine years prior, most in the Province of Maine. Unfortunately for later generations of Maine settlers, many patents were issued with insufficient attention to geography. Some were vague, while others clearly overlapped, fueling acrimonious land disputes that would take two centuries to resolve.

The men who obtained these patents became known as "proprietors," and a few of them succeeded in creating the first successful European settlements in what is now Maine. A fishing, trading, and farming community was established at Pemaquid in the late 1620s, followed by similar settlements at York, Cape Porpoise, and Saco in 1630, Kittery (1631), Scarborough (1632), Falmouth (1633), North Yarmouth (1636), and Wells (1642). New fishing stations were established at the mouth of the Piscataqua and at Richmond Island off Cape Elizabeth, and their personnel included female servants. These humble settlements were home to the first strain of European "native" Mainers.

The differences between the early settlers of Maine and Massachusetts Bay can hardly be overemphasized. They were drawn from opposing sides of a great struggle over the political, economic, and religious future of England. Seventeenth-century England was in the midst of a wrenching transformation from late medieval to early modern forms of rule, commerce, and worship. The Stuart kings stood in defense of the Anglican Church, manorial agriculture, and feudal monopolies with

limitations on commercial activity. They had the support of most of the landed gentry and the poor peasantry of the West and North, groups that would be hurt by the proposed changes. But the yeomanry—the emerging middle class of upwardly mobile farmers, merchants, and industrialists—wished to be unshackled from medieval constraints, including Anglican bishops, royal authority, and communal agriculture. Most sympathized with the Puritans, strict middle-class Calvinists from the wealthy, sophisticated counties of the East and South. Much conflict centered around the "enclosure" or privatization of communally farmed fields and pastures. Landlords and wealthier peasants

were buying up communal lands, evicting their tenants, and convert-
ing cropland to commercial sheep pastures to feed the expanding textile industry.

Most of coastal Maine's early settlers came from the West Country,
a rugged maritime region where respect for tradition, crown, and the
Anglican Church ran high. In one sample of 124 people who emigrated to Maine between 1620 and 1650, two-thirds came from the
West Country, with Devon alone representing nearly half of the total
and more than all the other regions of England combined. More than
a quarter of these early Mainers came from the ports and fishing hamlets of a single fifty-mile stretch of the South Devon coast between Plymouth and Teignmouth. Judging by their places of origin, the majority
of Maine emigrants were probably fishermen, sailors, or merchants
who had plied the cod trade in Newfoundland and were recruited by
Gorges's circle to man Maine's early fishing stations. Others came
from rural hamlets scattered across the moors and pastures of Devon, a
poor region where the enclosure movement had reduced many peasants to poverty. In the early 1500s, Devon's rolling hills and snug valleys were dotted with compact manorial villages surrounded by open
fields and pastures that for centuries had been communally farmed by
local peasants. But by the 1620s, Devon's fertile land had been divided
into tiny fields surrounded by tall, impenetrable hedgerows, each with
its own isolated farmhouse. Tenant farmers were pushed off the land
and into destitution. The region was noted for its high number of wage
earners, then the poorest, "meanest sort of people" in England. Many
were driven into the cities where a great number dwelled "in vaults,
holes, and caves which are cut or digged out of (or within) the rocke."
Not surprisingly, the West Country aligned itself with the king, who
wished to protect medieval institutions from capitalist-minded reform-
ers in Parliament.

The Puritan settlers of Massachusetts Bay came from a completely
different background. In a sample of 2,284 people who emigrated to
Massachusetts between 1620 and 1650, 43 percent came from England's
seven easternmost counties: Norfolk, Suffolk, Essex, Kent, Lincolnshire, Hertfordshire, and Cambridgeshire. These seven counties—the
furnace of the Puritan revolution—accounted for nearly two-thirds of
the colonists who came to Massachusetts with John Winthrop's "Great

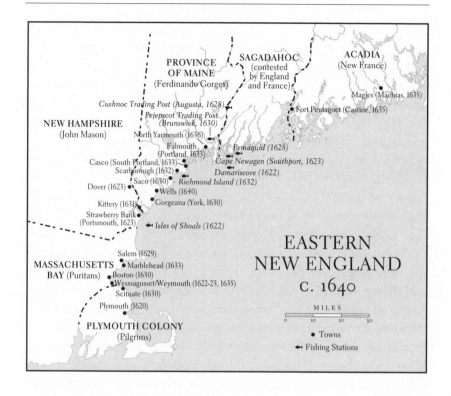

PROVINCE OF MAINE (Ferdinando Gorges)

SAGADAHOC (contested by England and France)

ACADIA (New France)

Magies (Machias, 1635)

Cushnoc Trading Post (Augusta, 1628)

Fort Pentagoet (Castine, 1635)

Pejepscot Trading Post (Brunswick, 1630)

NEW HAMPSHIRE (John Mason)

North Yarmouth (1636)

Falmouth (Portland, 1633)

Pemaquid (1628)

Casco (South Portland, 1633)

Cape Newagen (Southport, 1623)

Scarborough (1632)

Damariscove (1622)

Saco (1630)

Richmond Island (1632)

Dover (1623)

Wells (1640)

Kittery (1631)

Gorgeana (York, 1630)

Strawberry Bank (Portsmouth, 1623)

Isles of Shoals (1622)

Salem (1629)

MASSACHUSETTS BAY (Puritans)

Marblehead (1633)

Boston (1630)

Wesssagusset/Weymouth (1622-23, 1635)

Scituate (1630)

Plymouth (1620)

PLYMOUTH COLONY (Pilgrims)

EASTERN NEW ENGLAND C. 1640

MILES

0   10   20   30

● Towns

⊷ Fishing Stations

Fleet" in 1630. The remainder came from all across the realm, most led to the newly promised land by eastern-born Puritan ministers. The eastern counties were the most densely settled, urbanized, and educated part of England, with a burgeoning middle class and a long history of rebellion against arbitrary power. Across the sea, the eastern counties faced the Netherlands, the most advanced commercial and political nation in Europe, the continent's first republic and, arguably, its first nation-state. The east was profoundly shaped by Dutch civics, agriculture, engineering, art, commerce, architecture, and religion. The region had gabled houses, tulip gardens, and rich fields claimed from the sea. It also had a highly literate population of skilled artisans, craftsmen, and yeoman farmers, who participated in town meetings, served as selectmen, and accounted for the disproportionate share of England's artists, scientists, and scholars. It was also home to many textile mills, and to supply them the region's fields were enclosed at an early date.

There were plenty of extremely poor peasants here whose parents and grandparents had been pushed from their ancestral lands. But most emigrants to Massachusetts came from middle-class backgrounds and were the beneficiaries of the enclosure movement and other reforms, rather than its victims. During the English Civil War, many would return to fight against the king, the Anglican Church, and medieval constraints on the economic and political life of the country.

The differences between these groups were reflected in the settlements they built in New England. Massachusetts Bay towns were patterned after those of eastern England: nucleated villages of closely built houses constructed around long central greens like those left behind in Suffolk and Essex. Houses were built in the "saltbox" or "Cape Cod" styles common in Kent and East Anglia at the time. Communities were ordered and cohesive, with well-delineated private property and strong town governments. Puritanism was the only religion tolerated, and people of other faiths were often executed or banished. The Puritans lived in fear of the surrounding wilderness, whose inhabitants they imagined to be under Satan's sway. Towns were close to one another and connected by roads. Puritan settlers named these towns for the eastern English communities they'd left behind: Haverhill, Ipswich, and Groton (in Suffolk), Springfield, Malden, and Braintree (in Essex), Lynn, Hingham, and Newton (in Norfolk), and the south Lincolnshire port of Boston.

Maine's settlements, on the other hand, followed West Country models. Early Mainers scattered themselves across the landscape, creating dispersed ribbonlike settlements of isolated homes fronting rivers or the sea. Towns were far apart and separated by forests, swamps, and rivers, and almost all transportation was by boat or dugout canoe. The settlers may have distrusted the scattered Wabanaki in the area, but they conducted regular trade with them and enjoyed reasonable relations. Settlements were organized on the manorial model: tenants held inheritable, thousand-year leases to the land and paid annual rents to the patentee, who retained actual ownership. Anglicanism was the official religion, but other Protestant faiths were tolerated. West Country "longhouses" predominated, with a large manor house for the lord. Most town names were merely English or Wabanaki descriptions of the terrain like Black Point (now Scarborough) or Pemaquid ("extended land"). Other early settlements were named for West Country towns: Biddeford (Devon), Falmouth (Cornwall), Wells (Somerset), and Kittery (for Kittery Point Manor, Kingsweare, Devon); York was first named for Bristol, the great West Country port.

Early Maine and Massachusetts settlers came to the New World with different goals as well. Maine's settlers crossed the Atlantic for practical reasons. They hoped to better their lot in life by gaining access to land and fisheries resources on a scale they could never have dreamt of back in England. They left on individual initiative, and many went from farming two or three acres on an English manor to more than one hundred on a New England one. The Puritans, however, came on a profound spiritual endeavor to what they believed was the new Promised Land. Following their deacons, entire congregations moved to Massachusetts en masse. There they sought to create a new Zion, a "City upon a hill" that would act as a beacon of salvation in a sinful world. They thought themselves a chosen people and came to believe that their interests and God's interests were one and the same. And as they built their Calvinist utopia, they looked at their neighbors to the north with fear and contempt.

These rival societies shared only the understanding that manorial royalists and Puritan zealots would not live peacefully side by side for long.

⁓

As Puritans poured into Massachusetts, Ferdinando Gorges redoubled his efforts to build a royalist bulwark in New England. In 1635, he dissolved the Council of New England and divided its territory among the members. Gorges granted himself the territory between the Piscataqua and the Kennebec, "the Province of Maine." King Charles backed Gorges up, appointing the sixty-four-year-old knight governor general of all of New England and revoking the Massachusetts Bay Company's royal charter. Massachusetts simply ignored the rulings from London and carried on as if nothing had happened, and the king left it at that. He was having enough trouble trying to bring the Puritan-dominated English Parliament under control; if Gorges was to consolidate his control over New England, he would have to do it on his own.

The king had left Gorges with an extremely powerful weapon: a royal charter for the Province of Maine. This charter was unusual in that it gave the grantee almost unlimited powers. Gorges could make laws, ordinances, and constitutions—and establish the courts to enforce them. He appointed all judges, magistrates, and court officers in the province, and could remove them at will. He could raise troops and, if faced with "rebels, traitors, and seditious persons," could declare martial law and dispose of them as would "any captain general in the wars." The charter gave Gorges exclusive power to build, dedicate, and consecrate churches in his province; to levy tolls and duties; or to erect "forts, fortresses, platforms, castles, cities, towns and villages" in his new realm. In true feudal style, Gorges divided Maine into eight counties comprising several-hundreds, hundreds,* parishes, and tithings. He would employ a deputy governor, chancellor, treasurer, marshall, judge-marshall, admiral, maritime judge, master of ordnance, standing councilors, and, ultimately, Anglican bishops with cathedrals and retainers. The charter, in the words of the early-twentieth-century Maine historian Charles Banks, made Gorges "an uncrowned monarch in a little kingdom of his own."

Gorges had yet to lay eyes on Maine, but he planned to sail there and govern New England directly once he got his affairs in order. In the meantime, he appointed his twenty-two-year-old cousin, Thomas Gorges, deputy governor and sent him off to Maine to govern in his stead. Thomas, straight out of college and a childhood of wealth and privilege, was in for a few surprises when he arrived at Maine's greatest settlement, Agamenticus (now York), in June of 1640.

Instead of a teeming imperial and ecclesiastical capital city, Thomas Gorges was confronted with a rugged fishing village of less than one hundred souls living in drafty longhouses built on the remains of an Indian village. Point Christian, the governor's manor on the edge of town, was in great disrepair and furnished with "only one crock, two bedsteads, and a table board." Thomas wrote to his father that the house looked "much like your barn. . . ." The hamlet's tide-powered sawmill and gristmill—vital engines of growth—had been

---

*A subdivision of an English county consisting of "100 hides," a hide being the amount of land required to support one family (generally sixty to one hundred acres).

poorly built and were also falling apart. Wolves infested the surrounding woods, devouring the settlers' few animals at will. In the absence of proper government, Thomas found, the people of his province had begun to lapse into savagery. "Sin hath reigned uncontrolled," he wrote. "Justly hath [Maine] bin termed the receptacle of viscous men" and "a garden of vice." The settlers, for their part, worried that the young deputy governor would "draw them and theyrs into slavery." One local leader referred to him contemptuously as "the boy, Gorges."

But Thomas set about his task with care and diligence, allowing town governments to participate in decision making and routine administration. Effective courts were established, with provisions for jury trials. He had little contact with Indians—a second epidemic had completely depopulated the western Maine coast—but in his brief, friendly encounters with them he found them "very ingenious men only ignorant of the true wisdom [Christianity]. . . . Truly I take great delight to discourse with them." He advocated religious tolerance, writing to Sir Ferdinando that he "must of necessity tolerate liberty of conscience in many particulars." When antinomian leader John Wheelwright was driven from Massachusetts by the Puritan leaders, Thomas not only welcomed him to Maine, but allowed the religious dissenter to found the new settlement of Wells.

Thomas wrote detailed reports for Sir Ferdinando. The colony was surviving, but hardly thriving. "The winter was very tedious, the snow laying on the ground from the middle of [Sept]ember to the later end of March," he reported in the fall of 1641. "Mosquitoes are an exceeding great trouble to man and beast. We cannot sleep nor work nor idle comfortably for them, but the inconvenience of them would quickly be removed if the plantation flourished." The young deputy governor must have been stunned when he received his reply the following year. While the colonists were being eaten alive by insects, Sir Ferdinando had declared Agamenticus a chartered city, and extended its boundaries to encompass twenty-one square miles, renaming it Gorgeana after himself. Thomas was instructed to appoint a mayor, twelve aldermen, twenty-four councilmen, a recorder, town clerk, and "two to four sergeants to attend to the said mayor." Thomas wrote back that he could not fulfill this request for lack of people. "If you tie us to it," he pleaded, "every man in the plantation must assume offices."

Sir Ferdinando paid little heed to his deputy's advice and set to work on plans to make Gorgeana a cathedral city, the seat of the future Anglican bishop of New England.

But by now the English Civil War had begun, with Royal and Parliamentary armies clashing in full-scale battles from Yorkshire to Plymouth. Gorges, now in his dotage, sided with the king. Thomas, ironically a Puritan sympathizer, sailed home to fight for Parliament. And as this disastrous and bloody war swept England over the next six years, Maine, with all its unfulfilled promise, was left on its own, without a governor or outside support. In his moments of clarity, Sir Ferdinando probably assumed that once the king's armies put down the Puritan troublemakers at home there would be plenty of time to crush their Massachusetts colleagues. King and knight would rule their realms unmolested, and the proper order of affairs would finally be restored.

By 1649, King Charles had been tried and executed by victorious Parliamentary leaders, the monarchy had been abolished, and Puritans were leading the first and only republic in English history. England's new ruler, Oliver Cromwell, was in Ireland, leading his army's slaughter of tens of thousands of Irish "savages." Sir Ferdinando Gorges died in 1647, never having set eyes on his struggling colony.

These events had massive ramifications for the New England colonies. Maine's struggling royalist settlements not only lacked a government, they now had neither lord proprietor nor king. Their rivals, the radical Puritan leaders of Massachusetts, suddenly had the full support of their mother government. And the "savages" of New England, already decimated by disease, were about to confront a Puritan "Irish Solution" to their continued occupation of "Satan's" undeveloped New England real estate.

American historical myth holds that the Puritan fathers of Massachusetts stood for freedom, democracy, and religious tolerance. Nothing could be further from the truth. Back home in England, Puritans were a varied lot, constantly debating and compromising with one another on both theological and practical matters and nurturing notions of religious tolerance. Massachusetts's Puritan leaders were an entirely different animal: fanatical, zealous, and completely intolerant of any form of dissent. The Bay Colony divines had no need for debate: they already knew God's will. They considered themselves God's "chosen people," which meant not only that they could do no wrong, but that anybody who disagreed with them was in league with Satan. They were in New England on a divine mission to build a religious utopia and believed their interests and those of God were one and the same.

While other English colonies welcomed any settler with more than one leg, Massachusetts forbade anyone who failed to pass a test of their religious conformity from settling within its territory. Dissenters were excommunicated and banished from the colony. Some, like John Wheelwright, went to Maine. Roger Williams, banished for arguing that Indians owned their own lands and should be paid for them, founded Rhode Island. Quakers were particularly despised by the Puritan leadership for their dangerous notions of pacifism, equality, and tolerance; captured Quakers were disfigured for future reference, having their ears lopped off, their nostrils slit, or their faces branded with the letter *H* for "heretic." Not surprisingly, murderers, rapists, and "witches" in Massachusetts were executed by hanging; but equal punishment awaited those found guilty of adultery, blasphemy, idolatry, and sodomy, as well as teenagers who struck, cursed, or rebelled against their parents. Such draconian justice shocked contemporary Englishmen, including Thomas Gorges, who observed that these Old Testament punishments were outdated and inappropriate.

The Puritan leadership regarded the Indians the way Cromwell regarded the Irish: as uncivilized savages to whom normal moral obligations—treaties, promises, or forgoing the slaughter of the innocent—did not apply. When a group of dissatisfied Puritan settlers marched into the wilderness and founded a squatters' colony called Connecticut in 1636, the Massachusetts authorities engineered a genocidal war against area Pequot Indians to bring the region under their control through right of conquest. During this land grab, Puritan forces surrounded a lightly defended Pequot village and slaughtered virtually every one of the four hundred women, children, and old men they found there. Most were burned alive in their homes and survivors were cut down with swords. The slaughter so horrified the Puritans' own allies, the Narraganset Indians, that their braves refused to participate, admonishing their tactics as "too furious" behavior. The Puritans didn't stop until the Pequots had ceased to exist as a nation: their villages burnt, their children slaughtered, and the survivors scattered far and wide. Many more Indian tribes would share the Pequots' fate.

As Massachusetts grew, its leaders looked for new lands to conquer in God's name. After the defeat of the Royalists in the English Civil War, they set their eyes on the orphaned settlements of Maine. The Puritans regarded Maine's settlers as little better than the savages. That Maine was officially Anglican was bad enough, but the fact that it sheltered and tolerated Baptists, Quakers, and antinomians was downright sinful. They disparaged the Maine settlers as "wild English," though probably with some justification; early Maine court dockets were filled with cases of cursing, fornication, and drunken assaults. The Puritan leaders resolved to rescue Mainers from Satan's clutches, and hatched a plan that would ultimately place the province's land and resources in the hands of the Bay Colony's powerful oligarchy.

In 1651, Massachusetts announced, with a novel interpretation of its old royal charter, that it was extending its sovereignty over New Hampshire and southern Maine. The following year, commissioners were dispatched to the newly claimed settlements bearing articles of submission. New Hampshire's towns submitted promptly, but the communities of southern Maine were resistant. They had been governing themselves for nearly a decade since Thomas Gorges's departure, and some of the towns had even formed a compact and elected their own governor, Edward Godfrey of York. Popular opinion was sharply divided. Some argued that by joining Massachusetts the region might benefit from efficient courts and improved security against possible attacks by the French and Indians. Others sided with Godfrey, who wrote that he and other Mainers were "loath to part with our precious liberties for unknown and uncertain favors" promised by the divines in Boston.

Resistance to the Masschusetts commissioners' proposals was spirited, but ultimately futile. Kittery's residents were the first to submit, but only after a passionate, sometimes abusive debate that lasted for four whole days and resulted in the commissioners arresting at least one dissenter, John Burley, whom they charged with threatening them. In York, their records show there was a raucous daylong meeting at which Godfrey argued eloquently and exhaustively against submission. But at the end of the day, Godfrey mysteriously voted in favor of annexation along with a majority of those present. The record is silent on the means the commissioners used to prompt this amazing capitulation, but years later Godfrey told the English Parliament that on that day, "Whatever my body was inforced unto, heaven knows my soul did not consent." The inhabitants of Casco Bay and the Scarborough marshes, who had a separate government, ignored the commissioners' summons for years on end. But in 1657, the Massachusetts General Court had these communities' leaders arrested and dragged to Boston. Threatened with imprisonment or worse, the three men avowed allegiance to the Bay. Their communities followed suit almost immediately. By 1658, the Puritan conquest was complete.

Maine had become a colony of a colony, and would remain so for the better part of a century. It would prove the darkest, most tragic period in the area's history, and one that permanently shaped the identity of its people.

During the first twenty years after the Massachusetts takeover, Maine's English population more than doubled, from perhaps 1,200 people in 1650 to 3,500 in 1670. It also became more diverse, a mix of West Country "Old Settlers" and newcomers from Massachusetts and New Hampshire. Based on demographers' estimates that colonial New England's population doubled every twenty years from natural increase, it seems likely that the Old Settlers and their descendents probably constituted a comfortable majority in 1670. Genealogically, the influence of the seventeenth-century Massachusetts immigrants was fairly modest: many settled in the wild lands between the Kennebec and Pemaquid Point and were wiped out in the horrid wars to come. Culturally, however, their influence was lasting.

Massachusetts's rule put an end to the feudal system envisioned by the late Sir Ferdinando. Manorial estates were replaced by strong town governments led by "selectmen" who were appointed at annual meetings of the towns' citizens. Feudal land leases were replaced with private titles, including some extremely large tracts that would fall into the hands of a few Boston merchants. Congregational meetinghouses were constructed alongside Anglican and Baptist churches, often to be followed by town greens and the Cape or saltbox homes of eastern English provenance. While forced to tolerate religious dissent, Massachusetts courts sought to tame the troublesome Mainers; they cracked down on fornicators, drunkards, and the seemingly endless supply of people unable to refrain from abusing, cursing, and threatening Massachusetts officials. Boston merchants flocked to the region, monopolizing the sale of manufactured products and the purchase of the settlers' surplus of fish, farm products, and lumber. Visiting Maine in 1663, John Josselyn accused the Bay Colony merchants of gross exploitation: "they set excessive prices on [English goods, and] if they do not gain *Cent per Cent*, they cry out that they are losers. . . ." Fishermen traded underpriced fish for overpriced salt, gear, and spirits, "becoming thereby the Merchants slaves," and sometimes lost homes to them.

Of course, not all of Maine's population was English.* Despite epidemics, loss of land, and cultural erosion, Wabanakis were still the majority of Maine's population. In the early 1670s, they probably outnumbered the English two-to-one in what is now Maine and by many times more than that if one includes the Micmac bands east of the St. Croix.

Despite their superior numbers, the Wabanaki were now dependent on Europeans for a range of manufactured goods. Amid the epi-

---

*A non-English minority lived among the English, most of whom were shipped to New England against their will. Four hundred Scottish prisoners of war were shipped to New England in 1651 and sold into bondage for six to eight years apiece. Fifteen were sold to a Kittery sawmill operator, and at least ten more settled in York after serving indentures in New Hampshire. Puritan Massachusetts tolerated slavery, and merchants advertised their human cargoes in Boston newspapers until the end of the American Revolution. A few African slaves were purchased by wealthier Mainers, and some met ignoble ends. While visiting Cape Porpoise in 1663, John Josselyn encountered "a waggish lad" baiting his fishing hooks with a "drowned Negro's buttocks."

demics and the fur trade, the old ways of living off the land had come undone. In a society without a written language, skills must be passed from one generation to the next or they are lost entirely. Wabanakis now hunted with firearms which, while more powerful than bows, could not be replaced or repaired within the community. Metal knives and axes completely replaced those of stone; iron and bronze containers displaced their birch bark predecessors. Indians still smoked tobacco, but many succumbed to alcohol as well and were willing to pay any price to acquire it. But these goods—as well as gunpowder, shot, cloth blankets, and trinkets—had to be purchased from Europeans. For a hundred years the Wabanaki had something the Europeans also wanted: ready supplies of beaver skins that were of little value to the Indians but fetched great prices in Europe. By the late seventeenth century, New England's beavers had been all but exterminated by gun-toting Indian hunters. Europeans found their beaver elsewhere, while the Wabanaki were left greatly impoverished. They now had only one thing the English wanted: land.

Events in England further complicated the political landscape. In 1660, Oliver Cromwell's republic collapsed and the monarchy was restored. Two claimants approached the new king, Charles II, with designs on parts of what is now Maine. Ferdinando Gorges, grandson of the quixotic knight, lobbied for the restoration of his family's royal charter and payment of a decade of back rents by those living there, and dispatched commissioners to Maine to establish his government. Massachusetts Bay resisted, tossing some of Gorges's men out of their posts and arresting others. Gorges's prospects brightened in 1665, when the king annexed Maine as part of the new crown colony of New York (acquired from the Dutch at far-off peace talks). But they dimmed again three years later, when Massachusetts officials marched into Maine behind a small "troop of horse and foot" soldiers in flagrant disregard of the king's orders. Massachusetts consummated this bloodless coup by purchasing all proprietary rights to Maine from a frustrated Ferdinando Gorges for £1,250. The Gorges era was finally at an end.

The second claimant had better luck. Louis XIV of France—the Sun King who built Versailles—wanted the eastern half of the Gulf of Maine restored to France. Charles II was happy to oblige. Like his Stuart ancestors, Charles had both Catholic sympathies and enormous admiration for the centralized, absolute monarchies of Continental Europe. The two kings negotiated secret treaties with one another, and Charles repeatedly backed France in its wars with the Dutch. France had surrendered eastern Maine and the Maritimes to the English in 1654. But in the summer of 1667, Charles II returned the region to French control. Nova Scotia became Acadia once again.

Acadia's resurrection was good news for the Wabanaki. Since the time of Champlain, the French had proved reliable allies and trading partners of Wabanaki bands, from the Abenakis of the Kennebec to the Micmacs of Nova Scotia. Sixty French peasant families had been contentedly living at the head of the Bay of Fundy for nearly forty years, peaceably ignoring changes in government. They intermarried with area Micmacs, prompting a French missionary to predict the two groups would soon become "so mixed . . . that it will be impossible to tell them apart." Jesuit missionaries converted nearly all Micmacs to Catholicism, albeit a primitive, earthy form similar to that practiced by the devout, illiterate Acadian peasants. "The Acadians," historian Arthur Quinn has written, "were friendly neighbors who provided trade goods in exchange for fur, food during the hard months of February and March when the hunting was bad, and the occasional groom for the odd daughter. With such people the Micmacs could live peaceably." The new Acadian government, ensconced in a compact stone fort at what is now Castine on Penobscot Bay, happily supplied the Wabanaki with firearms, powder, and ammunition. More conveniently, the Penobscot fort's gunsmith repaired Wabanaki weapons. The French needed their Indian allies to keep New England at bay and generally treated them with fairness and respect.

In English Maine, relations between Indians and settlers were nuanced. Settlers on Monhegan and the Pemaquid Peninsula were but a few hours' sail from the French governor's fortress on the Penobscot, and feared attack by the French and their Indian allies. Tending fields or fishing gear on the wilderness frontier, Mainers dreaded sudden raids by the so-called "Frenchified" Indian bands: the Passamaquoddies and Micmacs living deep in Acadia under the "Popish" influence of Jesuit missionaries. But at the same time, relations with local Indians were generally positive. Of the four major tribes of English Maine, three had friendly relations with the Mainers: the Sacos, Kennebecs, and Penobscots. The fourth, the Androscoggins of western Maine, had been cheated and abused by a frontier trader and maintained a cooler stance. Compared to southern New Englanders, Mainers were better able to accept the Indians' way of life. Even the great Puritan propagandist William Hubbard had to admit that Mainers had been "in good correspondence with the Indians" for many years prior to 1675.

But in that year, disaster struck. As Mainers feared, outside forces instigated a terrible racial war that overwhelmed the tiny settlements of the "Eastern frontier." The tide of destruction came not from the East, but from the Puritan lands to the southwest.

In 1675, the much-aggrieved Indians of southern New England rose up in a massive rebellion that nearly succeeded in driving the Puritans out of North America. Though it is largely forgotten today, a larger proportion of America's population died in King Philip's War than in any other war in our nation's history. In less than two years, the Indians killed 3,500 colonists, destroyed fifty of New England's ninety towns, and set the region's prosperity back one hundred years. Through arrogance and stupidity, the Puritans essentially lost the war and had to be saved by their nemesis, King Charles II, who dispatched imperial troops and their Mohawk allies from the crown colony of New York to put down the rebellion. This imperial intervention cost Massachusetts much of its autonomy, and virtually exterminated the Indians of southern New England.

Proportionately, the English settlers of Maine paid the greatest price, with one in ten losing their lives and eight in ten losing their homes and sometimes the very towns they lived in. But Maine could have avoided the war altogether, had it not been for a series of bad decisions—and criminal acts—made by Massachusetts authorities and the settlers themselves.

As the war raged in Massachusetts in the early summer of 1675, the Maine frontier remained quiet. With the exception of the Androscoggins, tribal leaders went out of their way to show their goodwill toward their English neighbors. The leader of the Kennebecs, Mohotiwormet (whom the settlers called "Robin Hood"), even staged an elaborate ceremonial dance honoring his English allies.

Despite this, Massachusetts authorities insisted on disarming all Maine Indians, and soldiers were dispatched from York to friendly Indian villages to enforce these orders. But the Indians depended on firearms to hunt animals for food and trade, and taking their weapons was, in effect, a death sentence. Thomas Gardiner, a leading citizen of Pemaquid and former military commander, alerted the governor of Massachusetts of his folly. "These Indians amongst us live most by hunting as your Honour well knoweth [so I don't see] how we can take away their armes whose livlyhood dependeth on it," Gardiner wrote. "Indianes in these parts did never appear dissatisfied until their arms were taken away [and I expect] they may be forced to go to the French for releife or fight against us." In response, Governor John Leverett had Gardiner arrested and put on trial for treason.

Actually, at the time, the Indians had no way to procure weapons. The French fortress on the Penobscot had been destroyed by a marauding Dutch corsair, depriving the Indians of the services of the French gunsmiths. Without firearms, the Indians faced a winter of starvation. Even so, the Sacos, Kennebecs, and Penobscots remained peaceful. The Androscoggins immediately prepared for war.

A few weeks later, a murderous act by the crew of an English ship drove the Sacos to war. The sailors, drunk and milling about the Saco River area, noticed a canoe with an Indian mother and baby on board. Curious about a rumor that Indian children instinctively knew how to swim, the sailors overturned the canoe and watched the baby plummet like a stone. The mother dove into the frigid water and retrieved her son, but the child died shortly thereafter. Unfortunately for Mainers, the woman was the wife of the Saco leader, Squando, and the dead child was his son. The enraged chieftain mobilized his people for war.

In September, the Androscoggins took nearby English settlements by surprise. They burned down the trading post of the trader who had cheated them, then attacked the scattered homes of Falmouth, South Berwick, Wells, York, and finally Saco, where they were reinforced by Squando's warriors. Most of the homes in these towns were burned to the ground, often with the lifeless bodies of their owners inside. By the time the attacks abated in November, some 150 colonists had been killed, and others taken captive. The Sacos and Androscoggins took heavy losses as well—both on and off the battlefield.

That winter, Maine's Indians—friendly and unfriendly alike—faced starvation. Many died. Two Abenaki sachems (probably Penobscots) protested to the governor of Massachusetts in vain: "You came here when we were quiet and took away our guns and made prisoners of our chief sagamore and that winter for want of guns there were several who starved," they wrote. "Now we hear that you say you will not stop the war as long as there is an Indian in the country. We are the owners of the country and it is wide and full of Indians and we can drive you out, but our desire is to be quiet." The Penobscots shared their meager food supplies with starving Indian war refugees from southern New England and were soon reduced to scavenging animal bones for maggots and bonemeal. The food situation among the Kennebecs became so dire that large numbers fled eastward into Acadia to seek relief from the French and the Passamaquoddies.

In the spring, and many times thereafter, various Wabanaki leaders tried to organize peace talks with their Puritan counterparts. As authorities in Boston spurned Wabanaki advances, the Androscoggins and Sacos returned to the warpath, bolstered by small numbers of battle-hardened Wampanoag and Narraganset warriors, whose tribes had just been crushed in southern New England. Maine's settlers soon faced their wrath.

On August 20, 1676, a fisherman on Damariscove witnessed a horrifying sight. From the tiny palisaded fort perched on the ridge above the island's tiny harbor, the watchman could see all the islands and peninsulas of the mid-Maine coast from the mouth of the Kennebec in the west to the bold hump of Monhegan to the east. Only this morning, dozens of smoke plumes were rising across this vast tableau, one for each English home, fort, and settlement west of Pemaquid. The seas were dotted with the sails of dozens of boats converging on the island from every point and river, each overloaded with refugees. Within a day or two, Damariscove's narrow harbor was clogged with vessels, and fresh plumes rose from the remains of the mighty fort at Pemaquid Harbor.

Damariscove's dozen resident fishing families found themselves sheltering some three hundred mainland refugees—survivors of this massive Indian assault which had wiped out every settlement east of the Kennebec. Among the refugees was Sylvanus Davis from the large, fortified trading station on Arrowsic Island, located several miles inland on the Sasanoa River. An Androscoggin war party had executed a surprise attack several days earlier, infiltrating the fort and killing thirty-five of thirty-seven inhabitants. Davis himself had been gunned down while fleeing for the boats, but had crawled into a rocky crevice and hidden there for two days before making his way to Damariscove. Farmers from Sheepscot arrived with a traumatized young girl, the only survivor of a lightning raid on Richard Hammond's trading post on the east bank of the Kennebec in what is now Woolwich. As her family and neighbors were subdued or slaughtered, the girl fled into the woods, then walked twelve miles on Indian footpaths to the farming hamlet at Sheepscot. The farmers quickly gathered their possessions and fled south, driving their livestock before them, and warning every settler they encountered. Indians burned all that remained behind. Refugees from the Damariscotta, Boothbay, and Pemaquid areas reported that their neighbors on isolated farms had been carried away by the rampaging Androscoggins. Henry Champnois of what is now East Boothbay arrived clutching his sons and a gun he'd purchased from his friend Mugg Hegone, an Anglophile Kennebec sachem who later emerged as the Wabanakis' principal warlord. Pemaquid's two dozen residents were accompanied by Fort Pemaquid's eight-man garrison, who tried unsuccessfully to organize the terrified refugees to defend the tiny island.

At the time, Damariscove was one of the largest and most important settlements in the area, second only to Monhegan in tax assessments. In addition to the farms, fort, and fishing stages, John Wriford maintained an inn and tavern, but there were not enough provisions to support three hundred hungry refugees. When the bodies of two fishermen and their cattle were found outside their burnt homes on nearby Fishermen's Island a few days later, everyone crowded into their boats and fled east to the comparative safety of Monhegan.

For three weeks, Monhegan served as a lifeboat for some four hundred English settlers, fishermen, and mariners displaced by the Androscoggin assault. It was the safest place to go: the island was sufficiently tall and far enough from the mainland to prevent a surprise assault by Indians in fragile canoes. The summer and year-round fishing crews had great stockpiles of fresh and salt cod, while tavern keeper John Dolling maintained a large storehouse, as well as "barns, stables, orchards, gardens" and fields of Indian corn. Two of the Damariscove fishermen sailed to Boston to get help, while the rest of the island prepared to defend itself. Guards were posted, and every night twenty-five men were assigned to watch for approaching Indians. Finally the Damariscovers brought word that "it was in vain to expect any help from Boston" as it was "being questioned there what they had to do with those parts," i.e., Midcoast Maine. Running low on provisions, the refugees set sail for Massachusetts and New Hampshire. Many would never return to Maine's "cursed" shores.

While Midcoast Maine burned, Massachusetts was busy mopping up the last Indian bands in southern New England with the help of the Mohawks and royal forces. Flushed with victory, Boston finally did decide to dispatch an army to southern Maine made up of nearly two hundred English and Natick Indian soldiers under the command of Major Richard Waldron.

Waldron proved a terrible pick. Before the war, he had been a black marketeer in his native New Hampshire, selling liquor to the Indians in violation of Bay Colony law. He was contemptuous of them all, and had sanctioned the capture of friendly Wabanakis by Massachusetts slave traders. On his arrival in northern New England, he promptly turned a bad situation into a disastrous one. Waldron agreed to meet a delegation of negotiators from the peaceful Penobscot tribe at his Dover, New Hampshire, trading post. In the midst of a day of festivities, Waldron's men seized and disarmed the Indians. Only those Penobscots known to be peaceful were released, while dozens of others were killed on the spot or sold into slavery, including many Narraganset and Wampanoag refugees who'd taken shelter with the Penobscots. Waldron's actions carried a heavy price.

With news of this new treachery, the peaceable Kennebecs and Penobscots promptly went to war and quickly overwhelmed the wayward Massachusetts army. They were led by the formerly anglophile Mugg Hegone, a brilliant warlord who had lived with English families and understood their tactics. Mugg's forces received ample arms and advice from the governor of Acadia, Jean de St. Castin, an unusual French baron who lived in a wigwam in a Penobscot village and later married the daughter of a Penobscot chieftain. Allied with Androscoggins and Sacos, Mugg captured and occupied southern Maine's main fort in Scarborough, leveled the settlements of Casco Bay and Cape Neddick, the fishing station on Richmond Island, and even laid siege to poorly defended Boston. The following spring Mugg's forces sacked Wells, captured fishing vessels from other harbors, and then ambushed and destroyed a ninety-man Massachusetts force in Scarborough. Abandoned farms littered southern Maine and any settler who tried to fish, hunt, or tend fields risked ambush and death. Massachusetts, unwilling to contemplate peace, was now losing the war.

Royal authorities were appalled by the Massachusetts leadership's gross mishandling of the situation, which now threatened the security of England's entire North American empire. Finally, in the summer of 1677, the royals intervened. The king's brother and heir to the throne, James, Duke of York (later James II), reclaimed jurisdiction over Maine through his charter to New York and dispatched a small force to Pemaquid to set things straight. The warring parties were summoned to the rebuilt fortress and, under the king's flag, a peace treaty was negotiated.

The Peace of Casco, signed in April 1678, was a victory for the Wabanaki. The English acknowledged Wabanaki land rights and required each Maine family to make an annual payment of corn to the Indians. A royal commission blamed Massachusetts for starting and prolonging the war, citing their repeated mistreatment and humiliation of Indians. King Charles II declared that all of New England would now be ruled by a royal governor; Midcoast Maine was to remain part of New York as the "County of Cornwall." There, Mainers could return to their homes, but, to avoid future Indian conflict, no new settlers from Massachusetts would be allowed into the region. Further, Bay Colony vessels, fur traders, and herring fishermen were barred from the territory. With the Puritans at bay in "Cornwall" and cowed west of the Kennebec, Maine settled into an uneasy peace. It was not to last.

Over the next decade, settlers trickled back into Maine, rebuilding their burnt-out homes, barns, towns, and fortifications. Most did not pay the Wabanaki their annual quitrent, as required by the Treaty of Casco. The embittered settlers let their cattle wander freely through

Indian cornfields, where the beasts happily ate or trampled the crops. Southern Mainers took to setting large nets over the mouth of the Saco River, preventing great runs of fish from reaching Wabanaki villages upriver. In nearly all cases, the Indians' complaints were ignored by settlers and courts alike, driving racial tensions to the breaking point.

One day in August 1688, a group of Indians killed four or five cows that were destroying their crops near the Saco River. Despite the Indians' repeated efforts to get the settlers to restrain the errant animals, the Massachusetts authorities reacted severely to the crime. They seized twenty random Wabanakis and threw them into a Boston prison.

That summer, Indians raided North Yarmouth, Saco, and the settlements of Casco Bay. A war party rounded up and slaughtered all the settlers of Merrymeeting Bay in a "drunken carousal." Sheepscot, newly rebuilt, was burned again. So was Dover, New Hampshire, where the Wabanaki captured the infamous Major Waldron, hacked off his nose, and allowed him to pass out on his own sword. "The garden of the East," Puritan leader Cotton Mather declared, "was infested with serpents."

Again, cooler heads intervened. Edmund Andros, the royal governor of all of New England, was outraged that Massachusetts authorities had needlessly embroiled the "Eastern Territories" in another destructive conflict and tried to make peace. But in the midst of Andros's negotiations with the Wabanaki, ships arrived with momentous news from England. King James II, Andros's boss, had been deposed by Parliament and had fled to France. Massachusetts officials promptly clamped Andros in chains and ended negotiations with the Wabanaki.

In the spring of 1689, the Wabanaki resumed their war; it would continue, with only brief interruptions, for twenty-three years. For a quarter of a century, Maine was a scene of Balkan-like desolation, warfare, lawlessness, and ethnic slaughter. In 1689, all of Maine's settlers north of Wells—up to four thousand people—fled for their lives. Many of those who got away found themselves in the streets and poorhouses of Boston. Many of those who did not came to slow and gruesome ends. From 1689 to 1713, not a single English home stood in all of Maine north of Wells, which lies twenty-five miles south of what is

now Portland. Only three Maine towns remained inhabited throughout this period—Wells, York, and Kittery at Maine's southernmost
extremity—and even these experienced constant raids and massacres.
Seven hundred Mainers and an unknown number of Indians died in
this first quarter-century of war alone. When peace finally came in
1713 it lasted but seven years before the region plunged into a bloody,
six-year reprise.

Maine's Indian wars, which frequently involved French troops and
warships, were fought with unusual brutality. John Diamond, captured by Indians at Wells in 1692, was stripped, castrated, scalped,
stabbed, slashed, and stuck with firebrands in full view of his companions manning the town fort. English accounts describe many instances
of Indian brutality: scalping elderly women alive, chopping up children with hatchets, tearing infants from their mothers' arms and bash-
ing their brains out, and cutting open pregnant women and skewering
their fetuses in front of them. The English behaved no differently. In a
1724 raid on the Indian village of Norridgewock, English soldiers
slaughtered eighty Kennebec men, women, and children and a French
Jesuit missionary, then scalped the latter along with twenty-six of the
warriors. Massachusetts offered bounties as high as £100 per Indian
scalp, prompting many settlers to engage in "scalp hunting" expeditions. On several occasions, Wabanaki were killed or captured under
the flag of truce. In others, friendly Indian bands were slaughtered by
English soldiers in retribution for raids by French-backed Micmacs.

The devastation of the Indian wars left an indelible mark on the
character and outlook of Maine's people. Hundreds of their relatives
and neighbors had been killed, often in extremely grisly ways, and
many fled. Some had returned after the peace of 1699, only to lose
their newly built homes, barns, and fish houses when fighting resumed just two years later. Even those Mainers whose towns weren't
obliterated lived in constant terror of Indian attack. Two generations
of Mainers were born and raised amid southern Maine's killing fields,
where every trip to work the fields or fish the inshore banks exposed
settlers to ambush and death. Economic and social life deteriorated,
with many inhabitants reduced to the most miserable state of poverty.
By 1701, the situation was sufficiently desperate that even residents of
Kittery, York, and Wells started deserting their wasted land in droves.

Fearing the eastern frontier would become depopulated, the Massachusetts General Court forbade Mainers from relocating without their permission. Local court dockets became filled with alcohol-related crimes. Kittery, with nine hundred mostly impoverished residents, supported at least ten pubs in 1696. Life on the Maine frontier was a serious business, and those who survived under these conditions had to be stubborn, self-sufficient, and able to endure considerable physical and emotional punishment.

Maine's Wabanaki inhabitants paid the greatest price in these first four Indian wars. Unable to wage war and raise food simultaneously, the Wabanaki suffered repeated famines. In the winter of 1698, Cotton Mather reported, "both Indians and [their] English prisoners were starved to death. . . . Nine Indians in one company went a hunting, but met with such hard circumstances that after they had eat[en] up their dogs and their cats they dyed horribly famished." By the 1720s, starvation had forced most Maine Wabanaki to flee all the way to the shores of the St. Lawrence River in Quebec. At war's end in 1726, many lived in permanent refugee camps clustered around the Jesuit missions of St. Francis and Bécancour. Others removed to villages deep in Maine's wilderness interior, hoping to find peace in lands far from the English-infested coast.

Maine's true natives had lost their coast to newcomers. Now it would be the newcomers' turn to defend their homes from covetous and powerful outsiders.

FOUR

Insurrections

At the close of the fourth Indian war in 1726, Midcoast Maine was a desolate wasteland. The great stone fort at Pemaquid was in ruins and for many miles around it, all that remained of European settlement were burnt and looted farms, villages, fishing camps, and, undoubtedly, the remains of people who once lived in them. Maine's forests were reclaiming the land, spreading scrub and saplings across untended fields, pastures, and gardens. Some towns, abandoned since the great Indian assault of 1689, now were covered in full-fledged forests of forty-year-old pine and spruce. In southern Maine, most towns survived, though the people lived in desperate conditions. But east of the Sheepscot River not a single English settlement remained, save perhaps for the offshore fishing hamlets of Monhegan and Damariscove. Newcomers described the region as nothing more than a "howling wilderness."

But the region's natural resources continued to draw the attention of covetous outsiders. In Massachusetts, powerful land speculators, called the "Great Proprietors," were busily hatching plans to ensure that they would be the main beneficiaries of the region's future development. Gorges-era deeds were changing hands, maps were being consulted, and relevant Bay Colony officials were being bought or replaced. If things went as planned, the land speculators hoped their families would become a landed aristocracy that controlled New England's affairs much as the nobility controlled England itself.

Then, in 1729, these speculators heard the most horrifying news: the crown was seizing Midcoast Maine for its own purposes.

In the summer of 1729, Colonel David Dunbar, the Surveyor-General of His Majesty's Woods in America, arrived in Boston and informed Massachusetts governor Jonathan Belcher that all the lands between the Kennebec and St. Croix rivers were no longer under his jurisdiction. The region was to be annexed to the crown colony of Nova Scotia, effective immediately. Dunbar also told the outraged governor that he would soon sail for Pemaquid, where he would build a fort from which to govern the region as a brand-new royal colony, which would be called "Sagadahoc."

How could the crown seize this part of Massachusetts? Governor Belcher undoubtedly asked. The answer, Dunbar told him, was simple: Massachusetts had actually lost this stretch of Midcoast Maine many years earlier, when the French and their Indian allies had conquered it. The French, in turn, had just been defeated by the king, and so now Midcoast Maine belonged to His Majesty by right of conquest, to dispose of as he saw fit. Further, Dunbar's administration would not be recognizing any of the "ancient deeds" held by the Bay Colony land speculators. Instead, Sagadahoc's mighty forests were to be reserved for use as masts in His Majesty's every-growing navy. If Belcher was stunned by this turn of events, he must have been absolutely apoplectic when he learned that the entire plan had been Dunbar's idea in the first place. The governor vowed to stop the colonel, whom he later described as "the most malicious, perfidious creature that wears human shape."

This may have been an exaggeration, but Dunbar was certainly not the most diplomatic official in the empire. A proud, ambitious man born to a poor Scottish family in Northern Ireland, Dunbar had worked his way through the ranks of the English army, where he developed both an "impossibly bad temper" and friendships with some well-connected officers. One of his friends, Colonel Martin Bladen, had used his influence at the royal Board of Trade to secure Dunbar's royal commissions and approval for his Maine scheme. In New England, Dunbar pursued his plan with little diplomatic subtlety.

The first thing Dunbar required was settlers. He needed people as tough, fierce, and uncompromising as himself; self-sufficient men and women accustomed to the hardships and dangers of a war-ravaged borderland; people willing and able to fight Indians, Massachusetts land speculators, French raiders, or anyone else who might challenge the nascent colony. And Dunbar knew right where to find them: among his fellow countrymen in the northern provinces of Ireland. His quest would leave a permanent mark on the cultural fabric of coastal Maine.

The Scottish families of Northern Ireland were, to Dunbar's thinking, the perfect frontiersmen. Their ancestors had weathered seven hundred years of nearly constant warfare on the contested lowland borders of Scotland and England. This was the land where William ("Braveheart") Wallace and Robert the Bruce fought their respective battles, where anarchy reigned and life was often "nasty, brutish, and short." Borderlanders generally lived in dire poverty and were exposed to endemic violence, often without effective government of any kind. Survival required extreme self-reliance and the willingness to do anything to defend home and hearth or kith and kin against anyone who would do them harm, be they raiders, invaders, tax collectors, or surveyors. Suspicious of outside authority of any kind, the Scottish borderlanders valued individual liberty above all else, and often defended it by the most savage means.

King James I, who ruled England in the days of George Waymouth and John Popham, was the first to recognize the borderlanders' utility as frontline settlers. James was the monarch who finally brought peace to the borderlands because, in addition to being king of England, he was also, conveniently, King James VI of Scotland. But James had a new problem on his hands in 1603: how to pacify the "savage Irish" in Ulster, Munster, and other northern provinces of Ireland that had recently been conquered by English adventurers. He, like Dunbar a century later, looked to his countrymen for the answer. The king encouraged tens of thousands of Protestant borderlanders—most of them from the lowlands of southwestern Scotland—to cross the twenty-mile North Channel to begin new lives in Northern Ireland. There they became the Scotch-Irish, a people who have left a lasting mark on the history and culture of both Northern Ireland and the United States.

Northern Ireland, the settlers discovered, was much like home: a contested borderland marked by incessant violence and constant deprivation. At first, Ireland offered the Scottish settlers something they couldn't have back in Scotland: freehold farms on fertile land. But these farms occupied land stolen from their previous owners, Gaelic-speaking Irish "savages" who had been dispersed by English armies. The Irish, understandably, resented the new occupants, and large numbers of them turned to guerrilla warfare. Living in the forests and mountains, small bands of "wood-kerns" (guerrilla soldiers) raided Scotch-Irish farms, surviving on what they plundered. As in Maine, the natives repeatedly resorted to all-out warfare to force the newcomers from the land. At times the Scotch-Irish found themselves struggling not only with Irish guerrillas and English troops, but with the famine and disease that struck the region repeatedly in the opening years of the seventeenth century. To make matters worse, by the early 1700s most settler families had sunk into tenancy; forced to pay substantial rents to wealthy absentee landlords, many families lived in extreme poverty.

What better people to keep Maine "savages" at bay, Dunbar reasoned, than those who'd been knocking the heads of Irish savages for three generations? And the colonel knew that attracting them to the frontier would be easy. He could offer them what they most wanted in the world: their own land, free for the taking, a chance to exchange the "slavery" of tenancy for economic independence.

Dunbar didn't have to go far to find willing Scotch-Irish families. Conditions in Ireland had become so desperate that hundreds of families had already emigrated to New England. Once again, they had encountered harsh conditions, this time involving Puritans and climate alike.

In 1718, five ships arrived in Boston carrying 120 of these Scotch-Irish families, who had been lured by the promise of free frontier land. Receiving a hostile reception, they fled the city in two groups. One party went to the Bay Colony's western frontier and tried to settle in Worcester, but the people there denounced them as "Irish," burned down their meetinghouse, and drove them from the town. They then traveled to the New Hampshire frontier and founded the town of Londonderry. The second group sailed instead to the eastern frontier and spent a frigid and demoralizing winter on Casco Bay, near what is now Portland. In the spring the majority fled to join their countrymen in Londonderry; the others either stayed on Casco Bay or moved east to settle on the shores of the lower Kennebec. This latter group was soon joined by a fresh wave of several hundred Scotch-Irish immigrants, who settled on the shores of Merrymeeting Bay, a confluence of five rivers near what is now Bath, and founded the short-lived town of Cork. Wabanaki raiders destroyed the town a few years later, but the survivors remained in northern New England. By the time Colonel Dunbar showed up in Boston, several thousand Scotch-Irish were already living in Maine and New Hampshire.

Dunbar started a printed advertising campaign "in his Majesty's name," encouraging these Scotch-Irish settlers to join him at Pemaquid and promising to grant them free land under the crown's protection. Between 1729 and 1731, hundreds responded to Dunbar's call. Entire clans of interrelated settlers from County Antrim and County Tyrone moved en masse from New Hampshire to Dunbar's new settlements, founding Boothbay and Boothbay Harbor, Damariscotta and Newcastle, Bristol and South Bristol. Encouraged by their presence, hundreds more would follow in the decades to follow, turning Midcoast Maine into a cradle of Scotch-Irish culture.

These early-eighteenth-century settlers had a profound and lasting effect on Maine's social and cultural landscape, imparting a tradition of fierce pride, independence, and communal resistance to outside authority. From the original settlements of the Midcoast, the colonists' children and grandchildren fanned out to settle the upper river valleys and western Penobscot, while their great-grandchildren spread Downeast, creating the cultural framework to which later settlers would arrive. Today, a large proportion of coastal Maine's old families can trace at least a few of their lines back to these original Scotch-Irish settlers.

Conditions were difficult from the start. "[W]e proceeded to build us little huts and to clear and cultivate as we were able, an inhospitable desert, in the midst of savage beasts and yet more savage men," Boothbay settlers later reported. The lands were "naturally broken and poor" and the settlers "utterly unacquainted with the mode of managing lands in that state," so that "little of the neccesaries of life was raised from the soil." Dunbar had clearly expected the settlers to engage in fishing, having decreed that "forty feet upon the shore was to be common to all fishermen" so they would not be hindered when landing their boats or drying their catch. The first generation of settlers

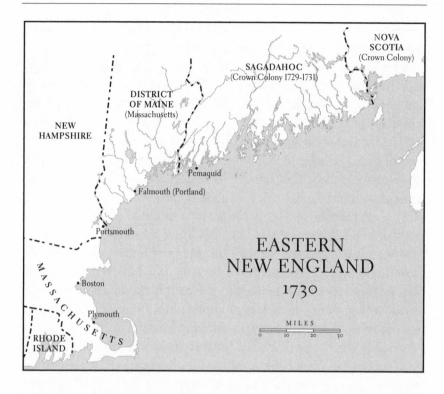

EASTERN
NEW ENGLAND
1730

apparently lacked fishing skills, however, compounding their suffering. Early settler Samuel McCobb recalled that in the early days the
settlers' "whole living depended on cutting firewood and carrying it to
Boston and other towns more than one hundred and fifty miles [away.]"
During many winters, settler John Beath recalled, the settlers would
have "inevitably perished from famine had they not been supplied
from the clam bank [which provided] their only food for several
months together."

They also faced political challenges. Massachusetts refused to recognize Dunbar's authority. In 1730 Governor Belcher even planned a
military assault to crush the new colony, but was foiled by King
George II, who specifically forbade him to carry out "a military expedition against . . . Pemaquid in order to remove several Irish Protestants
lately settled . . . there by Colonel Dunbar." In case those orders
weren't clear enough, thirty royal troops were dispatched from Nova
Scotia to garrison Dunbar's fort. And while Dunbar kept promising to

issue the settlers deeds to their land, rival claimants were showing up to survey, settle, or otherwise take possession of the area.

The settlers responded forcefully to any kind of outside intrusion, quickly earning the fear of people "from away." In 1732, Captain Stephen Lazabe made the mistake of sailing his four-man fishing schooner into Pemaquid Harbor in search of drinking water. The hapless Lazabe was confronted by "a file of men under armes" who seized control of his vessel and threatened to sink it with the fort's cannons. The Pemaquiders held Lazabe for three days and only released him after he signed "a note of hand for a sum of money." In another incident in 1730, Pemaquid settlers seized a sloop that had been taking on a cargo of wooden barrel staves, forced it into the harbor, and informed the captain that "in case he made any opposition they wou'd immediately shoot him." The captain left his ship and crew and fled to find help in York. After hearing his tale, the county sheriff set off for Pemaquid "with a company of Men to protect him from insults" but after hearing rumors that the settlers would kill him, he lost his nerve and returned home. Later that year, Josiah Glover was foolish enough to build a house in New Harbor on land his grandfather had settled before the Indian wars. He was soon confronted by "eight Irish men armed with guns and swords" who "many times threatened to sacrifice him, as their phrase was, and send him to the devil with all the New Harbor Proprietors." The settlers forced Glover to sail his fishing boat to Pemaquid to face Colonel Dunbar, but he slipped away in a canoe while they were sleeping.

But the settlers' worst foes were beyond their reach. The land they so vociferously defended was claimed by people far more powerful than Josiah Glover. Indeed, they were more powerful and better connected than Colonel Dunbar himself.

Word of the Dunbar settlers' antics received a cool reception in the drawing rooms of Boston.

By this time, the character of the Bay Colony's ruling classes had changed considerably. The religious zealots were gone, disgraced and discredited by their incompetent handling of the Indian wars. Now their grandchildren's generation was in charge, a generation more interested in building fabulous commercial fortunes than in creating a Calvinist utopia. Many of Boston's new leaders were from merchant families—the Belchers, Bowdoins, Brattles, Apthorps, Hutchinsons, and Waldos—some of whom had found wartime trade to be incredibly profitable. These families had a foolproof plan to transform themselves into a true New England aristocracy. First, they would use their political and family connections to buy vast swaths of unsettled Maine frontier land at astonishingly cheap rates. Then they would induce poor farmers and immigrants to settle on these lands as tenants. After that they could sit back and collect rents from the toiling farmers and, as land values rose, sell or rent adjacent plots for many times what they'd paid for them.

These Great Proprietors, as they came to be known, based their claims on Sir Ferdinando Gorges's century-old feudal grants. Some were larger than many European princedoms. The 1630 Muscongus Patent covered a million acres between the Medomak River and Penobscot Bay. The Plymouth or Kennebec Patent of 1629 was even larger: three million acres surrounding the Kennebec River that stretched from its mouth to Norridgewock, deep in Maine's wilderness interior. A third, the Pejepscot Patent, covered much of the lower Androscoggin Valley. Although of dubious validity, these grants had since been sold, resold, or inherited many times over the past four generations. Pooling their formidable resources into shareholding companies, the Great Proprietors bought these questionable claims from their various owners on the cheap.

But Dunbar's new colony threatened to stop the Proprietors in their tracks. Sagadahoc's boundaries incorporated half the Kennebec Patent and all of the Muscongus Patent along with several small claims. If it succeeded, the colony would render the Proprietors' titles as worthless as the paper they were printed on. Dunbar and his troublesome settlers, it was decided, had to be stopped at any cost.

The Great Proprietors pulled every trick in the book. They bombarded the Massachusetts General Court with calls for Dunbar's removal. Governor Belcher, himself a scion of a leading merchant family, appealed to the crown to reverse its decision and return Midcoast Maine to his control. But the man who came through for them was Samuel Waldo, the son of Boston merchant prince and Muscongus

Proprietor Jonathan Waldo. Dispatched to London by the Muscongus Proprietors, Waldo persuaded the Board of Trade to rescind its approval of Dunbar's colony. In 1731 the board handed down its final ruling: Massachusetts would control the entire Maine coast from the Kennebec to the St. Croix. The following year, Dunbar received orders to dissolve his government and abandon his post.

Dunbar followed his orders, but warned that his Scotch-Irish settlers wouldn't be so obedient. "[T]here will be a kind of warr 'tween these pretended proprietors and those that will go to settle upon the King's terms," he predicted, "for they will not quit the possession."

Samuel Waldo profited handsomely from his services. In gratitude, the other Muscongus Proprietors gave Waldo half the shares in the grant. To this he added shares belonging to his father, who had died while he was arguing before the Board of Trade. Within a few years, the egotistical merchant prince controlled 92 percent of the shares to the company's vast holdings, which came to be called, aptly enough, the Waldo Patent.

Though one Maine county and two of its towns were later named after him, Samuel Waldo was not a very sympathetic character. Born into considerable wealth, he went into business with money given to him by his father, importing "choice Irish duck, fine Florence wine, Negro Slaves, and Irish butter" and selling them from his elegant Boston home. Though he owned a business empire—trading operations in Boston, the West Indies, and Maine, a sizeable rum distillery and a chain of drinking houses, and paper mills and a large mast tree lumbering operation for the Royal Navy—he conducted his business affairs with the grasping frenzy of a drowning person.

"In all his undertakings [Waldo] was aggressive, ruthless, and avaricious, and in his dealings with others was without mercy," Maine state historian Thomas Griffiths wrote two centuries later. "He was greedy of wealth and ambitious for power, it was said, without a single generous impulse toward benevolence." Indeed, Waldo regularly betrayed or backstabbed not only employees, servants, and business partners, but his friends and family as well. After his father's death he tried to cheat his own siblings and children out of thousands of pounds. His case was so weak that he lost every suit against his family in the courts, despite his considerable political influence among judges, the governor's council, and the royal court in London. But Waldo was far more successful at deploying the legal system against people of lesser means. Richard Fry, a rag merchant who leased one of Waldo's paper mills, spent most of his life in prison, apparently because he refused a stingy offer from Waldo to buy back his lease. In the 1740s, Waldo foreclosed on his southern Maine business partner, Thomas Westbrook, in a bid to seize all of his assets. He even succeeded in having two Massachusetts governors sacked and replaced by successors of his choosing. In Midcoast Maine, Waldo would continue to conduct himself with characteristic ruthlessness.

To truly profit from his new wilderness princedom, Waldo needed settlers, and he went about acquiring them as if they were commodities, like duck, rum, or slaves. First there was the matter of determining what sort of product to acquire. They had to be Protestants, of course, though Waldo cared not whether they were Anglican or Calvinist. They had to be hardy and tenacious, able to survive and pay rents in the midst of the wilderness. And, most important, they had to have no better options, for surely they would take them before venturing out to Waldo's war-torn frontier. Waldo looked over at the Scotch-Irish settlers in Boothbay and other Dunbar settlements located just outside his grant and thought he saw just what he needed.

Indeed, this first wave of Scotch-Irish settlers was holding its own against ever-increasing odds. David Dunbar had promised to issue land deeds to the settlers he enticed to settle Damariscotta and the Boothbay, Bristol, and Pemaquid peninsulas. Unfortunately for the settlers, Dunbar was dismissed before he could have the deeds ratified, leaving the settlers without title to the lands they'd cleared and built their homes on. Soon, Boston lawyers started showing up in their towns, taking measurements and distributing threatening letters on behalf of prior owners or their heirs. With no hope of winning their case in Massachusetts courts, Dunbar settlers resolved "to keep their possessions till his majesty should see fit . . . to remove them." To show their loyalty to the king, as Boothbay settler William Fullerton later recalled, his community "never cut down . . . or destroyed any tree fit for any service as a mast in His Majesty's Navy, nor ever joined in any of the late unhappy disputes between [Massachusetts] and the Mother Country." Despite Massachusetts court rulings against them, the Dunbar settlers continued to occupy their land. While the record is silent on how they managed to defy the court's authority, their tactics probably resembled the actions of their countrymen on Georgetown Island. When Bay Colony authorities tried to serve a writ there in 1722, armed townspeople confronted them, threatening to bash their skulls in. "No officer should dare touch any man in the river," settler Samuel Rogers told one official, while neighbor Robert Poore urged, "Kill him, kill him, kill him." The settlers, it seemed, weren't going anywhere without a fight.

Waldo figured he could use men such as these. They had shown themselves to be the perfect frontiersmen, able to stand up against the very sorts of people who might threaten Waldo's less-than-watertight land title: rival claimants, nosy attorneys, or aggrieved Wabanaki bands. Waldo had to have some Scotch-Irish of his own.

Like Dunbar, Waldo started his recruiting drive among recent Scotch-Irish immigrants. Settlers were offered hundred-acre lots along the St. George River in what is now Warren on the condition that they construct a large log home, clear land for farming, and pay an annual quitrent of one peppercorn—the last item a symbolic acknowledgment of Waldo's lordship. Twenty-seven Scotch-Irish families took up the offer in 1735, moving to Warren from the Pemaquid, the Casco Bay area, and other parts of New England. Over the next few years, another forty families poured in. They settled what is now Thomaston at the head of the St. George, the river first charted by George Waymouth 130 years earlier. Some came more or less directly from Northern Ireland, others from Londonderry, New Hampshire. Local genealogies show that in the decades that followed, dozens of additional Scotch-Irish families arrived from Northern Ireland to settle among their countrymen on the Midcoast.

But with a million acres to develop, Waldo needed more settlers than the Scotch-Irish could draw in by word of mouth. To bring in more people, Waldo and his son began actively recruiting Protestant immigrants during their frequent trips to Europe. He hired agents

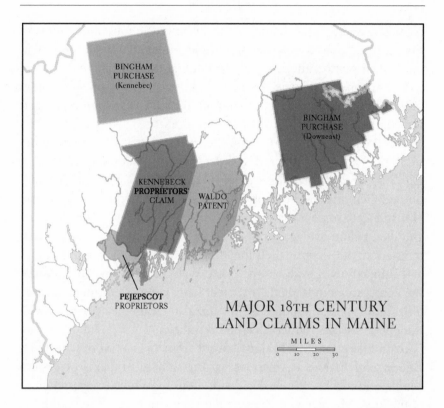

MAJOR 18TH CENTURY
LAND CLAIMS IN MAINE

MILES

overseas and took out advertisements in major German newspapers promising prospective immigrants free passage and, once they had lived in Maine for seven years, 120 acres of inheritable property. Immigrants were told that Midcoast Maine was a place where the "climate is acknowledged to be healthy, and the soil is exceedingly fruitful . . . and it yields all manner of fruit as in Germany, but hemp and flax in greater perfection." Waldo promised that on arrival, new colonists would find "necessary support for from four to six months," good roads, and frequent shipping connections to Boston and beyond.

Soon Waldo was importing settlers into Maine in wholesale quantities. In 1742, his agents shipped a cargo of 170 Palatinate Germans to what is now Waldoboro. A similar number of Bavarian and Hessian Germans arrived aboard the *Priscilla* in 1751 and another three hundred Germans followed in 1753. Waldo also recruited seventy lowland Scots, who settled among the Scotch-Irish of Warren, as well as twenty

New England Puritan families who became the founding fathers of
Friendship. Inspired by Waldo's example, budding aristocrats throughout British North America started rounding up German and Scotch-
Irish immigrants of their own; the holders of the Kennebec Patent
hired Waldo's very own agent to import thirty German families to their
vast Maine holdings.

For the European immigrants, the trip to Maine was extremely unpleasant. Many were abused and deceived by Waldo's agent, Joseph
Crellius, who cheated his "freights" out of their life's savings and
housed them in sordid conditions. Conditions at Crellius's facilities in
Holland were so poor that several of the colonists of 1753 became sick
and died before leaving Europe. Those who made it to Maine "were
transferred to a sloop, which they filled as close as they could stand,"
and shipped up to Waldoboro. There Waldo lodged most of them for
the winter in a crude shed, "sixty feet long, without chimnies, and utterly unfit for habitation." Many froze to death or "perished with
hunger or diseases induced by their privations."

Conditions on the Midcoast went from bad to worse. In 1744,
Britain and France went to war again, and the Indians of eastern
Maine and the Maritimes decided to help the French regain control
of the area. Micmac and Passamaquoddy warriors launched lightning
strikes throughout Midcoast Maine in 1745, attacking towns and mur-
dering settlers. The situation in Boothbay was so dire that the entire
community was abandoned for five years, the settlers taking refuge in
Massachusetts, "where all our little substance was soon spent in the
maintenance of our families so far from home." When they finally returned and rebuilt their cottages the Indians promptly "fell upon [the]
neighborhood, burnt barns, killed cattle, attacked the little garrison
kept by the people, and carried away a number of men, women, and
children into captivity." The remaining settlers were bottled up in the
garrison for months, unable to tend their fields, so that in winter "the
horrors of famine were in prospect." Raiders returned to the Midcoast
each summer until 1754, when warfare resumed in earnest.

All this fighting was making Waldo extremely nervous. As long as
the Indians were running around, burning towns and slaughtering
their inhabitants, it was going to be difficult to find new settlers will-

ing to pay top dollar for a bit of Waldo's little empire. He began lobbying in Boston for the construction of a new fort on the Penobscot River that would protect his holdings by cutting off the main line of supply between the French in Quebec and their Indian allies. It took four years to convince the Massachusetts assembly to fund the project, during which the war continued to intensify. But finally, in the spring of 1759, Governor William Shirley himself arrived at Waldo's estate at the head of a company of four hundred armed men. Waldo, delighted, joined the expedition as it traveled up the Penobscot and began constructing a fort that would, presumably, make his lands secure and profitable. But while walking along the eastern bank of the river, Waldo dropped dead from apoplexy. Governor Shirley's men buried him the next day on the site slated for his fort, which spared them the burden of hauling him back to Boston.

None of this did Waldo's settlers much good, however. The war lasted for nine years, during which the people all along the Midcoast "lived in continual terror and alarm from the savages who ranged the wilderness all around." Throughout this so-called French and Indian War, the people of Boothbay reported receiving no military or humanitarian assistance of any kind, "tho' numbers of our men were called into the Provincial Army and sent to the defence of other places." For fifteen years straight, Maine's wretched settlers lived in a terrorized state in which "scalping or captivity was frequently the fate of some, and ever the expectation of us all."

By the end of this sixth and final Indian war, the settlers had been reduced to dire poverty. A newly arrived parson found the German settlers north of Wiscasset living in "miserable huts, which scarce afforded them shelter from the inclemency of the weather in a vigorous climate. I might add many affecting instances of their extreme poverty— that multitudes of children were obliged to go barefoot through the whole winter, with hardly clothes to cover their nakedness,—that half of the houses were without chimneys—that many people had no other beds than a heap of straw—and whole families had scarce anything to subsist upon, for months together, except potatoes, roasted in the ashes."

Little did they know that the struggle to defend their land was just beginning.

In 1763, peace finally came. The French had been completely defeated and were forever ejected from the North American mainland. The Kennebec nation had collapsed and would never again function as a coherent tribe, while the Penobscots, ravaged by a smallpox epidemic, retreated into the interior. The Maine frontier, long synonymous with warfare and danger, had become safe for English settlement for the first time in nearly a century.

Despite Maine's desperate poverty and other trying conditions, plenty of people in southern New England were now willing to move there. The old, established towns of Massachusetts, Connecticut, Rhode Island, and southern New Hampshire were running out of the one thing every yeoman farmer wanted for himself and his children: land. Many New Englanders were reduced to renting land as tenant farmers or hiring themselves out as wage laborers, which meant they'd lost not only their economic independence, but their social standing and their right to vote as well. Many feared they would soon become landless peasants, beholden to the arbitrary whims of landed aristocrats—the very fate many had fled Europe to avoid. Facing the treacheries of New England's frontiers, then, seemed a risk worth taking.

We tend to think of the European settlement of North America as a great westward drive. But for the entire colonial period, the frontier generally expanded to the north, south, and east, from the established communities like Virginia and Massachusetts to the frontiers of Florida, northern New England, and Nova Scotia. In fact, wishing to avoid another protracted war with the Indians, Britain forbade colonists from settling west of the Appalachians. That left southern New Englanders with three options. Those who could afford to made the relatively expensive overland journey to Vermont and western New York. Poorer settlers simply booked cheap passage on coastal trading vessels and sailed across the gulf to Maine and western Nova Scotia in the hope of leading a freer life. Maine was, in the words of one settler, "an assalum for people . . . that could not live anywhere else."

Apparently, plenty of poor New Englanders were in need of asylum. In the decade preceding the American Revolution, Maine's population doubled to 47,000. The majority of this growth took place east of the Androscoggin River in Midcoast and Downeast Maine, where the population quintupled to more than 15,000. This great migration of land-hungry southern New Englanders moved Maine's eastern frontier from Monhegan to Machias and beyond. It spread to southwestern New Brunswick and Nova Scotia, accounting for many of the cultural and social affinities that bridge the Bay of Fundy to this day. The migration included New Hampshire Scotch-Irish, Cape Cod fishermen, coastal Rhode Islanders, Connecticut farmers, and a steady trickle of new settlers from Scotland and Ireland. But the migration consisted mainly of poor people from the small, thickly settled towns along the Massachusetts and New Hampshire coastline: places like Marshfield and Newburyport, Essex and Dover. They settled and intermarried with the Scotch-Irish of the Midcoast or the descendants of Maine's seventeenth-century settlers, whose great-great-grandparents might have sailed to the New World on the very same ships as their own ancestors. The families they founded on the coves, islands, and rivers of coastal Maine can still be found there today.

The new settlers soon discovered what their predecessors already knew: the ownership of Maine was largely in dispute. In Midcoast Maine, where most people settled, the Great Proprietors' claims—the Waldo, Plymouth, and Pejepscot patents—overlapped; somewhere amid these larger claims were ten smaller proprietary claimants, not to mention the Dunbar "squatters" of the Boothbay, Bristol, and Pemaquid peninsulas. They also discovered that the various land speculators rarely brought one another to court, for fear their tenuous titles would be overturned. Instead, they used the settlers as pawns: each land company pressed settlers to buy their titles, then sued those who purchased the titles of their rivals. As court cases were extremely expensive, time-consuming, and biased toward "men of consequence," the settlers had little hope of redress. "He who purchases [the deed] of one [claimant] is considered the enemy of the other," Brunswick area settlers lamented. "He is sued and at the end of seven years [of legal proceedings] it is of no consequence to him whether he wins or looses his cause [as] he is ruined in either case."

Indeed, the settlers found that the Great Proprietors had near-total control over the courts, law enforcement, lawmakers, and the government itself. The most powerful group in this period was the Kennebeck Proprietors,* holders of the Plymouth Patent, who laid claim to three million acres stretching from Freeport to Pemaquid and nearly a hundred miles inland. The Kennebeck Proprietors included John Hancock, the richest man in New England and future governor of the commonwealth. James Bowdoin, another wealthy merchant, also governed Massachusetts after a long stint as a leading member of the legislature. His sister, Elizabeth Bowdoin, was married to fellow proprietor James Pitts, a member of the king's council. Charles Apthorp, another fabulously wealthy Bostonian, was paymaster and commissary for the British army and navy in Boston, where colleague Benjamin Hallowell was comptroller of customs. Hallowell's son was married to the daughter of co-proprietor Silvester Gardiner, a Boston physician who built a fortune by monopolizing the import of pharmaceuticals to New England. William Vassall and his cousin Florentius Vassall built their riches on the backs of the African slaves toiling on their family's Jamaican sugar plantations.

Together, the Kennebeck Proprietors commanded a degree of influence over government policy that would have made late-twentieth-century corporate leaders green with envy. In the 1750s they curried the favor of Massachusetts governor William Shirley by secretly granting him a stake in the company. To protect their lands from attack, they got Shirley to build three massive forts on their lands at public expense. After receiving unfavorable judgments in property cases at York County courts, the Kennebeck Proprietors successfully lobbied the new governor, Thomas Pownall, to have Midcoast Maine broken off as a separate county. They then built the new Lincoln County Courthouse themselves in the company town of Pownalborough (now Dresden) and filled the judicial bench, sheriff's department, and county offices with friends and allies. In the 1790s, they repeated this exercise, breaking off their lands to create Kennebec County and appointing one of their own as well as one of their agents to the three-judge court,

---

*I have retained the archaic spelling of "Kennebec" in this context, as it has become the practice among historians of the period.

ensuring it would rule in their favor in any conflicts with squatters. Nor could a settler hope to have a case overturned on appeal: the Proprietors had their own lawyers appointed as appeals court judges. They were determined that their names would remain in posterity. Even today, Hancock, Vassall, Bowdoin, Pitts, Hallowell, and Gardiner each have at least one Maine town or county named after them, despite the fact that several of them defected to Britain during the Revolution.

Other proprietors were similarly influential. Samuel Waldo died in 1759, and his million-acre patent fell to his grandson Thomas Flucker, whose influence rivaled that of the Kennebeck Proprietors. Flucker was a representative to the Massachusetts assembly, a member of the governor's council, and then secretary of Massachusetts under Boston's infamous military governor, Thomas Gage. Thomas Hutchinson, leader of the Pejepscot Proprietors, served, sequentially, as Massachusetts's speaker of the house, chief justice, lieutenant governor, and governor. All believed that the elite were born to lead, and common men were obliged to follow.

In the late colonial period, the Massachusetts elite could generally count on the obedience of the common people. This was still the case in much of the District of Maine. Isolated by language, German settlers in Waldoboro and the Kennebec Valley generally did as they were told—much as they had back in the princedoms of Germany. The same was true of residents of the established towns of southern Maine, well on their way toward assimilation with Massachusetts proper. But, much to the Proprietors' surprise, the settlers of the Midcoast were far less cooperative. Most irksome were the Scotch-Irish, who, despite their acute poverty, had the audacity to behave as if they were equal to any man. Prideful and independent, the Scotch-Irish were inspiring and shaping similarly defiant attitudes among the impoverished New Englanders who settled among them. "I am worried day and night with the unruly people [in the Dunbar settlements]," an agent of the Kennebeck Proprietors reported in 1761, "for they oppose the Company in all shapes."

Indeed, Scotch-Irish settlers had the temerity to physically obstruct the Proprietors' schemes. In the 1750s and 1760s, the Kennebeck Proprietors tried to push squatters from the Midcoast by selling other settlers titles to the land they occupied. In Boothbay they sold most of today's Linekin Neck to new settler Benjamin Linekin, a transaction which upset the Montgomery clan, Scotch-Irish settlers who'd been farming the Neck for two decades. So in April 1755, the Montgomerys simply pulled down Linekin's house and carried away "both frame and boards" along with most of the home's contents. When the Linekins took the Montgomerys to court, a York jury found them not guilty, apparently because they did not find the Great Proprietors' titles legitimate. In June 1761, the people of Newcastle evicted another Kennebeck Proprietor tenant; they pulled down his house, fences, and timber stores and used them to fuel a bonfire. A few years later, thirty men "disguised in Indian dress" destroyed the Woolwich cabin occupied by tenants renting from the Clarke and Lake Company. The Proprietors' efforts to displace the squatters weren't working out so well.

Proprietors next tried evicting "squatters" and putting their tenants in the very homes they had built. This didn't work well either. When the Kennebeck Proprietors evicted James McFarland of Bowdoinham, they couldn't find anyone foolhardy enough to reoccupy his cabin, despite offering other impoverished, hungry squatters an entire winter's worth of provisions if they would serve as tenants. Frustrated with the situation, James Bowdoin ordered company agents to destroy the home. Similarly, proprietor Arthur Noble evicted the squatting owner of a Damariscotta sawmill and put his own tenant in his place; the aggrieved miller, Jonathan Cook, first tried to repossess his premises and, failing that, burned the structure down to deny it to Noble. In 1761, proprietor Silvester Gardiner visited the Sheepscot Valley himself to awe the "squatters" into compliance; settlers disguised themselves as Indians, surrounded the home where Gardiner was sleeping, and howled until the terrified plutocrat made his escape through a window.

As the situation worsened in the early 1770s, the inhabitants of Boothbay turned to the king for recourse. In a 1772 petition to George III, the settlers recalled how they had been harassed by "swarms of persons pretending themselves proprietors of our lands." Some settlers had "bought their lands three times over from three opposite sets of competing claim[ants]; none of whom have ever done anything to defend us from the others, and all of whom still leave us open to the challenges of we know not how many more; by one or another of whome we are daily threatened and disturbed," they wrote. "Permit us Great Sire, to cast ourselves, our wives and helpless little ones, at your Majesty's royal feet, humbly to implore a share in that Princely tenderness . . . to grant us, our heirs and assigns [land titles] in our several possessions in said Boothbay."

But before the situation could be resolved, something totally unexpected happened: the American Revolution.

Since the times of Gorges, Mainers had looked to the crown for relief from the excesses of their Boston overlords. Living in the colony of a colony, many settlers held royalist sympathies and the faith that the king would protect them from the grasping merchant princes of the Bay. But during the 1760s and 1770s, many settlers became disillusioned by a series of imperial policies that made their lives more difficult than they already were.

As settlers poured into the backcountry after the defeat of the French and Indians, they found themselves at odds not only with Boston's Great Proprietors, but with the crown itself. Many of the problems stemmed from the Empire's need for mast trees for its ever-growing navy. The monarchy claimed ownership of all white pine trees from Virginia to Nova Scotia, except for those already in private hands. Maine's coastal frontier was one of the few places where white pines grew on lands that were, arguably, still in the public domain. The crown wanted to keep it that way. It did its best to discourage settlement by proprietors and squatters alike by refusing to provide titles to either the Dunbar settlers or residents of the newly settled towns east of Penobscot Bay. Royal prohibitions on the lumbering of pine were doubly irksome to the Downeast settlers; there was little productive farmland in glacially scoured eastern Maine, so settlers were completely dependent on fishing and lumbering for their survival. The shipping of firewood, lumber, and barrel staves to wood-starved Boston was the settlers' only means of earning credit with which to purchase life's necessities. Prohibitions on the cutting of a key tree species denied them vital income. Downeast settlers were even more vexed when rumors began circulating that a group of English proprietors intended to revive a seventeenth-century claim to 100,000 acres of the eastern Maine coast.

But it was the so-called Coercive Acts of 1774 that permanently shattered Mainers' royalist sympathies. The draconian measures were meant to punish Massachusetts for the Boston Tea Party and other rebellious acts, but hurt Mainers even more than their Boston masters. Ordinary Mainers felt betrayed by the Massachusetts Government Act, which placed town meetings and local judicial appointments under the control of the new military governor of Boston, General Gage. Far worse was the Boston Port Act, which closed the port to colonial vessels carrying "any merchandise whatsoever" except for those carrying food or firewood to the city. The measure was harmful to Boston, but disastrous for Maine towns, where the economy was almost completely dependent on trade with the colonial capital. Downeast Mainers faced malnutrition, as they imported much of their food and supplies from Boston and could not raise their own on the rocky soil. The fact that certain loyalist merchant princes could continue shipping food, firewood, masts, and other military supplies to the city from other ports earned them the lasting wrath of their poorer, suffering neighbors. The situation proved explosive.

Some settlers decided to fight back. Angry militiamen from the frontier towns of Brunswick and Gorham raided the homes of loyalist merchants in wealthier port towns. The Brunswick militia, led by tavern keeper Samuel Thompson, captured several British sympathizers, forcing at least one to dig his own grave and make his last wishes before releasing him. Thompson's men also burst into the Lincoln County Courthouse near Wiscasset, harassed and humiliated the Kennebeck Proprietors' handpicked judges, and forced them to sign patriotic documents. But Thompson's most audacious act came in April 1775, when HMS *Canceaux*, a British sloop-of-war, called at Portland to protect a loyalist merchant's ships. Portland residents were already frightened—a number packed up their things and left town—before Thompson's men arrived on the scene. But fright soon turned to terror after Thompson and his men kidnapped the *Canceaux*'s commanding officer, Lieutenant Henry Mowatt, while he was visiting an Anglican pastor ashore. Many Portlanders fled the city, while others tried to convince Thompson to release Lieutenant Mowatt for fear that the *Canceaux*'s crew would bombard the town. Some city residents considered calling up the local militia to force Mowatt's release, but dropped the idea the following morning when more than six hundred cantankerous militiamen from the surrounding backcountry towns poured into the city to protect Thompson. After looting loyalist homes, Thompson's men released Mowatt and departed from the city. *Canceaux* soon left Portland, carrying a number of loyalist refugees with it. Mowatt would be back for revenge.

Just one month later, the residents of Machias did something even more outrageous. At the time, Machias was in a particularly vulnerable situation. The settlement was small (six hundred people), young (the first settlers had moved from Scarborough only twelve years before), and located so far to the east that the townspeople originally applied to Nova Scotia for the right to incorporate. Unable to raise sufficient food in the thin, rocky soil, Machias people suffered terribly when the British closed the port of Boston. "Potatoes were almost the only vegetable and of these there were not enough for their own consumption," a nineteenth-century historian recalled. Many feared a return of the "clam year" of 1767 when the supply ship from Boston was waylaid by ice and townspeople spent two wretched months foraging "a scanty subsistence from potato sprouts and remnants of starching-flour and from the clam beds." One person who was not suffering, however, was Ichabob Jones, a Boston merchant who dominated Machias's "lumber-for-provisions" trade with the far-off colonial capital. After the port closure, firewood became so scarce in Boston that people were burning fences and church pews for warmth. So when Jones approached British officials offering to ship them wood and lumber from Machias in return for foodstuffs, they happily granted him the right to pass through the blockade.

But Jones found the people of Machias much less accommodating. Many settlers were outraged when Jones's merchant vessels arrived under the protection of HMS *Margaretta*, a four-gun sloop-of-war. The leader of the local militia, Benjamin Foster, one of Jones's business partners, decided to do something about it. Summoning area men together, Foster attempted to ambush Jones and the *Margaretta*'s officers while they were at church. Jones fled into the woods and the officers to their ship, from which they threatened to bombard the town if Jones's lumber-laden ships were not released. The townspeople were not impressed. Instead of releasing Jones's sloops, Foster placed them under the command of Jeremiah O'Brien and his brothers, "a bold energetic Protestant family from Ireland." O'Brien's men, armed with pitchforks, clubs, and muskets, sailed out after the *Margaretta*. They soon overtook the ship, boarded her, and, in a bloody melee, captured her in the name of the Continental Congress. Several cannon were found in the hold, and the rebellious settlers used these to arm Jones's merchant vessels. When the armed schooner HMS *Diligent* and her tender arrived in town to investigate the *Margaretta*'s disappearance, O'Brien and Foster captured them as well, adding the vessels to the hamlet's growing naval flotilla.

Machias's bold actions triggered a series of events that turned all of Maine against the British. When word of the *Margaretta* incident reached Boston, Vice Admiral Samuel Graves, the senior British naval officer, resolved to punish the Mainers. Graves knew just the man to do it: Lieutenant Henry Mowatt, the officer who had been kidnapped by Samuel Thompson's militiamen. Mowatt sailed off to the east with four warships and orders to "chastise" nine rebellious coastal towns, "particularly Mechias [*sic*] where the *Margaretta* was taken, the Officer commanding her killed . . . and where preparations are now making to invade the Province of Nova Scotia." But unfavorable winds prevented Mowatt from reaching Machias, so he turned instead to a more personal target, Portland harbor. There, after a night's warning, Mowatt's ships commenced a full-scale bombardment of the city. "The streets were full of people, oxen and horses," a Portland resident reported. "The oxen, terrified at the smoke and report of the guns, ran with precipitation over the rocks, dashing everything to pieces and scattering large quantities of goods about the streets. . . . Bombs and carcasses, armed with destruction and screaming with fire, blazed dreadfully through the air and descended with flaming vengeance on the defenceless buildings." When the bombardment ended eight and a half hours later, Maine's largest town lay in ruins, with three-quarters of its buildings destroyed. To make matters worse, Gorham militiamen invaded the town, looting the homes of loyalists, real and imagined. News of the bombardment did little to win the hearts and minds of

Mainers, many of whom threw themselves in with radical backcountry settlers like Thompson, Foster, and O'Brien, and firmly behind the Revolution.

The conflict also strengthened ties between the settlers of Downeast Maine and western Nova Scotia, which included what is now New Brunswick. Outside of Halifax, Nova Scotians were generally sympathetic to the American cause, though most attempted to remain neutral in the conflict. "They refused to fight their blood brothers," historian John Barnett Brebner later wrote, "even . . . to the point of failing . . . to defend their homes against them." But some western settlements actively supported the Revolution. Lockeport and Port Mouton served as bases for American privateers raiding British shipping, while Yarmouth, Barrington, and the overtly rebellious Cape Sable fishing hamlets were havens for smugglers running the British blockades. In 1776, settlers on Passamaquoddy Bay and the St. John River in present-day New Brunswick even asked the Continental Congress to admit them as allies in the Revolution. Machias, for its part, became a haven for Revolutionary Nova Scotians. One such rebel, Jonathan Eddy, invaded Nova Scotia with seventy-two men in October 1776 and laid siege to a British fort in his hometown at the head of the Bay of Fundy before being dispersed by British troops. Another Nova Scotian, Scottish-born John Allan, invaded the St. John valley with forty men the following spring, but was also driven out by redcoats. General Washington himself ordered planners in Machias to give up on an even larger invasion plan that might have made Nova Scotia the fourteenth rebel colony.

But the Revolution did little to assuage Mainers' animosity toward their mother colony of Massachusetts. In 1779, British forces occupied Castine and much of eastern Maine, splitting the area off from the rebellious colonies. Eastern Maine became New Ireland, a new crown colony that was to serve as a homeland for British loyalists who were fleeing New England in droves. More than three hundred Maine and Massachusetts families moved to New Ireland, from which they raided Maine's poorly defended towns, including rebellious Machias, whose people resisted occupation. But apart from a wayward 1779 naval operation, Massachusetts made no effort to roust the occupation force. Even after the British surrendered at Yorktown in 1781, Boston expressed little interest in reclaiming its eastern colonial possessions. When the British finally abandoned New Ireland in 1784, Massachusetts didn't bother to send an official to Castine to see them off. To make matters worse, the British retreated only as far as Passamaquoddy Bay, where they established the loyalist town of St. Andrews on a peninsula that was arguably part of Maine. Some fifteen thousand loyalists settled in St. Andrews and other parts of the northern Fundy coast that are now in the province of New Brunswick, and continued to harass Downeast Mainers, seizing their fishing boats and trading vessels. These incidents convinced many Mainers that Massachusetts considered them disposable, hardly worth the trouble of defending. Maybe, some said, Maine should govern itself.

The most important legacy of the Revolution was the possibility of resisting power. Inspired by the Scotch-Irish and other frontier settlers, more and more Mainers were willing to stand up for themselves, their families, and the land they lived on. The Revolution, in their eyes, was a struggle for individual liberty, not merely a war of national independence. Since many of the Great Proprietors were loyalists and had fled to England during the war, Maine settlers concluded that their wilderness land claims were free for the taking. After all, most of the Proprietors' claims were based on royal decrees from Sir Ferdinando Gorges's day; how could they possibly be considered valid in the new, monarch-less American state? With the king out of the way, the settlers resolved that the wilderness belonged to no one, and became the property of whomever tamed and cultivated it. "A people who have been tutored in the school of freedom, and who have had the rights of humanity instilled with bloody strokes in the late American war, cannot easily forget the interesting lessons they have thus taught," declared James Shurtleff, a Litchfield settler. No "mode of oppression," he told his followers, is "more fatal to the natural rights and liberties of man than the monopolization of wild lands."

But back in Boston, the "ancient deeds" were again changing hands, and a new, even more powerful group of speculators were preparing to take control of Maine's long-contested coast.

While many of the Great Proprietors fled to Britain during the Revolution, in most cases their heirs were able to retain family claims in Maine. Massachusetts banished Benjamin Hallowell, but his grandson Charles Vaughan (who'd grown up on his family's Jamaican slave plantation) inherited Hallowell's stake in the Kennebec Valley. Vaughan expanded his holdings by marrying one of the Apthorp girls, whose parents had defected to England. Massachusetts confiscated Silvester Gardiner's 100,000-acre estate, but grandson Robert Hallowell Gardiner recovered most of it and became a leading figure in the town of Gardiner. The newly independent government confiscated the million-acre holdings of Waldo's heir, Thomas Flucker, who'd also fled to England. But Waldo's enormous patent was recovered—and greatly expanded—by the greatest speculator of them all: Flucker's son-in-law, General Henry Knox.

For twenty years, Henry Knox cast a long, broad shadow over the lives of ordinary Mainers. He was "a man of large, athletic frame, tall, deep-chested, [and] loud voiced," who weighed 280 pounds and lived a life of conspicuous consumption while condemning impoverished settlers as gluttons. He was a self-made man, the son of an impoverished Scotch-Irish immigrant, who dreamed of leading a new post-Revolutionary aristocracy. During the Revolution, Knox used his charm, grace, and considerable military expertise to rise rapidly through the ranks of the Continental Army, becoming a major general by the time of the British surrender. He fostered close friendships with many influential officers, including George Washington, who made him secretary of war in the first government of the United States. Anxious to make these ties permanent, Knox founded the Society of the Cincinnati, an elite club for veteran officers that included Washington and other prominent generals. Membership in the society was hereditary, passed down from one firstborn son to the next, triggering widespread fear that the generals intended to establish themselves as a hereditary nobility. (These fears were not unfounded; in fact, a Massachusetts legislative investigation ordered by John Adams concluded that the society was "dangerous to the peace, liberty, and safety of the United States" and forced Knox to drop the hereditary provisions.) Making full use of his hard-earned connections, Knox intended to build a personal empire based on land speculation on the Maine frontier.

He seized ownership of the Waldo Patent by exploiting his political connections with the Massachusetts elite. Most of Thomas Flucker's estate had been confiscated during the war, and Midcoast Mainers assumed these public lands would be distributed to actual settlers. Instead, Knox managed to exempt the one-fifth of the estate belonging to Flucker's daughter, Lucy, who was none other than Knox's wife. Wangling an appointment for himself as the government's agent in charge of the remaining two-fifths, Knox then sold the land to himself for next to nothing through the use of a series of front men. Finally, he collected exorbitant "agent's fees" from the government and wound up owning three-fifths of Waldo's vast princedom for nothing at all. In 1793 he purchased the remaining two-fifths from other Waldo heirs for $25,000, reuniting the patent for the first time since the late general's death.

Not content with merely controlling the coast of Muscongus and western Penobscot bays, Knox hatched a scheme to seize another three and a half million acres of public land on the upper Kennebec and Downeast coast—an area the size of Connecticut and Rhode Island combined. Knox got his war buddy, General David Cobb, speaker of the Massachusetts house, to waive a law that imposed a one-million-acre limit on public land sales. Then, operating through intermediaries, Knox and a partner purchased the 3.5 million acres with a tiny down payment. Knox planned to use this land monopoly to sell lots to land-hungry settlers for excessively high prices, a sale which would finance the original purchase and, later, make Knox exceedingly rich. But the land sold slowly, and in 1792 Knox was forced to sell these holdings to America's richest capitalist, William Bingham of Philadelphia. These lands, including most of the interior of today's Hancock and Washington counties, plus Trescott, north Gouldsborough, and a vast tract of north-central Maine, became known as the Bingham Purchase.

But Knox still had the Waldo Patent, and he intended to leave his mark on it. In true aristocratic style, Knox had a massive mansion constructed for himself atop a hill in Thomaston. Montpelier was "a spacious mansion of three lofty stories . . . and surmounted by a fourth, central and cupola-like, in the roof, together with stables, farmhouse, and other out-buildings . . . piazzas, balconies, balustrades . . . walks, summer-houses, gardens, orchards, well-arranged grounds, lawns, and forest openings." With twelve thousand square feet of living space, nineteen rooms, and twenty-four fireplaces, it was said to be "a much larger house in every respect than any other private house from Philadelphia to Passamaquoddy." Another visitor likened Montpelier to "the seat of a prince with an extensive establishment." Indeed, Montpelier was one of the models for Nathaniel Hawthorne's *The House of Seven Gables*, while the cruel and grasping Colonel Pyncheon was based on Knox himself.

Hawthorne's portrait was accurate; this new generation of Great Proprietors was extremely arrogant and held the greatest contempt for ordinary people. "Maine's Great Proprietors were well-educated, well-connected gentlemen convinced of their intellectual and moral superiority and of their paternalistic duty to direct the process of settlement," writes historian Alan Taylor in *Liberty Men and Great Proprietors*, one of the best histories of the period. Left to their own devices, the settlers would convert the frontier into "an asylum for the turbulent poor" where "the poor would remain saucy and uncooperative." Knox, Bingham, and other Proprietors imagined themselves as defenders of civilization who prevented the poor from escaping "the discipline of labor" by forcing them to hand over a large portion of their wealth as payment for the lands they occupied. Talleyrand, who visited Knox in Maine in 1794, dismissed Maine settlers as "indolent and grasping, poor but without needs," adding "they still resemble too much the natives of the country whom they have replaced." Bingham, failing to recognize that eastern Maine had a subarctic climate and that glaciers had scoured away most of its soil, blamed the settlers for the region's failure to thrive. Their "misery is attributed to the poverty of the country and not to its true cause," he declared, which was the "idleness and dissipation" of the settlers themselves. Knox was perennially flabbergasted by poor Mainers who failed to submit to his authority, and this seemed to be happening with ever-greater frequency.

❦

Knox, Bingham, and other land barons imagined that they could count on making a fortune because Maine was in the midst of another population explosion. As happened after the defeat of the French, the British defeat was followed by a mass migration of thousands of poor, land-hungry farmers into Maine from other parts of the Bay State. In the six years between 1784 and 1790, Maine's population nearly doubled, from 56,000 to 96,400. It grew by another 50 percent in the following decade, and reached 300,000 by 1820. Much of this growth took place away from the coast, as Massachusetts farmers spread up the relatively fertile Kennebec and Androscoggin river valleys. But some settlers also made their way to the Midcoast backcountry, joining third- and fourth-generation Scotch-Irish settlers in new squatter settlements in the backwoods of the upper Sheepscot Valley and on Penobscot Bay's rocky islands and unsettled western shore. Others streamed Downeast, peopling the harsh, rocky coast from Castine to the fledgling hamlet of Eastport, where they were perched within cannon range of the hostile loyalists of St. Andrews, New Brunswick. Virtually none of the settlers obtained titles from the land barons. They just made their way to the frontier and set about the difficult task of surviving on Maine's rugged coast.

Most settlers came to Maine not to fish but to farm, which made for a perilous existence. Maine's growing season is exceedingly short, and most coastal areas are plagued with thin, rocky, acidic soils, particularly east of the Penobscot. To make matters worse, wolves and wild bears preyed on settlers' livestock, while "amazing swarms of grasshoppers" frequently descended on their crops to destroy "a great part of the grain and grass and almost all vegetables that grew out of the earth." People were often reduced to near-starvation, compelled to dig up their seed potatoes or search the mudflats for clams. In at least one instance, children became sick after consuming the underbark of white birch trees in a desperate attempt to relieve their hunger.

Visitors to the Maine frontier in this period were astonished by the inhabitants' poverty. "Human nature, in some parts of the eastern country, makes a dreadful picture," one traveler reported. "To go into [Mainers'] log houses, and see half a dozen children almost naked and almost starved cannot fail to excite pity in the feeling mind." The settlers' homes, another reported, "could not be exceeded in miserable appearance by any of the most miserable in Europe." The French Duc de La Rochefoucauld-Liancourt, another of Henry Knox's aristocratic guests, sniffed that "Maine is the place that afforded me the worst accommodation. And considering how little reason I found to praise the accommodations of many other places; what I have now said of Maine must be regarded as an affirmation that the condition of life in that place is exceedingly wretched . . . this country is still in its infancy, and a languid and cheerless infancy."

So when agents of the Great Proprietors started coming around demanding rents or land payments, the settlers were understandably upset. Life was difficult enough without fattening the purses of absentee land barons, many concluded. As the settlers were many, the land barons few, and courts and law enforcement almost nonexistent on the frontier, most settlers followed in the footsteps of the Dunbar colonists. They decided to resist the barons and their claims to the land they lived on.

The Great Proprietors encountered trouble from the start. Before they could sell lots to settlers, they had to have the land surveyed, marked, and divided into townships and retail-size lots of one hundred acres or thereabouts. They went to the larger towns and hired impoverished day laborers to carry out the work, paying them well above the prevailing wage to ensure the job was done quickly. But as soon as a given surveyor arrived at a given backcountry surveying site, settlers appeared to drive him away at musket-point. Some were relieved of their maps and compasses, while others returned to discover that all their markers had been carried away in the night. When three of Henry Knox's surveyors failed to take the hint, the townspeople of Unity burned down two of their homes and killed the third man's horse. Knox tried to recruit leading settlers to his cause, granting them cheap land titles and other perks in return for assistance in bringing their rebellious neighbors in line. In 1788, Knox recruited Lincolnville mill owner George Ulmer in this manner, but Ulmer's neighbors quickly turned against him. When Ulmer tried to visit his hometown of Waldoboro the following winter, the townspeople surrounded him, "told him he was an enemy of the people; and that he should not leave [town] alive." Ulmer escaped, but over the next few years his mill was repeatedly vandalized. In Castine and Islesboro, Knox allies were beaten by angry settlers. Even Knox's own farm laborers rebelled, ransacking his estate on Brigadier Island and making off with its considerable store of rum. In 1795, Knox's agents warned him that Lincolnville's settlers intended to burn Montpelier to the ground.

Knox probably feared for his safety. Surrounded as they were by woods and linked to the outside world by the poorest of trails, it was nearly impossible to enforce the law in the backcountry settlements. On several occasions, sheriffs bold enough to try to serve arrest warrants or court summonses in the backcountry were ambushed and beaten by settlers wearing face-paint or disguised as Indians. John Trueman, an agent for one of the minor proprietors, was captured by such a band when he ventured into the backcountry town of Alna in July 1796. At the end of the encounter, Trueman stumbled into Wiscasset naked, his ears sliced and his horse and papers stolen. The assailants he was able to identify were rounded up and placed in Wiscasset's wooden jail. Word of the arrests spread like wildfire through the Sheepscot and Damariscotta valleys, largely settled by Scotch-Irish families from Boothbay, Damariscotta, and Warren. Almost a year later, on a March night, hundreds of axe-wielding settlers descended on Wiscasset, sealed off the town, and tore open the jail to release their comrades.* The settlers, Knox's agents warned, "are determined to prevent the survey of the lands on your patent as well as that of the [Kennebeck Proprietors] at the hazard of everything dear and valuable on Earth."

Indeed, resistance intensified in the first decade of the nineteenth century. Settlers stoned, plundered, or burned the homes of the land baron's agents and allies throughout the backcountry. In Albion, Belmont, and Jackson, as in Alna, armed settlers regularly donned Indian disguises and ambushed county sheriffs, stripping one naked and beating him with sticks; other "White Indians" seized intruding deputies, forcing them to watch as they killed, cooked, and ate their horses. The Proprietors' lawyers received death threats, crude drawings depicting their own hanging, and even the occasional delivery of an empty cof-

---

*Wiscasset's stone jailhouse, now a popular tourist attraction, was built in response to the jailbreak. Completed in 1811, the fortresslike building was designed to thwart any future chicanery.

fin in the middle of the night. At one point, Augusta's four-hundred-man militia was mobilized after settlers threatened to march on the town, destroy the courthouse, and slaughter the sheriff and all the Kennebeck Proprietors' attorneys.

But the settlers' bark was often worse than their bite. Wishing to avoid military intervention, they took great pains to ensure that nobody was actually killed in these encounters. During more than seventy years of violent resistance, only one person died: Paul Chadwick, a nineteen-year-old surveyor for the Kennebeck Proprietors who was executed in Windham in the summer of 1809 by Indian-clad settlers. Alarmed by the murder, other settlers persuaded the culprits to turn themselves in. At trial, however, local jurors declared the men not guilty, and all were released.

~

By now, the Maine resistance effort had taken on a wider political significance. Settlers now challenged not just the land barons, but the entire Massachusetts political establishment itself.

In the political landscape of the newly created United States, the Bay State was a stronghold of old-fashioned Federalist elitism. The Federalists championed a conservative vision of the new American society, a hierarchical one wherein common folk knew their place and gentlemen of property and influence were free to govern for the "common good." In Massachusetts, the Federalists maintained a near-total monopoly not only on political power, but on religion and higher education as well. Congregationalism remained the official state religion, its ministers, churches, and universities supported by citizens of all faiths through obligatory taxes. Leading Federalists could count on the support of sheriffs, courts, legislators, and other government officials because they controlled appointment to these positions. Knox, a leading Federalist, handpicked the federal marshal for the District of Maine and many of the district's judges, and presided over the legislative committee overseeing appeals against his own land claims. The Massachusetts senate was run by David Cobb, one of Knox's closest friends who also served as William Bingham's land agent. Knox's son-in-law, Samuel Thatcher, represented Massachusetts in the U.S. Congress.

These personal connections gave Knox, Bingham, and other Federalists the freedom to enact tax policies in their own favor; the poor were a matter of indifference. When settlers in western Massachusetts rebelled against tax foreclosures in 1786, Governor (and Kennebeck Proprietor) James Bowdoin dispatched an army to crush them. As secretary of war, Knox applauded the move. "The people who are the insurgents . . . feel . . . their own poverty . . . and their own force and are determined to make use of the latter in order to remedy the former," he wrote indignantly to Washington beforehand. "Our government must be braced, changed, or altered to secure our lives and property."

The settlers also felt that government had to change. In the early 1800s they were presented with an alternative.

Ten years earlier, Thomas Jefferson had built up a new party that challenged the age-old notion that politics should be left to the "well born." Instead Jefferson's party, the Democratic Republicans, put forward a truly revolutionary notion. America, they argued, should become a republic of independent, self-employed landholders. Government should, as much as possible, take the form of the New England town meeting, where the citizens voted directly on all measures affecting their community. Their representatives in state and local governments should not be their betters, but their servants. According to the Democratic Republicans, emerging aristocrats like Knox and Bingham had to be reined in or they would replace the tyranny of the English monarchy with one of their own. They also believed official churches like the Congregational Church in New England should be separated from the state to ensure religious freedom.

Unsurprisingly, the Democratic Republicans' message was enormously popular on the Maine frontier, where most settlers were independent small landholders belonging to Baptist, Methodist, and other "unofficial" faiths. Fed up with the land speculators and their Federalist allies in the Massachusetts house, backcountry Mainers rallied to the Democratic Republican cause. In 1805, a Democratic Republican candidate won Henry Knox's seat in the Massachusetts assembly, where the Federalist majority was growing thinner with each election. Federalists were alarmed. "Shall the squatters of Maine impose a Governor on Massachusetts?" asked the worried editors of Boston's *Columbian Centinel*, a leading Federalist paper, in 1806.

The *Centinel*'s editors didn't have to wait long for an answer. Mainers' overwhelming support for the upstart party allowed the Democratic Republicans to capture the Massachusetts governorship in 1807, a feat they began repeating on a regular basis. Midcoast settlers were so enthusiastic for the new party that they named their newly incorporated towns for Jefferson and his professed ideals—Liberty, Hope, Unity, Union, and Freedom—in striking contrast to the older towns of Waldo, Gardiner, Hallowell, Bowdoin, Waldoboro, and Vassalboro. To cap their victory, the Democratic Republicans forced the legislature to allow a referendum on Maine statehood in 1807, frightening the Commonwealth's Federalist establishment. "The squatters are about to manage their affairs in their own way," Federalist businessman Moses Greenleaf of New Gloucester proclaimed after the measure was announced. "Who knows amidst the revolutions that are impending what may await us?" But the "revolutions" would have to wait; the 1807 succession measure was defeated at the polls amid concerns about the economic consequences.

Henry Knox didn't live to see this Federalist defeat play out. On October 28, 1806, the gluttonous general swallowed a chicken bone and died from the resulting infection. After laying his body to rest in an elaborate Thomaston mausoleum, his family discovered that Knox had managed to wipe out his vast fortune. Knox had surrendered most of his remaining lands to his creditors, ruining the family. His friend William Bingham died in 1806 and, though Bingham was very rich, most of his Maine holdings were sold off on the cheap two decades later, having failed to attract settlers. The Federalists were on the wane.

But as it turned out, the Democratic Republicans weren't really the settlers' friends either. Jefferson, James Madison, and other party leaders were major landowners themselves, and had no intention of fomenting a populist revolution. Even in Maine, the party leadership was made up of upper-middle-class professionals—doctors, lawyers, and shipowners—from established coastal towns, and even included former agents and employees of the Great Proprietors themselves. Once in power, the Democratic Republicans didn't simply give the settlers the land they occupied; they offered a compromise solution and threatened to bring in the army if it was rejected. The settlers largely gave in.

The compromise, brokered in 1808, gave the rebellious settlers enough to pacify them and squelch the resistance movement. The new Democratic Republican government passed legislation that prohibited Proprietors from evicting squatters who had occupied land for at least six years. But the settlers would have to buy titles from the Proprietors at a reduced rate. In 1808 the land barons were selling wilderness lands for around $4 an acre. Under the new law, most settlers bought their land for between $2 and $3 an acre, paid over three years.

Wealthier settler families could afford these terms, but some twenty thousand poorer settlers could not, and migrated to the Ohio frontier in the coming years. This "Ohio Fever" drove so many families from certain parts of Maine that some Proprietors feared their lands would become completely depopulated. The "sober, industrious farmer and mechanic . . . [are] leaving every section of our District," Portland's *Eastern Argus* lamented, "even from the new settlements on the growth of which depend our general wealth and greatness."

But there were a few outright victors. In 1813, a government commission examined the land disputes in Boothbay, Damariscotta, and other Dunbar settlements of the Midcoast region. The commission concluded that most of the area's Proprietors possessed invalid titles, and ordered that the area's families be issued cheap titles from the government, which is all they'd wanted in the first place. In the end, most of these descendants of David Dunbar's Scotch-Irish settlers paid about thirteen cents an acre for the lands they'd clung to for so long.

The settlers' resistance had also laid the groundwork for an even greater achievement: Maine's secession from Massachusetts. They had brought down the Federalists within the District of Maine and given the Democratic Republicans enough strength in the Massachusetts assembly to force the 1807 referendum on secession. But Mainers, living as they were in a poor, underdeveloped province of 250,000, were not yet ready to step out on their own. Most reasoned that it was better to be a colony of a wealthy state than to be impoverished, isolated, and independent. But many minds were suddenly and profoundly changed by the behavior of Massachusetts during the War of 1812.

In the summer of 1812, after less than thirty years of peace, Americans were again at war with the British. President James Madison, a co-founder of the Democratic Republicans, declared war after years of British harassment of U.S. shipping and the repeated kidnapping and impressment of American sailors by ships of the Royal Navy.

But Massachusetts's Federalists were deeply opposed to "Mr. Madison's War" and openly sided with the British against the United States. Federalist bankers refused to loan money to the federal government, but advanced enormous sums to British authorities in Nova Scotia. New England merchants maintained a brisk trade with the enemy, while New England governors resisted Madison's request for troops. Some Massachusetts Federalists even argued that New England should secede from the nascent United States altogether.

Mainers paid the price for Massachusetts's pro-British policies. President Madison was so disgusted with Massachusetts's behavior that in 1813 he ordered all federal garrisons in the District of Maine to withdraw to more loyal states of the Union. William King, major general of one of the principal militia units in Maine, found his state suddenly defended by "a few invalids . . . who were retained on account of their indispositions."

In the summer and fall of 1814, British forces invaded and occupied eastern Maine without a fight. All of Maine east of the Penobscot River was incorporated into the British Empire. British warships captured Machias, burned Belfast, and reestablished a fortified naval base in Castine. Eastport residents were informed that their region was being "restored" to New Brunswick, while British troops ensconced themselves in a fortified compound above the town. British frigates sailed up the Penobscot to Bangor, where they seized all the ships in the harbor, plundered homes, and confiscated the money they found in the city's post office. Only in Boothbay were the Royal Marines repulsed by local militia. The Midcoast braced for an all-out British invasion. Bankers removed all reserves from the banks in Bath and in Wiscasset and transferred them to the relative safety of Portland. Many of Wiscasset's townspeople fled west, their furniture and belongings in tow. Militamen scrambled to fortify Portland. The coast sat on a knife's edge.

Meanwhile, down in Boston, Governor Caleb Strong called an emergency session of the Massachusetts legislature. But instead of responding to the invasion and occupation of a good chunk of the Commonwealth, legislators simply voted to further buttress Boston's defenses. Maine legislators returned home from the session to report that their colleagues "meant to say or do nothing" about the occupation. "No event in all the previous history of the union of Massachusetts and Maine," historian Ronald F. Banks later wrote, "so blatantly revealed the extent to which the interests of Maine could be sacrificed to those of Massachusetts proper."

Nor did the situation improve in the months that followed. President Madison wished to liberate Maine, and even nationalized part of the Massachusetts militia to do so. But when he turned to Boston bankers to borrow the money needed to equip the expedition, they refused, out of either ideological disagreement or because they had already loaned their capital to the British. Madison, humiliated, was forced to ask Massachusetts to loan the United States the necessary money. Not only did Governor Strong refuse this request, he leaked plans for the U.S. invasion of occupied Maine to the *Columbian Centinel*, which published them in their entirety. Madison had no choice but to give up his plans to liberate eastern Maine.

Governor Strong, for whom my hometown in western Maine is named, didn't just flirt with treason, he was involved in a full-blown affair. In late November 1814, Strong secretly dispatched an emissary to Halifax, Nova Scotia, to meet with the British commander there, John Sherbrooke. The unidentified emissary asked Sherbrooke whether Great Britain would "afford military assistance" to Massachusetts if it were to secede from the Union! While Maine's Democratic Republicans were unaware of this particular meeting, they accused many prominent Federalists of secretly meeting with the British in occupied Castine.

Massachusetts's collusion in the foreign occupation of Maine generated a groundswell of support for Maine statehood. The state's senators pushed for a new referendum on succession in the Massachuetts assembly. A "crisis has arrived when the District of Maine ought to legislate itself," wrote Samuel Whiting, an influential Bangor attorney.

"Released from the thraldom of Boston influence, we would not suffer this Eastern section of the country to fall into insignificance."

In February 1815, New Englanders learned of the British defeat at the Battle of New Orleans and of the peace treaty that had been negotiated back in Europe some days before the battle had started. The war was over, but Mainers had not been cured of their "separation fever."

Over the next four years, Democratic Republican politicians and newspaper editors clamored for statehood. "We are a mere province of our mother state, and our brethren in the West [consider] us an inferior race and totally incapable of self-government," the *Eastern Argus* wrote. "No one will deny . . . there is less literary emulation apparent in Maine than in any other section of New England [but] the cause of this may justly be imputed to our colonial state or dependency on old Massachusetts." The nonresident proprietors, the paper argued, had "impoverished the country . . . persecuted the people" and "driven many an honest man to seek a livelihood in a distant land." Sam Whiting appealed to his fellow Mainers to decide "whether you will place your District upon the elevated stand to which it is entitled . . . or whether you will continue your present Colonial vassalage."

Down in Massachusetts, more and more Federalists were of the opinion that maybe they would be better off if Maine went its own way. With Maine's ornery voters out of the picture, the Federalists would have a good chance of reasserting their dominance of the Commonwealth's political life. Despite the "Ohio Fever," the District of Maine's population was growing faster than that of the rest of Massachusetts, so things were likely to get worse for the Federalists over time. "The District has been considered as a sort of nursling, whose support cost more than its services were worth," the Federalist Boston *Advertiser* observed. "The citizens of this Commonwealth . . . have said 'if these people think they are oppressed, and are so anxious to get away from us, we can do very well without them; let them take their course, run and be glorified.' "

Mainers ultimately did just that. Early referenda were narrowly defeated because of concerns over the effect of a federal statute on coastal trade, which—due to a quirk of Maine geography—would have harmed the merchants of an independent Maine. Once the law was amended, Maine voters approved statehood by a wide margin.

On March 25, 1820, Maine became the twenty-third state in the Union. Under its new constitution, the Congregational Church was stripped of state sponsorship. Legislative seats were distributed based on population, rather than wealth, as had been the case in Massachusetts. Slavery was prohibited. And, in a measure reflecting the age-old concerns of Maine settlers, the state was specifically prohibited from conferring titles of nobility on its citizens.

After seventy years of resistance, Maine's ornery backcountry settlers had succeeded beyond their wildest dreams. But the future held some unpleasant surprises in store for their children and grandchildren.

PART THREE

Boom to Bust

FIVE

Boom to Bust

Fishing is central to the culture and economy of coastal Maine, but it hasn't always been so. It's true that fish underwrote the plans of Sir Ferdinando Gorges, attracted the first few generations of West Country settlers, and helped ensure the survival and expansion of the Puritans' New England empire. But from about 1650 to the early nineteenth century, fishing played an extremely modest role in the cultural and economic life of coastal Maine. Most of the families who settled coastal Maine in this period—Dunbar's Scotch-Irish, Waldo's Germans, and impoverished southern New Englanders—were farmers in search of land to clear and cultivate. Only when the thin, rocky soil failed to provide did they reluctantly turn to the sea.

The Ice Age was unkind to the Downeast coast, its great glaciers having scraped the topsoil away and dumped boulders in their wake. Farmland was hard to come by. Vinalhaven island, a nineteenth-century official reported, "is a huge mass of granite, with hardly a patch of soil large enough to warrant any one in engaging in agriculture." Further Downeast, settlers were only able to survive their first few years by lumbering their weather-beaten trees, as the land refused to produce even a subsistence level of food. Even in Southern and Midcoast Maine where soils were better, the harsh climate made farming difficult. In a good year, the growing season was a full month shorter than in southern New England. In 1816—remembered locally as "eighteen-hundred-and-froze-to-death"—Maine farms were struck with a killing frost every month of the year. Many settlers were faced with the realization that they could not survive from farming alone.

Fortunately, what glaciers took from the land they gave to the sea. The advancing ice had scraped rock from the shore and deposited it on the seafloor, forming undersea banks favored by a variety of sea creatures. It had also carved the coast into a ragged tapestry of bays, inlets, and islands. All the ingredients for a successful fishery were there: snug harbors for deep-draft vessels, vast habitat for fish and shellfish, rocky headlands on which to dry the catch, and accessible stands of wood to construct barrels, boats, and ships. "With so extensive a coastline and such excellent harbors for vessels and boats in the near vicinity of important fishing grounds," the U.S. Fish Commission declared in 1880, "Maine enjoys many advantages not possessed by other states for the prosecution of the fisheries."

Well into the second decade of the nineteenth century, the fishing fleet remained modest. In 1800, all Maine's fishing boats and vessels combined accounted for only 5,354 tons, the equivalent of two large five-masted schooners. More than half the total of this tonnage was in the form of boats of less than twenty tons: dories, small sloops, and other small craft confined to waters close to shore. In Boothbay, one of the early fishing centers, the larger vessels consisted entirely of "pinkeys," little two-masted schooners with a small covered cabin tucked in the bow. These were generally thirty-five to forty tons, or less than a quarter the size of the Pilgrims' *Mayflower*. In these small vessels, fishermen from Boothbay, Harpswell, Monhegan, Matinicus, Eastport, and the Isle of Shoals sailed days from shore to fish the offshore cod banks and the tide-scoured Bay of Fundy. In 1804, Vinalhaven fishermen were sailing all the way to Labrador—nine hundred miles by sea—in their thirty-ton, forty-eight-foot-long "Chebacco boats," small flush-decked boats whose holds they would fill with salt cod. Together, Maine's offshore vessels accounted for only 11 percent of the national fleet. But the settlement of Downeast Maine transformed Maine into the most important fisheries state in the nation.

English settlement did not spread to the eastern half of Maine until after the French defeat in 1763, and even then was retarded by the British occupation of the region during the Revolutionary War. University of Maine fisheries historian Wayne O'Leary has argued that eastern Maine "simply did not have sufficient population to take advantage of its resources and physical attributes" until about 1830, when the far-flung frontier settlements began maturing into established communities. Indeed, the population of the eastern coast exploded between 1790 and 1830. The population of Hancock County more than quadrupled to almost 23,000 in this period, while frontier villages like Bucksport, Deer Isle, Eastport, and Gouldsborough became thriving fisheries ports with several thousand inhabitants apiece. The Downeast coast, long empty, was suddenly dotted with boats.

Already propelled by the expansion of settlement, the growth of the fishing industry was further aided by U.S. government fishing bounties, which provided annual cash payments to owners of cod-fishing vessels. Politicians argued that these subsidies were a matter of national security, as they supported an industry that served as "a nursery for seamen" who could man the Navy's ships in time of war. There was some truth in the argument, but until 1819 the bounties were structured to favor Massachusetts's codfish aristocracy of wealthy shipowners and fish trading firms. Small-boat owners received a payment of $1.60 per ton of their vessel while those with larger ships got $4 per ton. But in 1819 Congress raised the rate for boats of thirty tons or less to $3.60 per ton, fueling a boatbuilding boom up and down the Maine coast.

Fishing afforded many coastal settlers the chance to make a living while retaining a large degree of social and economic independence— an important consideration for families who'd spent the previous three or four generations fighting the Great Proprietors. With the help of government subsidies, hundreds of families built their own inshore cod-fishing vessels. Others banded together to construct more substantial schooners capable of fishing distant cod-fishing banks far out in the Gulf of Maine or off the coast of eastern Canada. Cod was the fish of choice for several reasons. The government cod bounty alone increased a typical fisherman's income by about a fifth. Cod fishing was already the cheapest, easiest, and least risky form of deepwater fishing. Atlantic cod are laconic, gluttonous, tasty, and easily preserved by salting or drying—an important consideration before the invention of refrigeration. There was enormous demand for salt cod among the masses of poor immigrants arriving in the country's burgeoning urban centers as well as among the owners of large slave plantations in the Caribbean and the southern United States; for both groups, it represented a cheap form of animal protein. Nor did cod fishing require particularly fast vessels or expensive equipment. Cod-fishing techniques hadn't changed since Waymouth's day: once anchored on the fishing grounds, one just threw a baited hook over the ship's side, hauled in the fish, and repeated the process until the hold was full. Fish were then salted, dried in the sun, and transported to the cities and slave ports whenever convenient.

Fishing vessel ownership remained remarkably democratic throughout the early and mid-nineteenth century. Government figures compiled by O'Leary on the fishing fleet of eastern Penobscot Bay show that in 1829, the majority of the vessels were owned by the fishing captains themselves, and 72 percent by persons who owned no other fishing vessel of any size; twenty years later single-vessel owners still controlled 111 of 267 fishing boats and ships in the region. In the middle of the century, Matinicus Island was home to only fifteen families but had twenty-two vessel owners. Similarly, there were only twenty-five dwellings on Monhegan in 1869, but eighteen islanders owned vessels. Ownership tended to be more concentrated in Maine's larger ports such as Portland, Boothbay, and Castine, but even the largest owners were often self-made men from local families. Boothbay's largest fishing magnate, John McClintock, built a fleet of fourteen fishing schooners from modest beginnings as a hometown shoe store owner. Old Boothbay families owned much of the rest of the town's massive fleet, with Hodgdons, Barters, Lewises, and Montgomerys controlling eighteen bankers and schooners between them.

Ordinary crewmembers often held shares in the vessels they worked on and were not infrequently relatives of the captain, controlling shareholders, or both. The bounty law reinforced this democratic ownership structure as it required that owners share profits with their crew "in proportion to the quantities or number of said fish they may respectively have caught." Maritime historian Lincoln Paine observes that the law "was simply a codification of a fundamentally democratic practice that prevailed in the fisheries in the colonial period. The value of the crew's share differed from place to place—three-quarters, five-eighths, a half—but for the most part fishermen contributed the same share of the expenses of running the boat as they received of the profits."

The share system carried over into Maine's other fisheries. While cod fishing dominated the industry, some communities became major players in the mackerel and herring trade. Pursuing these fish required greater capital and risk-taking than did the cod fishery. Mackerel are fast schooling fish—here one day and gone the next—making them more difficult to locate and catch. Unlike cod, mackerel spoiled quickly even when salted, meaning they had to be rushed to market. But mackerel prices rapidly outstripped those for cod, and in the 1820s a few Boothbay and Eastport fishing captains decided to try fishing them during the midsummer lull in cod fishing. They didn't regret their decision. Within a few years Eastport's tiny harbor was crowded with forty large mackerel-fishing schooners employing nearly six hundred fishermen; there were days when three hundred mackerel vessels fished within sight of one another in the approaches to the Bay of Fundy. According to one resident, mackerel were so abundant in the area that "it was not uncommon to catch individuals weighing upward of two pounds within a few rods of the wharves." The fishing—done entirely with handlines and shiny metal lures—often reached fever pitch. Each of the fishermen "will haul in a jerk off a fish, and throw out the line for another with a single motion; and repeat the act in so rapid succession that their arms seem continually on the swing," an observer aboard a mackerel vessel recalled. "While the school remains alongside . . . the excitement of the men and the rushing noise of the fish in their beautiful and manifold evolutions in the water arrest the attention of the most careless observer."

One night in the early nineteenth century, a fisherman on Campobello Island on the Maine–New Brunswick border was rowing home late at night with a skillet filled with wood chips and campfire coals which he intended to use to light his kitchen stove. But while crossing the harbor the wind set the wood chips ablaze, bathing the bow of the man's dory in light. As he approached his landing he noticed that the waters around his boat were roiling with herring attracted by the light. His discovery revolutionized the herring fishery. By the 1830s hundreds of boats were out "torching" for herring each summer in the coves and harbors of eastern Maine. At night "the coves [were] most beautifully lighted up as with hundreds of lamps . . . heaving and falling with the motion of the sea," one observer recalled. Passengers aboard ships entering Passamaquoddy Bay saw such lights illuminating the indentations of the coast "in all directions." Other fishermen captured shoals of herring by constructing brush or wood-and-net dams, or "weirs," across the mouths of coves; at high tide the fish could swim over the weir and into the coves to feed, but were unable to escape when the tide fell. However they were caught, most herring made their way to smokehouses popping up like mushrooms in many outports. The little Downeast village of Lubec alone had twenty smokehouses in 1821, churning out more than fifty thousand boxes of herring annually. In the 1830s, Maine herring boats from Southport to Eastport were making annual 1,200-mile round-trips to the Magdalen Islands of Quebec to capture additional herring.

The golden age of Maine's fisheries was well under way.

By 1860, Maine had come to dominate the national fishing industry. The state had more full-time fishermen than any other—4,607 according to the 1860 census—and 21 percent of the national total. Mainers owned half of the nation's offshore fishing vessels, 57 percent of its tonnage of cod-fishing vessels, and 44 percent of its mackerel fishing tonnage. For decades, Maine fishermen also dominated the country's Grand Banks fishing fleet. They accounted for about half of the national cod catch, the majority of smoked herring production, and a significant proportion of the country's mackerel supply. In the overall value of its fisheries, Maine was second only to Massachusetts, where large merchant firms owned much of the fleet and could invest heavily in riskier, high-value fishing ventures.

Not surprisingly, fishing came to dominate life in coastal Maine at mid-century as well. Fishermen employed more than half the male workforce in the Boothbay region and the islands of Penobscot Bay; of Southport's 200 workers, 141 were fishermen. Lubec's smoked herring industry employed every man and boy over the age of ten, while every able-bodied man in Swan's Island went off to sea during mackerel season. Vinalhaven island had thirteen fish curing yards—enough to keep four cargo schooners employed just to move the finished product to market in Boston. Offshore fisheries alone represented the primary industry for thirty-two coastal communities; combined with the inshore, fishing employed at least ten thousand people, more Mainers than any other occupation except farming.

The success of Maine's fishing venture allowed it, in the three decades preceding the Civil War, to achieve a level of national economic importance never seen before or since. In the days when most of the country's goods moved back and forth on barges and ships plying the eastern seaboard, the Maine coast stood in the thick of national and international commerce. Skills learned in the fisheries—seamanship, boatbuilding, carpentry, and long-distance trade—led many coastal Mainers to careers in shipping and shipbuilding. Their merchant fleets, in turn, provided other coastal industries with regular access to distant markets, fueling a period of spectacular economic growth.

The fish Mainers caught were sold and eaten elsewhere, requiring fishermen to make expensive and time-consuming trips to bring preserved cod, mackerel, and herring to Boston, New York, New Orleans, or the sugar plantations of the Caribbean. As business boomed, more and more local merchants got into the act by building cargo schooners and square-riggers to carry fish and other products to these markets. Rather than return with empty holds, merchant captains looked for products that were in demand back at home. These coastal merchants carried food and manufactured goods up from Boston and New York to sell out of the stores they built in Maine's towns and outports. Others carried sugar, coal, or raw cotton from southern ports. But the most ambitious constructed full-rigged 300- to 900-ton oceangoing cargo ships to pursue the greater profits of what became known as the triangular fish trade. These ships sailed to the Deep South full of smoked or salted fish that were traded for bales of raw cotton. Rather than return to Maine, the ships crossed the Atlantic to Liverpool and other European ports where cotton was in great demand to feed the expanding textile mills. They then returned to Maine carrying manufactured goods and the one product fishermen could neither make themselves nor do without: the salt with which they cured their fish.

Others built family fortunes by building the ships themselves. In the age of sail, the Maine coast had everything a shipbuilding industry required. Sloping shores led to deepwater harbors with easy access to oak (for ship's ribs), white pine (for masts), spruce (for planking), and tamarack (which provided water-resistant joints). Boatbuilders who had cut their teeth building pinkeys and fishing schooners expanded their yards to lay down the keels of merchant ships of all sorts and sizes—from two-masted coasting schooners to the massive six- and seven-masted clipper ships that rushed cargo around Cape Horn to California's ports.

The growing fleet didn't just carry fish away from their ports. Maine woodsmen were pioneering the American lumber industry, floating millions of tree-length logs down the Kennebec, Penobscot, and other rivers flowing from the vast, roadless interior. Lumber barons bought up vast stretches of the northern Maine forest and dotted the lower river valleys with sawmills. By 1872 Maine had almost one thousand sawmills and woodworking establishments in operation, filling fleets of lumber schooners with nearly a billion board feet of lumber a year. Many of the mills were located in the frontier city of Bangor, which for a time produced more lumber than any other city in the world. Its mills poured so much sawdust and waste wood into the Penobscot River that the navigation channel sometimes became constricted to a narrow passage between great bars of waste. Bangor's poor scavenged the floating wastes in small boats and were able to salvage enough lumber to construct small houses.

On peninsulas and islands without lumber resources, people took to simply exporting the rocks themselves. In 1812, a Blue Hill merchant captain decided to ballast his ship with a load of granite cobblestones cut from a local quarry. Apparently they fetched a good price because within a few years dozens of quarries sprang up along the coast, exporting granite cobblestones, curbs, and hitching posts to the growing cities of the eastern seaboard. Boston capitalists purchased several granite islands and transformed them into small quarrying cities. By the end of the century, Maine led the nation in granite production.

Today, Dix and High islands, two small islands in the Mussel Ridge archipelago near Rockland, are usually deserted. But in the mid-nineteenth century they were home to nearly two thousand laborers, who cut granite with drills, hammers, and blasting powder. Dix alone had some 150 buildings, a railroad, and a meeting hall that could accommodate five hundred people. I remember exploring the two islands on foot as a kid, following a network of paths laid down for the old railway. In the woods I found rusting machinery, water-filled quarry ponds, and granite foundations of what must have been immense buildings. Along the rocky shore, discarded friezes and Doric columns lay camouflaged amid the granite boulders from which they were carved. The U.S. Treasury building and both the New York and Philadelphia post offices were built from Dix's bedrock. Both Boston's Museum of Fine Arts and the great columns of the Cathedral of St. John the Divine in New York were built with Deer Isle granite, while the Ellis Island administration building and the U.S. House of Representatives were constructed with granite shipped from Blue Hill. The New York Stock Exchange, the Library of Congress, the U.S. Naval Academy, the Brooklyn and George Washington bridges in New York, and the interior facings of the Washington Monument are all built from bits and pieces of the Maine coast.

Another Boston capitalist invested heavily in a Maine industry of his own creation. Until Frederick Tudor came along, ice wasn't used in American households. Without refrigeration, diet was based on the season and meat and fish were dried, smoked, or salted. But while attending a Boston party in 1805, the twenty-one-year-old heard his older brother joke that the ice on New England's ponds ought to be packed up and sold in the steamy ports of the Caribbean. The following year Tudor horrified his friends and family by doing just that. He shipped 130 tons of ice to Martinique, where he personally promoted sales by demonstrating how to preserve and use the novel product. But the ice melted quickly, along with $6,000 of the $10,000 he'd invested in the scheme. Undeterred, Tudor spent the next two decades perfecting the cutting, storage, and shipment of ice. He traveled throughout the American South and Caribbean extolling the virtues of chilled beverages, ice cream, ice-preserved foods, and medical ice packs. At one point he shipped New England ice all the way to India, selling the preserved cargo at considerable profit and reinvesting the money in a large Calcutta icehouse. By 1856, 130,000 tons of New England ice were being shipped around the world each year. Ice had become an important world commodity, and Tudor had become the "Ice King."

But Tudor's operations had a problem. In warm-winter years his ice ponds in Massachusetts and the lower Hudson Valley produced little ice, creating a considerable supply shortage. Then one day in 1824, a ship arrived in Baltimore with a load of beautiful blue ice cut from the clean waters of the Kennebec River. It proved especially tasty, and Tudor soon contracted with local Maine icehouses to supply his companies. By 1831, Tudor had built his own icehouses near Gardiner and other Maine towns. In warm-winter years, Maine's growing merchant fleet sailed with cargoes of ice as well as granite, lumber, and cured fish.

New industries drew new immigrants, but remarkably few came to the coastal settlements. In the summer of 1832, the roads from New Brunswick to Maine were clogged with thousands of impoverished Irish who had arrived in Canada on cheap British-subsidized tickets. But the Irish, like the French Canadians traveling south from Quebec, sought work in the lumber mills of Bangor, the textile mills of Lewiston, or with the construction companies building the new state capitol in Augusta. More Irish came in during the English-engineered Potato Famine in the 1840s, but almost all settled in just four towns: Portland, Bangor, Lewiston, and Ellsworth. Of the coastal outports, only Eastport, Calais, and Machias attracted significant numbers of Irish immigrants by 1850, mostly because the towns were located near the New Brunswick border. Small numbers of Irish, Finns, Swedes, Scots, and Italians were recruited to work in the granite and lime quarries around Penobscot Bay. But compared to other parts of the state and nation, coastal Maine remained relatively homogeneous throughout the nineteenth century. Newcomers came now and again, but, for the most part, the towns and outports of the Mid- and Downeast coasts remained peopled by descendants of the Anglo-Scottish settlement waves of the eighteenth and early nineteenth centuries.

Unfortunately, Maine's booming industries collapsed almost as quickly as they had risen.

The onset of the Civil War delivered the first blow, severing the salt fish and ice trade with the Deep South. Confederate warships plied the sea-lanes, capturing fishing vessels and cargo schooners alike and imprisoning their crews. Quarries, lumber camps, and fishing wharves grew quieter as more and more men left to fight on distant battlefields; 73,000 Mainers fought in the war, a higher proportion of the population than that of any other Northern state. More than 18,000 of them were killed or wounded. Family members who remained behind experienced severe wartime price increases that drove many smaller operations out of business.

Peace did not restore prosperity. The national economy was changing. Railroads were spreading across the country from east to west, connecting midwestern farms, Great Lakes lumberyards, and western stockyards with the burgeoning population centers of the East Coast. Maine's sparse population and irregular coastline discouraged railroad construction, and the state quickly became a backwater. Maine's lumbermen couldn't compete with their counterparts working the virgin forests of the Great Lakes and Pacific Northwest. And, as the century progressed, refrigeration destroyed the ice industry, concrete and steel frames savaged the granite quarries, and English-built iron steamships pushed Maine's wooden sailing ships out of the shipping lanes.

The offshore fishing industry faced even greater challenges. The cost of fishing gear and supplies increased enormously during the war, doubling the cost of fitting out a cod-fishing vessel. No sooner had the conflict ended than the new Republican Congress, strongly protectionist and suspicious of subsidies, made two decisions that proved devastating to small fishing operations. First, duties on foreign salt were increased by 800 percent. Then, in 1866, the fishing bounty was repealed, pushing hundreds of small fishing firms into bankruptcy.

Other small operators found they could neither afford nor compete with new fishing technologies adopted by corporate fishing companies. An Irish immigrant had introduced Massachusetts cod fishermen to "tub trawling," which proved far more efficient than the old hook-and-line method. Instead of fishing from a schooner's deck, fishermen were sent out from the main vessel in small dories. These boats were filled with tubs containing great coils of lines to which were attached hundreds of hooks; they played out their long trawls of baited lines and, a few hours later, hauled them up, hook by hook, to remove the cod that had happened by. The work was backbreaking and extremely dangerous: many dories were lost in fog, storms, and other accidents on the Grand Banks, which sit in the middle of the open North Atlantic. Tub trawling was also expensive, requiring the purchase of dories and ten times the usual quantity of hooks, lines, and bait. But a schooner equipped for dory trawling could catch as many fish in a day as the old handliners would in a week, and the fish tended to be bigger as well. For fishing captains who could afford it, tub trawling was the way to go.

Offshore mackerel and herring fishing was also getting more expensive. Mackerel jigging was made commercially obsolete by the purse seine, an enormous net, typically 1,400 feet long and 30 feet deep with floats, sinkers, and a great drawstring, used to corral an entire mackerel school and remove them from the water en masse. A skilled seining crew could catch as many mackerel in a single haul as a crew of mackerel jiggers might in several weeks. But fitting out a mackerel seiner cost two to three times more than a traditional mackerel catcher, largely due to the cost of the net. Purse seines were modified for use in offshore herring fishing, replacing simple gill nets of most of New England's Magdalen Islands fleet.

Between 1860 and 1900, Maine's offshore fishing industry quickly deteriorated as its enormous fleet of owner-operated vessels was bankrupted by the changes in law, markets, and technology. The fleet rapidly contracted, from 154,000 tons of offshore cod and mackerel vessels to 44,000, representing only a tenth of the nation's fleet. What vessels remained had been bought up by big firms that had the capital to compete in the new environment. Portland firms, minor players in the offshore fisheries before the Civil War, controlled nearly half of Maine's fleet by 1898. Across the state, independent fishermen abandoned the offshore fisheries, many selling out to wealthier operators in Portland, Boothbay, or Bucksport.

This consolidation worsened the lot of the average fisherman. The bounty law had required that owners share profits with their crews, making them coinvestors in the voyage. With the bounty law repealed, shipowners quickly switched to a wage system, greatly increasing their profits. On wages, offshore fishermen often took home little more than half of what they would have on the old share system. Fishermen who resisted the change to wages sometimes found themselves replaced by guest workers from the impoverished British provinces of New Brunswick and Nova Scotia, who would take whatever work they could get. Deep-sea fishermen were becoming, in O'Leary's words, "a maritime proletariat."

Fishermen reacted to these changes in various ways. A few accepted the harder work and lower wages of the big offshore fishing concerns. A larger number fled west in search of a better life as settlers on the fertile plains of the Midwest, where the growing soil was measured in feet, not inches. But a great number of them decided to stick it out on the rockbound coast. Building their own small boats, they set about fishing for whatever would provide a living on their own terms. Few could have guessed that the American lobster, that ungainly crawler that infested the bottoms of the coves and harbors outside their bedroom windows, would prove their lasting salvation.

Before the Civil War, deep-sea fishermen looked down on fishermen working inshore. Indeed, in those days, inshore fishing was at best a marginal occupation. There were fish to be caught, but few people to buy them. An inshore fisherman could preserve his catch, but with big offshore schooners flooding the docks with theirs, the price it could fetch was very low. Still, a great many Mainers engaged in inshore fishing in the early nineteenth century. Some were young people learning the ropes before signing aboard a Banks schooner, others old men no longer able to endure the punishment of the deep-sea fisheries. But a great many were farmers unable to feed their families from what the miserly land provided. "Most all farmers, like myself, were fishermen at times," declared N. V. Tibbetts, a Brooklin farmer who fished local waters for cod and haddock to feed his family.

But inshore fishing had some obvious advantages. The work was generally safer and easier than deep-sea operations. Grand Banks crews might not see their families for many weeks at a time, but inshore fishermen could usually sleep at home at the end of the day. And, because it required little capital investment, inshore fishing offered each fisherman a chance to be his own boss. That counted for a lot in families whose ancestors had fought the Great Proprietors to preserve their economic independence. As the offshore fishery shrank and consolidated, thousands of fishermen joined the inshore fleet.

After living on this harsh coast for several generations, European Mainers had learned to follow nature's round, switching their focus from one resource to another according to the season, much like the Wabanaki had before them. The mix and timing depended on where one lived. In eastern Maine most spent part of each day farming and the remainder fishing, according to the season: handlining for pollock or cod in the fall, digging the vast clam flats at low tide through the winter, and setting traps for lobster in spring and early summer. North Haven islanders pursued a similar cycle, but spent June fishing for hake, and stopped when huge schools of mackerel arrived around the island in the fall. Many trapped lobster in the mornings and manned small mackerel seines in the afternoon; lacking large clam flats, they spent the winter fishing for lobster and cod or preparing their gear for the busy spring season.

Bristol fishermen, by contrast, concentrated on fishing menhaden, which had become valuable during the war as a source of fertilizer and industrial oils. By 1878, the little town had become the center of the state's menhaden industry. Seven hundred people were employed by Bristol's eleven rendering factories and twenty-nine inshore menhaden steamers throughout the spring and summer when the fish were present along the shore. In spring they waded in creek mouths to net buckets full of spawning herring, and in winter trudged through the muck to dig clams. But in the fall, Bristol fishermen did what more and more fishermen were doing up and down the coast: setting traps for the hordes of lobsters scavenging the bottoms of local harbors, bays, coves, and islands.

Coastal Mainers had been catching and eating lobsters since Waymouth's day, but nobody had ever tried to make a living from it. Lobsters were tasty, plentiful, and easy to catch. In colonial days, a small boy could bring home enough to feed several families by simply wading along the shore at low tide and gaffing the huge five- and ten-pound beasts hiding among the rocks. Coastal New Englanders ate them in quantity, or fed them to prisoners and indentured servants in place of commercially valuable cod, mackerel, or grain. One group of indentured servants in Massachusetts became so upset with this diet that they took their owners to court, winning a judgment that they would not be served lobster more than three times a week. Lobsters were sometimes taken in great numbers and strewn on the fields as fertilizer. Well into the nineteenth century, fishermen were grinding up piles of lobsters and tossing them overboard in an effort to attract schools of mackerel.

But as the populations of New England and New York City grew, some fishing families started earning extra income by supplying nearby landlubbers with live lobsters. Boys and old men were sent out to the shore to set simple "hoop traps." These were built by hanging a shallow net around a three-foot-wide barrel hoop, which would be laid on the bottom. Two wooden half-hoops were bent above it, crossing at right angles in the center, from which fish heads or some other bait was hung. Lobsters would smell the bait and wander into the middle of the hoop to dine. At that point the trappers, who watched the traps constantly, yanked on the ropes attached to the hoop, lifting it from the bottom with the surprised lobster hanging in the bottom of the net. The lobsters were tossed into barrels with a little seawater in them and carted or rowed to the nearest town for sale.

But by the early 1800s, lobsters were getting harder to catch along the shoreline. In Maine and other rural areas, boy trappers started tending their hoops from small rowboats. Around rapidly expanding New York City, lobstering became a full-fledged occupation, with many men tending hoop traps set in ever-deeper water: ten feet, then twenty, thirty, forty, and more as lobsters became more and more scarce. By 1800, the city's fishermen could no longer meet the explosive demand for live or freshly boiled lobsters. Connecticut fishermen supplied a greater and greater proportion of the city's demand, sailing boatfuls of lobsters into the city every day in the spring and summer from as far away as New London. Soon lobsters were scarce there too. New York's restaurants and boiling houses could no longer obtain sufficient numbers of lobsters within a day's sail of the city.

But leave it to Yankee ingenuity to find a profitable solution. Sometime around 1800, a group of New London fishermen came up with a way to transport live lobsters from farther afield. They constructed a large tank in the hold of a small wooden sailing vessel, then drilled dozens of holes through the hull to allow seawater to circulate through the tank. The resulting vessel was called a "smack," and their wells could keep thousands of lobsters alive for several days, even a week or two, en route to New York.

By 1802, New Londoners were swarming the rich lobstering

grounds off Provincetown at the tip of Cape Cod. Tending traps directly from their smacks, the fishermen quickly filled their wells, sailed down to New York to sell the catch, then returned for more. Other smacks carried lobsters to Boston. So many lobsters were being caught off Cape Cod that as early as 1812 Provincetown's citizens appealed to the state legislature "to prevent the destruction of the lobster fishery in the town . . . and to preserve and regulate the same in the waters and shores of said town."

The first person to promote lobsters in Boston appears to have been a certain Benjamin Simpson, owner of a basement restaurant in South End, who "used to go out in the harbor in a little boat and catch them in [the harbor] . . . and then peddle them about the city." He was soon joined by a man named Newcomb, who built a ten-ton lobster smack and hired Massachusetts Bay fishermen to supply the vessel with lobsters as it made the harbor rounds. On arrival in Boston the lobsters "were boiled and peddled through the streets by venders" who carried their catch through the immigrant neighborhoods in wheelbarrows. By 1820, fleets of smacks carried lobsters to the city from Provincetown and other Massachusetts fishing hamlets.

Some of these smacks visited Maine as early as 1830, calling on the fishing hamlets at the end of the Harpswell peninsula, ten miles east of Portland. Harpswell, like other Midcoast Maine communities, had engaged in a very small-scale local lobster trade for many years. But Harpswell's fishermen had concentrated more time and effort on catching lobsters because they had a ready market in nearby Portland, whose population was swelling with Irish immigrant laborers. They also had plenty of good lobster bottom to trap on, and little competition to the west, where the coast turns sandy and is less hospitable for lobsters. The presence of these professional lobstermen attracted smacks to Harpswell. Within a few years, they were carrying Maine lobsters as far away as New York.

The first detailed accounts of Maine's lobster trade come to us from Elisha M. Oakes of Vinalhaven, who began carrying Harpswell lobsters to an East Boston dealer in 1841. Oakes made a round-trip once a week, carrying roughly 3,500 lobsters at a time in the well of his forty-one-ton smack, *Swampscott*. The season, he told fisheries agents many years later, ran "from the first of March until about the fourth of

July, after which time lobsters were supposed to be unfit for eating."
After that time the lobsters would have molted, and in their soft shells
they "were even considered poisonous." The average weight of marketable lobsters was three pounds, "and all under ten and a half inches
in length were rejected." Oakes worked with five or six fishermen, paying them three cents for each acceptable lobster early in the season, but
only two cents by May, when markets had become saturated. He recalled that around this time the fifty-ton New London smack *Hulda B.
Hall* was also visiting the region, having contracted four Cape Porpoise fishermen to fill its hold with lobsters, which they then carried to
New York.

By 1847, Harpswell's lobstermen were having a hard time catching
enough lobsters. Oakes decided to purchase a slightly larger smack
and began running up to the harbors around his native Vinalhaven in
Penobscot Bay. He was probably responsible for the beginning of commercial lobstering on North Haven the following year, when one fisherman began setting traps and selling market-sized lobsters to unnamed
"Boston smacks." In 1850, Oakes abandoned Harpswell altogether "on
account of the small size of the lobsters then being caught there." Operations were moved to Penobscot Bay, concentrating on the Mussel
Ridge Channel, an archipelago of islands that proved to be as rich in
lobsters as it was in granite. He hired just four fishermen, each of
whom could catch between 1,200 and 1,500 marketable lobsters every
ten days. "In Captain Oakes's opinion," a U.S. fisheries agent later reported, "the Muscle Ridges have furnished the most extensive lobster
fishery of the Maine coast."

But smackmen like Oakes were engaging the services of just a
handful of fishermen in 1850. The real catalyst for the growth of
Maine's lobster industry came not from Boston or New York, but from
a homegrown industry that got its start far Downeast.

In the 1830s, Upham S. Treat, a native of Prospect, Maine, made his
living smoking the great heaps of salmon caught each spring as they
migrated up the Penobscot River to spawn. In 1839, he and two of his
friends moved their operation to Calais on the salmon-rich St. Croix.
One of Treat's friends, Isaac Noble, was from Calais, and knew that

area's fish resources well. The other, Tristram Holliday, was from Scotland, where he had seen salmon being preserved in a novel fashion
imported from France: the fish were cooked, deboned, and packed in
airtight metal cans in which they could be kept edible for years. Treat
and Noble had never heard of such a thing; indeed, this "canning"
process had never been successfully attempted in the United States,
save for a small oyster-packing operation in Baltimore. But Holliday's
story intrigued them: What if they could replicate this technology
here, in eastern Maine? Then their remote location wouldn't be such
a liability in getting seafood to market. Hell, they could ship St. Croix
salmon to China if they wanted to. The three men formed a partner-
ship in 1842, moved to the coastal town of Eastport, and set about trying to can fish.

   Their experiments were conducted in the greatest secrecy, with no
outsiders allowed in their experimental bathing room. Working from
Holliday's fuzzy memory, they tried canning not only salmon, but haddock and lobster as well. Things didn't go well. They were short of
money, and the cheap cans they purchased sometimes exploded when
subjected to the requisite submersion in boiling water. Holliday didn't
know how to get all the air out of the cans before sealing them, leading
to further explosions in the bath. Some of their cans didn't explode,
but when the three men opened them weeks later the contents had
often spoiled. They needed some outside advice.

   The following year they traveled to Halifax, Nova Scotia, where
they found and hired a veteran Scottish canner, Charles Mitchell, and
brought him back to their secret Eastport laboratory. Mitchell knew
exactly what to do; he had spent a decade working in Scottish canneries and had even gone into business for himself after emigrating to
Halifax in 1841. Mitchell quickly got the assembly line in order, and
Treat, Holliday & Noble's factory began churning out one-pound cans
of lobster, the product they deemed to be most unique and profitable.
It was the first time anyone in the world had ever canned lobster, and
the second time Americans had ever canned anything at all.

   Treat scurried off to the major eastern cities with samples of their
product, which retailed for five cents a pound. Sales were slow at
first—shopkeepers were unfamiliar with canned goods and would
often only accept them on consignment. But the orders began to

come in, slowly at first, then at a remarkable speed. As the demand grew, one of their assembly line employees, Samuel Rumrey, took off with the secrets he'd learned and hired himself out to Boston investors. Next thing they knew, Rumrey was down in Portland operating the Bostonians' new lobster cannery. A couple of years later, Rumrey jumped ship again, and set up a new cannery in Harpswell. (His new employer, George Burnham, would go on to create the Burnham & Morrill canning empire, which lives on today in the form of B&M baked beans.) In 1850, these three lobster factories were practically the only canneries of any kind in the entire country. Two decades later there were hundreds.

From the start, the canneries encountered difficulties procuring lobsters. There were plenty of them out there on the coast of Maine, but almost nobody was fishing for them. Ironically, these early processors had to argue the merits of a commercial lobster fishery to the fishermen themselves.

Treat, Holliday, and Noble were in an especially awkward situation. They'd started their operations in Eastport with the idea of canning St. Croix salmon, but wound up concentrating on lobster. Unfortunately, nobody in Eastport fished for lobster as they were not thought to be present in large enough numbers to bother. The company was forced to purchase its own smacks and send them far westward in search of lobsters.

Smackmen, whether they worked for the fresh market or canneries, were the chief promoters of lobstering. A Gloucester smack crew introduced Swan's Island fishermen to lobstering in 1850, even providing them with traps with which to fill the smack's well. The Gloucestermen did not return, but the islanders must have been pleased with their income, because the following year they built their own traps and began selling to other smacks. In the spring of 1853, smack captain John D. Piper brought traps to Deer Isle and hired local shore fishermen to catch lobsters for him. Other early commercial lobstermen like those in Boothbay, North Haven, and Isle au Haut were likely induced to fish by visiting smackmen like Oates and Piper.

To recruit and retain lobstermen, the smack captains went out of their way to foster good relations with fishing families in remote out-ports. "The arrival of the smack is an important event," reported William H. Bishop, who visited the Maine coast in 1880 and wrote articles on the lobster industry for *Harper's* and *Scribner's*, the leading magazines of the day. "The skipper brings the news of the trade and the personal gossip of his circuit, and executes many small commissions for the household. . . . [He] endeavors to attach to himself his special gang [of lobstermen] and to make it as large as possible. To insure that they fish for him and no other he uses all the arts of a commercial traveler: . . . a slightly more favorable price here . . . an exhibition of jolly good fellowship there, [or] appeals to long-established usage and relations." Smackmen also supplied traps, lines, and other gear or household items on credit, at a time when few fishermen had much cash.

By this time, the old hoop traps had been replaced by the more sophisticated lath trap. These traps, invented in the early 1830s, looked very much like the wooden traps used in Maine as late as 1980 and still used today in parts of Newfoundland. Constructed of spruce slats, lath lobster "pots" were four feet long and two feet high, with a flat bottom and rounded top. The ends were covered with netting instead of slats, with a funnel-shaped opening in one end through which the lobster would enter, but had a difficult time exiting. Lobstermen placed the bait on hooks at the center of the trap, accessed via a small wooden door with leather hinges. Seeing a stack of these lobster pots for the first time, Bishop likened them to "a pile of mammoth bird cages."

Lath pots didn't need to be constantly watched over, so lobstermen could tend larger numbers of traps, only returning to check a given trap just once, perhaps twice a day. A typical lobsterman around 1860 tended twenty-five to fifty pots from an open dory. Usually each pot was marked with its own buoy, a hand-carved cedar or spruce spindle or a small keg attached to the trap with a tarred manila buoy line, or warp; occasionally two traps were fished in "pairs" marked with the same buoy line. Either way, the traps, which were weighted down with bricks or stones, had to be hauled up to the surface entirely by hand. There the fisherman hauled the trap onto the dory and removed the lobsters who'd wandered inside.

The catch in those days would astound today's lobsterman. Portland lobstermen in 1855 *averaged* seven four- to six-pound lobsters in
every pot, every day throughout the four-month season. (By comparison, today's lobstermen often find only one legal-sized lobster per trap,
and it typically weighs between a pound and a pound and a half.) In
Harpswell, the U.S. Fish Commission reported, "all lobsters weighting
less than two pounds were thrown away" because the canneries refused to buy such "small" specimens. Even so, two fishermen working
fifty to seventy-five traps together could expect "a daily average of 400
to 500 lobsters of marketable size." Fisheries agent John N. Cobb reported that "stories of the capture of lobsters weighing thirty, forty, and
even fifty pounds have been common" along the Maine coast. While
he couldn't verify many of the stories, Cobb did see a twenty-five-
pound lobster in 1899 at Peak's Island near Portland. "It had been
caught near Monhegan Island, and the owner was carrying it from
town to town in a small car, which he had built for it, and charging a
small fee to look at it," he wrote. In Saint George, William Bishop saw
"the claw of a lobster which in life weighed forty-three pounds" hanging on the wall of a building.

The fishermen rebaited the emptied trap and set it back on the bottom. Cod and haddock heads were preferred bait, but when they didn't
have any at hand, lobstermen turned to catching bottom-dwelling fish
like sculpin and flounder. Sculpin were often caught in the traps,
which they entered to gobble up smaller lobsters and crabs. Flounder,
then considered trash fish, were so common they could simply be
speared in shallow water on calm days; in rougher weather it was difficult to spot the flounder on the bottom, so fishermen would pour a
bottle of fish oil over the side to flatten the sea surface. The fish were
cut into small pieces and stuck on hooks inside the lobster trap.

Once the last trap was hauled, the lobstermen would row back to
their anchorage and unload their catch into a lobster car. These were
usually six-by-four-foot wooden crates tied to the dock or moored in
the harbor and kept mostly submerged for the benefit of the hundreds
of live lobsters stored inside. Often, "old leaky boats, especially dories,
furnished with a cover" were used as lobster cars. "If the open seams
do not afford a sufficient circulation of water" to keep the lobsters

alive, fisheries agent Richard Rathbun reported, "numerous holes are bored through the bottom and sides." There the lobsters remained until the arrival of the weekly smacks from Portland, Boston, or New York or the daily or thrice-weekly cannery smacks.

The smacks visited even the tiniest harbors, usually following a "rude sort of schedule" accurate "within a day or two." On arrival, the smack would sail alongside each lobster car and luff up its sails. The car's owner then climbed on top of the car, opened its door, and dipped the lobsters into the smack's iron weighing scoop which was then hoisted aboard with pulleys built into the vessel's rigging. Frequently rival smacks would arrive at the same time and, according to Cobb, "the bidding between the captains for the fishermen's catch gladdens the latter's heart and greatly enriches his pocketbook." Early lobstermen reported making good money. At a time when a dory was worth less than $20, a lobster trap cost less than a dollar to construct, and a new Grand Banks fishing schooner sold for $6,000, Boothbay lobstermen typically made $500 or more in six months of fishing.

On arrival at the cannery wharf, the smack's cargo, "clutching and flapping viscously, [was] unceremoniously transferred with shovels as though it was only coals." Workers then carried the lobsters into the cannery by the stretcher-full and dumped them into big copper vats filled with boiling water. The lobsters were cooked to well-done—about ten to twenty minutes—then dumped onto sorting tables to cool. "The scarlet hue [of the cooling lobsters] is seen in all quarters," Bishop opined, "on top of the steaming stretcher, in the great heaps on the tables, in scattered individuals on the floor, in a large pile of shells and refuse seen through the open door, and in an ox-cartload of the same refuse, farther off, which is being taken away as fertilizer." The lobsters were usually left to cool overnight before being dismantled by the staff.

A typical cannery employed about twenty-five people, roughly half of them women and children. The work was regimented, the workers organized into a lobster picking assembly line consisting of a "foreman, boilers, crackers, breakers, sealers, bathmen, tail pickers or shellers, arm-pickers, fillers, crowders, weighers, coverers, can-wipers, etc." Men, who were paid two to four times more than the women, were responsible for manning the boilers, breaking the lobsters into their constituent parts with cleavers, breaking the claw meat out of the shell, and pushing the meat from the tail sections. Women picked the meat from the arm segments with little forks and packed and weighed the cans. Then the cans were soldered and boiled another two hours.

The process consumed an extraordinary number of lobsters. It took four and a half to six pounds of live lobsters to fill a one-pound can with meat. The bodies were discarded along with the shells, forming great refuse piles behind the cannery shed. Some canneries gave the refuse away to local farmers by the wagonload. J. Winslow Holmes placed twenty-four young pigs on the refuse pile of his Boothbay Harbor cannery where they "thrived well." But most canneries simply dumped the refuse off the wharf—hundreds of tons annually at each cannery—transforming each harbor and nearby shores into a smelly mess of putrid shellfish.

The canneries spread like wildfire, and the lobster fishery followed. By the late 1870s, there were twenty-three from Portland to Eastport, engaging the service of 1,200 lobstermen. Together they churned out two million one-pound cans of lobster in two four-month canning seasons. These were distributed far and wide and introduced the American West and Southwest to lobster meat. Roughly half the production was exported to Europe, particularly England, where well-cooked meat found a ready market. Lobsters were canned from April to midsummer and again in the fall months. At other times, cannery owners found it more profitable to can fruits, berries, corn, or fish. By 1880, Bishop reported, the canneries were so numerous they could "hardly escape the notice of even the fashionable visitor to Maine."

"Fashionable" travelers didn't always like what they saw. Wealthy visitors to Mount Desert Island arriving by steamship at Southwest Harbor were greeted with the most stunning vistas of Somes Sound, the East Coast's only genuine fjord. Virtually all of them promptly fled to Bar Harbor, which became Maine's first and most exclusive resort town. The reason for their quick exodus, the editors of *Harper's* explained in 1872, was the presence of a large lobster cannery right at the steamship landing. "Now most of the visitors to Mount Desert, even the prosaic folk go prepared to enjoy the picturesque, the beautiful, the sublime," they sniffed. "Just as they are about to be ushered into this new world of romance and delight, to be met upon the threshold by thousands of lobsters, raw, boiled, cooked and canned, is discouraging to say the least."

But "fashionable visitors" were summering in Maine in ever-greater numbers after the Civil War. The arrival of the summer people would forever alter coastal Maine society, economics, and land ownership patterns. Their effect on the burgeoning lobster fishery was immediate and profoundly invigorating.

⌒〰〰〰

The summer trade began quietly, even discreetly, in the decades preceding the Civil War. A few adventurous families made their way up the coast by stagecoach or cargo schooner, escaping the heat and diseases of the cities to enjoy the "healthful" ocean air and clean and "invigorating" dips in the ocean itself. People didn't take vacations in those days—leisure was still a suspect activity among the wealthier descendants of the Puritan migration and an unattainable luxury for people of ordinary means. But, for those who could afford it, there was no shame in spending the summer at a health spa, recovering one's strength through rest, bathing, walking, dining, perhaps with a little fishing, hunting, sailing, or card playing on the side. As early as 1837, Boothbay had become "a favorite resort for invalids during the summer season, on account of the purity of the air and the facilities for bathing in clear water." Facilities were extremely modest. Boothbay's early "invalids" hired men to row them from Bath in open dories. On arrival they "either boarded in private families or camped on the shores, and any expenditures made by them were so small as not to be noticeable in the business affairs of the community."

A few artists spent their summers in Maine, boarding among the invalids and returning to the cities with paintings of a rugged, picturesque land where, in the words of one art historian, "nature offered assurances of both personal and national transcendence." One of the earliest was Thomas Doughty, who explored as far east as Mount Desert Island in the early 1830s, booking passages from harbor to harbor on small coastal sailing vessels. His paintings of fishing towns and the newly constructed Mount Desert Rock lighthouse were exhibited in Boston and London and attracted the interest of other artists. In the

1840s, Thomas Cole, Frederick Church, and other painters of the Hudson River School summered on Mount Desert, painting the stunning landscapes of the island that introduced wealthy Boston, New York, and Philadelphia families to the coast. To the south, New Hampshire legislator Thomas Laighton built Maine's first island resort hotel on Appledore in the Isles of Shoals, which was promptly filled with artists of all sorts; Nathaniel Hawthorne, Harriet Beecher Stowe, Henry Wadsworth Longfellow, and Sarah Orne Jewett were just a few of the guests.

Intentionally or not, the visiting artists' work promoted the Maine coast as a summer vacation destination. Each year, local families took in more summer boarders, and some built small hotels to meet the demand. At first most were teachers or college professors with free summers. But after the Civil War, summer vacations became fashionable among the nation's wealthy, who began arriving on the coast by the droves. They came in search of picturesque settings where they could, for a few weeks, relax in a simple, rustic setting and forget about the noisy, immigrant-choked industrial cities where they lived and to which they owed their fortunes.

The "rusticators," as these early vacationers called themselves, transformed the coast at an astonishing rate. From Kennebunk to Winter Harbor, simple boardinghouses gave way to rambling resort hotels. Bar Harbor was virtually unknown to the outside world in the 1840s. By the early 1870s it was home to fifteen large summer hotels. The largest of these, the Rodick House, grew to become the largest hotel in New England: It had six stories with 400 rooms that served 750 at mealtime and drew more than 3,000 to its biweekly dances. When Otis Waite visited the southern coast in 1871, two hotels were under construction on undeveloped York Beach, where horseback riding was "very pleasant, the horses' hoofs striking on the hard sand, making a fine accompaniment to the dashing of the waves. . . ." Old Orchard Beach's hotel had grown "within the last few years from an ordinary farmhouse to an establishment capable . . . of accommodating five hundred or more people." Wells's two large hotels overflowed with guests even though it was then "a resort for sportsmen rather than other pleasure seekers" on account of the large trout stream crossing the beach. By the early 1880s, grand hotels had popped up on islands all along the coast, from the Cranberry Islands off Mount Desert to the little islands of Casco Bay and Boothbay.

Shipping companies built fleets of passenger steamers to handle the inflow of well-heeled vacationers. Steamships ran from Boston to Belfast, with connecting service to the landings of dozens of exclusive summer colonies dotting the islands, peninsulas, and bays. By the 1880s, Portland, Bath, and Newcastle steamers made scheduled stops at tiny Inner Heron Island in Bristol, which had only sixteen cottages. Meanwhile railroads spread through the backcountry, linking Boston to Bangor, where a spur line carried passengers to within eight miles of the Bar Harbor wharf. In 1884, the year the spur line opened, the number of visitors to Mount Desert "more than quadrupled."

As the hotels grew ever larger, many rusticator families abandoned them, and instead built their own summer cottages where their families could enjoy the simpler life. Most were constructed in planned developments, with their own "reading rooms," tennis courts, and yacht clubs where cottagers could socialize far removed from the growing hordes of middle-class vacationers filling the hotels.

Developers fanned out across the coast, offering local families large cash payments for undeveloped oceanfront land. Boothbay residents watched as one development after another appeared on the shores of the region's many islands and coves. Judge J. B. Ham of Lewiston led a group that purchased tiny Squirrel Island from a local family for $2,200 in 1870. A few months later they'd constructed fourteen cottages, and within a year there was a steamboat landing, bowling alley, and a network of sidewalks. By the 1890s, Squirrel had become an exclusive little town with a post office, "reading room," newspaper, casino, chapel, store, two-hundred-guest hotel, and over one hundred cottages. Isle of Springs, purchased by Augusta developers in 1887, soon hosted twenty-five cottages, a casino, and a hotel for fifty guests. Similar colonies sprang up in nearby Southport, Capitol Island, Ocean Point, and Bayville. Boothbay judge George Kenniston got in on the act himself, heading a development company that bought up huge swaths of Monhegan in the 1890s and divided it up into sixty densely packed cottage lots spreading clear across the island and onto the great headlands on the back side.

But the rusticators soon had unwanted company. By the 1880s, Mount Desert, Islesboro, and other prestigious resorts had attracted the attention of the nation's ultrawealthy, war profiteers and industrial monopolists who had amassed unprecedented fortunes. Bar Harbor rivaled Newport, Rhode Island, as the summer capital of the Gilded Age's plutocrats. Newspaper publisher Joseph Pulitzer's "cottage" included a heated swimming pool, and the "Tower of Silence," a granite edifice with a soundproofed bedroom whose floor was mounted on ball bearings. *Liberty*, his three-hundred-foot yacht, contained a music room and gymnasium. Railroad owner John S. Kennedy's "Kenarden Lodge" cost $200,000 and was equipped with its own electric power plant. John D. Rockefeller Jr. bought 150 acres overlooking Seal Harbor and built a 107-room Tudor-style mansion for his family to spend their summers in.

The flashy, aristocratic lifestyle of the plutocrats upset many rusticators, who treasured the coast as a "scene of more plain living and high thinking." Edwin Godkin, a rusticator who spent his summers in Bar Harbor, complained bitterly of the arrival of the great cottagers, calling it "the great summer tragedy of American life." He compared their advance to the "hordes who issued from the plains of Scythia to overthrow the Roman Empire." Godkin found the plutocrats' flashy wealth disgusting:

> More cottages are built, with trim lawns and private lawn tennis grounds. . . . Then the dog-cart with the groom in buckskin and boots, the Irish red setter, the saddle-horse with banged tail, the phaeton with two ponies, the young men in knickerbockers carrying imported racquets, the girls with banged hair, the club, ostensibly for newspaper reading, but really for secret gin-fizzes and soda-cocktails, make their appearance with a number of other monarchal excrescences.

But both groups were displacing the families who actually lived on the coast. At a time when Maine's traditional industries were in decline, native landowners were probably happy to exchange some shorefront property for a little ready cash. In the mid-1870s, Mount Desert's native homes revealed their inhabitants to be in "a near approach to

poverty," according to visiting writer Samuel Adams Drake. The islanders, he wrote, were "in marked degree ... incapable of appre-
ciating the grandeur of the scenes with which they have from infancy
been familiar [and] look with scarce concealed disdain upon the admiration they inspire in others." Whatever the real source of their disdain,
natives often underestimated the value of seafront land to wealthy vacationers. A Bar Harbor property speculator is said to have purchased a
Bar Harbor lot from a local family for $200, selling it a few years later
to George Vanderbilt for $200,000. Monhegan's local assessors taxed
cottage lots at an average of only $0.08 a year in 1894, apparently un-
aware that each was worth many thousands of dollars.

The social condescension of the summer people had to have been
galling to the descendants of those who had struggled for their land in
the eighteenth and early nineteenth centuries. Society families must
have been taken aback by the natives' prideful insistence that they be
treated, if not as equals, at least respectfully. Writer Cleveland Amory,
who wrote about Bar Harbor society in the 1940s, collected a number
of stories in which Maine pride collided with visitors' arrogance. Jim
Foley, a native Bar Harbor carriage driver, apparently called all summer people by their first names and had little tolerance for their
criticism. When De Grasse Fox, a wealthy Philadelphia attorney, complained that Foley was driving slowly and asked if his horse was asleep,
Foley is said to have answered: "I don't know, but if you'll hold the
reins I'll get out and see." Bar Harbor paint shop owner Chet Sprague
was once summoned to a mansion where the lady of the house be-
rated him for allowing his mongrel dog to impregnate her pedigreed
Pekinese. Somewhere in the midst of the tirade, Sprague turned his
back on the enraged lady and started out the door. "Where are you going," she demanded. "Ma'm," Sprague responded, "I was just going
home to ask my dog if he'll marry your dog."

Defiant gestures aside, Bar Harbor's summer people called the
shots. J. P. Morgan, who arrived each year on his mammoth yacht *Corsair*, awarded a summertime household position in his mansion to the
prospective servant who reached his vessel first in an impromptu rowing race from the shore. Rockefeller, who brought an Armenian to his
mansion just to take care of his oriental carpets, gave strict orders

never to feed his night watchmen, even during the Great Depression. One watchman, Cecil Carter, later recalled Rockefeller to be the "meanest man that ever lived. . . . You always tipped your hat and never looked 'em in the eye when you talked." But Carter stuck with the job because his other alternative was surviving by "smelting fish, gardening, [and] digging clams."

The arrival of the summer people provided a great number of jobs to communities with few economic options. Hundreds of outport men and women found relatively well-paying summer employment as servants, cooks, gardeners, and coachmen at the grand estates of Mount Desert. In less ostentatious vacation spots, locals maintained the cottagers' homes, delivered their groceries, and taught their children how to handle the yacht club sailboats. In many towns, the summer population grew to exceed the year-round one, dramatically boosting everything from retail sales to tax receipts. By 1884, the summer trade was so all-important to Bar Harbor's economy that at the end of the season a local church member led the following prayer: "Oh, Lord, now that our summer visitors have departed, wilt Thou take their places in our hearts?"

The summer folk also provided a critical boost to Maine's inshore fishermen on the coast by eating a great deal of fresh seafood. An estimated 100,000 visitors stayed at the resort hotels each summer in the 1880s, consuming unprecedented quantities of fish, clams, and lobster. Tens of thousands of cottagers turned to local fishermen to supply the shore dinners, clambakes, and lobster boils that were fast becoming fixtures of the Maine vacation experience. On their return home to Boston, New York, or Philadelphia, many summer people continued to crave fresh seafood and so boosted demand in the urban markets as well.

The summer folk wanted to dine on all sorts of things. Clams, which diggers had previously shucked and pickled as cod bait, now fetched good money at resort hotels and Boston restaurants, which ordered them by the bushel. Canneries started buying them as well, shipping them all over the country for use in clam chowder. Sophisticated diners preferred fresh cod over salted fish, now spurned as poor man's food. Back in 1839, John Davis of Massachusetts had denounced hake and haddock on the floor of the U.S. Senate; dried haddock, Davis told his fellow senators, "is without reputation even in the hut of the negro, who is doomed to be its principal consumer. . . . The hake, however, yields a larger quantity of oil and is, therefore, held in estimation by those who catch it and are not compelled to eat it." But forty years later, both were in demand as fresh table fish in New England's finest dining establishments. And as iceboxes and refrigeration became commonplace during the 1880s, inshore fishermen found expansive markets for their catch.

Amid this fever for exotic foods, more and more out-of-staters became crazed for lobster. Fishermen found they could sell every lobster they pulled out of their traps in the early 1880s. At the height of summer, hotel owners would pay as much as five cents for a good, two-pound dinner table lobster, and most of the Boston, New York, and Portland smack captains would match the price. The live trade extended all the way to the extreme east of the state, where Eastport dealers bought large lobsters for three cents apiece, loaded them in ice-packed flour barrels, and shipped them off to Boston in the hold of the daily passenger steamship. Smaller lobsters were no longer discarded, as the canneries would buy them for $1 per hundredweight. The average size of cannery lobsters fell from more than three pounds to less than three-quarters of a pound, and each year Maine canneries processed hundreds of thousands of tiny half-pound "snappers" that were years away from sexual maturity.

The number of lobstermen exploded, from a few dozen in the late 1840s to 1,843 in 1880. Together they were catching more than 14 million pounds of marketable lobsters a year, of which two-thirds went to the canneries. Lobsters were fished year-round, and sturdy, purpose-built lobstering sloops were constructed in large numbers in Friendship and other Muscongus Bay towns. A fleet of fifty-eight smacks plied the coast for lobster, some of them equipped with steam engines and capable of hauling ten thousand lobsters in their wells. The canneries and smacks employed nearly one thousand more Mainers, and provided income to untold numbers of Canadian lobstermen now tending traps in New Brunswick and Nova Scotia. In the thirty years between

1850 and 1880, lobsters had gone from a cheap form of bait to a $430,000 industry, exceeding all other Maine fisheries save cod, mackerel, and herring.

The lobster craze prompted all sorts of risky experiments. Covetous of this new resource, the State of California made three unsuccessful attempts to transplant Atlantic lobsters to the West Coast in the 1870s, shipping them across the continent in special railway cars. The first shipment of 162 lobsters died in "an unfortunate accident near Omaha which precipitated their car into a river. . . ." In the second shipment, 146 of 150 lobsters died on the way, and the four survivors were never seen again after being dumped off an Oakland pier. Nor did anyone again see the two lobsters the experimenters dumped in Utah's Great Salt Lake en route. Not a word was heard from the twenty-one females that survived the third shipment after they were set free in San Francisco Bay. Later, the U.S. Fish Commission managed to introduce 590 lobsters to California and Washington state which, like their predecessors, vanished without a trace. Not to be outdone, the U.S. Navy dumped sixty-three hapless lobsters to the warm, briny waters of Chesapeake Bay. On completion of this mission, the officer in charge, Lieutenant W. M. Wood, said he would "trust they may be heard from in the future." They weren't.

Private investors had better success. Portland and Boston dealers started reliably shipping live lobsters as far as St. Louis by railroad in specially packed barrels. In 1877, the Portland firm of John Marston & Sons built a special lobster tank equipped with a seawater pump and shipped 250 Maine lobsters to England; 200 survived the trip and sold for sixty to seventy cents a pound—ten times what they'd paid for them. In the mid-1870s, Boston fish dealers fenced off a cove on Vinalhaven and began holding live lobsters through the summer and fall, selling them in early winter when prices were higher and the lobsters had grown larger. This proved so profitable that similar "lobster pounds" sprang up all over the coast in the years that followed. With pounds and new shipping methods, lobsters could be profitably stored and shipped to half the country. *Homarus americanus* had finally become big business.

As the industry grew, however, it became increasingly clear that the lobsters were shrinking. "At all points along the coast, from Cape Small Point to Pemaquid Point, the fishermen are agreed," fisheries agent Richard Rathbun reported in the early 1880s, "that formerly lobsters were very abundant and of large size, and that overfishing has reduced them in both size and numbers." Swan's Island lobstermen told Rathbun that over the past fifteen years, the average fisherman's catch had fallen from between 200 and 250 lobsters a day to only 75, while the average size fell from three pounds to two. North Haven lobstermen saw their daily catch fall from 1,500 to 400 pounds. Biddeford fishermen said their catch per trap had fallen by two-thirds since the 1860s, while lobster canneries started closing early in the season for lack of lobsters. "Lobsters are very small, scarce, and high," the Boston Fish Bureau reported from Deer Isle in 1882. "This season will finish them. Three years at most will close up every lobster factory in the State if something isn't done to protect them." Many feared Maine's lobsters would go the way of those in New York and southern New England.

Most fishermen blamed the decline on the lobster canneries, probably with justification. The canneries were consuming millions of juvenile lobsters before they could spawn. Many collected lobsters with smacks that had no wells, and in hot weather entire cargoes died before they could be canned. Sometimes ten or more tiny lobsters were needed to pack a one-pound tin.

As the situation became more serious, cannery owners lobbied state legislators to pass the lobster industry's first "conservation" measures. The resulting laws were designed to protect the canneries from the live lobster trade, rather than protecting the lobsters themselves. The first, passed in 1872, forbade lobstermen to keep egg-bearing females, which didn't affect the canneries because they bought lobsters too small to carry eggs. Two years later a second law forbade lobstermen to keep lobsters smaller than ten and a half inches from head to tail (a size that typically weighs 1.75 pounds) between October 1 and April 1. Since no canneries packed lobsters during those months of the year, the law had no effect on their business; it simply forced lobstermen to protect the canners' lobster supply during the months they were busy packing berries, corn, and other products.

The cannery-friendly laws angered people in the fresh lobster trade, who realized the destruction of entire generations of young lobsters was dooming the future supply of dinner-table-sized ones. "We catch [lobsters] faster than they can grow," declared dealer and lobster pound pioneer S. M. Johnson. "If we continue indiscriminate fishing, practical extermination must follow." A Biddeford lobsterman told fisheries agents that the new closed season law was "a mere farce" that "benefits the canneries to the injury of the fishermen and will result in the extinction of the lobster."

Fishermen across the state petitioned the legislature to crack down on the canneries, backed by Johnson and other lobster dealers, whose economic and political importance was increasing with each passing year. Soon the canners were on the defensive. In 1879 the state legislature limited the lobster canning season to four months in the spring and early summer. Live dealers lobbied for a year-round ban on the taking of small lobsters for any purpose, declaring the seasonal closure to be "utterly useless" in preventing the resource's destruction. Portland canners fought back, implicating Johnson's Vinalhaven lobster pound in the "wholesale slaughter of this fish, by rich corporations out of the state." J. Wilson Jones, a leading Portland canner, argued that instead of a minimum-size rule, "the fishing ground should be divided up so that one factory will not be competing with another on prices, making competition so close that neither the packers nor the fishermen have an interest in protecting the grounds. . . ."

Legislators were unimpressed by the canners' arguments. In 1883 they passed laws forbidding the taking of egg-bearing females and small lobsters less than nine inches long at any time of the year. Unable to secure cheap juveniles, canners moved their operations across the border to New Brunswick, which had no minimum-size laws. By 1889, when legislators restricted the canning operations to May and June, cannery production had fallen by 40 percent. Five years later the minimum size was increased to ten and a half inches, forcing the last cannery out of the state.

As the tide turned against him, George Burnham Jr., owner of the B&M canning empire, predicted the minimum-size rule would backfire for lack of support from the lobstermen themselves. "Do the fishermen throw the small ones overboard again to crawl into their traps and eat their bait, or do they take them ashore and boil them for the hens and other purposes, or destroy them in some other way?" he asked. "I am quite certain that the small lobsters once caught never again get the chance to eat bait from a trap."

Sadly, Burnham was right. Lobstermen largely ignored the new laws, crushing short lobsters as bait or taking them home for the family garden or dinner table. A large black-market trade developed around Massachusetts and New Hampshire lobster runners, who filled their smacks with shorts purchased from Maine lobstermen and sold them in their home states, which had greater minimum sizes. Warden N. J. Hanna estimated that Maine lobstermen were eating or selling over four million short lobsters each year, to the detriment of the fishery. There was little wardens like Hanna could do about it. Lobstermen could spot them coming from miles away and warned others with whistles and signal flags. Lobster smugglers carried word from harbor to harbor of a warden's approach, and resisted boarding inspections by sending the crew to "stand to the rail with bludgeons." Violations became so serious in the early 1920s that state fisheries authorities suspended lobster fishing in the Midcoast region for several weeks to protect the little softshell lobsters from poaching.

Meanwhile, the lobster population continued to show signs of distress. Catches peaked in 1889 at 25 million pounds and then began a steady decline. Maine landings slid to 17 million pounds in 1892, to 11 million pounds in 1898, and continued to languish well into the twentieth century. The destruction of juvenile lobsters played a part in the decline. But at the turn of the century, scientists began publishing the results of the first scientific surveys of lobster biology, reproduction, and behavior, which suggested a flaw in the current conservation laws. Francis Herrick of Western Reserve University discovered that the number of eggs laid by female lobsters increased geometrically as they grew larger: an eight-inch-long female typically carried half as many eggs as a ten-inch one, and only a quarter as many as a foot-long female. Herrick and other scientists argued that arresting the lobster's decline would require protecting very large lobsters as well as small ones.

Perversely, as the catch continued to fall, the number of lobstermen fishing for that catch increased dramatically. Between 1889 and 1898 the number of lobstermen jumped by a third, from 2,080 to 3,099. The fishery remained attractive because as supply fell further and further behind demand, lobstermen got higher and higher prices for their catch: average per-pound prices quadrupled between 1889 and 1898, then jumped again in 1904. Between 1905 and 1929, Maine lobstermen increased the number of traps they used by 62 percent and fished over ever-longer seasons, but their catch fell by 28 percent. Only the ever-increasing prices kept an economic disaster at bay.

The stock market collapse of 1929 dealt the final blow to the industry. By the 1920s, the annual catch was down to about five million pounds a year, a quarter of the levels of the 1890s. Lobsters were by then an expensive luxury item, and both demand and prices crashed during the Great Depression of the 1930s. "Lobsters are very scarce and the price so low that . . . a fisherman can't earn enough for a living not to mention keeping up his gear," one observer wrote the fisheries commissioner. The number of lobstermen fell by a third in the first three years of the depression. To make matters worse, hotels and restaurants started buying smaller, cheaper lobsters from Canada, which could now be shipped to New York and Boston by refrigerated railcars. Other traditional fisheries were also depleted: menhaden had been wiped out by overfishing in the 1880s; haddock catches were in free fall; hake, halibut, and mackerel landings all stood at a small fraction of their levels of thirty years earlier, while many clam flats were closed due to contamination from paper mills and sewage pipes.

The crisis had a silver lining, however, in that it transformed conservation attitudes along the coast, laying the groundwork for Maine's unusually successful late-twentieth-century lobster industry. In lobstering communities of the late 1930s, "people became convinced that those violating conservation laws were doing far more damage than previously thought," writes University of Maine anthropologist James Acheson, who studied the development of the conservation ethic within Maine's lobster fishery. Scientists reported seeing a marked change during the 1930s. Early in the decade, according to biologist Leslie Scattergood of the state marine lab in Boothbay Harbor, "violation of lobster laws was like rum running . . . everyone was doing it."

But by the end of the decade, major violations had ceased. Wardens reported greater cooperation from lobstermen, who by then generally observed conservation laws.

In this environment, Maine fish commissioner Horatio D. Crie pushed a radical new conservation law through the legislature in December 1933. Based on Herrick's findings, the new "double-gauge" law prohibited the taking of both small and very large lobsters. To make compliance easier, lobstermen were to measure the length of the animals' carapace, rather than have to manhandle a struggling lobster's tail section. Only lobsters that measured at least 3$\frac{1}{16}$ inches, but not more than 4$\frac{3}{4}$ inches, could be kept. The oversized lobsters would be returned to the water as breeding stock; the small ones were allowed to spawn once before being sent to the dinner table.

Before the vote, Crie promised fishermen, "if a double gauge measure is passed, you will see the lobsters continue to increase from year to year." So long as the measure was enforced, he predicted, "no one will ever have to feel disturbed about the depletion of the lobsters on the Maine Coast."

Fortunately, Crie's predictions held true, and Maine's lobster fishery stood poised at the beginning of an era of unprecedented prosperity.

SIX

Down and East

D uring the twentieth century, the Maine coast, long regarded as a land apart, became more closely drawn into the mainstream of both American society and its national economy than ever before. An environmental crisis on the sea and a sociological challenge ashore would profoundly alter the character and potential of Maine's coastal communities.

꙳

The Great Depression, the longest, deepest economic decline in the nation's history, drove tens of millions of Americans into abject poverty. A quarter of the American workforce could find no work, and even those who held on to their jobs often lost everything when four in ten of the nation's banks collapsed. Breadlines formed in the cities, and shantytowns sprang up at their outskirts. It was an event that shocked and scarred an entire generation of Americans.

Not so on the Maine coast. By the early decades of the twentieth century, Maine's coastal economy had been in decline for so long that it had nowhere left to fall. By the start of the Great Depression in 1929, many Mainers, especially in rural areas, were already as depressed as they could get; they had little more to lose.

Virtually every industry on the coast had fallen apart during the late nineteenth century: farming, fishing, shipbuilding, lumbering, and the cutting of granite, limestone, and ice. The nation's commerce abandoned the wooden hulls of Maine-built sailing vessels plying the Atlantic seaboard, shifting instead onto steel rails connecting the great eastern cities with the vast resources of the American West. The Maine coast, once at the heart of American commerce, had become an isolated backwater.

Maine's population growth stagnated and its coast became depopulated. Between 1860 and 1910, the U.S. population grew by two-thirds; Maine's grew by only 13 percent. During that same period, all of Maine's coastal counties actually shrank, save for York and Cumberland in the far south. The Midcoast region was particularly hard-hit: Lincoln County (which includes the Boothbay and Pemaquid peninsulas) lost more than a third of its people in that fifty-year span, while Waldo County (center of the backcountry resistance a century earlier) lost 40 percent. Forests advanced over the fields of derelict farmhouses, and the mudflats became littered with the rotting hulks of abandoned sailing ships. The great-grandchildren of backcountry resisters were abandoning their meager homesteads and heading west in hopes of a better life along the expanding frontiers of the American West.

Those who remained behind typically worked hard just to get by. "I never knew anybody around that was considered wealthy, able to step right out and buy a house or buy a horse or something like that. They always had to scrimp and figure it out somehow," fisherman Charles P. Dodge later recalled of his teenage years in turn-of-the-century Liberty and Isle au Haut, where his father farmed and kept horses. "Gorry, people were hard up in those days, you know, they'd hate to think of it now."

Many landless, jobless families were reduced to squatting on scraps of land that were so poor and isolated that even the local towns refused to annex them. "Of old, muskets drove the Abnakis off the coast of Maine," journalist Holman Day wrote in 1909. "Today, money is driving away another race."

> Cove and cape, the coast is pretty well monopolized by non-residents. . . . [The] queer squatter people who have been dispossessed . . . have hidden themselves in the deep gashes of the coast cliffs; their little huts are now at the head of crooked coves where pleasure craft do not venture; or they have located on little nubbins of islands that city people do not buy, for these islands may be approached only at flood-tide.

While at anchor off the southern end of Harpswell in or before 1915, yachtsman Edward P. Morris was approached by a rowboat operated by a child wearing "nothing but a tattered pair of trousers and the waist of a woman's dress . . . open down the front and with one sleeve torn half-way to the shoulder. With the alert look of a wild creature he rowed slowly round and round the yacht, silent, curious, unsmiling, not responding to offers of fruit, staring with his dark eyes."

On tiny Bush Island, a speck of land off of Phippsburg, Holman Day discovered a sick, hungry widow wasting away in a "wretched" hut, too weak to walk. Day alerted others to her plight and they brought her food regularly while Day searched for winter accommodations for the woman on the mainland. But when he returned he discovered that the woman's food was being stolen each night by one of Casco Bay's many "water tramps." There were at least a dozen of these "dory vagabonds" traveling the area, breaking into summer cottages, and consuming whatever food or fuel they found inside.

Other families were forced from island to island as the summer trade spread across Casco Bay. When Malaga, a small island just south of Bush, became a desirable destination for the summer tourist trade in 1912, the state removed its forty-five white, black, and mixed-race residents, imprisoning many of them at a state mental health facility for the rest of their lives. The state feared that the islanders who were not in detention might try to return to Malaga, since most of them were effectively homeless after their eviction. To discourage their return, state authorities moved the schoolhouse to the mainland and razed the rest of the structures on the island. Then they dug up all the corpses in Malaga's cemetery and moved them, tombstones and all, to the grounds of the mental hospital where some of their descendants and loved ones had been incarcerated.

Ironically, in the eyes of summer visitors, Maine's economic stagnation was one of its most attractive features. Industrialization, urbanization, and immigration had transformed their home cities. Many felt increasingly nostalgic for the quieter, cleaner agrarian life of their parents and grandparents; a homogeneous, Protestant New England that had vanished as Italians, Irish, and African Americans poured into the region. In the rural, deindustrialized towns and villages of coastal Maine, comfortable urbanites in Boston, Hartford, New York, and Philadelphia recognized their own past.

Writers extolled the Maine coast as an idyllic haven from the rat race of city life. Robert Herrick declared to *The Nation*'s readers in 1922 that "whatever may be left of that famous old New England, some time puritan and always protestant, will be found today more purely and abundantly in Maine than elsewhere. . . . It is the last stronghold of the Puritan." Summer people did not come to Maine "for either roller-coasters or dinner parties . . . [but] for the cool, clean air, for the blue hills and the bluer water, for rocks and sands and green trees," Harrison Rhodes wrote in *Harper's* in 1917. It is "for the country that they have come and for country life and country food and country sleep." In magazines, brochures, and public presentations, the Maine Central Railroad, desperate to replace vanishing freight traffic with passengers, aggressively promoted the state to city dwellers as "Vacationland."

Tourism exploded as middle-class professionals discovered what the rusticators had half a century before: the pleasures of the Maine summer. Traveling by train, steamship, and sometimes even with automobiles, modest businessmen, schoolteachers, doctors, and dentists followed the ultrawealthy to their summer retreats in Bar Harbor and Blue Hill, Camden and Boothbay, Kennebunk and Ogunquit. They built cottages, or bought abandoned farmhouses. They joined yacht, golf, and garden clubs. Their children learned to sail and play tennis as adults sat on their porches enjoying cool breezes and magical vistas offered by the surrounding ocean. As summer resident Edwin Mitchell later recalled, "no matter where on the coast you went, all were agreed that for health, history, or happiness it would be difficult to find a better place than Maine."

Coastal families benefited from the visitors' spending, even depended on it. The summer people needed to be fed and entertained. Their cottages, which outnumbered year-round homes in many resort towns, had to be built and maintained, carefully sealed up for the winter months and opened up in the spring. Maids, gardeners, cooks, and drivers were in great demand at hotels, boardinghouses, and cottages. Grocers, fishermen, boatyards, and farmers saw their sales jump in the summer months when the visitors were present and local people had more money in their pockets. Tourism had become part of the seasonal round, and in many towns and outports it was by 1920 the most important source of revenue.

But there was friction between locals and visitors over the way Maine life should be. Summer people wanted coastal Maine to remain pretty much as it was: a bucolic playground free of the hustle and bustle of modern life. Mainers wanted to regain the economic and social vitality their grandparents had enjoyed before the disasters of the mid-nineteenth century. These competing visions of Maine life were difficult to reconcile. Locals and summer people, though dependent on one another, were frequently at odds.

The wealthy cottagers of Bar Harbor aggressively fought local people's attempts to modernize their town. Their "Village Improvement Association" blocked the construction of a trolley line from the mainland, lobbied against utility poles, and even banned the possession or use of automobiles in the town until 1913, long after they had been introduced on the mainland. Owners of Islesboro's mansion-like summer cottages threatened to leave en masse if gasoline buggies were allowed on the island. They'd left their own automobiles back in the city with the rest of their modern problems and fought tooth and nail for two decades to prevent locals from using them to get around the thirteen-mile-long island. The struggle, described by one observer as "akin to civil war," didn't end until 1933, when locals unanimously voted to lift the unpopular ban. Several plutocratic families sold or dismantled their homes in protest, but most built garages on their compounds and became motorized year-round.

Some summer people lobbied loudly against the construction of the Bath bridge, which crossed the Kennebec to link Midcoast Maine to the rest of the world. Others fought smaller bridge projects along the convoluted coastline. "I once spent some time at Bailey Island in Casco Bay, but I have not been back since the bridge was built, and I have little desire to return," summer cottager Edwin Mitchell sniffed. "I have a horrid feeling that its island character, an important part of its charm, has been destroyed."

To stem the flood of development, wealthy summer residents pooled their resources to buy up vast tracts of wild land. The cottagers of Northeast, Southwest, Seal, and Bar Harbor on Mount Desert Island had the most ambitious plans. Harvard president emeritus Charles W. Eliot and eventually George Vanderbilt, John D. Rockefeller Jr., and other powerful figures staying there, concerned that the island would become overrun with middle-class excursionists, formed a land trust. "What needs to be forever excluded from the island is the squalor of the city, with all its inevitable bustle, dirt, and ugliness," Eliot explained in *The Right Development of Mount Desert Island*, a 1904 pamphlet describing the group's objectives. "Not even the appropriate pleasures and splendors of city life should be imitated at Mount Desert." Over the next decade, the trust controlled nearly six thousand acres of the island surrounding their resorts. In 1919 the group successfully lobbied the federal government to make their lands into Acadia National Park,* the first in the eastern United States, which had the added advantage of absolving the trustees of paying property taxes. Summer resident and trustee George Dorr was appointed as Acadia's superintendent, and promptly set about renaming many of its geographical features. At Dorr's insistence, Green Mountain became Mount Cadillac and Newport Mountain became Mount Champlain. Little Brown's Mountain was renamed for Charles W. Eliot's friend the historian Francis Parkman. Asticou Hill became Eliot Mountain, and Dry Mountain was renamed for Dorr himself. Rockefeller donated additional land to the park and built fifty-seven miles of carriage roads on which automobiles were expressly forbidden.

Confronted with such power and influence, Mainers felt their cherished independence slipping away. Their towns, their *country*, were being colonized by a ruling caste "from away," overlords who were quickly and efficiently seizing control of the coast's land, economy, and many of its political decisions. They even referred to local people as "natives." ("It is a wonder they do not call them aborigines," one writer observed.) And the natives, while increasingly dependent on the tourist trade, were growing restless. A 1914 newspaper article summarized Mainers' grievances:

> If we have any industry in the town, the rustikaters don't favor it, because it spoils the looks of the place and makes it harder for them to get help in the two months when they want it. We were

*The park was originally called Lafayette National Park, but was renamed "Acadia" in 1926.

going to have a caning factory here, and they prevented it. They don't want us to use the harbor for our fishing fleet, because they say it litters up the water; and they are paying big prices—bigger than we can pay—for the beach privileges. The rustikaters are gradually squeezing us out of our independence and into a dependence on them.

⌒﹏﹏

The Great Depression took some toll on the coast's tourism industry. The convoys of automobile excursionists vanished from Route 1, devastating families that had invested in tourist cabins and other roadside attractions to serve the new, middle-class visitors. Wealthy cottagers were hit hard by the stock market crash of 1929. Summer mansions cut back their staff. Others stood empty season after season or were listed for sale. A mysterious rash of fires burned several resort hotels to the ground.

But, by and large, the Depression was less devastating in Maine than in many other parts of the country. Most coastal Mainers had been just one step up from subsistence living before 1929. For most, it was easy to step back. Most family clans already had members who farmed, gardened, or fished for food, cut wood that could be sold or used as fuel, or knew how to hunt, berry, knit, and could build homes, barns, and boats. "The country people are the only people that can take it [in a depression], get something . . . in their stomachs, to actually live," said Walter F. Trundy, who served as town clerk of Stockton Springs for seven decades, from the recession of 1907 through the gas lines of the early 1970s. "We've got the . . . fundamental things you've got to have to survive." Or, as a coastal farmer told the *Bangor Daily News* in the 1930s: "We never worry about politics and depressions . . . down here, for if worst comes to worst, we can dig a mess of clams."

Indeed, as the Depression deepened, the national press noticed that New Englanders were weathering it better than most. "Panic possessed America, but New England wasn't quite so scared," wrote historian Bernard DeVoto, who toured the region in 1932. "The depression wasn't quite so black, the nightmare was not quite so ghastly. . . . [New England] had hard times for sixty years—in one way or another for three hundred. It had had to find a way to endure a perpetual depression, and found it." Perhaps, DeVoto argued, "the bankrupt nation might learn something from New England."

The lesson, DeVoto suggested, was that the Yankees' thrift, realism, and work ethic had spared them from "the disease of Bigness," the culture of greed and unsustainable growth that had brought America low. "Here, if you have a Buick income, you do not buy a Cadillac to keep your self-respect. You buy a Chevrolet." New England was earning a reputation for no-nonsense self-sufficiency at a time when this appeared a righteous alternative to the ills of the nation.

As the Depression deepened, some city dwellers retreated to northern New England in search of this bare-boned Yankee security. Unable to find work, one young professional couple in New York City "fled to the only place they owned in the world, a very small, very old house with kerosene lamps and no plumbing" on a small island in the mouth of the Kennebec River, opposite the site of the failed Popham colony. Ray Phillips, a food inspector in New York City, purchased a tiny wooden sloop in 1932 and sailed off to his native Maine. Fleeing the city's "traffic and dirt," Phillips wound up on Manana, Monhegan's small companion island, where he built a rambling shack and survived by fishing and shepherding. He lived there with his sheep and, later, a pet goose, until his death in 1975, by which time he had become a minor celebrity among the tourists and a mythic figure to young mainland children like myself.

But for the wider public, the most famous of these original "back-to-the-landers" were a pair idealistic intellectuals forced to the countryside by the economic and political circumstances of the day. Scott and Helen Nearing, unable to make ends meet in New York, took up subsistence farming in southern Vermont in 1932. They were vegetarian, pacifist, and decidedly skeptical of capitalism, which they believed "would be unable henceforth to provide an adequate, stable, and secure life even for those who attempted to follow its directives." They prepared for this future at their rural homestead, where they grew their own food, cut their own lumber and firewood, and tapped maple trees to make the syrup that paid their taxes and other unavoidable cash transactions. The book they wrote about their experiences, *Living the Good Life: How to Live Sanely and Simply in a Troubled*

World, would inspire a later generation of disaffected youth to follow in their footsteps. A great many of them chose coastal Maine, where the Nearings themselves fled in 1952 to escape the "disease of development" that had already reached their part of Vermont.

～～～

Mainers, with their long-term immunity to the development virus, continued scratching out whatever existence they could. As the world descended from depression to war, some enlisted, some found work building destroyers, minesweepers, and transports at newly revived shipyards, while others did what they'd always done: turned to the sea for sustenance.

Near-shore waters continued to provide incomes for people with few other options. Fishing inshore didn't require a lot of expensive equipment. Cod, haddock, and other bottom-dwelling fish were still caught from dories and small boats using the hundred-year-old "tub trawling" method: a long line of baited hooks set on the bottom and hauled back up by hand. Lobsters were still caught with wooden traps, though many fishermen had retrofitted their boats with small gasoline-powered engines, some of them salvaged from old automobiles. Shad, herring, and salmon were captured in stationary fish traps set in the rivers or coves where the fish came to spawn. Clams were still dug from Maine's broad mudflats with hand tools.

Offshore, the fishing industry was in the midst of a profound technological revolution. At its root was a revolutionary concept. Instead of trying to snare fish with baited hooks or cleverly positioned nets, weirs, and traps—all essentially stationary gear—why not take the gear to the fish and scoop them up wherever they might be hiding?

Europeans had been using mobile fishing gear for centuries. Ancient Romans had captured oysters by pulling a weighted net bag over the seafloor. Medieval Englishmen used a similar device to sweep rivers for fish, and their nineteenth-century descendants used steam-powered ships to drag larger net bags across the ocean bottom. But dragging was a clumsy undertaking. The mouth of the net was held open with a forty-foot elm beam which was dragged along the floor, where it often hung up on rocks and other obstructions. When a British naval officer tried to introduce Rhode Island fishermen to this form of dragging in 1850, it was ridiculed as "a very mean way of catching fish." But in the 1890s, British fishermen made a breakthrough that would change fishing forever. They replaced the cumbersome beam with a pair of small boards, one on each side of the net, rigged in such a way that when pulled through the water they flew apart like kites, pulling the net open. The lower mouth of the net was made of heavy chain, which weighed it down and could stand up to considerable punishment. They called it the "otter trawl," and it was lighter, tougher, and easier to handle than the old method. It also caught far more fish, and quickly came to dominate the North Sea fishing fleet.

The otter trawl was introduced to the Gulf of Maine in 1905 by Boston's Bay State Fishing Company, which built a fleet of 300-ton steel-hulled, steam-powered otter trawlers to ply New England's fishing grounds. The 115-foot vessels were equipped with electric lighting, steam-powered winches, and 150-foot-long nets with mouths that opened 80 feet wide. They could carry one hundred tons of fish in their holds, and they needed the space. By 1912, each of the Bay State Company's steam trawlers were landing two million pounds of cod, haddock, and other groundfish a year.

Conventional fishermen denounced the new technology, fearing it would wipe out both the fish and their relatively independent way of life. "It is labor independence against something not right," according to Gloucester fisherman Frank Nunan, who saw the trawlers as agents of industrial monopoly seeking "to control the fish business." In 1912, Congress ordered the Bureau of Fisheries to investigate fishermens' claims that otter trawling "is such an unduly destructive method that if generally adopted the lines and gear of ordinary fishing vessels will be continually carried away and destroyed and the fishing grounds quickly rendered unproductive." Fishermen believed the trawl nets killed both the fish eggs laid on the ocean floor and "very large numbers" of juvenile fish, "which are killed in the process of capture and thrown away." After extensive investigation, the Bureau's scientists recommended that groundfish dragging in New England should be restricted to Georges Bank, the South Channel, and Nantucket Shoals. Nevertheless, within a few years draggers of all shapes and sizes were operating throughout the region.

Dragger technology not only out-competed its predecessors, it rapidly improved in the years that followed. Diesel engines, introduced in 1920, were not only cheaper and safer than steam, they required fewer crew and less fuel storage. The economical diesels allowed smaller companies to engage in offshore trawling, while some inshore fishermen built forty- to ninety-foot diesel draggers for nearshore work. The technology was adapted to allow fishermen to dredge up scallops and oysters. And, in 1934, two Norwegians used an experimental drag to haul an entirely new resource up from the Gulf of Maine: "prolific shrimp beds" not far off the Maine coast. Within sixteen months, shrimp draggers were making two-thousand-pound landings at Portland's fish docks.

There were innovations on the waterfront as well. In 1922, the Bay State Fishing Company introduced the "fillet," a boneless cut of premium fish, which was sold fresh, canned, or smoked from centralized processing plants and was a huge hit with consumers. In 1925, Clarence Birdseye patented a method of flash-freezing fish on a commercial scale, and his General Foods Company began building a trawler fleet of its own a few years later. Fishing had joined the industrial age.

By the late 1930s, however, fishermen and fisheries scientists were seeing signs that the Gulf of Maine's living bounty was not infinite. The number of fish in this sea, once thought limitless, appeared to be shrinking. In some cases, whole populations of fish had vanished from places they had been found for as long as anyone could remember. After supporting fishing fleets for three centuries, the Gulf ecosystem was showing signs of weakness.

Halibut, a great flatfish that could weigh nine hundred pounds and measure nine feet in length, had once been so numerous they were "looked upon as a nuisance" by cod-seeking fishermen. When Bostonians developed a taste for halibut in the 1820s, fishermen were able to catch incredible numbers of the enormous fish. On at least one occasion, a vessel using the old hook-over-the-side method caught more than 250 in three hours; on another, a smack brought in twenty thousand pounds of halibut in a single day. But the halibut couldn't stand

up to the demand. Between 1902 and 1936, despite the vast improvements in fishing technology, the New England halibut catch fell from
13.5 million pounds a year to 2 million. "Long-liners and otter trawlers
search all the good ground-fish bottoms of the Gulf of Maine and its
banks so thoroughly and constantly that the halibut never have a
chance to reestablish themselves in any abundance," wrote Henry
Bigelow, the father of oceanography. The Gulf's halibut stocks never
recovered.

Out on Georges Bank, the favored ground of the otter trawlers,
haddock catches fell by two-thirds between 1929 and 1936. Winter
flounder, the mainstay of southern New England's small otter trawlers,
declined so severely that fishermen in the mid-thirties were forced to
find another species to fish, the previously spurned yellowtail flounder. A decade later the yellowtail fishery had been similarly depleted,
and government scientists reported that fishermen who had depended
on them could "find no other abundant species of similar value within
the range of their small otter trawlers." Only the stalwart cod stood up
to the increased fishing pressure on Georges.

Near-shore fish populations were also in trouble on the eve of
World War II. Maine's lobster catch stood at historic lows, prompting
the enactment of state fishery commissioner Horatio Crie's long-sought
conservation measures. Clams were in short supply due to over-
digging. Penobscot Bay clammers had seen their catch fall by three-
quarters between 1928 and 1930, and in 1937 Deer Isle's clam
canneries were open only one day a week for lack of clams. Maine's
catch of shad, a fish whose spawning runs choked rivers in colonial
times, had fallen to less than 15 percent of its turn-of-the-century level.
In the 1870s, Maine fishermen caught 150,000 pounds of Penobscot
River salmon as they swam upriver to spawn in the brooks and streams
where they had hatched. In 1920 they could catch only one-tenth as
much, probably because of pollution from paper factories and lumber
operations. By 1938 most "Penobscot" salmon sold in the United States
had been caught on rivers in Nova Scotia or British Columbia.

But, in human terms, the greatest loss in Maine fisheries was the
one that was least reported at the time: the destruction of near-shore
cod and haddock communities.

Landlubbers may imagine that New England's cod all belonged to one big, happy family, swimming about the region in search of food. But cod, like haddock and many other animals, actually live in separate tribes. Each tribe has its own habits, turf, and, in some cases, distinct physical traits. While they undoubtedly have relations with one another, much of their breeding, schooling, and feeding appears to be done within the group. In the 1930s, fisheries scientists had accepted that there were two distinct "stocks" of cod in the region—cod that lived on and around Georges Bank, and cod that lived inside the Gulf of Maine—and managed them as such. Fishermen, however, knew that the Gulf of Maine contained far more cod nations. There were cod that spawned and spent much of their time in and among the offshore banks of the Gulf; and there were cod that spawned inshore, right up inside Maine's bays and harbors, and appeared to reside in or near coastal waters for much, if not all, of the year.

Maine fishermen had relied on inshore cod from the times of the earliest expeditions. In 1605, George Waymouth's men were catching and subsisting on inshore cod caught beside Monhegan and Allen islands. Inshore cod, split and salted, filled the storehouses and drying racks of the seventeenth-century fishing stations at Damariscove, Monhegan, and Richmond islands. And they'd kept the small inshore fisherman going ever since. Inshore cod was the most important resource for most tiny outports until the advent of the lobster fishery in the late nineteenth century.

But while inshore cod stocks had always been targeted by fishermen, their spawning runs had not. "One of the interesting things about codfish and haddock is that they don't take the hook when they're spawning," says James Wilson, professor of marine policy at the University of Maine in Orono, who has studied the spawning runs. "The only way you can fish for them is with a jig and catch them by accident," by impaling a passing fish in the belly with your hook. Even when caught, the "ripe" cod weren't worth very much to salt-cod fishermen; their flesh was harder to dry and more difficult to preserve. On top of that, the spawning runs took place in late winter and early spring when drying was difficult and expensive. A fisherman might have to burn a great deal of firewood just to keep vats of curing brine from freezing solid. With little incentive to catch these inconvenient fish, few fishermen even knew of the existence of many of the spawning grounds until well into the twentieth century. But every March and April, countless multitudes of cod and haddock congregated on at least 140 separate spawning grounds between Monhegan and the mouth of the Bay of Fundy and did their thing, largely unseen and unmolested by fishermen.

By the 1930s, trawling and railroads had changed all that. In 1920, the Maine Central Railroad came to Rockland, connecting Midcoast Maine's primary fishing port with the great fresh and frozen fish markets of Boston and beyond. Frozen spawning cod and haddock tasted just fine, and the otter trawl made it possible to catch them. For the spawning fish, it was just a matter of time before their rendezvous were exposed.

The end came with astonishing swiftness.

By 1935, fishermen could find no cod or haddock in the upper half of Penobscot Bay, where they had once been prevalent. They continued to fish in the outer bay, first with small boats rigged with little otter trawls, later with larger draggers. By the late forties and early fifties, commercial quantities of cod and haddock could no longer be found in Maine's largest embayment. The story repeated itself up and down the coast and, in every instance, the cod and haddock never returned to their spawning grounds.

While state fisheries officials were aware of the collapse early on, no attempt was made to discover why it was happening. Penobscot Bay fishermen suspected that officials in Augusta ignored the issue because it might have implicated Maine's all-powerful pulp and paper industry, which owned nearly half of interior Maine and had reduced many Maine rivers to filthy, sometimes stinking, sewers. Indeed, later studies showed that paper mill pollution probably had despoiled the nursery grounds of upper Penobscot Bay. But that didn't explain why cod and haddock were also vanishing in unpolluted bays further Downeast.

The "inshore cod" mystery remained unexplored for two generations. But in the mid-1990s, Edward Ames, a fisherman-scientist from Stonington on Deer Isle, began interviewing dozens of old-time fishermen and pieced together a clearer picture of what had happened to the once-plentiful fish.

Ames collected detailed information on where and when the

spawning runs occurred, matching it to detailed electronic maps of the ocean bottom. Each year, the fish congregated briefly over patches of gravel or sand located in deep depressions that were exposed to strong tidal currents. Over and over, fishermen reported the same story: "once an inshore spawning ground lost its resident population, it remained barren season after season even when populations of spawning cod and haddock were present on neighboring grounds." The cod and haddock, to Ames's surprise, appeared to have behaved like salmon, mixing freely for most of the year, but splitting into genetically based "runs" at spawning time, each returning to a specific site to reproduce. When they vanished, they were gone for good.

Ames also uncovered clear evidence that overfishing was largely responsible for the disappearance of most of these stocks. Once a spawning run was discovered, the fishing pressure was unrelenting. Roger Beal Sr. of Jonesport related how in April 1942, he and his father had accidentally discovered a cod run just outside the harbor in Machias Bay. The first tow had come up with ten thousand pounds of five-foot-long cod from an area where they'd found none the day before. Their next tow blew their minds. As the side-rigged trawl net came up near the surface "all you could see was a big white ball," Beal told Ames. "And the whole net was filled from the cod end right to the mouth with those big codfish." The strain of the 30,000-pound catch broke their handling lines, forcing them to tow the bulging net back to the harbor, where they grounded it out at low tide for unloading. The following day they hauled in another huge catch. By the time the Beals got out for their third tow, other draggers had arrived, and within a few days a "formidable fleet" was sweeping up the massive fish. The following spring, more draggers arrived, but caught fewer fish. "By the third year, the spring run of giant Machias Bay codfish was broken," Ames wrote. "The bonanza was over."

But out on Georges and the offshore banks of the Gulf of Maine, the bonanza had yet to begin.

⌒﹏

By the late 1940s, Harald Salvesen was convinced that his industry was in trouble. Salvesen was a whaler, and the world was running short on whales. His firm, Christian Salvesen Limited of Scotland, was running out of its raw material with little hope of finding commercial quantities in the future. The company owned giant factory ships capable of processing and freezing at sea all the whales its catcher boats harpooned. They could operate for months at a time in the frigid waters of Antarctica, with fresh crew and supplies coming and going by smaller vessels. But now, clearly, Salvesen's firm needed to turn its expertise to something else. He would try to apply the same technology to the capture of fish.

The result was the construction of a most unusual fishing vessel: the factory-equipped freezer trawler. The *Fairtry*, the first of this class, turned heads from the moment it was launched in 1954. Salvesen's new ship was 280 feet long and weighed 2,600 gross tons, four times the size of a large side trawler. Her tall funnels, extensive superstructure, and numerous portholes gave the ship the appearance of an oceangoing passenger ship, but the gantry masts, winches, and other gear on the aft deck gave away her true purpose. *Fairtry*'s stern featured a gigantic ramp of the sort Salvesen's whaling ships had used to drag great whales aboard for processing. But *Fairtry*'s ramp allowed it to haul in nets filled with whale-sized hauls of fish instead. Once aboard, the fish were sent belowdecks to a state-of-the-art onboard processing plant equipped with automated filleting machines, a fish meal rendering factory, and enormous banks of freezers. Like the whaling ships, she could fish around the clock, seven days a week, for weeks on end, hauling up nets that could swallow the Statue of Liberty. To help her find and pursue large schools of fish, she had all the latest postwar technology: radar, depth sounders, and fish-finding sonar. She repeatedly returned to Britain in her first year with 650-ton loads of filleted codfish and other products made from more than 2,000 tons of cod swept from the Grand Banks of Canada. "Bags of twenty or more tons regularly inched up her stern like swollen sausages too big for their skins . . . only to get stuck in the rampway," William Warner wrote in *Distant Water*, the classic account of the factory-trawler era. Salvesen's "most serious problem was that *Fairtry* caught too many fish."

Other countries leapt into the fray. Within three years of *Fairtry*'s appearance, the Soviet Union had built twenty-four *Fairtry* clones, plus a dozen vessels of an even larger class. By the 1970s the Soviets had several hundred factory trawlers operating on the high seas. East and West Germany, Spain, France, Japan, and Poland each followed suit, building dozens of ships, some substantially larger than *Fairtry* herself. It wasn't long before these enormous ships turned their sights on Georges Bank and the Gulf of Maine.

꿈

While the USSR and other countries were building up their factory-freezer fleets, Maine's fishing industry was decaying. Not only were the waters of the Gulf of Maine becoming less productive, but the U.S. fish market had become flooded with cheap frozen fish caught by government-subsidized fleets from western Europe and Japan. There was little demand for the higher-quality fresh fish New England's fishermen brought in from the Gulf of Maine. Apart from a bizarre penchant for frozen "fish sticks" and other low-quality fish products, American consumers were still bingeing on meat and potatoes. Fish was still largely regarded as the food of the poor, or something Catholics had to eat for penance. Maine's lobster stocks were recovering in the 1950s, but lobstermen faced stiff competition from their counterparts in Nova Scotia and New Brunswick, who exported huge quantities of lobsters to the United States both on trucks and on the new car ferries running across the Gulf of Maine each day.

"Maine's once proud and profitable fishing fleet is sailing on a course that leads to extinction," the *Portland Sunday Telegram* reported in a front-page article in 1958:

> Cold, hard statistics indicate the fleet is now composed largely of old weary vessels manned by aging crews. Shipyards which once resounded to [the] construction of draggers and trawlers now are abandoned. Only one Maine yard has turned out a large fishing vessel in the past three years. The largest vessels in the 60 vessels in Maine's [offshore] fishing fleet average close to 30 years old. . . . And, for what has long been considered a young man's trade, today's fishermen are ancient mariners. The average age of crews is 40 and is constantly on the way up.

With their profits shrinking, offshore boat owners were unable either to buy new vessels or to adopt the latest technologies. While

Europeans were perfecting their massive factory-freezer trawlers, New England's offshore fishermen generally went to sea in antiquated side trawlers built before the war. By the late fifties, Maine fisheries commissioner Ronald W. Green was warning that if something didn't change, "the state's fishing industry may cease to exist."

But things were about to change, for the worse. Starting in the early sixties, those vessels that made it to the offshore banks faced the most daunting competition imaginable. Great fleets of Eastern bloc factory-freezer trawlers descended on Georges Bank, crowding out the relatively tiny vessels from Maine and New England. The Soviets arrived first, in 1961, "sweeping up and down Georges with their ships paced out in long diagonal lines, plowing the best fishing grounds like disk harrows in a field," as Warner described it. They were soon joined by distant-water fleets from other Eastern bloc countries, plus those from West Germany, France, Japan, and Mexico.

By the early 1970s, more than two hundred foreign fishing vessels were fishing New England waters in a given month. Some trawled as far up the Gulf as Jeffrey's Bank and Cashes Ledge, less than thirty miles from Maine shores. "Sometimes they'd come in kind of close looking for perch when cod and haddock got scarce," recalls Rockland dragger owner Frank O'Hara Sr., whose grandfather founded one of the country's first steam-trawler companies in the 1930s. "So we would see them, but weren't pushed off the bottom by them. Still, weather is weather, and in the fog or night when you're in a ninety-foot boat you gotta get out of the way of a 250-foot trawler steaming or towing down on you."

On Georges, the foreign fleets were so large, so closely packed on the banks that observers likened them to great floating cities. "Ships of all kinds could be seen sweeping the fishing grounds in every direction: small otter trawlers, purse seiners, medium-sized stern trawlers twice as long as New England's largest fishing boats, and . . . larger stern trawler factory ships," wrote David Boeri and James Gibson in their account of the era, *Tell It Goodbye, Kiddo*. "Purse seiners and otter trawlers are transferring their catches to 600-foot-long factory ships for processing, while a whole support fleet of oil tankers, fresh water tankers, repair and salvage vessels, tug boats and base ships moves among the vessels of the fishing fleet." By night, one Coast Guard pilot said, the fleet looked like New York City.

Scientists later estimated that during the first decade after the foreigners' arrival, fishing pressure increased *sixfold* in the waters off the United States' northeastern seaboard. Overall landings tripled in this period, with the foreigners taking the lion's share. (In 1968, for instance, U.S. fishermen caught 556 million pounds of fish in the Gulf of Maine and Georges Bank, while the six largest foreign fleets caught 1.2 billion tons, or more than twice as much.) But, from the fish's perspective, the landings of saleable, adult fish were only part of the story. To process fish efficiently, factory trawlers needed large numbers of similarly sized animals of the same species. When a haul of their vast nets turned out to have improperly sized or mixed species, fishermen dumped the contents overboard, covering the ocean surface with dead and dying fish. If the trawl contained the right type of fish its contents would be sluiced down to the processing deck and sorted. But trawl nets don't just drag up the right kind of fish. Groundfish draggers of all sizes pull up everything in their path, and little of it survives the pressure changes and crushing forces it experiences as it's hauled from the bottom. All these unwanted creatures—undersized cod, haddock, and flounder, adult crabs, starfish, lobster, sharks, skates, coral heads, and a hundred other undesirable species—the so-called by-catch, would be sent overboard through special discard chutes. The United Nations later estimated that for every four tons of fish that were landed worldwide, another ton or more of other creatures were discarded as by-catch.

The foreigners massed their incredible fishing power on one fish species after another, depleting one stock and moving on to a new one. First they fished herring and whiting. Then they targeted haddock, cod, and flounder, redfish and pollock. By the mid-seventies, U.S. fisheries scientists reported that all major finfish stocks off the northeastern seaboard were "fully exploited," while haddock, Georges Bank herring, and other stocks were "demonstrably overfished." In the late sixties a U.S. trawler brought its nets up from 1,000-foot-deep water off Rhode Island and caught a large lobster with tagging information painted on its shell in Russian, indicating that the Soviets were becoming interested in the crustacean.

The Soviets never actually targeted lobsters, but Maine's inshore fishermen were feeling the effects of their intensive trawling. Fish populations that normally migrated to Maine from the southern banks—herring, whiting, and pollock—were being cut off at the source, Commissioner Green reported in 1970. Maine fishermen were certainly catching fewer of these fish. They'd caught four million pounds of pollock in 1960, but only 800,000 in 1970; herring landings fell by more than 80 percent in the same period. In 1977, Mainers only managed to land 250,000 pounds of whiting (or "silver hake"), down from fifteen to twenty *million* pounds in the 1950s and 1960s. Other species were also in sharp decline. In 1950, even after the destruction of the inshore spawning runs, Maine fishermen caught seven million pounds of haddock; in 1974 they could land only 228,000 pounds, a decline of 97 percent. Of all the major fisheries, only lobster landings remained stable. Within the industry there was a growing sense of doom. "Within ten years there will hardly be a fishing industry left in New England," Captain Tim Asbury of the Portland-based fishing vessel *Sandra Ann* predicted. Something clearly had to be done.

Distant-water fishing fleets were wreaking havoc all across the North Atlantic. The Grand Banks, the world's greatest fishery, was being decimated by huge fleets of factory-freezer trawlers. The huge ships hit virgin fish stocks in the high Arctic of Norway, Canada, and Greenland. Soviet fleets swept the grounds of southern New England, the Caribbean, the North Pacific, even the Antarctic. But there was little governments could do about the destruction of the fish off their respective coasts. Under international law, beyond three miles from shore the seas belonged to everybody, and to no one.

Tiny Iceland was the first to stand up to the foreign fleets. Living near the Arctic Circle, Iceland's 200,000 citizens counted on fish to finance the purchase of all manner of goods imported from the outside world. Unsurprisingly, Icelanders demonstrated a willingness to do whatever was necessary to protect fish from the beginning. On gaining independence from Denmark in 1944, they took the unprecedented step of extending their territorial waters from three to four miles from shore. And when British trawlers began hammering area fish populations in the 1950s, Icelanders felt their national survival was at stake. They had to protect the fish. So in 1958, Iceland unilaterally extended its territorial seas from four to twelve miles; In 1971 it extended it again to fifty miles, and a few years later, two hundred. From the outset, the outside world vehemently protested. Britain dispatched a fleet of warships to protect its trawlers, but Iceland would not back down. Their tiny coast guard fought three bloodless "cod wars" with the Royal Navy. Shots were fired, ships rammed, and nets cut. For a time, Iceland even refused to give British warplanes access to the massive NATO base in Keflavík. Finally, in 1976, Iceland gained recognition of its two-hundred-mile "exclusive economic zone." Soon thereafter, nations around the world, including the United States and Canada, declared their own two-hundred-mile zones.

The U.S. decision was greeted with enthusiasm within New England's long-suffering fishing industry. The 1976 Magnuson Fisheries Management and Conservation Act forced foreign fleets off all but the most remote sections of Georges Bank and out of the Gulf of Maine altogether. Some details needed to be worked out with the Canadians, as they claimed large parts of the Gulf and Bank for themselves. But with the vast European fleets gone, fishermen figured that from now on, things were going to be just great. "For many U.S. fishermen, the 200-mile economic zone is construed as a cure-all for their particular problems," the *National Fisherman* editorialized, while cautioning that it would take time for both fish stocks and the industry to rebuild. Fishing, it appeared, was finally on the mend.

〜〰〰

While factory trawlers were invading the seas, a different sort of invasion was taking place ashore. More and more people broached the coast every year in search of Vacationland.

When Maine humorist John Gould was a boy nearly a century ago, his hometown of Freeport had a single automobile: an early-model Overland. Gould remembers riding around on its hood when the townspeople celebrated the end of the First World War. "Route One was paved in Freeport village but that's all," he recalls. "The rest was a dirt road all the way to Newburyport [Massachusetts], where there was a steep hill and people would get stuck on it." Even into the twenties and thirties, getting to Maine from Boston and New York wasn't easy, and people tended to stay for weeks or months at a time once they made it to their destination.

After World War II, however, the middle-class residents of the great Washington-to-Boston megalopolis purchased cars, big powerful ones that had no trouble with the hill in Newburyport. And from 1947 they could charge into Maine on the Maine Turnpike, one of the first high-speed, controlled-access highways in the nation. The Turnpike Authority could brag that "few people in Maine—or anywhere in America—had ever had a chance to travel at sixty miles-per-hour before." Spurred by the new expressway, tourism swept up the coast like a tidal wave in the 1950s. Annual tourism revenues jumped by nearly a third between 1944 and 1946 to $110 million, and grew by a whopping 225 percent over the next ten years. The summer tide surged to the farthest extremities of the Downeast coast, bringing significant numbers of sightseers and cottagers to places like Corea, Machias, and Eastport for the first time. Southern Maine's seaside villages found themselves completely inundated by a great throng of vacationing humanity.

As the rest of the eastern seaboard became increasingly suburbanized, outsiders became more captivated by Maine's anachronistic character. Urbanites contended with an increasingly dehumanized environment of strip malls, expressways, and cookie-cutter "neighborhoods" surrounding abandoned and decaying inner cities. For Bostonians, New Yorkers, and Washingtonians, Maine represented solace and sanctuary, a vital antidote to the problems of late-twentieth-century urban life. People came to Maine to recharge their batteries and connect with family and nature amid its quaint and unspoiled rural Yankee landscape. From afar, writer and seasonal resident José Yglesias wrote, "Maine is not a place, but a metaphor."

This mythic Maine, promoted in the pages of the L.L. Bean catalog and Yankee magazine, remained at odds with the harsh realities of year-round life. Vacationers left after Labor Day, but many Mainers faced nine months of uncertain employment on farms, timber lots, fishing vessels, and the floors of fish processing plants. Virtually all of the coast's year-round economy was based on the extraction of natural resources, which were seasonal, subject to wild swings in demand and prices, or both. The tourist industry kept many communities afloat, but it provided mostly low-wage jobs that vanished in the fall. With half its jobs unable to offer full-time work, Vacationland was populated year-round by the working poor. In 1960, 23 percent of Maine families were classified as poor according to federal standards, and the coastal counties east of Brunswick were the poorest in the state.* In the late sixties, two-thirds of rural families were classified as poor, with one in five living in outright poverty. Maine's per capita income in 1966— $2,477—was the lowest in New England and thirty-eighth in the country. But unlike its competitors in the Deep South and Appalachia, Maine's cost of living remained high. Food, electricity, and transportation were expensive in Maine, not to mention the cost of heating a home through the state's long, cold winters. In studies that took these factors into account, Maine consistently ranked as the first, second, or third poorest state in the nation.

Real estate development may have pushed the hermits and "dory vagabonds" off picturesque shores, but tens of thousands still lived in squalor in tar paper shacks and ancient trailers tucked away on back roads few summer visitors even knew existed. There were places even locals rarely ventured, backwoods enclaves inhabited by extended clans of "wild folk" to whom local lore ascribed all manner of sins, from inbreeding to homicide. Where I grew up there was Happy Valley, where in 1967 families of eight or twelve lived in one- or two-room shacks without refrigerators or running water. "This is one of the most concentrated pockets of rural poverty in the state, with overcrowded homes, sanitation problems, and a certain amount of discrimination from the surrounding populace," a Portland reporter wrote of the Valley that year. "Unfortunately, officials say several Happy Valley children have dropped out of school because of their embarrassment over the condition of their clothing, prior education, and a certain amount of teasing from the town children." Twenty years later being from

*These coastal counties comprised five of the six poorest counties in the state, with a third of Waldo County residents classified as poor, and 42 percent of those in Washington County. Only Aroostook County in far northern Maine had comparable figures—31 percent—ranking it just ahead of Lincoln (30.1 percent), Hancock (29.7 percent), and Knox (28.2 percent).

Happy Valley still carried a stigma at my high school, while in Phippsburg, the children and grandchildren of Malaga islanders were disparaged more than eighty years after their ancestors' eviction.

Perhaps the slurs on Malaga and Happy Valley children were
rooted in fear, as many Mainers themselves lived only a step or two
above such abject poverty. In Waldo County, in 1967, where nearly a
third of families lived on less than $2,500 a year, social workers re-
ported that many children enrolled in Head Start had never eaten
green vegetables in their lives. "We find most of the families go heavy
on potatoes, bread and homemade biscuits," county Community Action Program director Winifred Black told a reporter. A few miles from
the shoreside mansions of Islesboro, underweight children were "living on tonic and potato chips," while sick, elderly couples were discovered without food and supplies. Other families pieced together a living
from scraps of seasonal work and by building things they needed from
piles of machinery, appliances, and vehicles discarded by others. "I
take someone's rubbish and make somethin' out of it," junk-pile owner
Ervins Bubier of Perry told a documentary team from Portland's Salt
Institute in 1988. "Someone with a fancy-fancy house will complain
that we got a lot of junk here" in the front yard, Ervins' wife, Donna,
explained. "But he's got to have it."

"This Maine is frustrating," novelist and native son Sanford Phippen writes. "It is hard on people. It is a life of poverty, solitude, struggle, lowered aspirations, living on the edge." As opposed to the idyllic
retreat summer people embrace, Phippen describes a Maine that is
"cold, dark, and often deformed."

Phippen grew up in the late forties and fifties in Hancock, a small
peninsular town east of Bar Harbor, where few homes had flush toilets
and many lacked running water. "My family was poor, but because we
had enough to eat, and just about the entire population of the town
was in the same boat, we didn't know it," he later wrote. In winter, his
family ate a lot of deer meat and clams and Phippen went to school in
some summer kid's old clothes. But in summer he was down at exclusive Hancock Point, mowing the rusticators' seaside lawns, serving
food and carrying firewood for wealthy vacationers at the colony's
summer hotel. He's been writing about how that felt ever since.

"You want so badly to fit in and be accepted by these people," says

Phippen over pizza in Orono, where he teaches English to high school kids. "They look nicer, they seem to have the world by the balls, the way they talk. They seem so alive in that world, while you feel like a clod. And yet, you're from Maine: it's *your* world, they're just here for two or three months. But you try to talk to them and they may be very nice to you on the surface, but there's this awful thing that's underneath there . . . they're laughing at you the whole time."

Phippen vividly recalls seeing his first summer person's cocktail party while delivering laundry his mother had done for a Hancock Point cottager. "I was probably fifteen or sixteen, jeans and a T-shirt on, my mother out there in the car with her bandanna on," says Phippen, who later wrote the scene into his novel *Kitchen Boy*. "The cottage door opens and here's this magnificent view of Bar Harbor [across the bay] with the twinkling lights and these lovely people dressed differently from my relatives. It was foreign, absolutely foreign." Before the hostess spotted him and brought his mother's money, there was an awkward moment where the guests looked at him "like I was a black kid who came in the front door instead of the kitchen." That moment has always stuck with him, that moment when it first hits you that you can be an alien in your own backyard.

There was—and in many places still is—an imperial dynamic in the relationship between Mainers and summer people. The latter, after all, lived in "colonies," surrounded by and dependent on the labor of "the natives." They were generally wealthier, more educated, and better connected than the locals. They spoke, dressed, and behaved differently from the locals and, while in Maine, generally socialized among themselves. There are plenty of exceptions, of course; witness egalitarian Monhegan, or the many hundreds of summer people who have put down roots and "gone native." But, by and large, Maine summer life had always been split into two castes, the colonists and the colonized.

Here lies the root of the resentment and hostility some Mainers display toward "summer complaints" and others "from away." For nearly three centuries, the people of the coast had fought those who sought to lord over them. Now many were becoming dependent on "foreigners" who were buying up the best land and could be arrogant or condescending when dealing with locals. Resentment festered as the postwar

tourism boom transformed many Southern and Midcoast towns beyond recognition. In Boothbay Harbor, the fish processing plants were
torn down to make way for hotel complexes. When a fire tore through
the Fisherman's Wharf chandlery and fish market in 1958, it was replaced by a motel and gift shop operating under the same name. Fishing vessels were pushed from the adjacent waterfront, which was filled
in to make a large seaside parking lot. "I'll say to people I'm from
Boothbay Harbor, and they'll say, 'Oh, that's a lovely town,' and I'll
wince," comedian Tim Sample told *Down East* in 1989. The land on
which his family ran a shipyard was covered in condos in the mid-
eighties, denying his father's explicit dying wish. "I feel like saying that
in 1957 it was a lovely town," Sample said. "Going back now—it's just
ravaged." Such scenes repeated themselves from Kittery to Camden
and beyond.

Mainers relied on tourist spending, of course, and many families
invested in hotels, gift shops, and other seasonal businesses. But
when Labor Day came and the visitors departed, Mainers breathed a
collective sigh of relief. For eight months, at least, they again had their
hardscrabble coast to themselves.

❧

In the early 1970s, the strangest thing started happening in the farming villages and fishing outports of rural Maine. While local youth
continued to depart Maine in search of a better life—thirty thousand
Mainers fled the state every year—*city people* began showing up to
take their places. This was surprising in and of itself: Didn't they realize that, for three seasons anyway, Maine remained in the depths of a
century-long depression? Didn't they see that farms were going bankrupt and foreign ships were offshore, sweeping up the fish? What,
many locals wondered, were these flatlanders thinking?

But things got stranger. On arrival, many newcomers embraced the
very privations local people were struggling against. They bought
bankrupt farmhouses and began tilling the land, apparently oblivious
to their proven economic failure. Some seemed content, even pleased,
to live without electricity or running water. Others even built ram-
shackle houses or shacks deep in the woods, hopelessly remote from

the nearest utility lines, and happily lit their homes with kerosene lamps. Some failed even to build driveways to their backwoods homes. They did many of the things impoverished Mainers did—cut their own wood, grew their own food, hauled water from wells, and built their own tools, homes, and furniture—but they did them *voluntarily*.

These were, of course, the "back-to-the-landers." Inspired by Scott and Helen Nearing's *Living the Good Life*, thousands of young idealists fled the cities and suburbs seeking solace from the turmoil of the times: the civil rights movement, Vietnam, the assassinations of Robert F. Kennedy and Martin Luther King, the paranoid dementia of the Nixon administration. Some shivered through the winter in their families' uninsulated summer cottages. Some came to raise their own food, to raise their children away from the perceived madness of mainstream life. A few established hippie communes or alternative schools where the dying dreams of the sixties might live on. Others just wanted peace and quiet, and became country doctors, rural schoolteachers, artists or artisans. They came in pursuit of the Maine myth, not for the summer, but for a lifetime.

The first person to examine this wave of in-migration was University of Maine sociologist Louis A. Ploch, who became curious as to who these people were, where they were going, and what changes they were making at the local level. Some 36,000 people were moving to the state every year in the early 1970s, offsetting the out-migration of young Mainers. In 1975, Ploch sent questionnaires to thousands of in-migrants who had recently swapped their out-of-state driver's licenses for Maine ones. In this way, he learned that the typical migrant came not for better pay, prestige, or power, but for a better quality of life. Most had come from northeastern cities or suburban counties with a population of half a million or more, and a plurality settled in Maine towns with less than two thousand residents. They tended to be younger, better educated, and had fewer children than the people they settled among. And while Ploch generally regarded the new migration as a good thing, he found many Mainers were more skeptical. The "average Mainer perceives the model immigrant to be a malcontent (if not a hippie) who has come to Maine to take advantage of what we have with little thought of making any contribution in return," he wrote in 1976. Friction was likely. "The migrants have come here to get away from the kinds of trends they perceive to have been undermining more urban communities," he said that year. "They will resist efforts to greatly change their perceived image of Maine."

These tensions were in the air that year in Waldoboro, once the domain of Samuel Waldo and Henry Knox, still populated by descendants of the original German and Scotch-Irish settlers. After decades of stagnation, some seventy families had moved to Waldoboro in the first half of the 1970s. In 1976, three Bates College students interviewed dozens of townspeople, and nearly all the newcomers, to figure out how the two groups perceived one another. In both groups, a majority felt that relations were acceptable, but 40 percent of locals and more than a quarter of the newcomers felt there was conflict between the groups. Newcomers expressed concerns about the provincialism of the townspeople and their lack of concern about the environment, zoning, and land use, which, one newcomer said, "is in a total state of havoc." Locals complained that the newcomers sought to change things for the worse. "It seems to me that it's not to Maine's benefit to have out-of-state people coming here with the same ideas and attitudes that made where they came from so putrid," said one. Another said: "We as independent Maine people . . . resent people from urban areas who want all the beauty of Maine life but want all the conveniences of urban life." While many of the complaints on both sides were not backed up by statistics—most locals said they supported zoning, while most newcomers were retired or self-employed and so did not compete for jobs—the two groups were not seeing eye to eye.

For older Mainers, the hardcore back-to-the-landers sometimes appeared humorous, naive, and a little misguided. "We've had locate in town here several of the so-called hippies; I got one up on the hill here," Stockton Springs town clerk Walter Trundy told a University of Maine folklorist in 1973, at which point Trundy was ninety-four years old. "He comes in from New York a couple of years ago and . . . he's got an Indian band around his head there, full of business. . . . He wants to farm, he wants to do something, and he don't even know how to do it. He can't even drive a nail." Trundy had good-naturedly tried to teach his new neighbor some fishing and animal husbandry skills, but he had his doubts as to whether the wayward fellow would make it.

Indeed, many newcomers did not make it. Some were unprepared for or had underestimated the harsh realities of rural Maine life: bitterly cold winters, social and geographical isolation, and a shortage of cultural, entertainment, and economic opportunities. "I can remember a town meeting in the late seventies when we were having quite an influx of people," recalls Joyce Benson of Troy, now an analyst for the State Planning Office. "This woman got up and said what a horrible community we were, that she'd expected a barn dance and bean supper every night. She was in tears, she was so disappointed. We were like, we're working hard to make a living and we're so tired we just want to go to sleep."

People who couldn't bear the poverty and isolation abandoned their farms and moved to suburban Portland or back whence they came. For many would-be Nearings, "the good life" ended in divorce. "Every couple we knew in our back-to-the-land days got divorced, ourselves included," one of my friends' parents recalled. In each case "one spouse found they needed more out of life than just watching the broccoli grow." Confirming the trend, the editor of *Farmstead*, the Freedom-based magazine of the back-to-the-land movement, moved to New York in 1985 to help the Hearst Corporation devise new circulation strategies for *Esquire, Marie Claire,* and *Country Living.*

But while the homesteading movement wilted, in-migration and the tourist trade continued to grow. During the 1970s, Maine's population grew by more than 131,000, or nearly 14 percent, with in-migration accounting for more than half the growth. When Louis Ploch repeated his survey in 1980 he found the in-migrants were coming for the same "quality of life" reasons, but that they were moving into small towns around Portland and Bangor, creating Maine's first true suburbs. The in-migration, Ploch predicted, would continue "for the foreseeable future."

After 1980, the physical landscape began changing as well. In popular resort areas like Camden, Kennebunkport, and Boothbay Harbor, real estate speculators constructed homogenous waterfront condominium complexes with little regard for the towns' architectural character. These suburban pods were wildly popular with out-of-state investors who had no desire to return to these communities year after year. They purchased their "units" as investments, leasing them for the summer to whatever vacationing family wanted them. Instead of new summer colonies, developers were creating anonymous, money-making stables that filled with transient visitors. (At one condo complex on Rockport harbor, only one in six units was owner-occupied in 1982.) Speculators paid outrageous sums for these attached apartments. In 1981, the average three-bedroom home in York County sold for $53,000, at a time when condominium units started at $75,000 and often sold for a quarter million or more. Longtime summer visitors regretted the passing of the quaint summer scene of the past.

Indeed, by the mid-1980s, Boothbay, Camden, and the towns of the southern seacoast were completely overwhelmed by a seasonal tourist tsunami that grew greater and lasted longer year after year. In 1985 a whopping 6.3 million tourists visited Maine, or six for every man, woman, and child in the state. Of those, three million went to the once-sleepy seaside villages between Kittery and Old Orchard Beach— more than one hundred for every year-round resident. Tourism had exploded to a $1.6 billion industry employing more than 57,000 people, with half the jobs and a third of the spending concentrated in York County's seven little tourist towns. Dock Square at the heart of Kennebunkport had turned into the epicenter of a summer-long traffic jam, while Old Orchard Beach had become a sprawling honky-tonk resort looking very like its counterparts on the Atlantic shores of New Jersey or Maryland. "As a native living in a little, small colonial town," Kennebunkport resident Ann Little told *Salt* in 1987, she hated to see it "change so drastically that nobody likes it."

But tourism was big business in a state with few other options, and Maine tourism authorities were promoting the coast with gusto. The Maine Tourism Bureau, whose budget tripled to $3 million in 1987, commissioned an advertising agency to create a new marketing campaign. What they came up with was straight out of the old Maine myth: "Maine: The Way Life Should Be." "Living here is like living in a [Norman] Rockwell painting," the campaign declared without irony. "In Maine, Americana is not a façade, but the heartfelt pride of our residents."

Out on the sea, however, life was definitely not as it should have been. What happened in New England after the passage of the Magnuson Act is a sad tale of scientific hubris, political cowardice, and plain, old-fashioned greed. The establishment of the two-hundred-mile limit should have been the climax of a story with a happy ending for fish and fishermen alike. Instead, it was merely the second act of a tragic opera, one in which few actors would be left standing when the curtain finally dropped.

Things began auspiciously enough when Magnuson went into effect in March of 1977. In the coming months, New England fishermen experienced an immediate rise in their catches. Groundfish landings jumped by 34 percent, scallops by 50 percent, and the average offshore crewman was taking home more than twice as much money as the typical factory worker each year. Many offshore fishermen, encouraged by new federal subsidies, promptly ordered new and more powerful boats. They were joined by doctors, lawyers, and other wealthy landlubbers who, taking advantage of tax loopholes, banded together to buy trawlers of their own. "The tax credits were really for farmers to buy tractors, to stimulate agriculture," says Rockland trawler fleet owner Frank O'Hara Sr. "But the smart lawyers and tax accountants decided to see if they could apply it to boats. It stimulated the fleet, alright." As these vessels were completed between 1976 and 1979, the number of medium-sized groundfish vessels jumped by 75 percent, while the number of trawlers over 125 gross tons jumped by 144 percent.

But out on Georges Bank, groundfish populations were dangerously depleted from the foreign fishing bonanza. From the day the foreign ships left, the resurgent New England fleet started hitting the surviving fish, and hitting them hard. Without some sort of intervention, the weakened fish stocks might be pushed over the edge into a full-scale collapse.

The Magnuson Act had created a mechanism for managing the United States' new fisheries resources. The National Marine Fisheries Service (NMFS), an agency of the Commerce Department, was instructed to monitor the fish populations, forwarding stock assessments to the newly created New England Fisheries Management Council, a public-private regulatory body dominated by representatives from the groundfishing industry itself. The Management Council's scientific committee reviewed NMFS's stock assessments, and forwarded recommendations to the Council proper, which was solely responsible for setting quotas for the total allowable catch of each species in a given year. NMFS and other federal authorities were only allowed to intervene if the Council failed to take measures to ensure the "optimum yield" of fish over the long haul. Unless that happened, NMFS was to stick to monitoring the fish stocks and the grounds themselves, enforcing whatever measures the Council adopted.

Unfortunately, there were serious problems at every stage of this chain of command.

To begin with, NMFS's stock assessments weren't as accurate as the scientists of the day thought they were. "It was scientific hubris," says resource economist James Wilson, who was chairman of the New England Fisheries Management Council's scientific committee. "In 1977 we walked in—myself included—with the idea that we could manipulate the stocks, that we could measure their behavior, set their quotas or figure out the right number of boats necessary to harvest them and create 'maximum sustainable yield' fisheries. We saw it as a technical, expert problem. Smart guys would figure it out and tell the New England Council what to do and if they were smart they would follow our advice. But while we had really good, very sophisticated scientific models, we never bothered to validate them against the real world."

In 1977 and for decades to follow, fisheries science was dominated not by marine biology, ecology, or oceanography, but by statistics. Fishing quotas were based on polling and demographic modeling techniques, computer models, and logarithmic calculations; ecological relationships were largely ignored. Instead, each species was managed in a near-vacuum, as if its health were unrelated to the creatures it ate, competed with, or was eaten by. Fish were managed not as wildlife, but as if they were some commodity like corn, soybeans, or pork bellies. "Because we thought we were so good at this stuff, we didn't think it was necessary to ask the basic questions like: Why do migration patterns occur the way they do? Why the fish occurred when and where they did. What the effect of fishing was on the bottom habitat or on the age structure of the fish," Wilson says. "We had a theory that said the only thing that mattered was the number of fish, so NMFS annual surveys counted the fish, and nothing else." As a result, Wilson's committee recommended groundfish quotas to the Council that were optimistic at best.

But even these quotas were often watered down by the Council, which was controlled by groundfishing interests. In 1977, the Council's first year, Georges Bank fishermen caught their annual quotas of cod, haddock, and yellowtail flounder in just *six months* of fishing. Following procedures set down by the Magnuson Act, NMFS stepped in and closed the fishery. Groundfishermen went ballistic, barraging the Council with protests of financial hardship. The latter responded by raising the quotas for the following year, even though the stock assessments before them indicated the fish population needed more, not less protection. The same process was played out the following year, and the year after that, and so on for more than a decade as the fish quietly spiraled toward oblivion.

As if weak science and oversized catch quotas weren't bad enough, NMFS was unwilling or unable to enforce the quota system out on the banks. On Georges Bank, where a handful of NMFS agents patrolled ten thousand square miles of fishing grounds, cod, haddock, and other fish were being systematically decimated by massive and widespread poaching. In the spring of 1980, the Boston Fish Market was glutted with cod and haddock illegally caught from the closed spawning grounds on Georges Bank. *National Fisherman* reported that enforcement agents had been overwhelmed when the "usual handful of violators ducking in and out of the closed area [were] replaced by a large number of vessels from Gloucester, Boston, and New Bedford, which descended on the area in blatant disregard of the rules." NMFS officials estimated that illegally caught haddock made up as much as 90 percent of the total catch. "The fish are coming in right and left and . . . we know where they're coming from. . . . Everybody does," one skipper told *National Fisherman*. "Haddock were reported as flounder, and dealers were neglecting to report catches at all," says environmental attorney Peter Shelley of the Conservation

Law Foundation. "There was an atmosphere of almost total lawlessness. These were the last buffalo hunters and they were out there on the Banks just letting it rip."

This atmosphere of unfettered greed did more than simply undermine the fish populations the offshore industry depended on. It cost the United States access to vast stretches of the Gulf of Maine.

Even after 1977, the Gulf wasn't an American sea, of course. Its eastern shores belonged to Canada, which had declared a two-hundred-mile limit of its own in 1977. In addition to the Bay of Fundy, the Canadians laid claim to much of the eastern Gulf, including a large swath of Georges Bank, based on an "equidistant" line drawn between New England and the Canadian Maritimes. Washington did not accept this border, instead insisting that Georges Bank was "a natural prolongation of U.S. territory" and should belong to the United States alone. But like good neighbors, the two countries agreed to allow their fishermen to continue as they always had while the diplomats negotiated a final settlement of both the boundary and some sort of fisheries treaty to allow each other to continue fishing throughout the Gulf.

For months, diplomatic notes were passed back and forth between Ottawa and Washington pointing out the deficiencies of one another's claims. Diplomats even sparred over which country had rightful ownership of Machias Seal Island, a rocky, treeless promontory ten miles off the Maine coast inhabited by thousands of noisy seabirds and two Canadian lightkeepers. The United States argued that it had "sovereign title" to the puffin-infested island under the peace treaty that had ended the American Revolution. Canada countered with "conclusive documentary evidence" of British and Canadian control "including continuous and unchallenged occupation since 1832." As tempers flared over such issues, each side extended its claims toward the other's coastline.

As the haggling continued, New England fishermen expanded their operations in Canadian waters, antagonizing Canadian fishermen and officials. When the New England Council raised quotas for cod and haddock in 1978—and refused to establish any regulations for pollock—Ottawa canceled the interim fisheries agreement, kicking U.S. vessels out of all undisputedly Canadian waters. "Canada has consistently managed the stocks for the long term interest of the country," regional fisheries director Doug Johnston said in the spring of 1978.* "The U.S., however, fishes the same area without restrictions and with escalating effort," making negotiations all but impossible.

Then, pressed by southern New England groundfishing interests, the State Department foolishly played hardball on the boundary question, insisting on U.S. sovereignty over all of Georges Bank. Unable to come to an agreement over the boundary, the two countries decided on binding arbitration before the International Court of Justice in the Netherlands. The two sides also signed a fisheries treaty that would have allowed for shared fishing regardless of the outcome of the boundary dispute; but the Senate refused to ratify it, fearing that it would amount to "an unfair giveaway of important stocks" if the United States won its full claim.

In their 1984 decision, the justices at The Hague did what any clear-headed negotiator knew they would do. They split the claims down the middle, awarding Canada a valuable chunk of Georges Bank and much of the eastern Gulf offshore from Maine's Downeast coast. Overzealous fishing as well as overzealous bargaining had exacted a heavy price: New England fishermen had now lost any right to fish in these waters.

Frank O'Hara Sr. was one of those who paid that price. He was in the midst of modernizing his fleet of stern trawlers, which went for redfish in waters near the Nova Scotia shore. In the early eighties, my family regularly walked down the hill from my grandparents' house to watch O'Hara's state-of-the-art trawlers slide down the ways of James Stevens's shipyard. Bedecked with colorful flags, the big blue 120-foot trawlers slid into the harbor as the crowd cheered and a band played a

*While Canada was, indeed, attempting to manage its Atlantic fisheries in a sustainable fashion, it failed spectacularly. As a result, the Grand Banks of Newfoundland, probably the greatest groundfishery the world has ever seen, was stripped of cod, destroying the foundations of outport life across the province. For a detailed account of this tragedy see Colin Woodard, *Ocean's End: Travels Through Endangered Seas* (New York: Basic Books, 2000), pp. 57–95.

rousing chorus on Lobsterman's Wharf. "Everyone had said, 'We'll have this negotiated fishery with the Canadians and we'll have our historic fishing patterns—they'll have theirs and we'll have ours and we'll live happily ever after,' " O'Hara recalls. He ordered three big trawlers. By the time the *Ranger* and *Enterprise* hit the water, the interim fisheries agreement had collapsed. When *Constellation* was launched, the grounds O'Hara had been fishing had been awarded to Canada. "The line is fifty miles from Mount Desert Rock, so you can see it doesn't give you too much water to fish in." Meanwhile "the volume of those species was going down all the time. Things got tough." *Constellation* was retooled to fish for "underutilized species" like squid and mackerel. *Ranger* and *Enterprise* tried to earn their keep chasing eversmaller schools of groundfish, but the numbers just wouldn't add up.

All over New England, new boats were being added to the fleet at a time when U.S. fishing grounds had shrunk by 27 percent. More and more boats were fishing in a much smaller puddle, increasing pressure on stocks that were already overfished. By the mid-1980s, the New England fleet was catching twice as many fish on Georges as the population could withstand. From 1980 on, NMFS forwarded surveys to the New England Council showing that groundfish stocks were shrinking, but the Council refused to take meaningful action. When NMFS tried to intervene, the groundfishermen's allies in Congress forced the agency to back off. Congressmen Gerry Studds and Don Young wrote to the secretary of commerce that "federal funds and employee man-hours . . . surely can be spent in a more productive fashion." Six New England senators, including William Cohen and George Mitchell of Maine, declared that the Council and the fishing industry "have acted responsibly—and commendably" and that the "precise causes for any decline in the New England fish stocks are unknown and subject to considerable scientific and technical debate."

On the water, it was clear what was happening. "You could tell the stock was in trouble," O'Hara says. "It had gotten low during a period when the puddle was smaller and the boats that were out there had better nets and electronic equipment." As catches continued to fall, O'Hara's ships gave up on New England altogether. The Rockland-based company dispatched them, one by one, to the Pacific to fish the still-rich grounds around Alaska; they still fish there today. Other vessel owners began to go bankrupt. Yet the Council continued to set quotas exceeding what their own scientists said the fish could withstand; at one point, fishermen were catching 70 percent of the total Georges groundfish population *every year*.

The trawlers were damaging the banks in other ways too. As their population collapsed, the surviving schools of cod, haddock, and flounder retreated into smaller and smaller areas. The territory they abandoned was quickly taken over by dogfish and skates, whose numbers exploded on the Banks. The hated dogfish—Henry Bigelow called them "sea wolves" for their nasty temper and voracious appetites—was taking over the ecological niche occupied by cod and haddock since long before Waymouth's day. The trawl nets were also tearing up the bottom, destroying the sponges, stony corals, brushy bryozoans, tube worms, and other bottom plants and animals that provided food and shelter to small cod and other juvenile animals. Later studies showed that otter trawls typically scooped up ten to twenty pounds of these creatures for every pound of commercially useful fish they caught. Les Watling, a benthic oceanographer at the University of Maine's Darling Marine Center, has hours of "before-and-after" videotape showing the effect of such trawls: gardens of life in one segment, mud and debris in the other. He likens the effects to clear-cutting in forests, and says it takes months or years for an area to recover from a single trawl. Unfortunately, few areas get that break. In the Gulf of Maine, the area of the ocean bottom swept by trawlers each year was equal to the entire area of the Gulf. On Georges Bank, trawlers passed over a given spot, on average, three times a year. Of course, fishermen didn't trawl either area at random. Trawls were concentrated in precisely the areas where commercial fish lived, probably disrupting most of their habitat dozens of times each year. The bottoms of the Banks and the Gulf were being turned into a wasteland.

The failure of New England management was so acute that it required the intervention of a then-obscure conservation group to protect the groundfish from total annihilation. In 1988 and 1989, the Conservation Law Foundation started getting calls from fishermen pleading that they take a look at what was happening out on Georges. "We were getting these messages, many of them anonymous, saying 'You gotta take a look at what is happening out here,' " says Peter Shelley, head of

CLF's Rockland office. "I mean, everyone knew this fishery was headed for a crash. All the Council's documents showed they were overfishing, and yet they wouldn't do anything serious to stop it." NMFS and the Commerce Department had been cowed into not intervening to save the fish.

CLF decided to take a wild shot: they'd sue the Commerce Department for failing to protect the fish as required under the Magnuson Act. "We had no expectations of winning," Shelley recalls. "Nobody ever wins these kind of suits."

But what CLF didn't know was that NMFS was desperate to stop what was happening on the Banks. The 1991 CLF suit gave them the chance they needed. "The agency very quickly settled with us," Shelley says. "We served as the political lightning rod, while NMFS had a court order to stop the overfishing."

The suit forced the Council to take the only step that could protect the fish at this late stage: a complete ban on groundfishing over large parts of Georges Bank.

The closure, which went into effect in 1994, had profound effects on Maine fishermen. Some effects were direct and immediate. Dozens of trawlers from Portland, Rockland, Boothbay, and other Maine ports had fished Georges since 1977. Now they were forced off the Banks and onto Jeffrey's Bank, Cashes Ledge, and other minor banks in the U.S. portion of the Gulf of Maine, where there were fewer fish. They also faced new regulations that limited the number of days they could spend at sea.

But for other Maine fishermen who'd always fished the inshore grounds in the Gulf, the indirect effects were the worst. When NMFS closed Georges, all the big offshore trawlers and scallop dredgers moved into the Gulf to fish. Gulf of Maine cod weren't that healthy to begin with. In 1991, New England vessels had caught a record-setting 17,800 metric tons of Gulf cod at a time when scientists estimated the combined mass of the entire population of adult spawning cod at only 21,200 metric tons. The cod catch went into free fall after that, plunging to 7,900 metric tons in 1994, and 6,800 in 1996. Each year, fishermen were catching more than 70 percent of the adult cod population, but again the Council refused to take the necessary steps to protect the fish. In 1997 they began tightening the number of days vessels were allowed to fish, but the following year scientists reported that spawning cod "is projected to decline to the lowest level ever observed." Indeed, the total weight of spawning cod in the Gulf stood at one-fifth of its level in the 1960s. Something drastic had to be done.

The endgame came in December 1998, when the Council finally decided to institute rotating closures throughout the Gulf's cod grounds. New catch limits were imposed, then tightened, fixing a daily quota of only two hundred pounds of cod per day at sea. Haddock, flounder, and other species were also in decline. Maine's fisheries had become a mere shadow of their former wealth.

To cap off this depressing tale, in 2000 even the spiny dogfish was in trouble. Deprived of groundfish, fishermen had begun targeting the ill-tempered creature to sell to English fish-and-chips shops. Landings had risen 500 percent between 1989 and 1995 to 50 million pounds a year, and fisheries authorities realized that the slow-maturing shark might go the way of cod and haddock. The Council intervened, introducing strict quotas "intended to end targeted fishing for dogfish . . . [and] promote rebuilding."

But there was one bright spot in the dark cloud hovering over Maine's working waterfronts. One species had defied all predictions of its demise, growing in strength and value as other creatures collapsed before the might of modern fishing technology. Scientists and regulators scratched their heads in wonder, and fishermen gave thanks that the American lobster was riding high.

PART FOUR

The New Frontier

SEVEN

Triumph of the Commons

I followed Bob Steneck as he stepped overboard and into the cold sea. I vanished into the sunlit green, braced for the numbing shock of 55-degree water, but the thick wetsuit seemed to be doing the trick. Encased in a half inch of neoprene, I felt only a slicing pain on my forehead. As my head bobbed back to the surface, I felt the spot: there was a small gap between the top of my mask and the insulated hood of my wetsuit. The pain was from the chill of the water.

Bob took his regulator out of his mouth. "All set?" he asked. "Okay, let's go see some lobsters." We purged the air from the chambers of our dive gear and descended into the sunny haze below.

We were diving in the Thread of Life, a narrow passage squeezed between the eastern shore of the South Bristol peninsula and a thin line of islets and nasty ledges marching south toward the open Atlantic. Steneck, a professor of oceanography at the University of Maine's Darling Marine Center, has spent plenty of time in the Thread of Life in recent years because the creatures he studies love the place. It was July, a time of year when *Homarus americanus*, the American lobster, crawls up into these relatively warm, sunlit shallows to shed its shell and grow.

I couldn't see much of anything as we slowly fell toward the bottom, but I was surprised by how bright it was down there, with as much light as the clear tropical seas where I'd done all my previous diving. The Caribbean and Central Pacific are crystal clear, but here in Maine I felt like I was falling through a slow-motion blizzard. Sunlight reflected off a million little particles suspended in the chilly waters, reducing visibility considerably. Scientists call the stuff "marine snow," and it's one of the reasons the Gulf is so productive. Most of the snow is produced by microscopic plants and animals as they happily go about their business in the sunny surface layer. It's rich in nutrients, and as it slowly settles on the bottom, the snow is gobbled up by a whole array of creatures, including shrimp, clams, mussels, and scallops. They, in turn, feed fish and, of course, lobsters.

I myself was settling out on the bottom, which suddenly appeared out of nowhere just five feet beneath me. I added some compressed air back into my gear and hovered next to Bob, surveying the lobster bottom.

We were only twenty feet down, but already beneath the marine snowstorm, peering at our surroundings through the gentle snowfall. We floated above a patchy meadow of two-foot-tall sea grass growing on a smooth plain of sand sloping toward the open ocean. Here and there small, transparent shrimp darted along the bottom. A fish-sized rock crab, alarmed by our presence, retreated backward to hide in the shadows beneath a clump of eelgrass. But I didn't notice any lobsters until Bob, swimming ahead of me, began pointing out little piles of sand dotting the bottom every few feet. I drifted up to one and, to my surprise, found myself face-to-face with a one-pound lobster, hiding in the little foxhole it had dug for itself. At first it didn't seem to notice me — lobsters don't see very well — but then its antennae suddenly shot to attention and it raised its arms, claws wide open, defying me to come any closer. As I drifted past, it continued waving its claws at me like a punch-drunk boxer. *Move it along, you!* A few seconds later, I was face-to-face with another foxholed lobster, and the sequence was repeated. A few feet later, a one-clawed half-pounder lunged at me from his sandy den. The bottom, I started to realize, was dotted with lobster burrows spaced five to ten feet apart, giving the sandy plain the appearance of the Colorado prairie after a prairie dog infestation.

Lobsters were everywhere.

Bob swam into an eelgrass meadow and, pushing the fronds aside, revealed a lobster beneath almost every clump. Occasionally he shot one hand toward the lobster and, as the lobster lunged in that direction like a faked-out goalie, quickly grabbed the animal by the back with his other hand. As we made our way across the deepening eelgrass, Bob handed me one lobster after another, pointing out their particular attributes. They came in a range of sizes, from four-inch-long two-year-olds to a feisty pound-and-a-halfer who would have looked nice on a dinner plate. He pointed out which were males and which were females—if you flip them over and look at the underside of the tail, the two foremost pairs of swimmerets give them away. The male's are hard and sharp to assist in copulation; the female's are small and flat, and the rest of her swimmerets are feathery so she can carry eggs around. Bob pointed out that nearly all of the lobsters had a long, straight, pencil-colored line down the back of their body shell (or *carapace*), an early sign that they were preparing to molt. Others were missing claws or antennae, particularly those caught in open sand burrows. Smaller, weaker lobsters were forced to settle out here on the sandy bottom where there was less cover, kicked out of better habitat by larger ones, Bob later told me. He calls this sand the Thread of Life's "low-rent district."

Further into the channel, the bottom was deeper, colder, and rockier. Forty feet down off Crow Island, we swam through 50-degree water over a massive kelp-covered boulder field. Under the brown canopy of kelp, big dark rocks lay here and there amid great, low heaps of rounded, football-sized stones called cobbles. These were decorated in a lavender-pink patchwork of coralline algae and littered with the largest mussels I'd ever seen. These were horse mussels, and looked like the blue mussels found on dinner plates and rocky shores at low tide, except that they measured four to six inches long. I tapped on one, and it closed its shell so quickly that the tip of my rubber glove got caught in its mouth; I had to take a moment to pull myself free. Bob later told me that horse mussels don't taste as good as blue mussels and, in any case, nobody harvests them because of their bright orange meat. This is probably a good thing. Unlike their tasty cousins, horse mussels are slow to grow or reproduce, and scientists estimate the largest ones to be as much as sixty years old. Here and there the rocks were colonized by anemones, their many delicate arms swaying in the undersea current. Despite their camouflage, I spotted a baby flounder or two lying prone on the bottom. But at first, the only sign of lobsters I saw was an empty pile of recently molted shell.

That changed the moment Bob started poking around in the rocks. Almost without fail, each time he lifted a rock or cobble, a cloud of sediment burst forth as a hidden lobster launched itself away with a sudden contraction of the tail. With uncanny skill, Bob managed to block with his free hand. The lobster would then jet backward in the other direction, only to encounter Bob's other hand. Within a few seconds, Bob would have fumbled his way to a capture, and handed the annoyed lobster over to me. The first one was a mere five inches long, but as feisty as a lapdog. Bob pointed out its gender, then moved along to a nearby boulder. I gently released my captive with a little underhand toss and watched him start settling to the bottom, his little antennae at attention and claws flailing. Bob was twenty feet ahead, quickly capturing another lobster, and I started swimming over to him. But just as I reached his side, I felt a sharp little tug on the knee of my wetsuit. Perplexed, I lowered my head for a view down my front side. The little lobster had pursued me and was now latched on to my knee, tugging away as if to say: *I'll get you for this!* I easily released myself from his grip and let him go, but he immediately started chasing me again. I had to take a ten-yard detour before he gave up the chase and returned to his lobstery business.

Meanwhile, Bob was up ahead, catching a lobster under almost every stone he turned. He pointed out lobsters hiding under boulders, under kelp, even beneath a long length of algae-covered rope lost by some fisherman. We came across a lost or "ghost" lobster trap sitting on a bed of cobbles. The four-foot-long wire box looked enormous sitting on the bottom, in part because peering through a scuba mask is a little like looking into a fish tank: everything appears 30 percent bigger than it really is. It was obvious that its owner had lost the trap quite some time ago, as it was now thickly covered with algae and a brightly colored crusty substance that I later learned is a strange colonial organism called a sea squirt that filters tiny bits of food from the water. Pleased with this decor, a good-sized dinner lobster had made his home inside this ghost trap and could be seen lounging securely within, entirely uninterested in our comings and goings. I swam on.

Then, up ahead loomed another great wire box, this one clean, with a nylon warp line tied to one end that rose up and vanished into the sunny green glow overhead.

I drifted across a sandy patch and settled down beside the forest green trap. A half-dozen lobsters were visible inside, most hanging around in the first of its two chambers, in the middle of which hung a nylon mesh bag filled with ripe-looking herring. A large rock crab clung to the underside of the bait bag and was shoveling little bits of herring into its mouth with its claws. Another lobster was crawling around the outside of the trap, clearly trying to find a way in, while those inside made aggressive gestures toward it. Under the entrance to the trap—a funnel-shaped piece of netting—yet another lobster had burrowed right under the trap. When I approached to investigate, he charged out to defend the trap from me. Another clung to the back wall, this one with a normal-sized tearing claw and an itty-bitty crusher claw, the latter regenerating after a recent amputation. When we came across other traps, we witnessed similar scenes.

The bottom was clearly covered in lobsters, including plenty of young ones. In fact, surveys of baby and adolescent lobsters taken by Steneck and Carl Wilson, the chief lobster biologist at Maine's Department of Marine Resources (DMR), found that in prime lobster habitat like the Thread of Life and the mouth of Penobscot Bay, lobsters are found in an average density of nearly *one per square meter.* That's a young lobster, on average, every six feet or so in every direction across vast stretches of the seafloor. Diving in the Thread of Life that summer, there seemed to be even more than that.

Which leads us to the Great Lobster Mystery. For nearly three decades, federal fisheries managers have warned that the lobster stock is so severely overfished that a tragic, codlike collapse is inevitable. Instead, Maine's annual lobster catch has exploded, from 20 million pounds in the seventies and early eighties to around 50 million pounds today, and scientists like Steneck see little evidence that fishermen are hurting the lobster population. "Lobsters may be globally unique in that their population keeps growing despite high rates of exploitation by fishermen," Steneck had told me earlier, in his laboratory. "That's almost heresy to say in a world that's so seriously overfished, where so many stocks have been entirely extracted. But lobsters have shown themselves to be highly resilient."

Lobster have been resilient indeed. At the height of the nineteenth-century lobster boom, Maine lobstermen were tending somewhere between 50,000 and 100,000 traps. Today there are more than three million, a thirty- to sixty-fold increase over the stock-crushing fishing pressure of that first lobster boom. And over the twentieth century, the lobstermen who fished those traps kept buying larger, more powerful, and better-equipped boats. Each generation has been capable of fishing farther, faster, and in worse conditions than their parents were. Fishermen can scan the bottom to find lobster habitat. They can locate traps with precision accuracy using global satellite positioning technology. And their catch—once spurned as the food of the poor—has become a signature luxury food sought by diners from Bangor to Boston and Berlin to Beijing.

Scientists warned early on that the lobster was being overexploited, and that another 1930s-style crash was in the works. In 1965, Robert Dow, research director of DMR's predecessor, the Sea and Shore Fisheries Department, estimated that 90 percent of all legal-sized lobsters in Maine's waters were being caught and eaten every year. If something wasn't done to reduce the number of traps in the water—then less than one million—lobstering would "degenerate to sport fishing," journalist Bill Caldwell concluded at the end of an extensive exposé on the controversy. But twelve years later, Maine's catch remained stable at around 19 million pounds, while the number of traps in the water had doubled to 1.8 million. "It's just a matter of time before [the lobster stock] crashes," Dow's successor, Vaughn Anthony, warned in the spring of 1978. "We should see it in a year or so." Instead, the 1979 catch was 22.1 million pounds, the largest since 1963, without any reduction in the number of traps. "Over-exploitation certainly does exist now," DMR biologist James Thomas told reporters the following spring. "They're fishing the lobster population way over the maximum that it can support."

But lobstermen, like their groundfishing counterparts, refused to act on the scientists' advice. Instead of decreasing the number of traps in the water, they continued to increase them. And as groundfish stocks collapsed, more and more fishermen switched over to full-time lobstering in an effort to support their families. Between 1973 and 1998, the number of fishermen earning the majority of their income from lobstering jumped from less than 2,500 to nearly 5,500. Concerns about future restictions also pushed the increasing number of lobstermen to fish more and more traps; the total number of traps in use in Maine waters climbed steeply from about 1.8 million in 1980 to over 3 million in 1999. Every model, every scientist, any rationale observer could see that the lobster fishery was about to follow cod and haddock into oblivion.

Instead, landings exploded.

Maine lobstermen saw their combined landings jump from a respectable 21.7 million pounds in 1988 to a new all-time record of 30.8 million pounds in 1991, more than 25 percent greater than the peak catch of the nineteenth-century boom. In 1994, the catch jumped to a shocking 38.9 million pounds, only to leap to a stupendous 47 million in 1997. In 2000 it hit a staggering 57.2 million pounds, only to be topped in 2002, when Maine fishermen landed 62.3 million pounds of lobster.

And while Steneck and his colleagues continued to find young lobsters under practically every stone from Crow Island to Criehaven, federal fisheries managers continued to maintain that the lobster stock was overfished. "Every time the scientists say the stock is about to collapse, there has been a groan from the industry," says James A. Wilson of the University of Maine, who remembers how fisheries managers in the late seventies were convinced that groundfish were rebuilding and lobsters were about to collapse. "Clearly, the model they are using is not one that hits the nail on the head."

Hitting that nail on the head has never been more important. A lobster collapse would be devastating to the coast's working waterfronts. With most of Maine's other marine resources in a state of decline or outright collapse, lobsters are practically the sole economic underpinning for Maine's fishing industry. These feisty, omnivorous creatures are the lifeline supporting all of the coast's year-round island communities from Monhegan on east to Vinalhaven, Isle au Haut, and Frenchboro. They're the main reason there's still a commercial fishing culture in old fisheries centers like Portland, Boothbay, and Rockland and provide one of the few ways for young people to stay on and raise a family in their native outports, be it Corea or Beals, Jonesport or Stonington. Maine's seven thousand lobstermen earn between $150 and $180 million a year catching lobsters; the overall economic effect of the industry is estimated at half a billion dollars annually.

The lobster has, rightly or wrongly, become a symbol of Maine as a whole. Lobsters adorned our license plates for nearly two decades, and a lobster boat now cruises across the top of our driver's licenses. When we travel around the country and people learn of our place of origin they invariably evoke one of three keywords: Stephen King, L.L. Bean, and, of course, lobster. Maine, in turn, has vigorously defended its icon from outside intrusion. It's illegal to touch, molest, or possess an undersized lobster, unless, like Steneck, you have the proper permits. From 1941 until 1973, it was illegal to sell or even possess a crawfish, langouste, or spiny lobster—fresh, frozen, or otherwise—within the state of Maine. This official effort to ban the lobster's competition was eventually challenged by the Maine Restaurant Association, which got the state legislature to change the law. Another state law banning the importation of picked lobster meat from other states was overturned in 1968 by a panel of federal judges who declared the measure unconstitutional. However, the industry has run such successful promotion campaigns that virtually any *Homarus americanus* caught anywhere from North Carolina to Newfoundland winds up being marketed as "Maine Lobster."

Indeed, it's hard to imagine Maine without lobster fishing. But, if marine scientists like Bob Steneck are right, we may never have to. It appears that lobsters and lobstermen may have reached a complicated symbiosis, one with few precedents in the postindustrial world, but with many antecedents going back to the dawn of human history. If the symbiosis can be preserved, large numbers of both lobsters and lobstermen could be around for a very long time to come.

⁓

Lobsters make for an unlikely icon. They're neither soft and fuzzy, like China's pandas, nor regal and majestic like African lions or the elephants of the Indian subcontinent. They display few behaviors that humans can relate to, such as carrying their young around in cute little pouches or singing songs to their mates while perching in a nest. Instead, lobsters are armored and buglike, cold-blooded omnivores from an alien realm few humans ever visit. Hiding in the gloom beneath rocks and burrows, feasting on rotting bait and occasionally on one another, they provided little fodder for the poets and painters of the Romantic age. There's little nonsense with a lobster, just a tenacious will to hold down its turf and get what it needs to survive.

In basic design, *Homarus americanus* resembles a self-propelled Swiss Army knife, with deployable appendages for every occasion. Around the mouth is an assortment of forks, clamps, brushes, paring knives, and crushing devices, which have been likened to a sausage machine. There are retractable stalks for each eye, long whiplike antennae for touch and smaller ones for smell. There are walking legs and cleaning brooms, plus long sets of swimming paddles, modified in the female for clutching eggs. In all, the lobster has twenty pairs of appendages, not counting the muscular tail, with which it can launch itself backward more than twenty-five feet in a single second. Additionally, each of its ten legs is covered in thousands of sensitive smelling hairs, capable of sniffing out food or predators as the lobster treads along the bottom.

Lobsters look helpless and ungainly when sprawled upon a kitchen table, but in their own environment they are surprisingly fast and agile. They are almost neutrally buoyant, and practically float as they tiptoe across the bottom on their walking legs. Their main antennae twitch back and forth, scanning their surroundings for vibrations, while their vast array of smelling sensors sift the water for chemical traces of food, friends, and foes. They can use their swimmerets to paddle along above the bottom and raise their large claws to deter potential enemies.

American lobsters are found from North Carolina to Labrador, even in parts of northern Europe, but are most plentiful in the Gulf of Maine, particularly along the rocky, convoluted shores of Nova Scotia and Maine. But wherever they find themselves, lobsters do their best to secure snug, solitary homes, and will vigorously defend them from intruders. In the Thread of Life, the strongest lobsters appropriate lost traps or snug caves beneath boulders or cobbles, while others dig niches under kelp and eelgrass, or simply burrow holes in the sand. While visiting a large outdoor lobster pound on Southport in the late nineteenth century, Francis Herrick, the father of lobster biology, found lobsters hiding at the end of five-foot-deep burrows in the pound's muddy banks. When he stuck an oar down the hole, the lobsters would seize it in their claws, refusing to let go even when dragged from their burrows. "The pile of dirt and the broken clam shells which are sometimes seen near the hole of the lobster," he wrote, "recall the excavations of the muskrat."

Lobsters feed on most anything: mussels, crabs, hydroids, starfish, small fish, and dead creatures of many sorts. They will happily feed on a person, should they find a dead one in their habitat, and will just as happily dismantle a smaller lobster alive, picking him clean, even consuming the shell if molting is close at hand. In natural pounds, Herrick found that lobsters were constantly digging up the bottom in search of clams and other mollusks, sometimes digging craters two feet across and half a foot deep. "In a large lobster pound at the Vinal Haven Islands I have seen the muddy bottom scored in all directions, the work of lobsters in their search for clams," he wrote. "One was reminded of a pasture in which the soil had been rooted up by pigs." A fisherman told him that when left unfed, pounded lobsters "will soon turn over the bottom as effectively as it could be done with a plow." In Herrick's day, inexperienced pound owners could lose as much as 20 percent of their stock in a few days' time as softshell lobsters that had recently shed their old armor were devoured by larger rivals. In the wild, adult lobsters are hunted by skates, rays, sharks, and, until recently, cod and other groundfish, which would happily swallow them whole and digest them at their leisure.

Despite their burrowing instinct, adult lobsters move around a great deal. In the spring, millions begin crawling toward warming waters near the shore from the deeper water where they've wintered, apparently in an effort to find food, shelter, and water of the right temperature. "They want to grow fast, reach sexual maturity, and reproduce as much as they can in the time they have," says Win Watson, a University of New Hampshire zoologist who studies lobster. "I think they're seeking the optimal temperature to do that, avoiding water that's too cold and will slow them down into a kind of torpor, or water that's so warm that they are unable to maintain their rate of metabolism." In the fall, the chill winds begin lowering the temperature of the seafloor in Maine's coves, bays, and inlets, and the lobsters begin the long crawl back to the deep, where the water temperature remains stable in winter. Tagging studies have shown that most lobsters, most of the time, confine their wanderings to this seasonal, inshore–offshore migration. But some lobsters, for reasons known only to themselves, suddenly embark on long coastal journeys. In one massive tagging study of tens of thousands of lobsters caught in Connecticut, most were recaptured in the same general area. But a couple dozen of these lobsters marched right out of Long Island Sound, crossed the two-hundred-mile-wide continental shelf, and trundled over the edge where they were captured in thousands of feet of water. Some tagged lobsters have been shown to travel as much as four miles in a single day, while others stay close to their burrows for the entire season.

Many of the lobsters coming ashore have nearly outgrown their own shells and are preparing to shed them. Some of them will seize this rare chance to mate as well. Lobsters can only have sex just after the female has shed, as her hard shell blocks access to the critical anatomy. It's a bizarre process that researchers have only recently gotten a handle on.

Few scientists have spent as much time studying the sex lives of lobsters as Diane Cowan, whose passionate interest in these crustaceans has led her to be described as the "Jane Goodall of Lobsters." She started studying them for a school report as a seventh grader in upstate New York, and by the time she was in high school her classmates had nicknamed her "the lobster lady." She studied lobsters in graduate school at the Woods Hole Oceanographic Institution on Cape Cod. When she moved to Maine, she supported her field research on intertidal lobsters by waitressing at an Orr's Island seafood restaurant that was willing to schedule her shifts around the tide charts. She later founded the Lobster Conservancy, a Friendship-based nonprofit dedicated to basic, hands-on lobster research.

While at Woods Hole, Cowan set up a reasonably convincing subtidal lobster habitat inside a large aquarium tank, pumped natural seawater through it, and stayed up night after night watching the lobsters inside do their thing. Each night, "M-5," the tank's dominant male lobster, would march from shelter to shelter, evicting the occupants, and then return to his own shelter and await admirers. The four females, impressed with this display, ventured out in turn to investigate M-5's shelter, generally spurning the smaller, subordinate males. During these "dates," the females made no secret of their interest in M-5. Each stuck her head into the shelter and peed inside. M-5, apparently pleased with the attention, fanned his swimmerets to draw the urine cloud in and around him. "Like dogs, lobsters probably have informative urine," Cowan says. "It may be a way of communicating gender, age, molting status, and even dominance." But the biggest surprise was yet to come. Each of the females, in turn, moved in with M-5 for a few days, during which time they shed, copulated, and then hardened up under his protection. Amazingly, the females had staggered the timing of their molts, so that each of them could mate with M-5, instead of smaller, less desirable M-6, alone and possibly frustrated in his shelter at the other end of the tank. When Cowan filled the tank with females, most put off molting altogether and those who did molt lost claws or walking legs in the process. Female lobsters were clearly capable of controlling their molting process, and went out of their way to shed with a dominant male present.

Shedding is already an amazing, risky, and exhausting feat. With copulation thrown into the mix, it's a wonder the females survive at all.

Lobsters are constantly growing, but as with humans and many other animals, their growth rate is fastest in the early years. Hatchlings expand so quickly, they are forced to molt three times in their first month of life, and will shed their shells a couple dozen times before they reach legal size, a process that can take anywhere from five to seven years. Each molt increases the lobster's size by about 10 percent, and allows it to grow 50 percent heavier. As adults get larger, they need to shed less and less often. A three- or four-pound female may only molt once every three to five years, which also means she can have sex only a few times each decade.

Several weeks before it sheds, a molting lobster begins forming a soft new shell underneath its old one, drawing minerals from the long median line that runs down its back. If the lobster has lost any limbs, it begins regrowing them, and they poke out of the amputated area like little buds. When it decides to shed, the lobster pumps itself full of water, forcing the old shell to begin to come apart where certain plates join. It then rolls onto its side, and the back of the carapace pops up from the tail like a reverse-facing automobile hood. At this point the lobster has been forced to shut down its gills and pump most of the blood out of its claws and other appendages. It then pulls its front half out of its old shell, withdrawing its soft, squishy body, legs, eyestalks, antennae, and other body parts from their hard molds and restraining tendons. The lobster is even able to pull its big claws out through its narrow arm joints completely intact. (If something goes wrong, the lobster will sacrifice a claw or limb to escape, and will begin growing a new one in the next molt.) After all that, it's comparatively simple to remove its tail from the back section of the shell and the lobster body from its hard, heavy mold. The entire process can take as little as five minutes, or as long as an hour. The exhausted lobster then rests, pumping itself up like a water balloon, and begins the weeks-long process of hardening up its new, larger shell. Often it will eat its old shell to scavenge some of the necessary minerals, sometimes hiding some of it under rocks or in its shelter for later consumption.

When mating, however, the female doesn't get much rest at first. Once she has gained enough strength to stand, the hardshelled male marches up, flips her over on her back, and penetrates her twin sperm receptacles with his rigid front swimmerets. In a few seconds, her sperm storage reservoir is filled and the female escapes from under her partner with a powerful tail flip. She will spend the next week or so inside his shelter, while he guards the door against the hungry and horny alike. After that, she departs for her own shelter and is often replaced by another shedding female.

The female can carry the male's sperm around with her for months, even years, before putting it to use. She might even save some to use for a second batch of eggs. Either way, her eggs develop for months inside her body before she releases them onto the underside of her tail, where they pass through a stream of stored sperm before attaching themselves around her feathery swimmerets. At this point the eggs are dark green and extremely tiny—about one-sixteenth of an inch in diameter. There are also an incredible number of them, from about 5,000 in a small adult female to as many as 100,000 in a five-pound matriarch. The eggs cover the underside of the tail like great wads of caviar or miniature berries, leading lobstermen to refer to egg-carrying lobsters as "berried" females. A female will carry her eggs around for ten or eleven months, gently aerating them with her swimmerets. There they hatch into tiny "pre-larvae," each less than one-sixth of an inch long, which cling to her tail until their mother decides the time has come to release them into the wide, dangerous ocean. When that hour comes, she places herself below an appropriate current or water mass and fans her babies away with her pulsing swimmerets. They rise immediately toward the sunny ocean surface, molting for the first time on their way up. Now proper larvae, these tiny floating lobsters begin a two- to three-week-long oceanic journey few of them will survive.

～～

Since Herrick's day, scientists have known that lobster larvae spend ten to twenty days afloat, whisked along by wind, tide, and currents, while most every creature they encounter tries to gobble them up. Nobody has any idea how many survive this free-floating period, but it is probably considerably less than one in one thousand, possibly one in ten thousand. Lobsters need lots of eggs because very few ever get the chance to grow to adulthood.

Until recently, scientists assumed that the supply of eggs was the most important factor in assessing the health of the lobster population from one year to the next. Fewer females presumably meant fewer eggs. Fishermen were catching an awful lot of young females before they had a chance to breed for the first time, because Maine's minimum size allows lobstermen to keep teenagers that haven't quite reached maturity. So when their statistical models started showing that lobstermen were catching more than 80 percent of a given generation of female lobsters every year before they had an opportunity to breed for the first time, the scientists concluded that the species was in trouble. They called for measures to reduce fishing pressure and increase the minimum size, but lobstermen resisted. Instead of crashing, the population grew; still, fisheries managers stood behind their models.

Bob Steneck was one of the first scientists to break rank. Maine's lobster stock wasn't overfished at all, he argued, and the evidence was crawling around out there on the bottom of the Thread of Life, Mussel Ridge Channel, and hundreds of other lobster grounds for anyone with a scuba tank to see. Maybe the critical "bottleneck" for a given generation of lobsters wasn't the supply of mature eggs, Steneck thought, but the number of larvae successfully reaching the bottom to become baby lobsters.

For the first ten to twenty days after hatching, lobsters are almost entirely at the mercy of ocean currents. The tiny larvae can swim a little, but just enough to shift their position within a veritable river of fast-flowing water: they have little control over where they end up. After their fourth molt—when they look like half-inch-long scale replicas of an adult lobster—the tiny, free-floating lobsters are ready to settle on the bottom where they will spend the rest of their lives. When they reach water of a certain temperature, the baby lobsters drop to the bottom like raindrops. Steneck wondered if the recent lobster boom could have something to do with where the ocean currents were carrying these "new settlers," and the type of bottom they found. Maybe more settlers were landing on the cobble nursery habitat they thrived in. Maybe there was a relationship between the number of settlers arriving on the bottom in a given year, and the number of adult lobsters appearing in traps in the same area years later. Such a discovery could revolutionize the way scientists monitor the health of the American lobster.

Baby lobsters don't move around a lot. Something would quickly gobble them up if they did. So Steneck figured the best way to locate lobster nurseries would be to find out where juvenile lobsters lived in great numbers. And to do that, Steneck took the then-revolutionary step of asking lobstermen for help. Lobstermen saw undersized and oversized lobsters every day in their traps, and had a pretty good idea of where and when to find them. "We'd ask lobstermen if we could come along and tag and record each one that comes up," he recalls. "We've approached hundreds of lobstermen, and almost every one wants to be involved. We just have to get our butts out of our office chairs and onto their boats and they're great." Clear juvenile hot spots emerged, most of them in and around areas with particularly huge lobster landings, like lower Penobscot Bay. But surveying the quarter- or half-pound juveniles was one thing—at least they went into fishermen's traps for a snack. The tiny settler lobsters weighed a fraction of an ounce and didn't go anywhere. How could they ever be counted?

One of Steneck's graduate students, Rick Wahle, came up with a solution. He built himself a sort of underwater vacuum cleaner, allowing him to suck up and count all the little lobsters in a given sampling area, then release them, unharmed. "No one knew exactly where the lobster nurseries were until we developed this suction tool," says

Wahle, now a research scientist at the Bigelow Laboratory for Ocean Sciences in Boothbay Harbor. "It opened a window on a whole segment of their life history that nobody had a handle on."

Using the lobster vacuum, Wahle and Steneck discovered that Maine's baby lobsters are concentrated in cobble-covered bottoms that provided them vital shelter. In some areas, average densities of tiny, newly settled baby lobsters reached almost seven per square meter of the bottom, compared to almost zero for sandy, featureless bottoms. When Wahle built his own cobble field in the middle of a large sandy plain, the density of tiny lobsters jumped tenfold. As they continued experiments and surveys, a clearer picture emerged. Baby lobsters that settled out of the water on sandy or muddy bottoms were quickly eaten by predators, usually in less than twenty-four hours. But the vast majority of those that settled on cobbled bottoms and found shelter not only survived their first day, but were still alive three or four years later when they started showing up in lobstermen's traps. "There's a clear link in space between where we see high settlement densities [of tiny lobsters] on the coast of Maine, and where we see high landings [of adult lobsters] by lobstermen," he says. "What we're working on now is determining if there's a link in time between when we see good larval settlement and when we'll see good landings five to seven years down the road when those lobsters reach harvestable size."

Tracking a given "year class" of baby lobsters as they grow up isn't easy. Individual lobsters grow at different rates, and scientists have no way to determine a given lobster's age. A lobster that's just reached the legal size could be anywhere from four to nine years of age depending on water temperature, food supply, or past injuries, which may have required it to divert energy to regenerating a lost limb. To build an accurate population model for the fishery, researchers will need to get a clear idea of how such factors affect a given generation's growth.

Diane Cowan is trying to get a handle on lobster growth and is doing it with her Goodall-like commitment to field research. She lives alone now among her study lobsters on Friendship Long Island in Muscongus Bay. Her house has no running water or utility connections, but stands next to a cove that some nineteenth-century entrepreneur gated off to create a lobster storage pound. The six-acre cove is the largest of three Muscongus Bay pounds donated to her Lobster

Conservancy in 1999, and is now a giant lobster research facility. She has been collecting huge five-pound lobsters to monitor how they behave and how quickly they molt and grow. "I won't be able to spy on them quite as well as I could in the aquarium [at Woods Hole], but it's going to be a lot closer to their wild habitat," she says. "We just don't know a lot about these large lobsters."

But Cowan's signature research is on the growth and abundance of small juvenile lobsters, ones with a carapace length of less than two inches, and often as little as half an inch. She studies them without scuba gear, submarines, or vacuum devices. For a few days each month, when the very lowest tides briefly expose their subtidal habitat, she goes out on the slippery, rockweed-covered rocks of her island and literally picks them from beneath their little rocky hideouts.

Late one neap tide afternoon in late October, Diane picked me up from Friendship with her skiff and we sped off to an isolated cove on the back side of Friendship Long Island. It was one of those crisp, clear fall evenings when the air was still enough to make out the sound of a cormorant's flight a half-mile away. The lowering sunlight sharpened every crease and contour of the island's exposed rockweed skirt, as we clambered awkwardly along the water's edge in our rubber boots. Diane raced against the setting sun, flipping over likely rocks and adeptly seizing the tiny, tail-flapping creatures underneath. She had a stack of little plastic dishes and placed a tiny lobster in each. By the time the tide shifted, I was crouching amid dozens of dishes, each containing a little one- to five-inch-long scale replica of the lobsters I'd been eating all my life. In the fading light, Diane began recording her catch. She pulled out a little hand-held scanner and ran each tiny lobster under it like a grocery clerk might run your groceries. To my surprise, one of them caused the scanner to beep. "This one's been tagged before," Diane said with a smile. The scanner reported the tag number, allowing Diane to find out where it had been previously caught and how big it was then. We measured each lobster, recorded whether its crusher claw was on the left or right (lobsters, like people, can be right- or left-handed), and added other various personal details. Then Diane inserted a tiny, splinter-sized tag between the joint-plates and into the flesh of one of its tiny legs, and ran it across the scanner to determine its number. The lobsters will molt their shells, but the tag will remain with them inside their new shells. With the help of Rockland's Island Institute, Cowan's studies have expanded to dozens of sites across Maine and New England and are helping build the database scientists will need to understand how the Gulf of Maine grows so many lobsters.

While scientists now have a pretty good sense of where the lobsters' nursery grounds are, it's still not clear where they are coming from. Since larvae float in currents for ten to twenty days before settling, their mothers may be concentrated far from the prime lobstering grounds of Maine's Midcoast region, which have the greatest nursery grounds and commercial landings of anywhere in the United States. Lewis Incze, an oceanographer at the Bigelow Lab, has been trawling Maine's coastal currents with a special larval sampling net, trying to determine where they come from. The results are intriguing: The largest concentration of newly hatched larvae isn't in the Midcoast, but way Downeast off Cutler, Eastport, and New Brunswick's Grand Manan Island. The largest concentration of fully developed larvae — the ones about to settle on the bottom — is found farther west, near the entrance to Penobscot Bay. This discrepancy has led to what Incze calls the "lobster larvae superhighway theory," which hypothesizes that a large proportion of Maine's lobster supply comes from eggs released by brood lobsters around the Canadian border and transported a hundred miles or more to their nurseries by the westward-flowing Eastern Maine Coastal Current. While there appear to be local brood stocks as well, it's clear that the health of the lobster population in any one area may not only be dependent on lobsters far away, but on the currents themselves. "We expect that fisheries landings are driven in significant part by the supply of larvae transported to the area," Incze explains. "Right now most fisheries policies assume the ups and downs of a population are determined by the activities of the fishermen. But it may have a lot to do with oceanographic factors."*

*A number of fisheries scientists outside of Maine do not accept this theory and believe the state's lobsters are, in fact, overfished. Andrew Rosenberg, dean of life sciences at the University of New Hampshire and the former deputy director of the National Marine Fisheries Service, describes the sustainability theories of Steneck and his colleagues as part of "the Wizard of Oz School of Management." They "want to spin around and click [their] heels three times

Oceanographers suspect that the explosive increase in the Gulf of Maine's lobster population since the late 1980s may have to do with some sort of natural shift in the oceanographic cycle. In its current state, more larvae are delivered to their nursery grounds than were in, say, the sixties and seventies, when lobster landings were less than half what they are today. "The North Atlantic Oscillation influences the flow of currents into the Gulf of Maine and we know it has an effect on shrimp," says Neal Pettigrew, a physical oceanographer at the University of Maine in Orono. "It's all speculation at this point, but it's the kind of thing that might have a significant effect on larval delivery."

But while ocean currents may wind up explaining the recent explosion in lobster landings, they don't explain why lobstermen—unlike most of their fellow fishermen—haven't wiped out the brood stock itself. The scientists know there must be lots of big, breeding females out there somewhere—Steneck and Wilson have been working with lobstermen, submarines, and remotely operated vehicles, both inshore and offshore, to try to find and quantify them. But to answer why the brooders are still there, all one needs to do is go out to sea with a Maine lobsterman.

Jennifer Elderkin keeps her lobster boat in a narrow slit of a cove on the west side of Southport Island, just a few miles from the one-room island schoolhouse my mother attended in the 1950s. Southport, though connected to Boothbay by a swinging drawbridge and thoroughly colonized by retirees and summer cottagers, still has an untrammeled feel. As Jennifer and I row across the dawn-painted water, sandwiched between seaweed-covered ledges and spruce-scented forest, it feels like we're setting out from some remote outport. Behind Jennifer's thirty-two-foot lobster boat the cove opens out onto the wide-

---

and wish that there were more fish out there," he says. How can a fishery be sustainable, Rosenberg argues, if more than 90 percent of each generation of lobsters are caught in the very first year they reach legal size, meaning they have only had a chance to spawn once, if at all? Since lobsters can live for many decades, the age structure of the population is also completely out of whack, he says, and fishing pressure has grown dramatically, classic indicators of overfishing. Rosenberg's conclusion: "I think it's a disaster waiting to happen."

open Atlantic which continues, uninterrupted, all the way to the tropical isles of the Caribbean.

Jennifer grew up on Southport, where her mother's family has lived for generations, but she hadn't planned to take up lobstering. She had tended a few traps from the time she was old enough to handle a rowboat and, later, earned money for school each summer hauling fifty wooden traps by hand from a small skiff, or sterning for her father. "Fishing was something I enjoyed, but I never entertained it as a career because it just didn't seem like a thing that women did, and I was a little hung up on that I guess," she says. "But also I'd see the people from Connecticut and New Jersey and New York who come for their summer vacations and shop at L.L. Bean and they've got their Volvos and you know their life looks pretty good. So, I says, that must be what success is in an urban or suburban area—let's go to it." She took business in college, moved to New York City, and took a job with Xerox. She loved the city, but when a family member passed away a few years later she got to thinking about her priorities and, before she knew it, found herself back on Southport, tending traps from Joe's Gut in a little eighteen-foot boat. "Fishing just kind of found me again and I gave in to it."

Ten years later, Jennifer has worked her way up to *Pat's Girl*, a modern thirty-two-foot fiberglass lobster boat that her husband, a professional builder, assembled in their backyard. *Pat's Girl* is a far cry from the open dories and working sloops of the late nineteenth century. Like most Maine lobster boats, she retains the high bow and wide, stable stern of the Reach Boat—a fast, tough open workboat built by Downeast Maine fishermen in the late nineteenth century. Reach Boats were originally driven by a small square sail but were easily converted to engine power when that technology appeared in the early twentieth century. Wilton Frost and Harold Gower, two innovative Nova Scotian boatbuilders living in Jonesport in the 1910s, introduced many trademarks of the modern lobster boat, including the wooden shelter amidships. In subsequent years, the lobster boat grew bigger, and its hull has changed from wood to fiberglass. Its engines grew larger and more reliable, and were adapted to drive ever-better powered trap haulers, while the wheelhouse gathered an array of electronics: radios, radar, fish-finding sonar, and satellite positioning systems. All of this apparatus allowed lobstermen to fish more traps, farther from home, in worse weather conditions and greater safety and comfort than their grandparents and great-grandparents would have imagined possible.

It's a good thing too, because as Jennifer and I set out and start hauling traps, the wind starts really picking up, and the mouth of the Sheepscot is soon covered in angry little whitecaps. Jennifer usually fishes alone, but on this day I am acting as a novice sternman, impaling ripe, squishy herring on the skewerlike baiting needles as we run between her brightly colored pot buoys. Things go fine for the first hour or so: I have never gotten seasick, even when on a ship battered for three days straight by sixty-mile-an-hour winds and forty-foot seas in Antarctica's notorious Drake Passage. But as we pass outside Lower Mark Island—once home to an island hermit, but now denuded of trees by the acidlike feces of its enormous cormorant population— *Pat's Girl* starts rolling pretty hard every time we slow down to pick up a trap. Something in the rank odor of the putrid herring seems to be crawling slowly into the back of my throat and settling there, poking sadistically at my gag spot. Holding my breath helps for a little while, but it must be giving my skin a shade of green, because pretty soon Jennifer suggests I get some fresh air outside the shelter and let her bait the needles for a little while.

As Jennifer approachs her next trap buoy, she throttles down *Pat's Girl* so that we coast right alongside, within range of her boathook. With a quick jab under the base of the buoy, she hooks the trap line and pulls it in. In a quick series of movements, she runs the line through a pulley that hangs over the water and back down onto the wheel of the powered trap hauler and sets the buoy on the deck. With the flick of a control, the hauler whines to life, quickly hauling in the cold, dripping trap line—or warp—and coiling it neatly on the deck near Jennifer's feet. A few moments later, the first trap breaks the surface. Jennifer stops the hauler and pulls the trap over and onto the starboard rail, the counterlike lip on the right side of the boat where she tends her traps. Even after hauling more than a hundred traps, I felt a rush of excitement each time a trap came up, wondering what the sea had left inside. Many lobstermen I've talked to say they still enjoy that moment of expectation, day after day, season after season, as they open their presents from the deep.

Several crabs are clinging to the walls and ceiling of the trap. A couple of tiny, half-pound juvenile lobsters sit in the "kitchen," the first of the trap's two chambers, looking perplexed at their sudden, waterless predicament. A green urchin and a pair of larger lobsters sit in the second chamber, or parlor. The big access door on top of the modern traps can be opened in a flash—they are kept shut by the marine equivalent of a bungee cord—but Jennifer wires hers shut. If she didn't, Jennifer says, the area's plentiful seals might open the traps and happily consume their contents, which doesn't do much for her bottom line. On other parts of the coast, lobstermen even tie their traps shut with their own distinctive knots so they can know if another person has been raiding them. Jennifer pops the door open and gently tosses the juveniles back over the side. One of them looks quite surprised at what is probably his first flying experience, his long antennae standing erect in the air, searching for answers before splashing into the sea. She puts each of the larger ones in a long wooden tray in the wheelhouse to be measured later, on the way to the next trap. Meanwhile, I detach the old bait bag, shake the remaining herring goo over the side, and use the baiting needle to replace it with one of our freshly loaded nylon bags. Then I struggle with the stubborn rock crabs, slowly prying them from the wire mesh walls of the trap. I haven't mastered the proper technique, which is to whip them off quickly like an old Band-Aid. Nine out of ten times, the crab is flicked off and over the side unharmed. But sometimes they leave a claw behind, clamped to the trap wall, which the crab will have to regenerate in its next molt.

While I fight with the crabs, Jennifer has turned the trap hauler on again, which starts pulling up the second trap. Here in the mouth of the Sheepscot, lobstermen fish traps in pairs—two traps strung together on the same buoy line—because strong tides make longer strings impractical. In other areas, lobstermen may fish only a single trap per buoy or, alternately, in strings of three to six traps, with a buoy on each end of the string. One deepwater lobstering operation out of New Hampshire fishes in federal waters using strings of a dozen or more traps, but that's illegal in Maine waters, which extend to three miles from its shores. Different types of nylon line have made longer strings more practical. Generally the warp connecting the buoy to the first trap (and the second buoy to the last trap in longer strings) is made of a heavy nylon that sinks in water, keeping it from getting hung up in propellers and other surface obstructions. But the warp connecting the traps to one another is usually buoyant, floating above the bottom to keep it from getting hung up on rocks. Sometimes when both trap buoys have been lost to propellers or other surface challenges, lobstermen have been able to salvage their traps by dragging a grappling hook over the bottom and catching the floating loop of line between traps—an impossible operation in the days of tarred cotton lines.

I close the freshly baited trap and push it a little farther down the rail as Jennifer swings the second trap down next to it. There's another two or three rock crabs clinging to the mesh, and two undersized lobsters huddling in the corners. They all go back in the water to live another day, stomachs stuffed with herring at Jennifer's expense. (Do they pull this scam off every week?) But in the parlor there's a nice pound-and-a-half female, and when we turn her over we see that she's carrying thousands of tiny eggs on the underside of her tail. "Berried female," Jennifer says as she inspects the lobster's tail fins for a V-notch mark. This one hasn't been caught before, which is unusual. More than 70 percent of all egg-bearing lobsters caught in Maine waters already have a V-notch, according to catch survey data collected by Maine lobstermen that is currently being compiled by Carl Wilson at the Department of Marine Resources lab in Boothbay Harbor. (Carl, DMR's chief lobster scientist, is the son of fisheries scientist Jim Wilson and was Bob Steneck's student; yes, Maine is a small state.) Some Maine lobstermen voluntarily V-notch unberried females as well, further increasing the breeding supply that supports their fishery. Sifting through the survey data, Wilson has found that approximately 35 percent of all legal-sized females that are caught by Maine lobstermen are thrown back. Scientists long pooh-poohed Maine lobstermen's enthusiasm for V-notching, arguing that it made little difference, but not anymore. "We're always talking about management failures with just about every fishery out there," Carl says. "Maybe this is something that works." In any case, Jennifer is V-notching this one. Using a special paper punch–like tool provided by DMR, she clips a small nick in one of the berried lobster's back tail fins and gently returns her to the water. Because the V-notch is still detectable after one or two molts, this female will never wind up on the dinner table if she sticks to Maine waters. Unfortunately, lobstermen in other states and out in federal waters do not V-notch, though there's increasing pressure to do so. Nor do most states have a maximum size law, which Maine lobstermen believe protects an uncatchable stock of big breeders lurking, undetected, out on the bottoms of the Gulf of Maine.

The traps are both rebaited and closed and Jennifer circles the boat around to the right location and prepares to let them go. This is done by simply dropping one of the traps from the moving boat, usually while moving at full speed toward the next trap buoy. The sinking trap rapidly plays the line out from the coil near Jennifer's feet, pulls the second trap down the length of the rail and over the side of the stern, then the rest of the line, and, finally, the buoy. That fast-moving rope is one of the most dangerous hazards lobstermen face. If you catch your foot in the rope or the rapidly unwinding coil, you could be whisked right overboard and down to the sea bottom as your lobster boat rushes off at full speed. I catch myself getting too close to the outgoing line on more than one occasion that day, and even experienced lobstermen admit to having a close call once or twice a season. Most lobster boats have a shut-off switch for the engine located back at the stern, so that its outgoing owner might have a chance to stop the boat while being dragged over the side. Jennifer also has a dive knife attached to her foul weather gear, just in case. "It's another chance," she says.

Astern, the pair of lobster traps had vanished beneath the sea, leaving only a buoy to mark their existence.

⌒⌒⌒⌒

Until very recently, nobody really knew what happened in and around lobster traps while they "soaked" on the bottom. Scientists and lobstermen generally assumed that the traps were pretty effective snares. During the few days between hauls, a handful of lobsters were thought to enter the traps through their funnel-shaped opening to dine on the bait inside the first chamber, or kitchen. After stuffing themselves, they were thought to have great difficulty finding their way back out through the narrow end of the funnel. Befuddled, many lobsters were presumably fooled into climbing through the second funnel to the parlor, the dead-end second compartment. Small lobsters could get out of the parlor through special escape vents, but legal-sized ones had little hope of finding their way out of the trap.

As it turns out, just about all of these 150-year-old assumptions are completely wrong, and Win Watson of the University of New Hampshire has the videotape to prove it.

Like many lobster scientists, Watson wondered why state and federal stock assessments had gotten the lobster stock so wrong. He suspected that part of the problem lay with the surveys themselves. The National Marine Fisheries Service takes the pulse of the lobster population in two ways. One is by trawling the bottom and counting how many lobsters show up in the nets, along with cod and haddock and other commercial species they need to assess. Problem is, when trawling one tends to avoid the very rocky habitats lobsters thrive on, for fear of tearing the net; burrowed lobsters may avoid being caught altogether. The other method was much better: go out with the lobstermen and see what they actually catch in their traps. But nobody knew anything about the relationship between the number of lobsters caught in a trap and the density of lobsters on the bottom. Without that information, stock assessment models would remain little better than guesswork, so Watson put on his dive gear and set out to find some answers. Instead, he found himself with a host of new questions.

Watson and his students took a straightforward approach: they dove down, carefully surveyed a section of relatively sandy bottom, and counted all the lobsters living there. Then they dropped a trap down, let it soak for a day or more, and hauled it up to see how many came inside. Presumably, the more lobsters were on the bottom, the more they would find in their trap. But wherever Watson went, he caught the same amount of lobsters. "We'd dive in one area and wouldn't see any lobsters and we'd catch three or four lobsters in each trap," he recalled. "Then we'd go somewhere with a lot of lobsters and we'd still catch three or four lobsters in each trap." They closed the escape vents on the traps and got similar results, except there would be fifteen or twenty lobsters in each trap instead of three or four. "So we wanted to know why there was this disconnect, why the traps weren't collecting lobsters in proportion to their density."

To solve this mystery once and for all, Watson attached an underwater video camera to a standard trap and dropped it down to the sandy seafloor off Portsmouth, New Hampshire. Given that hauled traps in the area usually contained only a handful of lobsters, he expected the tape would show a modest number of the animals approaching the trap.

But when Watson's team hauled the trap and looked at the first time-lapse video they were totally stunned by what they saw. "The numbers of lobsters were just amazing," Watson recalls, with lobsters scuffling and fighting over the trap, often within a few minutes of its arrival on the bottom. "It looked like an anthill."

Day or night, the trap attracted a huge crowd of hungry lobsters and crabs, though the latter were often put in their place by the bullying lobsters.

But the biggest surprise was that the lobsters were happily wandering in and out of the traps at will. On the video, lobsters of all sizes crawled in and out of the funnel-shaped entrance as they pleased. In test after test, only 6 percent of the lobsters that entered the trap failed to find their way out again. Ninety-four percent marched out through the entrance or escape vents, their stomachs filled with UNH herring. The biggest impediment they faced wasn't the trap, but the other lobsters, who did their best to chase newcomers away from the bait. "Outside the lobster trap you can see them chasing each other away. It's nonstop," Watson says. "A lobster enters and chases others away until a bigger one comes and chases him away. So at any given moment if there's somebody in the kitchen, no one else can enter easily until it finishes eating and leaves. So it's sort of like trying to catch guys in a men's room where you only have one stall."

Legal-sized lobsters that wound up in the rear chamber or parlor did have more difficulty finding their way out again, but very few lobsters made that mistake voluntarily. "The ones that go into the parlor tend to go there accidentally," Watson says. "They get scared by something, do a sudden tail-flip or something and end up in the parlor."

So what really determines the catch in a given trap? When I last spoke to him, Watson was working on what he calls the "restaurant hypothesis." "You pull up the restaurant and you catch whoever happens to be in there at the time," he suggests. If that is even half-true, it would explain why stock assessment models are so far off. But whatever is going on, it's clear that the lobster traps may be doing the animals more good than harm. One of the reasons the lobster resource is so healthy may be that Maine lobstermen are, in effect, ranching lobsters: raising them at feeding stations and occasionally harvesting some of the herd. If so, traps are only part of the answer. Canadian lobster populations thrive all summer despite the fact that there are no traps in the water from June to November, when the shedders are most ravenous. The traps—in conjunction with V-notching, size restrictions, and oceanography—are just one part of what appears to be a truly sustainable fishery.

Lobstermen who have seen Watson's video often react with a combination of surprise and amusement. "It's pretty discouraging to think that here we as intelligent human beings have been trying our best to harvest this thing that has no brain to speak of and they're outsmarting us," says Pat White of York, chief executive officer of the Maine Lobstermen's Association. "But it may be that part of the success of our fishery is due to the fact that our traps are as inefficient as they are."

The last trap hauled, Jennifer points *Pat's Girl* toward Georgetown Island, a large, automobile-accessible island lying opposite Southport on the far side of the Sheepscot River. Jennifer measures the potential keepers, and I finish putting rubber bands on their claws with the help of a clever metal banding tool. Some of the lobsters put up a fight, flailing their claws around, but most seem resigned to capture. We put the newly banded lobsters into a large metal holding tank through which water circulates—a half-dozen hardshells on one side, a small army of shedders on the other. The tank's holding somewhere between one and two hundred lobsters by now, easily enough to fill a typical bathtub to the rim.

We pull into Five Islands, a small hamlet and summer colony near Georgetown's southern end, and make for the lobster dock or "buying station." This one is on a float attached to a retail lobster wharf. Dozens of customers eat their lobster lunches on outdoor picnic tables and admire the stunning view of the harbor, its five little islands, and the mouth of the Sheepscot. Jennifer sells her lobsters here because it's one of the closest buying stations to her mooring, just a mile across the water on Southport. Few landbound Southport residents ever visit Five Islands; it's a seventy-minute, forty-mile drive each way by automobile. But Jennifer sees Georgetown lobstermen on the water every day—they're her neighbors—and they lobster side by side in many parts of the river. She shops and socializes in Boothbay Harbor, but knows very little about the lobstering scene there, or even that on the other side of Southport, which is foreign lobstering territory and, in any case, relatively inconvenient to visit by water.

After a short wait for the lobster boat in front of us, we pull in and unload Jennifer's catch. The buyers at the dock weigh the lobsters while carrying on a lively banter with Jennifer, who orders some tubs of bait. Jennifer has kept track of the catch throughout the day, making cryptic marks in a little notebook in the wheelhouse—it's hard to play the scales with lobstermen. The buyer tallies up the hardshells and softshells separately, taps on a calculator and announces the final price. With a nod, the lobsters are on their way up the gangway toward the lobster shack. Some of them will be in the bellies of vacationers before sunset. The softest softshells—the ones that feel almost leathery to the touch—won't keep well and will probably be steamed and picked for lobster roll meat later that day. A couple are on the way home with me, to be wolfed down with drawn butter and a side of freshly steamed mussels from the seafood market.

While many of Jennifer's lobsters are consumed locally, these days that is hardly the norm. Once lobsters are landed at the dock, they have joined a massive, global distribution system that links lobstermen on Southport or Monhegan with consumers in New York, Los Angeles, Brussels, or Tokyo.

A fair number of Maine's lobsters wind up on Sprucehead Island, the road-accessible island south of Rockland where William Atwood runs the state's largest live lobster shipping operation. Six million pounds of lobster pass through Atwood's holding pools each year, en route from the dock to restaurants, supermarket chains, and seafood markets across the country and both oceans. "It's a lot of lobster," says Atwood, a bearded ex-Marine with an easy laugh, standing in the middle of his cavernous lobster warehouse. Most of the floor space is flooded knee-deep in refrigerated seawater in which hundreds of plastic bins are submerged, each filled with lobsters of a given size and condition. Several guys are wandering around the holding pool in rubber hip-waders, moving bins around the pool or pushing them through an opening into the adjacent packing chamber, which is similarly flooded. The building can hold a quarter million pounds of live lobsters at any one time, but it isn't meant to house them for very long. "We really don't want to keep a lobster more than a week if we can help it," he says. "We're strictly volume and we've got to keep them moving."

And move they do. In the packing chamber, employees pack live lobsters in 25- to 50-pound boxes and stack them, wrapped in insulating foil, in big 2,500-pound metal air cargo containers called LD-3s. Trucks trundle in and out of the parking lot outside, bringing new, unsorted lobsters in from buying stations all along the Midcoast and carrying the LD-3s off to airports in Boston, New York, and Newark. Sometimes they are flown out of Bangor, the only Maine airport capable of handling the wide-bodied aircraft that carry LD-3s. Smaller lobster orders are packed in special FedEx shipping cartons and whisked away by their drivers each afternoon. It's July, so the shedders are in and many are too soft to make long-distance journeys. These get steamed in a huge stainless steel vat and are picked for their meat at an incredible speed by a team of expert pickers. Atwood has shipped orders as large as 80,000 pounds all at once in a single aircraft. When the Safeway supermarket chain decided to do a live lobster promotion on the West Coast a few years ago, Atwood and other lobster dealers got together to charter an entire 747 freighter to fly a quarter million pounds across the country all at once. "Even using all the scheduled planes going out there, there was no way to move that many," he says. At Christmas, dealers often have to charter airlift capacity to get live lobsters to Europe, where Maine lobster has become a Parisian holiday tradition. When Hong Kong was returned to China in 1997, 4,000 pounds of Atwood lobster graced the official banquet tables.

Bill Atwood's family has been moving lobsters for three generations, possibly longer. His ancestors lived on Cape Cod until the eighteenth century, when they joined the migration to the fishing grounds
of Cape Sable, Nova Scotia. His grandfather took the family back to
Massachusetts, where he worked for one of the big Boston lobster
companies, and his father built his own lobster business there. As a
child Bill played in the plant amid a throng of workers packing lobsters into wooden barrels that were shipped out by rail. After a devastating fire in the early 1950s, Bill's family moved their operations to
Midcoast Maine, and as soon as Bill got his driver's license he was off
driving trucks of lobster in from Canada or down to market in Boston.
By the time he started his own business on Sprucehead in 1962, more
and more lobsters were leaving New England by aircraft. The first experiments were shaky. According to family legend my grandfather was
involved in one of the pioneering flights in an army surplus DC-3. En
route to California the plane encountered heavy weather, the shipping
barrels poured open, and the cockpit was breached by several angry
hardshells. Other pioneers watched their aircraft deteriorate as dripping saltwater corroded the frames. But now the airlines have gotten
the system down, and neither lobsters nor their salty drippings escape
from their packaging.

Lobstermen often say that the middlemen are the only people who
really make any money in their industry. While there's clearly money
to be made moving lobsters, it's not an undertaking for the faint of
heart. There are enormous risks and uncertainties in moving a live,
wild-caught, highly perishable product over great distances. From the
time they are purchased at the dock, the lobsters start losing weight
through excretion of water or, if they are not fed copiously, loss of tis-
sue. Bill Atwood sees his lobsters lose 2 percent of their weight just in
the time it takes to move them to the holding tanks from his buying
station across the street. "Every time we buy a hundred pounds of lobster we only ship ninety-eight, at best," he says. "That's a hidden cost
that drives you crazy." In the middle of the summer he can only ship
half the lobsters he buys from lobstermen; the other half, too soft to
survive shipment, are boiled and picked for meat, but that's much less
profitable than selling the live animal. Atwood doesn't keep his lobsters long, but many dealers do, maintaining enormous holding

pounds, which they fill with cheap lobsters during the fall glut, hoping to sell them in the winter when the price rises. A lobster pound might hold 100,000 pounds of lobster—one on Deer Island, New Brunswick, holds well over a million—which can yield a tidy profit if everything goes smoothly. But all sorts of things can go wrong. There are diseases that can wipe out an entire pound stock, as can an especially deep winter freeze. As time passes, more and more lobsters may die from natural causes or the stress of pound life, and some may even be stolen by thieves, human or otherwise. Even if all the lobsters survive, profits are unpredictable. When a large pound unloads its stock, the price can fall precipitously. Some Canadian pound owners have even switched to using special indoor holding facilities, where lobsters can be stored in a state of semi-hibernation in near-freezing water for as long as six months, spreading out the winter supply, and so keeping prices and profits low for pound owners of all sorts.

Then there's shipping. A canceled flight or serious truck breakdown can spell disaster for a lobster shipment, because even refrigerated lobsters can't last more than two or three days in their light shipping boxes. Major disruptions to air traffic can result in enormous losses. Live lobster shipments were banned for a few days in advance of the 1981 air traffic controllers' strike because the airlines didn't want to be liable for strike-related shipping losses. Unable to get his product to the West Coast, one small Rockport dealer reported losing $75,000 in orders. Two thousand pounds of Atwood lobster were destroyed on September 11, 2001, when the Los Angeles–bound 757 they were aboard struck the World Trade Towers. Tens of thousands of American lobsters spoiled in shipping containers that were stranded at airports across the country during the ensuing air traffic shutdown. Prices remained depressed for months afterward, triggering substantial losses for winter lobstermen and conventional pound owners alike.

But, crises aside, lobster demand has grown at least as fast as the catch itself. Maine's overseas exports of lobsters grew by 65 percent in the last five years of the twentieth century. The European Union market for U.S. lobster doubled to $250 million annually between 1995 and 2000, with Italians leading the way both in growth and total consumption. Spanish demand more than doubled over the same period as chefs discovered its utility in making top-notch paella. Nova

Scotians—the only people who catch more American lobsters than Mainers do—saw live exports jump by over 40 percent in just three years in the early 1990s. Before the 1997 Asian financial meltdown, Nova Scotians alone were flying more than half a million pounds of live lobsters to South Korea every year, and over 1.7 million pounds to Hong Kong, many of them originally caught by Maine lobstermen. *Homarus americanus* is the most valuable fishery in all of Canada, and the third in the United States. The lobster business has clearly come a long way since the days when lobsters were used as garden manure.

But lobstering presents a peculiar paradox. The marketing and distribution of lobster—like many seafood products—is a high-tech, capital-intensive industry operating on a global scale. But, strangely enough, the actual harvesting of lobster is still undertaken not by corporate conglomerates with large, industrial-scale vessels, but by a diffuse fleet of tiny boats, each owned and operated by independent, self-employed individuals. Lobstering, unlike shrimping, groundfishing, or, say, Bering Strait crabbing, is essentially an artisanal enterprise, a peculiar anachronism in early-twenty-first-century America. People are so accustomed to the image of the independent lobsterman and his boat, they rarely ask themselves how it is that such a lucrative, globalized fishery has not consolidated under external control. Indeed, would the lobster fishery be so successful, so wonderfully sustainable, if lobsters were being harvested by wage employees of some subsidiary of Unilever, Nestlé, or Tyson's Foods? It's a situation that runs counter to the logic of laissez-faire capitalism—the triumph of the small and "inefficient." But it also flies in the face of a four-century-old theory of natural resource conservation that argues that the sea and its creatures must be, in effect, privately owned if they are to be protected. Indeed, Maine lobstermen are clearly participating not in a "tragedy of the commons," but a triumph.

⌒⤳

In 1968, a biologist named Garrett Hardin published an article in the journal *Science* that transformed the way many experts think about the management of fishing banks, public forests, the open range, and other common property. Imagine, Hardin asked, a village commons, a pasture where anyone in the community is free to graze their animals.

The arrangement, he argued, is doomed to tragedy. Each herdsman, "as a rational being," will pursue his own self-interest by putting as many animals as possible on the commons. While this arrangement may work "for centuries," he argued, eventually a time will come when "tribal wars, poaching, and disease" no longer keep "the numbers of both man and beast . . . below the carrying capacity of the land." Then the villagers, "locked into a system that compels [each] to increase his herd without limit," will overgraze the land, destroying the resource for all. Indeed, this very "tragedy of the commons" had already played out on public ranges of the American West (where ranchers knowingly overgrazed land to maximize short-term profit), Yosemite National Park (a public resource which even then was being loved to death by overwhelming numbers of visitors), and the fishing banks of New England and Atlantic Canada, then being devastated by factory-freezer trawlers. The commons, Hardin argued, must be closed for the good of all.

Curiously, the intellectual origins of Hardin's argument trace back to the seventeenth-century English philosopher Thomas Hobbes, a man whose ideas helped drive some peasants out of the English countryside and onto the coast of Maine. Having lived through the anarchy of the English Civil War, Hobbes concluded that men were selfish beings who would destroy one another in pursuit of their own interests unless kept in check by some sort of coercive authority: a landowner, dictator, or king, for instance. Such notions fit nicely into the political agendas of many would-be capitalists, including feudal landlords who wished to seize control of their serfs' commonly held pastures and farms. While Hobbes served the Earls of Devon in the early 1600s, many Devonshire peasants were driven from their ancestral farms to make way for large, privately held sheep farms. A large proportion of Maine's settlers in this period came from Devon and other counties where this so-called enclosure movement was in full swing.

But for all of the strengths of their arguments, both Hardin and Hobbes shortchanged the commons themselves. England's village commons worked remarkably well for more than six centuries preceding their seizure by the landowning class, providing farmers with grain, meat, milk, and wool while avoiding ecological tragedy. They succeeded because, contrary to Hobbes's assumptions, the local community cooperated to regulate the use of their commonly held resource. Through informal customs or formal councils, villagers made and enforced collective decisions about everything from the number of animals on the pastures to the sharing of local water supplies, the timing and sequence of crop rotations, the correct time to plant or harvest, and even the use of local woodlots. Overgrazing did become a major problem on English pastures, but only after they were privatized to form large-scale sheep farms. Even today, traditional village institutions continue to successfully manage community-owned meadows and forests from the Swiss Alps to the mountains of interior Japan. In fact, since Hardin wrote his article, researchers have discovered scores of successful community-managed property arrangements, from the jungles of India and Southeast Asia to the submerged coral reefs surrounding the tiny islands of the Central Pacific. It turns out that in some situations, the "village" way of doing things works a whole lot better than either privatization or draconian government intervention.

Which brings us back to Maine. Unbeknownst to most lobstermen, the Maine lobster fishery has become the source of great excitement and revelation for many of the world's leading property theorists. The traditional system by which Maine and Maritimes lobstermen have long managed their fishery has literally become a textbook example of how communities successfully protect and defend the resources they depend upon. In the midst of the world's ongoing fisheries crisis, many political economists have begun to agree with what Maine's lobstermen have been saying all along: let us manage this ourselves, we know what we're doing. It's even changing the way the "experts" and so the officials at places like the World Bank, the U.S. Agency for International Development, or the European Union think about local ways of resource management. And if this Downeast way of doing things winds up saving some African village from destruction at the hands of some wrongheaded World Bank program, the villagers will have a humble, hands-on University of Maine anthropologist to thank for it.

As a doctoral student in the 1960s, James Acheson was focused on Mexico, studying the way of life in a furniture-making town in Tabasco. But after finishing his degree, Acheson turned back to his northern New England roots. While his fellow anthropologists were out documenting the way people live, work, and war in East Africa, the South Pacific, or the Amazon Basin, Acheson focused his research on his home state of Maine. For more than three decades, he's been researching and writing about the social structure of Maine's lobstering communities from Bailey's Island to Brooksville. His 1988 book, *The Lobster Gangs of Maine*, shed light on the way lobstermen manage each other, enlightening many state officials, federal fisheries managers, and other outsiders. "The whole theory of common property resources like lobster assumes they're bound to be over-exploited," he says. "That's nonsense."

In theory, up until the late 1980s, any Maine resident could buy a state lobster license, some traps, and a boat and head out lobstering. But, as many would-be lobstermen have discovered over the years, this approach doesn't work in practice. Truth is, much of the coast's "lobster bottom" is divided into informal territories, each of which is controlled and defended by the lobstermen of one or more nearby harbors. Through custom, peer pressure, and the occasional extralegal act, the lobstermen of each harbor have long conserved their lobstering turf; they determine who fishes it and, to a certain extent, by what means. In most places, the members of each harbor gang largely police themselves. Violations of conservation laws like the taking of undersized, oversized, or egg-bearing lobsters aren't tolerated, as they are seen to jeopardize the future of the shared lobster resource. As most lobstermen live in the same town, send their kids to the same school, and rely on one another in emergencies, social sanctions can be more effective than a dozen wardens. They also keep nonmembers from lobstering their turf. An intruder may go out to haul his traps, only to find they've been emptied beforehand, or that their buoys are missing altogether. Thousands of dollars' worth of his traps can vanish in the first "killer fog." It usually doesn't take long for the uninvited newcomer to give up or try his luck elsewhere.

If somebody wants to take up lobstering, they first have to gain the acceptance of local lobstermen. Until recently, this process was informal and was generally based on the personal characteristics of the applicant. Acheson found that things went smoothest if the applicant was the child of one of the harbor's lobstermen, although most local teens were accepted without much resistance, even if their parents had moved to town from away. An adult outsider, on the other hand, was likely to meet stiff resistance, particularly if he or she had another form of income or planned to engage in part-time fishing. "In the eyes of most local people, such a man is a 'hog' and can never be accepted into the gang," Acheson wrote. Lobstermen in one of the harbors he studied related how a man from New Jersey with another form of income showed up with a huge number of traps and "plenty of unwanted advice" for local lobstermen. "He lasted approximately two weeks in the fishing business," Acheson learned. "Eventually he was forced to leave town."

Of course, all sorts of outsiders do take up lobstering. Witness Monhegan, where the majority of lobstermen were born out of state. For such people, success often depends on being someone the established fishermen know, like, and respect. Take Jean Symonds, who has been lobstering out of Corea for more than thirty years. When Jean first came to this no-nonsense Downeast fishing hamlet in 1970, she was a very unlikely applicant. She was a woman in her mid-thirties, Massachusetts-born, and newly arrived from Washington, D.C., with no ties to fishing in Corea or anyplace else for that matter. She and her partner, Dorothy Kemske, a retired army colonel, had just bought property on the harbor and had opened a grocery store at the base of one of the fishing piers. But when Jean expressed an interest in trying lobstering, her neighbor, Clifford Young, gave her some wooden traps. "I'd never been on the water and I didn't even know how to rig a trap," she laughs. But local kids showed her how, and she was soon tending her traps from a small rowboat and loving it. Her traps were never harassed, even as she graduated to larger boats, though one time she opened her trap to find an enormous lobster inside with rubber gloves on its claws. "Nobody ever did anything but help or made any issue at all," she says. "I don't know why they were so good to me." But other residents point to her considerable generosity and commitment to the community, which includes arrangements for her wharf to remain in the hands of fishermen, not cottagers, after her death.

Once accepted into the community, a lobsterman gains the right to fish within the territory it controls. Most harbors have a swath of exclusive territory close to home from which they repel any trespassers, plus areas shared with neighboring harbors, from which third parties are excluded. Lines are distinct, marked by geographical features like points, islands, or channel markers, and by GPS coordinates farther from shore. "You know when you cross a certain line and if you don't know, you will know," says Harvey Crowley of Corea, longtime head of the Downeast Lobsterman's Association. "There'll be nothing verbal, but somehow or another they're going to let you know." Methods of discouraging trespassers vary from harbor to harbor, but typically a first-time offender will find a couple of half-hitches tied around the spindles of his misplaced trap buoys as a warning. This then escalates to emptying the traps of lobsters and leaving the doors open or replacing the crustaceans with a threatening note or some other scarecrows. If the interloper still doesn't take the hint, he may find his buoys missing altogether, which often means that he can't retrieve his expensive traps from the bottom. Shafmaster, the New Hampshire–based offshore lobstering company, has regularly found itself the target of angry competitors, particularly when it has tried to drop its massive, forty-trap strings in federal waters close to Maine fishing grounds. In 1988, Shafmaster reported that some enterprising lobstermen had dragged one of its mile-long strings of traps all the way across the Canadian border, where they were seized by fishery agents. The company's manager had to travel all the way to Halifax to claim the gear.

Usually lines between harbors are respected, but sometimes one harbor will decide to push the line or annex a piece of territory from a neighbor. Sometimes the weaker harbor will give up, such as when Matinicus, weakened by the World War II draft, ceded its Seal Island grounds to competitors from Vinalhaven. One way or another, matters usually get settled without involving the marine patrol or mainland police. After all, both sides in a dispute know that if things escalate into a trap-cutting free-for-all, everyone involved will wind up a loser. Given the number of lobstermen and harbors out there, the territories system has kept the peace remarkably well.

But every once in a while—perhaps once in a decade—things do get out of hand and a full-scale lobster war will erupt between harbors. Old-timers recall widespread wars around the offshore islands of Penobscot Bay in the 1930s and 1940s in which hundreds of traps were destroyed, fishing docks were burned to the ground, and a few fishermen shot. In the early 1950s, a major dispute broke out between the lobstermen of Matinicus and those of Criehaven, which sit next to each other in a remote archipelago twenty miles out to sea. "My Lord, those guys on Criehaven were shooting over the heads of any people from outside their island who tried to put traps there," recalls attorney Stanley Tupper of Boothbay Harbor, who was Maine's fisheries commissioner at the time. "Finally I had one of my wardens come back telling me he had to get way down in his boat because the bullets were coming so close to his windshield. . . . They played rough in those days." In the early 1980s the federal government had to step in to quell a massive border war between Maine and New Hampshire lobstermen. The action, sparked by a black market trade in lobsters too small to land in Maine, but legal in New Hampshire, eventually led to a Supreme Court decision pertaining to the shared border. Monhegan and Friendship have been antagonists for as long as anyone can remember, with a number of skirmishes and small-scale cutting wars over the years.

On the whole, most lobstermen say they get along just fine with their counterparts from neighboring harbors. For some the central nemesis isn't their fellow lobstermen, but the scientists and government regulators with their regulations and endless talk of a lobster crash that never comes. "Scientists! If we were wrong as often as they are they'd shoot us," says Colby Young, a Corea lobsterman and co-owner of the famous Young Brothers boatyard and a man who doesn't mince words. "I've been dealing with them now since 1959 and they haven't gotten any farther then telling you the temperature of the water—and the Coast Guard can tell you that. They don't have a clue, they just keep guessing and we pay for it!" Sometimes fishermen lose their patience, taking lobster-war tactics ashore. In 1975, after explaining a new fisheries bill to a group of Vinalhaven lobstermen, fisheries economist Jim Wilson was escorted off the island at gunpoint by two angry fishermen. "I saw the boat that was picking me up to go to North Haven and got out of the truck and started walking down this long spindle pier, two planks wide, leading over the mudflats," he recalls. "Soon as I did, these two guys who'd been following me jumped out of their truck, pulled out their rifles, and started walking down to the pier behind me." No shots were fired and Wilson lived to speak to North Haven's displeased fishermen later that day.

⟡

In Boothbay Harbor, territorial defense can extend all the way to the Lobstermen's Co-Op parking lot, as I learned the morning I went out lobstering with David Norton, one of the Co-Op's founding members.

Following David's instructions, I'd driven down to town shortly after dawn and pulled into the gravel lot across the street from the Co-Op pier. As I was pulling on my boots and gathering my work gloves and lunch pail, a fisherman arrived in the lot and parked his pickup next to me. He hopped out of the truck and received my greeting with the cool facial set of a state trooper who's about to ask for your license and registration. "You fishin' today?" he said, more of a challenge than a question. I affirmed that I was going out with someone. "Oh, yeah? Who with?" he said, glowering grimly. But at the mention of David's name a magical thing happened, so fast I think my jaw may have dropped. The man's face transformed in an instant, as if a mask had suddenly been torn off, revealing a warm, smiling grandfather with twinkling eyes. "Oh, David, he's a great guy!" he exclaimed, clapping me on the back. "Come with me!" He led me past a huge truck offloading tubs of bait and down to the lobstermen's wharf, perched over the harbor amid the still-slumbering waterfront hotels. Still smiling ear to ear, he introduced me to a couple of other fishermen. "This fella's goin' out with David," he said. We shook hands warmly and somebody pointed out the whereabouts of the nearest coffeepot. As I chatted about the weather and what-not with the coffeepot crowd, I noticed the older fellow was wandering ahead of me down the dock, greeting the other men in turn before pointing me out to them with the words: "He's goin' out with David." I wondered if my reception would have been different if I were going out with a less popular lobsterman, or if I'd turned out to be an auditor from the Internal Revenue Service. I looked down over the rail: yes, the water was definitely over my head.

David Norton pulled up to the float a few minutes later in *Suzanne B.*, his thirty-two-foot lobster boat. I quickly learned that David is one of the nicest people you're likely to meet, which may be part of the reason everyone on the dock was so welcoming. I helped Mike, his sternman, load the boat with tubs of putrid menhaden and redfish "racks," what's left of a redfish after a machine has removed the boneless fillets. As we cast off, Mike started making shish kebabs, mixing menhaden and redfish as he stuck them on the needles. In less than a minute David's already picked up his first buoy and started hauling. We're so close to the float that he's able to continue a conversation with one of the guys on the pier while he pulls up his first string of traps. The atmosphere is completely different from Monhegan or West Southport, where you get the sense you're fishing along the Atlantic frontier. For the first half hour or so we creep quietly along in the crowded harbor, plucking strings of the traps hidden between million-dollar yachts. A dozen other lobster boats are doing the same, their running lights prominent against the early-morning light. Even as we work our way out of the inner harbor and into more open water on the east side of Southport, it feels like we're fishing on the village commons. Other lobster boats are always nearby, often within shouting distance. The marine radio, set to the Boothbay Harbor gang's channel, chatters constantly as the lobstermen spar and joke with one another. Occasionally somebody forces the fleet to listen to their favorite music by holding their microphone against their stereo's speaker for a minute or more. The windows of a thousand summer cottages look on from every shore. As the day progresses, crowded excursion boats pass close by from time to time, a hundred tourists gawking at whatever David and Mike are doing. In summer, Boothbay Harbor lobstermen don't have much privacy, even on the water.

The pace is different too. When I'd been out with Jennifer Elderkin and John Murdock, they were generally fishing pairs, hauling and rebaiting two traps for each buoy they picked up. But in the Boothbay area, lobstermen generally fish strings of six traps, and in the summer shedding season the buoys are often fairly close to one another, so there's almost no pause from one string to the next. David swings one trap after another onto the starboard rail and has just about enough time to open it, remove the lobsters, and push it down to Mike for rebaiting by the time the next one pops above the surface. As Mike rebaits the traps with fishy shish kebabs, he puts the readied traps on the stern fantail. When it's time to set them he pushes one over as David runs to the next buoy. The weighted trap plays out the line and pulls its fellow string mates over the rail one by one. By the time the buoy hits the water with a splash, we're nearly to the next string. The pace is almost industrial: David and Mike process their traps with assembly-line intensity, filling the storage tanks with softshells at a remarkable pace.

David Norton comes from a fishing family in Camden, but when he first moved down to Boothbay Harbor in 1970 he had no intention of fishing. He tended bar at the Thistle Inn, back in that pub's glory days, when all the region showed up after work and often left in each other's cars because their own were blocked in. "These lobstermen would always be in there and I thought: this is great, these guys earn a living and yet they're always in here," he says with a laugh. "I didn't realize that they were the ones who didn't work too hard!" One of his older friends encouraged him to come out lobstering with him and, ultimately, to buy his boat and traps and take his place in the fishery. "Nobody ever bothered me. Probably a lot of the guys didn't even know I was there at first, thought it was the same guy fishing."

David says the traditional territories system has been extremely important for the fishery. "If you didn't have that, you'd have chaos out there," he says. Instead, despite the growing number of lobstermen in the region and the close proximity of rival harbors, relations have remained civil almost the entire time David's been fishing. "Every now and again something will happen and you'll get upset, but you're not going to start whacking the guy's traps," he says. "You might see him at a basketball game that night, or his kid and your kid might be friends. When you used to know everyone you were fishing with, it helps a lot."

But Boothbay Harbor, like the rest of the coast, is changing. Since the collapse of groundfishing, more and more fishermen have turned to lobsters. The number of boats and buoys out on the water has exploded, growing to the point where lobstermen no longer know everyone in the harbor and, thus, have a harder time detecting trespassers or discouraging bad behavior. When David started lobstering in 1971, he had an older mentor with him who taught him proper manners. One day David was getting ready to set a string of traps near another lobsterman's traps inside Grimes Cove on Ocean Point. "This older guy, he'd been fishing since the 1930s, and he said, 'No, that guy there is an old man and has been fishing there for forty years. We'll stay outside [the cove] and not crowd him,' " he remembers. "It was just something you didn't do. But nowadays you have a lot of people who came out and just started fishing and didn't have an old guy to go out with to tell them, 'You don't do this, you don't go there.' A lot of younger guys fish anyplace, wouldn't even think of it." In another decade or two, David wonders if the old ways may get lost altogether.

But at the same, the traditional way of doing things has been endorsed by Maine lawmakers for the first time in history.

By 1995, Maine legislators had despaired of ever finding statewide solutions for some of the lobster industry's intractable problems. The number of traps in the water had grown to 2.4 million, up from 1.6 million in 1986, and many lobstermen felt they could catch just as many lobsters with fewer traps, if only a trap limit could be agreed upon. The fishermen switching over to full-time lobstering as other fisheries declined made the fisheries even harder to manage. But the situation varied enormously from region to region, even from one harbor to another. Many fishermen in Casco Bay were tending as many as 1,800 traps, and in summer the area became so congested with snarled buoys that fishermen started calling it the "Bay of Pigs." But while many Southern Mainers clamored for new trap and license limits, Downeast lobstermen argued that these made little sense. Many Downeast outports were losing population as young people moved away in search of better economic opportunities. Even the most aggressive lobstermen rarely fished more than 600 traps because the region's powerful tides—approaching thirty feet in Passamaquoddy Bay—made long strings impractical. When it came to lobster regulation, one size definitely did not fit all.

So in the spring of 1995, Maine legislators took a bold step. They handed much of the responsibility for managing the fishery over to the lobstermen themselves. Through two years of negotiation, lobstermen agreed to divide the coast into seven zones, each of which would be governed by a council of lobstermen elected by their local peers. These councils could recommend local rules on a whole range of issues from trap and string limits to the number of new licenses to be issued and the eligibility requirements for new applicants. The councilors' recommendations needed the support of two-thirds of the lobstermen in their zone, giving every license holder a say in what would happen. Never before had the state shared so much management responsibility with the fishermen themselves.

In the years since, the new system appears to have maintained broad support, particularly Downeast. "It gives us a voice to speak and control our own area, whereas before we were never heard," says Harvey Crowley, who was chairman of the Down East Lobstermen's Association when the zones were being created. "The southern part of Maine, their fishery is so different, and we couldn't fish with their habits. But it seemed like they had a better voice, better lobbyists in the legislature than we did. . . . I think zoning is better for the whole coast." Pat White of York, chief executive of the rival Maine Lobstermen's Association, agrees. "You can't paint it all with one brush when it comes to regulations," he says. "This gives fishermen a lot more opportunity to participate in the process, and people from all over the country are wondering how it will work out."

The experiment hasn't been without its problems, particularly when traditional harbor territories come up against the new zone system, as when Friendship lobstermen figured they would fish anywhere they pleased within their zone, including the waters around Monhegan. Monhegan's 1997 legislative victory resulted in an official endorsement of their traditional territory, which became a locally managed subzone. Isle au Haut rushed to follow suit, and many mainland fishermen feared that if every island grabbed their turf, there would be few places to fish. For now, state authorities have taken a step back from considering more subzones, and Isle au Haut lobstermen remain inundated with boats from nearby Stonington, which has a larger gang and is linked to the mainland by bridge.

The zones law has also pitted full-time and part-time lobstermen against one another, particularly in the more crowded harbors of Midcoast Maine. Every zone in Maine has imposed a limit of eight hundred traps per fisherman, but in the Boothbay region's zone, lobstermen passed a limit of only six hundred traps. "Everybody who has a license gets a vote, and so this zone is controlled by people who might have only four, five, twenty, or twenty-five traps. If they make me take

half my traps out of the water then they're going to catch more lobsters, and I'm going to catch less," says David Norton, who fished
1,300 traps before the limits were imposed. More irksome to full-
timers is the fact that while they've been forced to radically cut back,
many part-timers have doubled or tripled the number of traps they use,
often right up to the local trap limit. As of 1999, the number of traps in
state waters had actually increased by more than 600,000. But with
many zones issuing only one license for every three that are retired,
the overall trap numbers will eventually decrease.

By early afternoon, David and Mike have tended their last traps and
we head back to the Co-Op, our storage tank filled with hundreds of
pounds of lobster. At the float, Mike and I sort the lobsters, separating
soft from super soft, filling one tub after another and setting them on
the dock. When we finish, the landing is crowded with crustaceans,
and another boat is coming in with more. There's clearly no shortage
of lobsters here today, and everyone on the coast hopes that remains
the case forevermore.

EIGHT

Brave Old World

A t the dawn of the twenty-first century, coastal Maine was starting to look more and more like the rest of the country, particularly if you were a motorist driving into the state from the "other" forty-nine.

High-speed, multilane highways sucked motorists over the Piscataqua River from New Hampshire and whisked them past the forests and subdivisions of Greater Portland's sprawling suburbs, which blend with those of Brunswick. There, coastal travelers exited onto a new connector road, lined with newly paved strip mall developments, that links them up with U.S. Route 1. They whizzed along to Bath and over the Kennebec River on a four-lane, controlled-access highway, which finally petered down to two amid the strip malls and car dealerships of Woolwich. For the next thirty miles, Route 1 still cut a wide slash through woods, fields, and front yards: twenty-four feet of travel lanes lined with six- to eight-foot shoulders and graded grassy slopes like those on the sides of interstates. This expansion wasn't arbitrary. Even in the dead of winter Route 1 was afflicted with rush hour traffic, while, in summer, traffic backed up for miles on either side of Wiscasset, one of the few towns in these parts that didn't have a bypass.

But in the town of Warren, 140 miles from the New Hampshire border, everything changed. Most drivers turned onto Route 90, a faster, wider, more direct path through the backcountry to Camden, Belfast, and the Downeast coast. On Route 1, however, traffic thinned and the shoulders narrowed. The great trees drew close, embracing the quiet road in a leafy canopy. The road meandered through hayfields and past stone walls built by settlers brought here by Samuel Waldo and houses built in the days when Henry Knox ruled these parts. Passing under spreading oak, maple, and chestnut trees, past farm stands and grazing livestock, one had the feeling of having finally reached Maine, the way many of us remembered it. It was a temporary feeling. A few miles later the sprawl returned, continuing almost unabated for miles to come.

The signs first appeared on the roadside in the summer of 1999: little vinyl boards staked in front yards and along that quiet stretch in Warren amid the bees, black flies, and lengthening hay. "Don't be fooled," one suggested to passing drivers, "Wider Is Not Wiser." "DOT: What about our homes, our dreams, our way of life?" another asked the Maine Department of Transportation. A third proclaimed, simply, "Stop the Widening!"

The signs were put up by local residents who had learned that the state was planning to "improve" this two-mile stretch of highway. According to the DOT, traffic was expected to increase from nine thousand vehicles a day to twelve thousand twenty years hence. For safety's sake, Route 1 had to be upgraded. "This road is part of the national highway system," DOT spokesman Bruce Van Note explained, "and that requires certain standards because travelers from other parts of the country expect certain kinds of roads." The solution: add eight feet of shoulder on each side of the road, six of it paved, and knock down ninety large trees, or "deadly fixed objects" in the DOT's vernacular. When the $3.4 million project was completed, DOT planners assured, Route 1 in Warren would finally look like Route 1 to the south.

Steve Burke didn't think this sounded like much of an improvement. First of all, the road would widen right into his front yard, toppling the century-old maple there and bringing traffic closer to the steps of the old farmhouse where he lived and ran his graphic design business. And the state's rationale for the project didn't make much sense either. When an ambulance rushed by his home, it was invariably on its way to an accident on "improved" parts of Routes 1 and 90; people tended to drive more carefully on his winding section of road. DOT's own statistics showed that his section of Route 1 had a significantly lower rate of serious accidents than the widened roads nearby. As for traffic, the DOT's estimates failed to account for the 2006 completion of a major highway bridge in Augusta which would divert much coastal through traffic away from the area. As for the rest, why not designate faster, shorter Route 90 as "Route 1-A," an alternate bypass for through traffic? But most of all, Burke feared that the DOT's plan was a step onto a path that would end in strip malls, subdivisions, speeding cars, and the death of community. He'd seen it happen to his hometown on Cape Cod. In fact, he'd moved to Maine in the 1970s to escape the advancing sprawl. And he wasn't going to see it happen to Warren without a fight.

Most of his neighbors felt the same way and banded together to put up signs and lobby the DOT to cancel the project. But the DOT stuck by its projections and its plan. The project, Commissioner John Melrose announced, would go ahead in the summer of 2002.

The DOT got more than it bargained for.

As the project lurched forward in the spring of 2002, dozens of protesters from across Knox County were holding sunset vigils twice a month at the busy turnoff to Route 90. Local artists gathered to paint the condemned trees. Letters poured in to local newspapers. Then the big papers in Portland and Bangor picked up the story, and soon television news crews were shooting spots from Warren. The little 1.6-mile widening project was becoming a statewide issue. But the DOT stuck by its guns.

When workers arrived to begin clearing trees in mid-June, things started getting out of hand. For three days, protesters tried to block work from going forward. They sat on new utility poles, preventing crews from raising them. They chained themselves to one another and to the trees. They chanted "Shame!" at the contractors and tried to rally passing motorists with "Stop the Widening" signs. TV crews, the Knox County sheriff's patrolmen, and state police interceptors converged on the rural road. By the time the trees were cleared, seventeen people had been arrested and carted off to jail, including a man who'd threatened to kill the protesters. For the DOT, it was a public relations disaster.

It's tempting to say that the descendants of Samuel Waldo's Scotch-Irish settlers had risen up to resist this assault on their land by yet another powerful, absentee interest, confronting surveyors and sheriffs just as their eighth, ninth, or tenth great-grandparents did. But while this was undoubtedly the case with a few individuals, the vast majority of the Warren protesters were born out-of-state—aging back-to-the-landers like Burke who'd seen what sprawl can do to a place. In fact, the widening had the support of the area chamber of commerce and two of Warren's three selectmen. According to some locals, the protests were just another attempt by outsiders to keep Maine quaint at the price of keeping its people poor. Roads are infrastructure, infrastructure means jobs, and the more jobs the better. "You've got a lot of people who were coming from areas that were congested and built up and they came here looking to retire and don't want the community to change," explains James Raye, a native son and former mayor of nearby Rockland. "But I have children and I want them to have the job opportunities that let them stay around here because it's a great place to live."

For others, native and nonnative alike, uncontrolled development is threatening the very qualities that make Maine unique. "There's this attitude that landscape and nature should just be pushed aside in favor of more pavement," says Susan Beebe, a Camden artist who was arrested for refusing to climb down from one of the condemned trees during the Route 1 standoff. "Warren is just a microcosm of what's happening all over the place."

At the root of such protests is a struggle for Maine's identity that is complicated by the historical relationship between natives and newcomers, between Maine and Massachusetts, and between local control and that of distant government. "What you see in many of these debates is that technical issues about economic changes or highway safety get dressed up and are masquerading for fundamental visions of what Maine is and ought to be," says Charles S. Colgan, a community planning specialist at the University of Southern Maine's Muskie School of Public Service in Portland. "Maine has a strong sense of place and when anything comes along that challenges that, people get motivated."

These days, Maine's sense of place is under constant threat. During the 1990s, Maine's coastal counties grew at a remarkable rate as more and more people moved in from out of state to retire or raise children. York County in the far south grew by 13.5 percent, three times the state's overall growth rate, while most other coastal counties grew by between 9 and 11 percent. And most of that growth has been taking place in traditional farming and fishing hamlets in the backcountry or down the peninsulas. During the 1990s, the coast's larger cities and towns barely grew or even shrank, but many traditional farming and fishing towns saw their populations jump by 20, 30, even 50 percent. Cushing, a hardscrabble Midcoast fishing hamlet, grew by more than a third as wealthy retirees bought up bucolic shoreline property. Scarborough, a sleepy bedroom community set amid Southern Maine's greatest salt marshes, swelled by 36 percent to nearly seventeen thousand people, making it larger than the neighboring city of Saco. Meanwhile the cities of Portland, Bath, and Rockland actually lost population. The coast's human population isn't just growing, it's spreading out.

Richard Sherwood, a census expert at the State Planning Office, has been trying to get a handle on what is driving the coast's sprawling growth. Poring over data from the federal census and Louis Ploch's landmark migration studies, Sherwood has identified two major trends that are changing the region's social fabric. Young Mainers are moving out of the state—more than 90,000 in the 1990s—leaving grammar school classrooms emptier than demographers would expect them to be. But those people are being replaced by a slightly larger wave of thirty-somethings and early retirees moving in from out of state. Around 110,000 moved in during the 1990s, Sherwood estimates, including an unusually large number of ten- to seventeen-year-old children, who fill middle and high schools. As a result, newcomers now make up a significant share of Maine's coastal population. Sherwood has found that approximately one in ten residents of most Southern and Midcoast counties in 2000 have moved there since 1995. "People moving to Maine probably have an image of living in the quiet countryside, on the lakes and the coast," he says. "Meanwhile people in the traditional town centers are going ten, fifteen, twenty miles out into the countryside where land is cheap, taxes are lower, and they can afford a mortgage or a lot to put a trailer on." The result, Sherwood says, is "the ongoing suburbanization of Maine."

This transformation has triggered a number of baleful effects on the culture, environment, and economy of the coast. In July 2001, Greater Portland had the worst sprawl in the entire Northeast and the ninth worst in the United States, according to a nationwide study conducted by the Brookings Institution in Washington. Between 1982 and

1997 the Portland metro area's population grew by only 17 percent, but the amount of rural land converted to urban uses increased by 108 percent—five times the rate of population growth. "Sprawl isn't on the way," the *Maine Sunday Telegram* editorialized. "It's already here."

Nor is sprawl confined to Maine's largest urban area. From Kittery to Searsmont, new driveways, house lots, and subdivisions appeared every few months on rural roads and once-forested shorelines. Trees have been cleared to improve the view of a large island summer home overlooking the remote anchorage where George Waymouth's party fished for cod and kidnapped Wabanakis. Audacious McMansions have cropped up on the summits of the Camden Hills and the shores of Mount Desert Island. Based on current trends, Evan Richert, the former director of the State Planning Office, has predicted that by 2050 Southern Maine will be an urbanized extension of Greater Boston, and a swath of the coast extending as far as Bar Harbor will be effectively suburban.

On behalf of the State Planning Office, Richert traveled to towns up and down the coast explaining to audiences what a change from rural to suburban really means. "It's a fundamental reorganization of the way land is used," he says. "At its essence, rural land is organized around production. It's farms and fishing piers and woodlots, gravel pits and quarries." Suburban land, on the other hand, is ultimately organized around consumption: the buying and selling of real estate, of scenery, privacy, peace and quiet. A low-density suburb of two-acre home lots may look like the countryside, Richert told his audiences, but it's really a collection of homes in a park, "a cartoon of rural." The cartoon and the real McCoy make very poor neighbors, and when they are put side by side conflict inevitably arises. Suburbanites' desire for peace and quiet is threatened by the noise and havoc of a lumbering operation, the unpleasant odors from the fish plant or a newly fertilized field, or the early-morning racket of departing lobster boats. And by force of numbers, wealth, and influence, suburbanites almost always triumph over their rural adversaries, who are slowly pushed out of the picture, soon to be replaced by strip malls, marinas, and new subdivisions. "It's not something where you wake up one day and all the bad stuff has happened at once," Richert explains. "It proceeds quite inconspicuously, in a way that separates cause from effect."

One of the first effects of this shift is the disruption of wildlife. Suburbanization involves a fragmentation of the landscape: the five-thousand-acre woodlot gets hacked into fifty-acre estates, the five-hundred-acre farm into two-acre building lots, and soon there are very few large blocks of land left. Problem is, most wildlife species need large home ranges in which to live, reproduce, and feed. When a 2,500-acre block of land is cut down to 20 acres, 80 percent of the resident species vanish. Bobcats, owls, hawks, bear, foxes, moose, and many songbirds disappear, replaced by bluejays, skunks, raccoon, and squirrels. "This is the habitat we all use for wildlife hunting and trapping and all those things," says Amanda Russell, who is trying to protect large blocks of land in Edgecomb, where she sits on the town planning board. "When it goes, we lose part of our culture and character."

There are financial costs as well. As the population has spread out, town services have had to follow, at a cost entirely out of proportion with the actual population increase. Take roads, for instance. During the 1980s, when Maine's population grew by 10 percent, the total number of miles driven grew by nearly *sixfold*! In the 1990s, as people moved farther and farther from their places of work, the average commute grew by more than 25 percent to forty-five minutes per day, forcing towns to buy more snowplows, pave miles and miles of dirt and gravel roads, and upgrade the roads they already had. The State Planning Office estimates that in the late eighties and early nineties, Maine was adding more than one hundred miles of town-maintained roads every year.

For Maine towns, by far the largest expense is paying for the school system. Given that the number of public school students in the state has been falling for three decades, one might think that school construction costs have been modest. Not so. Between 1975 and 1995, state government alone spent three quarters of a billion dollars on school construction while the number of students sank by about 25,000. "While we were closing schools in the service center communities—in my hometown of South Portland we closed five of them—we were building new schools ten miles away," Richert told his audiences. Meanwhile, school districts spent more and more on busing. By the late 1990s, Maine school buses traveled an average of one mile per student every day.

Crime has dropped in Maine, but the number of policemen has grown because of the state's sprawing development pattern. Cars have gotten cleaner, but Maine's automobiles are creating more pollution because they are being driven farther each year. As more natural landscape is converted to lawns, roads, and parking lots, runoff is polluting lakes, rivers, and estuaries. "I think there's a tremendous misunderstanding of the costs of this kind of development," Richert says, leaning back in his office chair in Portland. "There are solutions, but people have to first accept that they have a problem. I'm afraid I think that's a long shot."

We Mainers don't want to believe that we're becoming suburban. Generations of people have moved here precisely to escape suburbia—its congestion, alienation, and mind-numbing conformity—for the solace of Maine's untrammeled beauty. The native identity is completely wrapped up in the coast's rural character: hunting and fishing, access to the shore, lakes, streams, and forests is regarded as a near birthright. The coast's rural past allowed local people to "run our own affairs" and "settle things ourselves" on a hamlet-by-hamlet basis, with common sense trumping detailed regulations. Describe a cliché Mainer—rugged, individualistic, outdoorsy, no-nonsense, practical in dress, egalitarian in outlook—and you have a list of characteristics that are the polar opposite of suburbia's: manicured, conforming, officebound, climate-controlled, status-minded, exclusive, possibly gated and guarded. The coast's identity is tied up in what it is not: rush hours and parking lots, business suits and flashy jewelry, cubicles in the corporate office building or identical homes lining labyrinthine networks of curving streets and cul-de-sacs. But somewhere, in the backs of our minds, we know it's coming. It's spreading out from Boston, absorbing southern New Hampshire and slipping over the Piscataqua to plant subdivisions along the southern coast. It's engulfed Greater Portland, swallowing farms and fishing piers from Scarborough to Cumberland, and hopped up the expanding commuter ways to Brunswick,

Augusta, Belfast, and beyond. We even have our own term for it: "Massification." And while this Massification has brought Maine unprecedented wealth, expanding opportunities, and a good many wonderful people, there's also a sense that something vital is being lost.

Richard Barringer, a professor at the Edmund Muskie School of Public Service at the University of Southern Maine, has been watching Maine's quiet transformation for more than thirty years. "If you want to see what Maine looked like in 1965, you have to go to Nova Scotia and Prince Edward Island," he says, gesturing toward the Maritime provinces, hidden somewhere beyond the low-slung Portland skyline. "If you want to see what it looked like in 1940 you'd have to go to Newfoundland. And that's just because of the inexorable spread of this national culture that we are a part of."

Since he first came to Maine in the late 1960s, he's watched the state become gradually absorbed into the national economy. The shoe, paper, textile, and fish factory jobs that once formed the backbone of statewide employment have largely disappeared, replaced by the more skilled office, education, and health care professions. Fishing and other natural-resource-dependent jobs have fallen from 6 percent of the state's jobs in 1959 to just over 1 percent in 1999, while high-tech jobs have had almost the opposite trend. "We look much more like the rest of the country," says Barringer, who was an adviser to several Maine governors and even ran for the post himself in the 1990s. "The upside is that you don't see the same kind of blinding poverty that I saw here in the 1950s and 1960s. Our standard of living is higher. But with that has come a lot of changes."

Take Dogfish Head on Southport, the road-linked island where my mother grew up and where Jennifer Elderkin still lives. Richard Barringer has ties there too. His wife's family owned a summer cottage there for more than a century. In fact, her great-great grandfather, a Civil War veteran from Attleboro, Massachusetts, bought a piece of land near Dogfish Head in the early 1880s. The family camped in tents the first few summers, enjoying the wild promontory and its sweeping views of the Sheepscot River. Then they built a small cabin, the family's summer retreat, which remained essentially unchanged for nearly a century. Barringer remembers that even into the early 1970s Dogfish Head itself, whose beaches had once served as the local steamboat landing, was still regarded as common property, though a local farmer technically owned it. "Families went out for the Fourth of July celebrations and people would be out there all the time," he recalls. "It was just part of island life."

But in the mid-1970s the farmer died and his children put the land on the market. An out-of-state family quickly snapped up the land, built an imposing home, and posted NO TRESPASSING signs that blocked access to the Head and its beaches. "They were a Connecticut family and in Connecticut, private property is not for trespassing," Barringer says. Dogfish Head transformed rapidly from there, as more properties were sold or subdivided. It is now ringed with large, multi-million-dollar houses with expensive cars in the driveways, resembling an exclusive suburban neighborhood. "One of the traditional values of Maine was that if you had money and showed it you were not welcome. There was no flash. If you owned a Cadillac, well, you wore a checkered jacket when you drove it. But all that's changing. New values are coming in, and they're completely different from what came before."

Indeed, since the beginning of the twenty-first century, the small towns of the Maine coast have been attracting a new sort of people, heretofore rare outside of Greater Portland. They are wealthy retirees, often quite young, attracted by the coast's incredible scenery and still ample supply of developable waterfront property. Unlike the rusticators, artists, and back-to-the-landers of the past, the newcomers haven't come in pursuit of the Maine Myth, for that fleeting, summer-warmed taste of New England's lost agrarian past. It's not that the newcomers reject this Maine Myth; they aren't even aware of its existence. As a group, they tend to be entirely unschooled in Maine's cultural background, ignorant of the divisions between natives and strangers or the complex social rapprochement that has developed between the great-great-grandchildren of the rusticators and their year-round neighbors. For many of these newcomers, the Maine coast is simply an attractive place to buy property, construct a massive trophy house, and stake out one's own, private bit of coastline.

Oblivious or uninterested in where they've arrived, newcomers give themselves away with decidedly un-Yankee displays of wealth, taste, or downright foolishness. There's Texas millionaire Charles

Butt, owner of the H-E-B supermarket chain, who moved power lines and blocked traffic on one of Mount Desert Island's few roads *for ten hours* in order to move a fifty-year-old apple tree twenty miles to his summer estate. There are the untold hundreds of homebuyers who settle on the shores of some "quaint" fishing harbor only to clamor for noise ordinances to stop lobstermen from leaving the harbor early in the morning as they need to. Some give themselves away by putting up NO TRESPASSING signs at beaches, islands, and swimming holes that have been frequented by locals for centuries. Others simply plop down an absurd-looking trophy home—an uncoordinated hodgepodge of bulges and rooflines—amid a neighborhood of traditional capes, mowing down old-growth trees and blueberry barrens in favor of office park landscaping: square, knee-high shrubs isolated from the lawn in pools of chopped brown tree bark. Suburban Boston arrives plot by plot, forever erasing landscape and memory in favor of meaningless uniformity.

Mary Brewer is worried about another aspect of the ongoing real estate boom along the coast: the toll it is taking on the region's cultural fabric. A lobsterman's wife and longtime editor of the *Boothbay Register*, Brewer has become increasingly concerned about the changing cultural landscape on the Boothbay peninsula, which has attracted more than its fair share of retirees in recent years. And in the summer of 2002 she set out her concerns, loud and clear, on the *Register*'s editorial page. What we are witnessing, she warned, is nothing less than "the death of the Maine coast native."

The problem boils down to money and taxes. As city dwellers, retirees, and telecommuters have poured into coastal hamlets, buying farmhouses, waterfront home lots, and rural subdivisions, they've triggered a veritable explosion in property values. After the next property revaluation, many local people are forced to sell homes that have been in their families for generations simply because they can no longer afford the new property taxes, which have tended to increase very sharply if one lives on or near the water. In the seventies and eighties, Southern and Midcoast residents could still trade the family homestead for a house in the woods on one of their town's back roads, which was also where young people bought property and put up their house or house trailer. But by the 1990s, the back roads of Boothbay and other Midcoast towns were pretty much built out, and taxes were increasing just about everywhere. Local people—young and old alike—are now being displaced much farther afield to far-off backcountry towns. There are young lobstermen who commute nearly an hour to Boothbay Harbor each morning from their homes in the backwoods of Jefferson or the suburbs of Augusta. Similar situations are found from York to Corea and beyond.

"I can count on one hand how many lobstermen I know who live on the water anymore," Mary Brewer says, leaning back in a chair in her tiny office as the downtown Boothbay Harbor traffic passes by the window behind her. "We're lucky because we still live on the water, but we pay for it."

Mary and her husband, Butch, have lived in their home for more than forty years, buying it for $7,200. When it was last appraised fifteen years ago—for $224,000—the revaluation assessor took one look at it and told the Brewers, "Wow, waterfront. You know you could get a lot of money for this if you sold." Mary is still indignant about that. "Some of these out-of-state assessors don't share Maine people's love for their homes, I mean they just don't get it," she says. "To them it's a piece of real estate and if you can make good money on it then why in God's name wouldn't you want to sell it. I've tried repeatedly to say, 'It's my home, I don't want to sell it and make good money. I want to live there until I die.'" Her home is probably worth close to half a million today, but she has no intention of ever selling.

Many of her friends and neighbors felt the same way, but were forced to sell when they could no longer afford rising property taxes. "Old people on a fixed income are forced into making these decisions. I've seen it happen over and over," she says. "Every time you lose a piece of waterfront property—might be a little natural clapboard old building that was somebody's workshop or fish house—and boom! Down it comes and up goes this really expensive home. And people say, 'Gee, that's nice.' But is it? It's not the Maine that many people came to love years ago. That's disappearing. To find it now I think you really have to go east almost to the Canadian border!

"We've got to do something, and not just here but statewide, or all of a sudden the Maine people are all going to be from Massachusetts and New Jersey and Pennsylvania," Brewer says. "The people who are moving here are really nice and try to help the community but the fact is they are literally displacing a lot of local people who can no longer afford the real estate in their own hometown. I think that's sad, and I don't think those [recently arrived] people want to see that happen either."

From the editorial pages of the *Register*, Brewer has argued for the creation of some statewide mechanism by which properties are taxed on their current use rather than their potential market value were they to be subdivided. Others have suggested that there be tax breaks for property owners who agree not to sell their properties on the open market, but with provisions that would allow them to pass them down to immediate family members.

"I truly don't know what the exact answer is, but I hope I live long enough to see some changes," she says. "I really do."

The Ralph W. Stanley Boatyard has been a fixture of the Southwest Harbor waterfront for more than half a century, but the Stanleys themselves have been on Mount Desert Island far longer than that. The first Stanleys came to the island shortly after the French defeat in the 1760s. During the boom years of the mid-nineteenth century, Ralph Stanley's great-grandfather owned a fleet of fishing schooners. With the arrival of the millionaire "cottagers" in the late nineteenth century, Ralph's grandfather took Rockefellers and Vanderbilts out sailing on Somes Sound. His father lobstered out of Southwest Harbor between the world wars, when the waterfront was crowded with canneries, fishing wharves, and boatyards.

Ralph Stanley started his own yard in the 1950s, on Clark Point Road, a long, thickly settled street running along the north side of the town's narrow harbor. He first built wooden lobster boats but, as fiberglass displaced wood, he turned to building and repairing wooden sailboats, skiffs, and cruisers. Other wooden boatbuilders switched to fiberglass or went by the wayside, but Ralph Stanley carved out a niche, designing and constructing unique wooden boats for the island's very wealthy summer residents. Today his work is known to wooden boat aficionados across the country, and in 1999 the National Endowment for the Arts awarded Ralph a National Heritage Fellowship, the nation's most prestigious honor in folk and traditional arts.

Now the yard is run by his son, Richard Stanley, who grew up amid the wooden masts, planking, and half-finished hulls in the family's cavernous boathouse. But as Richard, forty-one, looks back at the demographic and cultural changes Southwest Harbor has undergone in recent years, he wonders if there's any future here for those who would build boats, haul traps, or simply try to hold on to homes that have belonged to the same family for generations. "They want to make this into a residential community, but that's not what this town is about," he says, referring to the newcomers who now control municipal politics. "If you make it a residential community then you've got a dead town, you've got no future, and the young people have to move away."

During the 1980s and 1990s, a flood of wealthy homebuyers descended on Mount Desert Island, quickly buying up every available property in posh villages like Northeast Harbor, Somesville, and Seal Harbor, long the preserve of wealthy summer cottagers. As the supply of properties dwindled in the late 1990s, buyers turned their attention to Southwest Harbor, a workingman's town whose lobster canneries and fish piers had kept cottagers at bay since the steamboat age. Homeowners were inundated with unsolicited offers for houses they hadn't put up for sale. Bidding wars erupted over prime lots, with people offering many times more than the market had previously borne. And as properties changed hands, tax assessments on everyone's properties exploded. In 1999 alone, the tax bill of the average shorefront property owner rose by 100 percent. The town's other boatyards have since moved elsewhere, as have many longtime residents unable to pay the new taxes or to resist staggering offers for their homes.

The Stanleys' tax burden has jumped as well, but Richard says they've been able to weather the increases because they pass the costs on to their customers, who are not particularly price sensitive. But the yard is threatened by another aspect of Southwest Harbor's real estate boom: the values and attitudes of the town's new residents.

Richard remembers his father going out in the yard on a recent Sunday morning to do some work on a sailboat mast. As often happens, Ralph needed to do some finishing work with a power planer. But a few minutes into his job, his wife answered a phone call from the neighbors, who'd thrown a big bash the night before and wanted to put a stop to Ralph's racket. The request was ignored, but Richard says the town has since imposed noise ordinances to protect late-night revelers from being awoken by early risers.

"Years ago, things worked simpler, neighbors worked with neighbors, you knew everybody," Richard says as he guides a hand chisel along a section of an overturned Herreshoff sloop in his workshop. "It's not just local people who've lived here forever. I mean, there've always been people moving in and out of here; it's always been that way. But when a person moved into town they got to know people. Nowadays it just ain't that way."

He stands up straight, whisking away some tiny wood chips with his free hand, and gestures with his chisel toward a fish dock out in front of the open door of the boathouse. "They come here on vacation or whatever and they say, 'Oh, what a wonderful place to live.' And then they move here and they discover that, oh, God, there's all this noise. The lobster boats are going out early in the morning! The fish bait stinks! The lobster traps are unsightly because when they haul them up and they sit out they start stinking." Richard's pacing along the shop floor now with a theatrical grin, throwing his arms in the air. "Funny thing is, these people have moved here to get away from it all and the first thing they do when they get here is try to change it to the way it was where they came from."

Richard contends with a whole slew of new regulations that will be familiar to suburban readers, but are completely at odds with a working waterfront. In addition to noise ordinances he faces "ridiculous" buffering requirements mandating that he screen his "unsightly" boatyard with landscaping and attractive fencing. An expansion of his boathouse has been blocked by height restrictions, and he's prohibited from operating a marina from his prime harborfront location. But what Richard finds most irksome is the fact that, were he starting out today, it would be illegal for him to operate his boat storage business on Clarks Point Road. The town zoning code forbids it. He's flabbergasted that while the town increases restrictions on commercial activities, they spent over $10,000 in taxpayer funds to build a "welcoming gateway" at the entrance to town. "Instead of maintaining our water pipes, they've gone out and cut down a couple of perfectly good spruce trees and planted a couple of little plants so the town crew had something to do," he says with a laugh, tossing his hands in the air. The town, he fears, is being changed into "a Newport, Rhode Island," a manicured haven of mansions requiring only enough working people to "mow the lawns, fix the car, and keep the store shelves stocked."

Nor is Richard alone in feeling this way. David Rockefeller Jr., grandson of the late John D. Rockefeller and a summer resident of nearby Seal Harbor, shares many of his concerns. The whole coast, he says, will remain under increasing development pressure, pressure that could easily destroy the culture and landscape that's attracted people to Maine for nearly two centuries. "I don't think you want to make Maine into sort of a lobster form of Disneyland," says Rockefeller, whose family set up the Maine Coast Heritage Trust, which protects open spaces along the coast. If communities fail to look ahead, he says, they could wind up "killing the goose that lays the golden egg." Towns need to start looking at issues like the balance of properties winding up in the hands of part-time residents and the availability of affordable housing for year-rounders, he says, if they are to avoid losing one of their greatest assets: the Maine people themselves.

When it comes to multigenerational ties to the land, few Midcoast residents have Linda Sicotte beat. Her maiden name was Linda McFarland, and her kin have been living on the Pemaquid Peninsula since 1729 or 1730, when David Dunbar lured them here to build his fort, promising them free land in the crown colony of Sagadahoc. The rest is history: wars with the Indians, the insurrection against the Great Proprietors, the struggle to earn a living from the frost-plagued fields and the ice-cold sea. Linda hasn't traced her family history back to those colonial days, but for as long as anyone can remember, McFarlands have been living on the McFarland Shore in New Harbor, a quiet fishing hamlet on the eastern shore of Pemaquid Neck, three miles north of where Colonel Dunbar built his fort. But over Linda's lifetime—less than half a century—the McFarlands have vanished from McFarland Shore.

Linda has lived in New Harbor for most of her life, though when asked about this she, like others, sheepishly admits that she was actually born at Miles Hospital, twelve miles away in Damariscotta. At the time of her birth, the family owned all of the McFarland Shore. But her parents were far from rich. Her father, Harold "Biscuit" McFarland, was a fisherman and small boatbuilder at a time when neither profession paid very much. "Dad didn't have an off-season," she recalls. "He went from lobstering to shrimping to alewifing in the spring, and then he'd build and repair boats, make the head nets for the lobster traps, and carve his old wooden buoys by hand. Then he'd be back to pretty much fishing." As time passed, he grew to hate going on shopping trips to Damariscotta, population five thousand, because the shopping center and tourist traffic had changed it so. "It was becoming like a city for him," Linda recalls. "If we took him to a town like Bath [population: 10,000], he'd hem and haw about it. Saw his first McDonald's there and hated the place, hated it!" She paused, thinking back on it a moment. "Guess he wasn't a restaurant person. But he had been a cook on many of the boats he went [herring] seining on, but the recipes I wouldn't tell ya because it would make you ill."

As Linda was growing up, her father and other relatives sold off the Shore in bits and pieces, until finally there was nothing left. "We don't own any of it now," she says, "except for the last eleven acres my niece was able to buy. All the rest is owned by out-of-staters."

Linda recalls having unambiguous childhood feelings about the out-of-staters. "I despised them," she says. "I could see my grandfather's land being scuppled up for little or nothing. And even though they bought the land from us and liked the view, I guess they felt we were beneath them." One day, when she was nine, Linda was riding a horse down one of the woods-lined roads leading to the shore that had belonged to her grandfather. "At one point this car came up by me and it was from New York. They kept tooting on their horn and my horse would jump at the sound. Finally they come up and told me I had to get off the road. They said, 'We own this property.' Well, I told them, 'If it hadn't been for my grandfather you wouldn't have owned any of this! I'm a McFarland and I have a right to go down to the shore any time I want!' " When the New Yorkers consulted their deeds they discovered young Linda was right: the McFarlands had preserved access rights to the road. But for Linda, the bitterness remains. "Now the McFarland Shore is still named that, but there are no McFarlands there."

Linda's father died in 1987, less than two years before McDonald's opened a restaurant near the shopping center in Damariscotta. "After they'd been open for six months they had this grand opening with balloons and Ronald McDonald and all that, so I took my kids there," she says. "Well, kids being kids, they had to go to the bathroom while we were standing in line. So my friend takes her daughter and my daughter and heads back towards the restrooms. But she comes back a few minutes later and says, Linda, there's something you need to see."

Linda, leading her son by the hand, left the line, negotiated her way past the throngs of children, and turned the corner to another seating area, the walls of which McDonald's had decorated with vintage photographs depicting local scenes in an effort to connect with the community. She stopped at the end of a long row of people waiting for the restrooms and turned to her left. Her jaw dropped. There, staring back from a framed photograph, was her father, straining alongside six of his buddies to haul in a seine net bulging with sixty thousand bushels of herring. It was the first time she'd seen her father since his death. "It just horrified me it was so overwhelming. I got emotional and I grabbed my kids and I ran out to my car. I couldn't bring myself to go back inside."

Now, fifteen years later, the striking photograph of the New Harbor fishermen and their record catch still hangs at McDonald's, and has been published by local papers and *Down East* magazine, becoming a minor icon of the Maine identity. Today, Linda also sees it as homage to her father's way of life, one she's watched slip away with the generation that lived it. But she says she'll never forget the shock of seeing the photograph for the first time, her father in his hat and foul weather gear, pulling on the net above that new McDonald's dining table.

❧

Samuel Waldo and Henry Knox are long gone. But there is a new Great Proprietor in the counties that bear their names, one who has succeeded in transforming this hardscrabble region at a pace his eighteenth-century counterparts could only have dreamed of.

In the 1960s and 1970s, the western shore of Penobscot Bay included some of the poorest towns in the state. Even into the early 1990s, Rockland and Belfast were still sad, anemic little cities, whose traditional industries—fish packing in Rockland, chicken processing in Belfast—had collapsed. Between them lay quiet, picturesque Camden, Rockport, and Lincolnville, residential towns relying on summer tourists, cottagers, and retirees to make ends meet. From the guides at the Knox mansion replica in Thomaston to the secondhand shop proprietors along Route 1 in Searsmont, many locals made what they could in the summer season, then did their best to survive through the long, cold winter.

But in 1993, Charles Cawley showed up, and the lands of the old Waldo Patent would never be the same.

Cawley, the chief executive of MBNA, the nation's largest credit card company, was no stranger to Maine. The son of a New Jersey banking executive, Cawley had spent childhood summers at his grandfather's Lincolnville home. As a teenager he worked summer jobs at his grandfather's garment factories in Belfast and Camden, and, after making his millions, he purchased a palatial summer home for himself outside Camden. In the early 1990s, Cawley decided he wanted to spend more time at his Camden home and, given Maine's relatively low property and wage costs, figured he could take a large chunk of his corporation with him to Midcoast Maine.

Given the region's history of resisting the ambitions of great men, one might have imagined that Cawley would be doomed to failure. He had a well-established reputation as an aggressive, acquisitive tycoon, the corporate equivalent of Maine's eighteenth-century land barons. Like Knox and Waldo, he had a very un-Maine penchant for flashy, over-the-top displays of wealth and privilege. He kept one hundred vintage roadsters as well as the company's sumptuous yacht, helicopters, and guesthouses. He decided to construct an oversized driveway on his sprawling estate and reportedly only obtained the required variance permits from the town after much of the work was completed. He threw a birthday bash one summer, and his well-heeled guests managed to wake up half of Knox County in the middle of the night as their private jets soared homeward from Owl's Head's tiny airport.

Like those of the Great Proprietors, Cawley's business interests benefited from close contacts with high-level political figures. George W.
Bush was one of Cawley's personal friends and in 1999 came to Cawley's Camden home to attend a fund-raising event in his honor. During the 2000 presidential campaign, MBNA and its senior employees
were the Bush campaign's single biggest contributor *nationally*; their
investment was likely returned many times over when the new president pushed through massive tax cuts for the extremely wealthy. Cawley and his fellow MBNA executives also gave lavishly to Maine's
Republican senators, the Republican National Committee, and particularly to those congressmen and senators who supported an extensive 2001 overhaul of the nation's bankruptcy laws. *Business Week* later
reported that the legal changes, which made it harder for ordinary
consumers to seek protection from credit card debt, boosted MBNA's
profits by around $75 million a year.

But unlike Knox and Waldo, Cawley wasn't coming to the region
with demands that pushed people off the land. To the contrary, his
company offered large numbers of the sort of well-paying jobs that
might keep people from having to leave in search of work. MBNA
started its operations in Maine as a modest affair: forty employees answering phones at an abandoned mill in a downtown Camden mill
site, which the company transformed from a dilapidated fire hazard to
a comfortable office complex, decorated in MBNA's hallmark green
and beige. But Cawley was just getting started. Over the next six years
his Delaware-based company rapidly expanded its Midcoast operations. MBNA's Camden facility grew from forty to four hundred employees. It bought up modest homes and decaying structures on the
south side of Rockland's harbor and built a campus for another one
thousand employees. It purchased the side of one of the seaward-
facing hills between Lincolnville and Belfast, plopping down a twenty-
nine-acre recreational complex in the midst of a deer wintering yard.
In Belfast, MBNA constructed a brand-new office complex with
360,000 square feet of workspace—as much as three large Wal-Mart
stores—where it employed another three thousand people. By 2000,
MBNA had become the Midcoast's largest employer and the fourth
largest in all of Maine. The average wage in Waldo County, where
Belfast is located, jumped by 26 percent between 1995 and 1999,

while the unemployment rate fell by 45 percent. Meanwhile, the company gave lavishly to local institutions, renovating libraries and airport runways, building youth centers, and helping to finance the expansion of the Farnsworth Art Gallery and the nonprofit Island Institute. At Christmas one year, MBNA "adopted" sixteen local families, providing them with food and gifts.

Not everyone was happy with the new Santa Claus, however. Paul Cartwright, a carpenter and Camden selectman, feels MBNA has changed his town's character, bit by bit, for the worse. "They're very controlling, and they want an environment that's clean and compliant, with no challenges to their mode of operation," he says. He finds the continuous presence of MBNA security patrols throughout the town a little spooky, as he does the teams of street sweepers MBNA sends out in the fall to pick up every last leaf on sidewalks near company properties. It bothers him that the skate park and youth centers the company built in Camden are "swarming with employees" and bristling with security cameras. "The old youth center was this funky little place in the old Lions Club building. We pitched together to pound nails and build partitions and kids were there and all," he says. "But MBNA built this complex for hundreds of thousands of dollars and it's decorated in their image and there are regulations for everything. I mean, there's a regulation that says you cannot sit sideways in your chair, which isn't really conducive to sixteen-year-olds."

Other local critics hate the way MBNA throws their money around. When the company encounters a building they don't like, their normal procedure is to buy it and tear it down, even if the building could have easily been moved to another location. One Easter the company planted hundreds of tulips around their Camden campus, which died the next day in seasonably cold temperatures. Earlier, at its grand opening celebration in Camden, MBNA decided to improve the backdrop by placing a flock of live ducks on its millpond, their wings clipped to prevent escape. According to the *Maine Times*, the unfortunate creatures were caught up in the strong spring currents and, unable to fly, were swept over the mill's old dam to their deaths.

But, for all its influence and ostentation, Cawley's company has far more supporters than detractors in the communities where it operates. While Mainers in other parts of the state are almost unanimous in their concerns about the effects of, say, the influx of retirees on the character of their towns, most people in Rockland, Belfast, and Camden have only good things to say about their new corporate neighbor. That's because, for all its faults, MBNA has given these communities a new lease on life.

James Raye grew up in Rockland in the late sixties and early seventies and served as the town's mayor in 1999–2000. He remembers a run-down working town where opportunity was thin on the ground. Raye's parents worked in the fish processing plants, which were pretty much the only steady jobs around. "It was tough. There were a lot of hard workers making very little money," he recalls. "There were a lot of barrooms and a lot of barroom activities—fights and stuff like that. There weren't a lot of alternatives to the fish plants beyond going to Shop and Save and running a cash register." But with the fisheries' collapse in the eighties, the trawlers moved away and most of the fish plants went out of business. "It was absolutely devastating. People just looked at one another and said, 'What are we going to do?' "

In the 1980s and 1990s, thousands of retirees moved into Camden and other neighboring towns, starting the familiar cycle of escalating property values, increased taxation, and gentrification pressures. "You started getting people from away coming here from areas that were all congested and built up who had the opportunity to purchase some property here at pretty inexpensive rates," says Raye. "They were looking to retire and come to a Sleepy Hollow–type bedroom community. And they didn't like seeing anything happen that would change that." When MBNA arrived in town in 2000, Raye says, it was these folks who were most upset.

But Raye, who works for an insurance company, says MBNA has been a blessing for the town. The company has brought jobs and tax revenues to the once blighted city. Its donations helped the Farnsworth Museum become a major regional tourist destination, the anchor for a vibrant gallery scene along Main Street. People who otherwise would have been forced to sell and move away are now staying, and young people, including Raye's daughter, have found quality jobs at MBNA. "Their medical care programs are second to none. They have vision and dental and disability and 401(k) plans with matching funds," he says. "They've really brought up the standard around here. People aren't going to get away with paying $5.50 [an hour] with no health in-surance and working on Christmas Eve. Nowadays, if you want to be doing that, you'll be working alone."

Farther east, however, the discussion at gas stations, fish houses, and town meetings isn't about how to deal with sprawl, development, and corporate influence. For while retirees and young professionals have swept up the coast, transforming communities from Kittery to Mount Desert Island, much of the rest of the state remains as it was: impover-ished, isolated, and neglected. In this, the "other Maine," people are angry at DOT for *not* improving their roads. Instead of fighting by-passes, towns fight one another for the chance to be connected to a controlled-access highway. From the western foothills to the fogbound coast of Washington County, people are worried not about managing growth, but about keeping their communities alive.

Back in the days of the Great Proprietors, William Bingham tried and failed to bring settlers and development to his vast holding in what is now Washington County, the easternmost swath of the Maine coast. Despite being the wealthiest businessman in the country, Bingham was unable to overcome the obstacles to settlement: poor soils and fierce tides, profound cold and even more profound isolation from the rest of New England. Two centuries after his death, the lands in and around the old Bingham Purchase remain poor, remote, and thinly settled. Over the past several decades, Washington County has had the highest unemployment and poverty rates of any county in the state, ac-cording to state economist Laurie LaChance. In fact, her office pre-dicts that in 2005, per capita income in Washington County will be only half of that in Cumberland County, which contains Greater Port-land. The differences between the regions, LaChance says, are "major and growing."

In the fall of 1998, the *Bangor Daily News* published a six-part se-ries on the growing gulf between the "Two Maines" that focused pub-lic attention on the phenomenon. "Maine is grappling with a problem plaguing many areas of the nation where traditional rural natural-resource industries have failed, while new high-tech business has taken off in nearby cities," the paper reported. As chip manufacturers

and retirees moved into the south—and traditional fishing and manu-
facturing industries declined elsewhere—the historic fissure between
the two Maines had widened into "a new Gulf of Maine," reflected in
everything from incomes to politics to school spending. Governor Angus King called the divide "the most serious problem facing Maine" at
the time.

As the fissure widened, there was also growing resentment in
the "other Maine" for the "Massified" south. Shortly after the *Bangor
Daily News* series ran, Robbie McKay, a Kingman-based property
rights activist, went so far as to start a petition drive calling for northern
Maine to secede from the rest of the state. Jeffrey Jacob of Corinna
wrote the *News* suggesting that the new state be named "Maine" because "that way all we have to do is rename everything from Augusta
to Kittery as North Massachusetts, a name that more fittingly describes
their political sentiments." Another reader, Ray Leighton of Limestone, suggested that when Quebec finally seceded from Canada,
northern and western Maine and "the whole of Washington County"
should join it to "form a new nation."

But, presuming Leighton's suggestion doesn't take hold, residents
of Washington County had best prepare themselves for what is coming
their way. Because, despite their long-standing poverty, Downeast
Mainers live on what is perhaps the final stretch of undersettled and
underdeveloped coastline on the entire U.S. eastern seaboard. As
other parts of the coast are bought up and built out, development pressure will increasingly spread Downeast and, if the experience of Hancock County and the Midcoast is any guide, change will be swift,
bewildering, and permanent. But, Mount Desert Island aside, Downeast communities still have time to learn from the experiences of their
Southern and Midcoast neighbors, managing growth before growth
starts managing them.

⌒⌒⌒

West of the Penobscot there is a growing realization that ignoring development pressures only makes them worse. "Coastal and southern
Maine have to face the fact that growth is inevitable. Boston has one of
the most overheated housing markets in the country and it's like pok-

ing at a boiling pot: we're going to get some of it splashed our way,"
says Portland Realtor and legislator Ed Suslovic, one of the state's most
vocal advocates of "smart growth" planning. "The question we have to
ask ourselves is: are we going to deal with it responsibly or are we going
to stick our heads in the sand and wait twenty years to find ourselves
building bypasses on top of bypasses?"

The only way to deal with development pressure, Suslovic has long
argued, is to plan for it. This requires adopting a notion that may seem
paradoxical at first: when defending a place's rural character, high-
density development can be your best friend.

On a crisp fall day in 2002 I found myself clambering through a
stretch of scrubby woods sandwiched between Route 1 and the Maine
Turnpike in Scarborough, one of Portland's fastest-growing suburbs.
Along the way my guide, developer John Chamberlain, was describing
what he hoped would become of this, one of the last large developable
properties in this part of Scarborough, a town of 16,000 where Maine
sprawl has taken hold. "The entrance road will go through here," he
said, marking a straight line through a stand of trees with his out-
stretched arm. "This hill," a wooded hump just to our right, "will be
bulldozed into there," an abandoned gravel pit overgrown with scrub.
According to the blueprint John had given me, roads would circle
through the pine trees ahead, lined with homes, parks, brick row
houses, even an apartment building or two. There would be sidewalks
and porches, back alleyways, esplanades, and old-fashioned lampposts.
Altogether, the proposed subdivision would have more than four hundred units, plus shops, trails, and possibly a second-floor office or two.
"It's just going back to the way things were done in the twenties and
thirties," explained John, a South Portland native who runs ALC Development with his brother, Elliott. "We think it's a better way to build."

The idea behind the Chamberlains' ambitious Dunstan Crossing
project was simple: build a traditional village-style neighborhood instead of an automobile-oriented subdivision. Their plans included
public parks, pedestrian-friendly tree-lined streets and esplanades, and
a mix of buildings including single-family homes, condos, row houses,
housing for the elderly, shops, and apartments. The developments'
streets, parks, and hiking trails all would have been open to the public,

and its homes were to be located close to the streets, to which they presented front porches or stoops rather than driveways and garage doors.

Advocates of this "back to the future" approach argue that by encouraging walkable, compact, and diverse neighborhoods, towns can reduce traffic, preserve open space, and grow at the same time. "For two hundred years we grew in a rather good way in this country," says Andres Duany, coauthor of *Suburban Nation*, who is widely regarded as the father of this "New Urbanist" approach to town planning. "We made towns and villages that were walkable, diverse, and compact and they've served us well. It's the human habitat . . . a place where you can actually walk to most of your daily needs." Duany, a Miami town planner who has promoted this line of thinking in cities across the nation, says the problem with current development is that the key ingredients of the human habitat are being kept separate from one another, creating an unhealthy, unsustainable, and ultimately unaffordable pattern of growth, or simply "sprawl." Housing, schools, businesses, and services are typically isolated from one another in pods linked by high-speed collector roads, forcing people to get in their cars to do even the simplest tasks. Walking becomes unpleasant and often dangerous, while every mall, school, or office park becomes marooned in a sea of parking. "What we're suggesting is not at all radical," Duany says, "it's just putting the pieces back together again in a way that makes sense."

Nationally, New Urbanism is usually promoted as a way to use urban design to make suburbs more livable. But in Maine, it has been embraced by smart-growth advocates as a way to preserve the rural character of coastal communities in the face of creeping suburbanization.

Under Evan Richert, the State Planning Office embraced the approach and has tried to encourage towns to plan ahead, designating areas where higher-density, village-type growth will be encouraged and others that will remain open space. To bolster their case, SPO officials point to their 1998 survey showing that 49 percent of prospective Maine homebuyers would be interested in living in a traditional neighborhood like downtown Portland or the village centers of Wiscasset, Damariscotta, or Camden, whose compact streets are lined with trees, shops, apartments, and residences. "There are a considerable number of folks who want to live in rural areas on three or five acres and don't want to live in town, and our approach says that's okay," says John DelVecchio, a community planner at the State Planning Office. "We're saying we at least ought to be providing an alternative for those who'd prefer to live in towns where they can walk to school, work, or shopping."

Ironically, current zoning rules in most Maine towns virtually mandate sprawl, and have made traditional neighborhoods illegal. "There are a handful of developers trying to do higher-density, village-type traditional neighborhoods, but we make that almost impossible because of minimum lot sizes, road frontage, growth caps, and extensive street-width requirements," Suslovic says. "If Wiscasset village burned down today it would be illegal to rebuild it anywhere in the state."

The Chamberlains discovered the hard way just how difficult it is to fight sprawl-making zoning laws. Although they owned the Scarborough land outright and the parcel was zoned for high-density development, the Chamberlains needed special permits *not* to build a sprawling subdivision because the town's zoning ordinances mandated two football fields' worth of open land around every home. The brothers opened the design process to the public, holding open meetings to garner suggestions and ideas about how it should be designed. They were instrumental in getting DOT to address long-standing traffic problems at a nearby intersection, and they even offered to give the town $1 million to buy and preserve farmland on the other side of the Maine Turnpike. But after more than three years of negotiating and hundreds of thousands of dollars in extra costs, the Dunstan Crossing project was rejected by a townwide public referendum by a resounding 4:1 margin. Critics felt it was just too big for their once-rural town.

Instead of the four-hundred-unit neighborhood, the Chamberlains will probably build a traditional sixty-five-unit subdivision on the property—a land-devouring project that requires no special approval whatsoever. By their calculations the town budget will lose $40,000 once this low-density, cookie-cutter development is completed because, in the long term, the cost of services to the area will exceed tax revenues collected from it. By comparison, the Chamberlains estimated that Scarborough would have realized a net gain of $250,000 a year from the Dunstan Crossing plan, which uses services like roads, water, sewage, and school busing far more efficiently.

Other Maine towns still have the chance to decide if and where these kinds of developments should be encouraged. Amanda Russell, who sits on the planning board of Edgecomb, a still largely undeveloped town at the base of the Boothbay peninsula, says this kind of long-range planning is essential. "You look at the maps—the soil maps, 911 maps, tree growth maps, wetlands, tree-growth—and it jumps at you where there should be growth and where there shouldn't be," she says, seated at the kitchen table of her farmhouse. In Maine, towns have a variety of tools that can be used to channel growth to particular areas and away from others, including voluntary conservation and tree growth easements, the lease or purchase of development rights, and zoning changes. Local and national land trusts can play a role as well, by buying and preserving natural areas. "We want to stay rural, so we're looking for a place in our town that will be left for growth, so that other areas can be preserved for rural uses," Russell says.

Unlike their counterparts in many other states, Maine towns exercise considerable control over local affairs, including zoning and planning rules. While this has guaranteed local control over many aspects of civic life, the "home rule" system has made it nearly impossible for Mainers to plan on a regional level. "The problem we have in Maine is that land use planning is fiercely defended at the local level but none of us live locally," says Nigel Calder, an Alna writer and ocean navigator who became active in planning routes for a controversial new highway bypass around Wiscasset. "It used to be that you went to work in the town you grew up in, but now where we live isn't closely related to where we shop, work, or play. We're planning land use at the town level when most of us are living at the regional level." That makes it extremely difficult for towns to manage or resist regional-scale changes, such as the arrival of a Wal-Mart or Home Depot. "Big box retailers plan regionally and have region-wide effects on businesses and growth, but because of the lack of regional planning [in Maine] these big corporations can just come in and play one town off against the other."

"You can't solve a regional problem at the municipal level," agrees Suslovic, who argues for the creation of some sort of regional entities through which clusters of towns can plan land use and share services and expenditures like police, fire, or the hiring of tax assessors. "Until we have a regional structure everything the towns do on their own is really nibbling at the edges of the problem."

As with the problems of sprawl and development on land, shoring up Maine's working waterfronts will require taking a longer view and planning more carefully for the future. There's a great deal at stake for the cultural fabric of coastal Maine, where fishing has long provided the essential thread. At this writing, the incredible abundance of American lobster is holding Maine's fishing communities together, but, as rural Mainers know well, it's risky to have all of one's eggs in a single basket. Fishermen traditionally moved from one species to another, as one fish population or another went from boom to bust with the seasons or longer-term cycles. Coastal Mainers need cod, haddock, and other decimated fish populations to come back because with both fishing and ecology, diversity is strength.

Scientists have long argued for an ecological approach to fisheries and oceans management. But at the dawn of the twenty-first century, efforts to move in that direction have been hampered by the incredible shortage of information on how the Gulf of Maine and other marine systems actually function and change over time. The oceans—impossibly huge, deep, and inhospitable to humans—have been notoriously difficult and expensive places to study and explore. Monitoring their health was an all but impossible task before the computer revolution of the 1990s. There were simply too many factors to keep track of—constantly changing currents, wind patterns, and nutrient levels flowing over a bottom with features as complex and varied as those on dry land. Back when even the most basic data had to be collected manually by divers, submarine pilots, or dredge crews—and collected on clipboards and processed with calculators—getting enough information to see the big picture was often a futile task.

But technology is finally coming to the rescue. Whereas advances in satellite, sonar, and computer technology once helped fishermen overwhelm the fish populations they depended on, the latest advances in these fields may help scientists and fisheries managers avoid such collapses in the future. Perhaps it's fitting that many of these technologies are being perfected just off Maine's shores.

Since 2001, the federal government has spent some $3 million a year to fund the Gulf of Maine Ocean Observing System (GoMoos), a network of offshore buoys, shore-based radar, and orbital satellites that is now constantly monitoring ecological conditions within the Gulf. Nine rugged oceanographic buoys scattered throughout the Gulf collect data on the strength and direction of wind and waves as well as the temperature, salt content, and strength of surface, mid-water, and bottom currents. The buoys then upload the data to computers at the University of Maine in Orono on an hourly basis. These computers also collect data from GoMoos's four ocean-observing radar stations ashore and from three satellites peering down on the Gulf from space. The radar stations, whiplike antenna systems standing outside lighthouses on Cape Cod and Cape Sable and in Saco and Penobscot bays, are able to monitor changes in surface currents and wave patterns from one end of the Gulf to the other. NASA and NOAA satellites contribute detailed images of the Gulf's surface that not only reveal sea surface temperatures, but also concentrations of phytoplankton, the tiny marine plants on which the Gulf's fish life ultimately depends. All this information is digested and wired to an office suite in downtown Portland, where GoMoos's staff post it on the Internet for all to see.

GoMoos, a consortium of research institutions, nonprofits, commercial associations, and state and federal agencies in New England, Maritime Canada, and Washington, provides all of this information on the marine environment free of charge, much as the National Weather Service does for the atmosphere. As of the summer of 2002, GoMoos was the most sophisticated ocean observing system on the continent, a prototype for a national network with the potential to transform the nation's ability to manage its oceans.

While GoMoos's data is available to everyone from fishermen to search and rescue teams, it represents a particularly large boon for marine scientists. For the first time they can tap into a database of the basic oceanographic information most need to understand the environment in which their experiments are taking place. It's the sort of information that could help Bob Steneck and his colleagues figure out where lobster larvae travel and hatch, or allow fisheries managers to "see" water movements that determine the distribution of herring, shrimp, and other species off the coast of Maine. "This generates a wealth of basic data on the Gulf that I could never generate or maintain with a research grant," says Lew Incze, a University of Southern Maine researcher who is compiling a Gulf-wide census of marine life. "It's the backbone of information that researchers like me need to test ideas about what is going on out there in the ocean."

GoMoos is already having an effect on the management of the region's shrimp fishery, which has long suffered from grossly inaccurate population predictions. "The shrimp seasons have been the exact opposite of what [fisheries managers] said it would be," attests David Norton, who takes a break from lobstering in midwinter to set traps for shrimp. "Now I get worried whenever they say there'll be a good year." The problem the scientists have had is that the cold-loving shrimp only come into the Gulf of Maine when icy Arctic waters bring them here, and that happens in some years and not others. Scientists have had a very hard time guessing where the currents would go. But now GoMoos is providing an "early warning system" for shrimp fishery managers. One of the system's buoys is stationed at the main deepwater entrance to the Gulf off Cape Sable, Nova Scotia. Here it can detect the arrival of deep cold-water currents several months before these shrimp-laden waters arrive in, say, David Norton's home port of Boothbay Harbor. "When you're managing this fishery using a fishing-pressure model and not taking these oceanographic factors into account, you'd be just tearing your hair out," says Philip Bogden, GoMoos's CEO. "Without this information you just wouldn't know."

Best of all, GoMoos is an extremely profitable public investment: the system is expected to have a return of $33 million a year on a $3 million budget. It reduces the cost of natural disasters and oil spills by improving the accuracy of search and rescue operations, and it helps to enhance marine habitats and the fish stocks that depend on them. And that, Bogden says, will continue to win over legislators in Augusta and Washington. "If you give me a buck and I give you ten," he asks, "are you going to do it?"

At this writing, it looks like the answer will probably be "yes." A handful of congressmen and senators, including Maine's Olympia Snowe and Susan Collins, are pushing a plan to create a federation of observing systems that would monitor most of the U.S. ocean realm, which extends to two hundred miles off our shores and islands, including Hawaii, Guam, and the Aleutians. The system, which would incorporate GoMoos, would cost $100 million a year to operate, but would generate several billion dollars in savings and increased fisheries revenues.

c~~~~

While satellites and buoys provide continuous information on the movement and properties of the water in the Gulf of Maine, other researchers in the region are developing a complementary technology: one that allows us to see the bottom itself in ways previous generations of marine scientists would never have thought possible.

Ocean engineer Larry Mayer says he will always remember the day he showed Nova Scotia scallop fishermen what his high-tech sonar mapping technology could do.

He sat the fishermen down at his lab at the University of New Brunswick in Fredericton in front of a twelve-foot glass screen. There Mayer displayed his research team's new "chart"—a high-resolution, three-dimensional model of Brown's Bank, a key scalloping ground at the entrance to the Gulf of Maine. Using a joystick, the fishermen flew through seascapes they'd fished their whole lives, seeing rocks and crannies as small as seven or ten feet across and likely scallop habitats hidden on the hilly terrain more than three hundred feet below the surface.

Then one burly six-foot-six scalloper walked up from the back of the room, tears in his eyes, and touched the screen where a rocky crag was displayed. "I always thought it looked like this," he said. "Now I know."

Mayer, now the head of the University of New Hampshire's Center for Coastal and Ocean Mapping, assembled the vivid images by scanning the seafloor with a new technology called multibeam sonar. Ordinary depth sounders found aboard most recreational boats these days send a single beam of sound down to the bottom, calculating the depth based on how long it takes the echo to return. Rather than a single ping, multibeam systems send dozens, even hundreds of beams simultaneously, allowing ocean mappers to construct detailed 3-D maps of structures on the bottom. The technology was originally developed by the U.S. Navy in preparation for the apocalypse; undersea mountains and canyons apparently exert enough gravitational pull to make militarily significant alterations in the trajectory of intercontinental ballistic missiles, so it was essential the mountains be precisely mapped. The Navy designed multibeam for this purpose, but paid little thought to its utility in underwater mapping. Once the cold war ended, the Canadian Hydrographic Survey brought in Mayer's team at UNB to develop software that would allow survey ships to make better navigational charts. It worked like a charm, yielding startling 3-D color images of harbors, fishing banks, and underwater wrecks.

On his office laptop, Mayer showed me his team's new computerized multibeam chart of the entrance to the Piscataqua River, which divides Kittery, Maine, from Portsmouth, New Hampshire. On the screen we flew over rolling sand ripples and rocky outcroppings, and passed between the sharply dredged shipping channels leading to Kittery's busy naval yard. Individual boulders, some no bigger than coffee tables, stood out starkly amid the gently undulating sand and sloping mud bottoms. In some areas, the chart included such detailed imagery that individual lobster traps were clearly visible on the seafloor in sixty feet of water. Elsewhere he showed images of sunken cargo ships, their funnels and superstructure clearly visible despite being hundreds of feet underwater. There were images of sunken Sherman tanks his team located off the Normandy invasion beaches in France, and others from Georges Bank where the bottom is crisscrossed with the long plowlike furrows that bottom trawlers leave behind them. In all the images, resolution was directly related to depth. In twenty feet of water, Mayer's maps revealed rocks as small as a basketball, while in four thousand feet of water, the smallest objects were about the size of a modest home.

Mayer's team has even been able to recognize the difference between sand, mud, gravel, and rocky bottoms by analyzing the qualities of returning sonar beams, which are distorted based on the texture and solidity of the bottom. That's allowed ocean mappers to make considerable headway in what is perhaps the "holy grail" of underwater cartography: being able to map likely bottom habitats from the surface. "We can't see individual animals—say a lobster—but we can map the types of seabed they like to live on," explains John Hughes Clarke, who became head of the University of New Brunswick's Ocean Mapping Center when Mayer moved to UNH. "That has some dramatic applications."

For scientists who study bottom-dwelling creatures, it is the difference between night and day. "When we drop our cameras and other instruments over the side we're really running blind most of the time," explains Les Watling, a benthic oceanographer at the Darling Marine Center. Watling studies worms, sponges, and other creatures that live on the ocean bottom, and has discovered several species of beautiful cold-water corals living in the deep canyons of the Gulf of Maine. "Multibeam mapping allows us to pinpoint places and things we might want to study," he says. "We don't have much multibeam mapping in the Gulf yet," he adds, "but we could sure use it."

Fishermen could become important beneficiaries of the technology as well. Clark's team is using multibeam to map potential sturgeon spawning habitat in New Brunswick's Saint John River. Nova Scotian scallopers were so impressed with Mayer's maps that one of the larger companies purchased a million-dollar multibeam system of their own and have used it to pinpoint the gravelly bottoms scallops like. It has allowed them to fill their individual, government-imposed scallop quotas in one-quarter of the time it used to take, while dragging their dredges over one-third as much bottom, reducing collateral damage to other organisms. It's been good for fishermen and fishing banks alike. "But if you did this without firm quotas, it would be a disaster," cautions Mayer, who says he's "lost a lot of sleep" worrying about the potential abuses of the technology, which, like so many technological advances, could be used for good or evil.

The fisheries collapses in the Gulf of Maine and elsewhere have generated a scientific consensus on the need to take a more sophisticated approach to managing human activities on the ocean. In New England, many scientists and conservation groups are pushing the federal government to create a network of marine protected areas that would, in effect, zone the seafloor much as people already zone activities on land. Some areas might be zoned for aquaculture operations, others for oil drilling and compatible fishing, a third opened and closed to bottom trawling in multiyear cycles to allow any one area to recover. Some areas might be closed in certain seasons to protect fish as they gather to spawn or lay eggs, while a few might even be closed altogether to serve as natural reserves free from disturbance.

Scientists say the latter, fully protected reserves, would serve as an important "insurance policy" to protect biodiversity, habitat, and spawning fish against our still-considerable ignorance about the oceans and how to sustainably use what's in them. In places like New Zealand, where a few "no take" marine reserves have been in place for decades, scientists now find twenty-five to thirty times as many crayfish and rock lobster within the reserves as there are outside them, while fishermen report a strong spillover effect in the surrounding fishing grounds. "Right now it's like we have a few oases in the desert," says Bill Ballantine, a marine biologist at the University of Auckland's Leigh Marine Laboratory and one of the world's leading experts on marine reserves. "If we had an intelligent system, a proper network, then there wouldn't be a great difference between what's inside the reserves and what's outside."

By providing the big picture, GoMoos and multibeam surveys will be of enormous assistance in determining where and what sort of marine protected areas or marine reserves should be established in the Gulf of Maine. But that will still leave a great deal of ecological detective work to tease out the details, the sort of down-and-dirty fieldwork that Bob Steneck, Rick Wahle, Carl Wilson, and others have been doing on the American lobster. The same services are required for lots of other species, from cod and haddock to muck-dwelling worms and stately humpback whales. "We're not making very good use of the information that we already have in hand about the oceans, but we could be making even better decisions if we had better and more information," says Jane Lubchenco of Oregon State University, one of the nation's premier marine scientists. "We're never going to understand everything about these ecoystems, but we can do a lot better if we have a handle on what the natural fluctuations and biological processes are like."

In their effort to get a handle on these sorts of issues, field scientists in Maine are increasingly taking a page from Steneck's playbook by collaborating with fishermen themselves. "The first step of the scientific process is observation, and fishing is all about observation," says Don Perkins, president of the Gulf of Maine Research Institute in Portland, which specializes in drawing fishermen and scientists together for collaborative research projects. "Scientists bring methods and expertise in exploring the questions that arise from those observations," he says.

Perkins says his institute serves as combination "matchmaker and marriage counselor" between the groups and their distinct and sometimes contradictory priorities and professional cultures. Indeed, herring fishermen have begun using their own vessels to help scientists survey stocks of the notoriously elusive fish, and so have greater faith in the scientists' data. "Now it's the herring industry that's pushing the [fisheries managers at NMFS] to develop a better fishery management plan," he says. The institute helped Maine and New Hampshire fisheries managers organize the first regular survey of their states' inshore cod, haddock, and flounder stocks using an out-of-work Portland fishing trawler and its crew. The owner of one fishing trawler, Cameron McLellan, recently approached Perkins's office looking for scientists to help him undertake a detailed study of the impact of trawlers on bottom habitat. At this writing, the project was under way, using McLellan's own vessel as the primary research platform. "If I were a scientist who needed to go down and study something two hundred fathoms down, I'd pick a fishing vessel over a chartered research vessel if the option was available," Perkins adds. "The fishermen are just brilliant at operating in these environments." Add fishermen and scientists together, he says, and "the two are greater than the sum of the parts."

I don't know whether one can "save" Maine's land, sea, and culture from the forces that are dismantling it. I know that things change— places, people, ecosystems—and that adaptation has been the hallmark of success since the universe was born. The Gulf of Maine didn't even exist ten thousand years ago, the Maine coast less than half that time, with Europeans living on its shores for a mere four centuries. If the native Mainer is a nascent, homegrown culture or ethnicity, it's one born over little more than two centuries, shaped by military, economic, and environmental challenges every bit as serious as the ones before them now.

What worries me about today's crises is their fearsome combination of speed and intensity. Coastal Maine has become integrated with the global economy at a time when people and capital move at an astounding pace, overwhelming zoning boards and fisheries managers alike. The unquenchable demand of Asia's great fish markets creates and destroys fisheries for urchins, whelks, and other strange creatures before scientists can even develop a management plan. A fishing hamlet is transformed into a retirement colony so fast that the newcomers never even realize what was there and what has been lost.

New people, as Richard Stanley says, have always been moving to the coast, and thank goodness for that. Before, most came to embrace and revel in Maine's unique character, albeit sometimes an idealized version of it. There's much less of that today. People are coming for property bargains, for a trophy house near a golf course with a good hospital nearby, for a dog park and a community center with familiar landscaping, curbside recycling and quaint, tidy waterfronts, even if they've just moved to Boothbay, Port Clyde, or Corea. Many are coming not to embrace Maine, but rather to remake it in the homogenized image of Suburbistan. It's a world that won't be compatible with fish piers and bait trucks, town meetings and deer hunting season, lobstermen, lumbermen, and worm diggers. I wonder if, twenty years from now, Maine will look and feel any different from any other low-density suburb in the great East Coast megalopolis. I wonder if anyone will even remember what came before.

Then I'm reminded, week in and week out, of Maine's practical, independent-minded civic character. Our poor, backwater state has led the country in everything from recycling bottles to securing health care for low-income citizens, from confronting the excesses of drug companies to enacting policies to reduce greenhouse gas emissions. Our legislators developed laws recognizing key aspects of our lobstermen's traditional management practices, while scientists and fishermen are adapting cutting-edge technologies to better understand and protect the ecosystems our fishing industry depends on. There are popular movements afoot to reform state property tax laws so they protect current owners from market bubbles, while citizens' groups have sprouted up all along the coast to find solutions to sprawl, road congestion, and the loss of farms, forests, and accessible shorefront. When Wal-Mart announced plans to open a superstore in Bangor, opponents created a lobbying group against it, while Wal-Mart supporters paid farmers to plow and plant the fields where it would be located to prevent any endangered species from moving in and upsetting the process. Mainers, whether they've been here a few decades or a few generations, still get engaged in local politics with an intensity that residents of few other states can match. Grassroots civics, perhaps, will be the coast's saving grace, a force even the most oblivious of newcomers may come to appreciate.

The morning after Trap Day on Monhegan, most of the working guests returned to the mainland with the *Laura B.*, accompanied by a Dumpster's worth of compressed trash and a small cache of empty natural gas cylinders. The island resumed its ordinary winter pace. I walked through the village without seeing another soul, though I could hear the sound of conversation in the tiny post office where the postmaster was sorting the contents of mailbags carried out by the *Laura B.* The next boat—the next mail—wouldn't arrive until the day after tomorrow, and I would be returning with it.

As I walked, the village slowly gave way to forest, the houses retreating from the road and one another, tucked away in their own evergreen chambers. At one driveway entrance someone had festooned a large pine tree with old lobster buoys, lending it the appearance of a gigantic Christmas tree. Not far beyond, the forest closed in all around and the rutted dirt road gave way to a narrow path of dark, foot-packed soil. The trees grew larger as I made my way across the island, culminating in a large old-growth stand known, appropriately, as Cathedral Woods. Then, as I approached the island's back side, the path vanished into sheets of exposed granite, reduced to imagined lines between markers of piled stone.

At the crest of this final hill I emerged from a last stand of wind-beaten trees and onto the crest of Black Head, a near-vertical wall of dark granite rising up from the crashing, sizzling sea 150 feet below. Guillemots and herring gulls bobbed in the surf between fish-finding plunges or soared beneath my rocky perch, tracing circles in the air before landing on their own tenuous perches farther down the wall. Looking south along the shore the scene was repeated on White Head and Burnt Head, Monhegan's other bulwarks against the sea. From here one can see across the ocean for miles and miles, from the dark green sweep of the mainland shore to the scrubby, treeless outer islands of Penobscot Bay, each clad in its winter plumage of rust and tan. In the past four centuries, empires have come and gone, whole civilizations have vanished, and great schools of fish have been swept away, but the view from Black Head has changed very little. Apart from the Monhegan lobster boats tending their traps along the bases of the cliffs, there was little to remind one of the twentieth century's arrival, to say nothing of the twenty-first. The island trust negotiated by Sherman Stanley and Ted Edison has spared Monhegan from the suburbanization pressures faced by people inshore; these days, one builds in the vicinity of the village, or not at all. And in the half-century since the trust was negotiated the idea of a wild, publicly accessible back side has become a deeply ingrained part of island identity, even a birthright. Most islanders would no more want to see a mansion atop Black Head than a mainlander would want to see the Grand Canyon subdivided into exclusive house lots. The islanders had the foresight to see that, left to its own devices, development would diminish Monhegan into a shadow or caricature of itself, and they took steps to enhance the prospect that their island would grow and develop on its own terms. The back side would remain as it was, ensuring that, whatever happened, the island would retain its half-wild character.

This is not to say that the island has eschewed change: quite the contrary. Over the past twenty years, Monheganers have built a power plant and a cell phone tower, installed fail-safe pumps and connected home computers to the Internet. Garbage, once "sent overboard," is now compacted and shipped to the mainland for disposal, and the island government even sponsors a free recycling program to cut down on the island's refuse costs. Most island lobstermen have traded the small wooden boats of the early 1970s for large, powerful fiberglass vessels equipped with the latest technology, which make winter fishing far safer and more comfortable. Landlubbers have replaced hand pumps with running water, and remodeled their homes with the latest insulation, reducing the need to surrender most of the home to the cold in midwinter. "Most people living out here aren't trying to live like it was two centuries ago like in Colonial Williamsburg or something like that," Bill Boynton had explained to me back in July. "Having safe, reliable, twenty-four-hour electricity is something most people want." The improvements, he said, have probably helped keep the year-round community from shrinking more than it already has, from roughly one hundred winter residents twenty years ago to less than seventy today.

"People often take out this interview I gave to the [New York] Times in 1970 where I said, 'Anything that makes living on Monhegan easier is a step in the wrong direction,' and they beat me about the head with it," Doug Boynton said with a smile. "Guess your viewpoint changes after a while. Mine certainly has! I mean we do have electricity and phones and the Internet and when people first move out here they more or less expect to have running water in the wintertime. But there's still seven months of the year where the island is pretty much the same as it has been for a long time." There is, he said, "no Nantucket in the winter."

On my final morning on Monhegan, not long after sunrise, I made my way down to Swim Beach to soak in the scenery one last time. Manana stood as a shadow against the orange-washed sky as seabirds flew overhead en route to and from their morning feeding. Small rowing skiffs hung from their moorings as the tide gently flowed through the harbor; all the lobstermen were out on the yawning sea around us, tending their traps on the vast ocean from their rugged little boats. During the night, somebody had left a pile of bright red lobster shells near the water's edge, remnants of the season's first feast. As the sun slowly climbed the sky, the sea quietly crept up the shore, rolling and caressing the shells for a time before carrying them away in its timeless, all-consuming embrace.

Notes

ONE: **Monhegan**

PAGE

3 Seven thousand lobstermen: Maine Department of Marine Resources, *Lobster Zone License and Trap Tag Annual Summary 1997 to 2003*, as posted on their website 20 August 2003. The exact number of commercial lobster license holders was 7,096 in 1997, 7,325 in 2000, and 6,871 in 2003.

9 Ted Hoskins bio: Abby Zimet, "Mission for God," *Portland Press Herald*, 13 February 2000, p. 1A.

10 Fish house, Stanley family history: Ruth Grant Filler, *Monhegan: Her Houses and Her People, 1780–1970* (Melrose, Mass.: Mainstay Publications, 1995), pp. H-5, 39, H-43; Charles Francis Jenny, *The Fortunate Island of Monhegan* (New Bedford, Mass.: Reynolds Printing, 1920), p. 70; Charles Rawlings, "The End of an Era," *Saturday Evening Post*, August 1953; Stanley Family Genealogy, unnumbered file, Monhegan Museum, Monhegan, Me.

11 Monhegan's conservation past: Rawlings (1953); James A. Acheson, "Lobster Traps Limits: A solution to a communal action problem," *Human Organization*, Vol. 57, No. 1 (Spring 1998), p. 47.

12 Monhegan-Friendship lobster war: Author's interview, Douglas Boynton, lobsterman, Monhegan, Me., 19 July 2000; author's interview, Zoe Zanidakis, lobsterwoman, Monhegan, Me., 16 July 2001; author's interview, Marge Kilkelly, state senator, Edgecomb, Me., 7 May 2001; Walter Griffin, "Monhegan asks state to help stem lobster war," *Bangor Daily News*, 25 September 1997; Edie Lau, "Monhegan lobster war draws in state," *Portland Press Herald*, 17 June 1996; Bruce Kyle, "Fishermen skirmish over rights," *Bangor Daily News*, 6 June 1996; Bruce Kyle, "Corrections," *Bangor Daily News*, 21 May 1996; Denise Goodman, "Island sees threat to livelihood," *Boston Globe*, 13 October 1997, p. B1.

19 On painters in Maine: Arnold Skolnick, ed., *Paintings of Maine* (New York: Clarkson Potter, 1991); Pamela J. Belanger, *Maine in America: American Art at the Farnsworth Art Museum* (Rockland, Me.: Farnsworth Art Museum, 2000); Earle G. Shettleworth and W. H. Bunting, *An Eye for the Coast* (Gardiner, Me.: Tilbury House, 1998), p. 130.

22 Geographical statistics on coast, islands: Philip W. Conkling, *Islands in Time* (Rockland, Me.: Island Institute, 1999), p. 15; Lincoln P. Paine, *Down*

East: A *Maritime History of Coastal Maine* (Gardiner, Me.: Tilbury House, 2000), p. 4.

24 MBNA and Matinicus: Author's telephone interview, Stefan Pakulski, community development consultant, Portland/Rockland, Me., 19 November 2002.

25 Zoe Zanidakis quotes, bio: Author's interviews, Zoe Zanidakis, lobsterman, Monhegan, Me.: 16 July 2001, 18 July 2001.

26 George Brackett's *Novelty*: Shettleworth and Bunting (1998), p. 128.

26 Elva Brackett buys Monhegan House: Filler (1995), p. H-19.

28 Lobster license #1A: Phyllis Austin, "Friendship Man, 94, Gives Up Lobstering," Associated Press, 1987, undated clipping from Monhegan Historical and Cultural Museum, File 1246: 87-1-53.

30 Mary Brewer quote: Author's interview, Mary Brewer, newspaper editor, Boothbay Harbor, Me., 9 October 2002.

32 Statistics on New England fisheries collapse: official commercial landings statistics from the National Marine Fisheries Service, available at www.st.nmfs.gov. Halibut figures are for the Atlantic halibut.

33 Sherman Stanley quotes: Author's interview, Sherman M. Stanley, retired lobsterman, Monhegan, Me., 19 July 2001.

34 Shermie Stanley quotes: Author's interview, Shermie Stanley, lobsterman and harbormaster, Monhegan, Me., 20 July 2001.

37 Bill Boynton quotes: Author's interview, Bill Boynton, art gallery owner, Monhegan, Me., 18 July 2001.

37 On Doug and Harry Odom: Author's interview, Tralice Bracy, museum curator, Monhegan, Me., 4 December 2001; Author's interview, Harry and Doug Odom, retired lobstermen and storekeepers, Damariscotta, Me.: 3 October 2001; see also Colin Woodard, "Brothers on the Rock," *Island Journal*, Vol. 19 (2002), pp. 32–37.

39 Barbara Rumsey quotes: Author's interview, Barbara Rumsey, Boothbay Region Historical Society director, Boothbay Harbor, Me., 9 October 2001.

40 Rumsey's research: Barbara Rumsey, "The Changing Face of Boothbay, Part I," *Boothbay Register*, 7 September 2000; Barbara Rumsey, "The Changing Face of Boothbay, Part II," *Boothbay Register*, 14 September 2000, p. 19.

40 James Stevens quotes, bio: Author's interview, James P. Stevens, retired shipyard owner, Boothbay, Me., 10 October 2001; "James P. Stevens," obituary, *Boothbay Register*, 11 July 2002.

42 Bruce Reed quotes; digging industry: Author's interview, Bruce Reed, wormer, Wiscasset, Me., 11 October 2001; Barbara Rumsey, "Shutting off access to the flats for clammers and wormers," *Boothbay Register*, 27 January

2000; Barbara Rumsey, "Opening access to the flats for clammers and worm-ers," *Boothbay Register*, 3 February 2000.

47 Zoe Zanidakis quotes; *Survivor* **appearance:** Author's interview, Zoe Zanidakis, lobsterman, Rockland, Me., 16 July 2002; *Lincoln County News*, 4 April 2002.

TWO: **Dawnland**

51 All Rosier quotes in this chapter are from: James Rosier, *A True Re-lation* (1605), as published in David B. Quinn and Alison M. Quinn, *The En-glish New England Voyages 1602–1608* (London: Hakluyt Society, 1983), pp. 250–311.

52 Southampton: "Southampton, Henry Wriothesley, 3rd Earl of," in *The New Encyclopedia Britannica*, 16th edition, Micropedia Volume XI (Chi-cago: Encyclopedia Britannica, 2002), p. 48; Thomas Bethell, Daniel Wright, Joseph Sobran, Harold Bloom, et al., "The Ghost of Shakespeare," *Harper's*, April 1999, pp. 35–62.

54–55 Gosnold and Pring quotes: *Brereton's Briefe and True Relation of the Discoverie of the North Part of Virginia* (1602), as published in Henry S. Burrage, *Early English and French Voyages* (New York: Scribner's, 1932), p. 331; *The Voyage of Martin Pring* (1603), as published in Burrage, p. 345.

55 Davies quote: *Relation of a Voyage to Sagadahoc* (1608), in Burrage (1932), p. 402.

56 7,500 miles of coast: Philip W. Conkling, *From Cape Cod to the Bay of Fundy: An Environmental Atlas of the Gulf of Maine* (Cambridge, Mass.: MIT Press, 1995), p. 21.

56 Northeast Channel: Conkling (1995), pp. 29, 35, 65, 78.

57 Sixty rivers, 250 billion gallons: Conkling (1995), p. 63.

57 Ecological importance of tides: Conkling (1995), pp. 49–50, 65; Harry Thurston, *Tidal Life: A Natural History of the Bay of Fundy* (Camden East, Ontario: Camden House Publishing, 1990), pp. 24–25.

57 Seabirds/great auk: Quinn and Quinn (1983), pp. 260, 306; Farley Mowat, *Sea of Slaughter* (Shelburne, Vt.: Chapters, 1984), pp. 18–19, 27 (on the great auk); Nicolas Denys, *The Description and Natural History of the Coasts of North America* (Toronto: The Champlain Society, 1908), p. 109 (on eiders).

58 Sturgeon: 400 lbs. from Clayton W. Mayers, "Caviar from the Ken-nebec," *Down East*, August 1964, pp. 46–47, 53.

58 Oysters: George Brown Goode, *The Fisheries and Fisheries Industries of the United States*, Section V, Volume 2 (Washington, D.C.: Government Printing Office, 1887), pp. 512–514; as for their size, James Josselyn says his were nine inches long when shucked and Mowat (p. 198), quoting Denys, describes Gulf of St. Lawrence ones as big as a shoe.

58 **Lobsters gaffed from boats:** This was done off the coast of Nova Scotia during Robert Davies's 1607 expedition. Quinn and Quinn (1983), p. 422.

60 **Wabanaki population in 1605:** Harald E. L. Prins, "Turmoil on the Wabanaki Fronter, 1524–1678," in Richard W. Judd et al. (eds.), *Maine: The Pine Tree State from Prehistory to the Present* (Orono: University of Maine Press, 1995), p. 98.

60 **New England Indian population in 1605:** Howard S. Russell, *Indian New England Before the Mayflower* (Hanover, N.H.: University Press of New England, 1980), pp. 26–28; Francis Jennings, *The Invasion of America: Indians, Colonialism and the Cant of Conquest* (New York: W. W. Norton, 1975), pp. 29–31.

60 **Champlain and Smith quotes on fields:** Russell, pp. 9–11.

60 **Geology of the Gulf of Maine:** Conkling (1995), pp. 34–36.

61 **Functional youth of the Gulf:** Conkling (1995), pp. 71–72; Bruce J. Borque, "Prehistoric Indians of Maine," in Judd et al. (1995), p. 17.

61 **Paleo-Indians to modern Indians:** Borque in Judd et al. (1995), pp. 15–21.

62 **Wabanaki common property:** Prins, "The Children of Gluskap: Wabanaki Indians on the Eve of the European Invasion," in Emerson W. Baker et al. (eds.), *American Beginnings: Exploration, Culture, and Cartography in the Land of Norumbega* (Lincoln: University of Nebraska Press, 1994), p. 98–99; Russell (1980), p. 21. Intrusion "punishable by death" according to Jennings (1975), pp. 67 and 71.

62 **Wabanaki use of resources:** Prins in Baker (1994), pp. 99–100; Russell (1980), pp. 21–22; Prins in Judd (1995), pp. 99–101.

62 **Biard quoted:** From Prins in Judd (1995), p. 99.

63 **Agricultural practices:** Prins in Baker (1994), p. 104.

63 **Deer parks:** Jennings (1975), pp. 61–62, 65. He says on p. 65: "After contact with Europeans, some Indians came to speak of their deer as 'sheep.' " Russell (1980) describes deer parks and moose on pp. 125, 179.

63 **Use of marine resources by Indians:** Russell (1980), pp. 111, 123–124; Prins in Baker (1994), pp. 102–3.

63 **Damariscotta oyster bank:** Rufus King Sewall, *Ancient voyages to the western continent: Three phases of history on the coast of Maine* (New York: The Knickerbocker Press, 1895). The Damariscotta oyster banks were measured in the nineteenth century and found to be "one hundred and eight rods long by eighty to one hundred wide, and twenty-five or six feet deep."

64 **Gluskap:** Colin G. Calloway (ed.), *Dawnland Encounters: Indians and Europeans in Northern New England* (Hanover, N.H.: University Press of New England, 1991), p. 7.

64 Passage to Allen Island: Quinn and Quinn (1983), pp. 261–262.

64 Incidents at anchor in Allen Island: Quinn and Quinn (1983), pp. 262–267.

64 Wabanaki descriptions: Quinn and Quinn (1983), pp. 267–268; see also Prins in Baker (1994), pp. 107–109.

64 Indian trade networks within New England: Prins in Baker (1994), p. 106; Steven L. Cox, "A Norse Penny from Maine," in William W. Fitzhugh and Elizabeth Ward, *Vikings: The North Atlantic Saga* (Washington, D.C.: The Smithsonian Institution Press, 2000), pp. 206–207.

65 Indian trade with Dorset and Thule Eskimos: Patricia D. Sutherland, "The Norse and the Native Americans," in Fitzhugh and Ward (2000), pp. 238–247; Cox in Fitzhugh and Ward, pp. 206–207; author's telephone interview, Steven L. Cox, Wiscasset and Augusta, Me., 23 August 1999; author's telephone interview, Patricia Sutherland, Washington, D.C., and Hull, Quebec, 23 February 2000.

65 Cartier's encounters: Samuel Eliot Morison, *The European Discovery of America: The Northern Voyages* (New York: Oxford University Press, 1971), pp. 369–370.

65 European goods in Maine: Bruce Borque and Ruth H. Whitehead, "Trade and Alliances in the Contact Period," in Baker et al. (1994), p. 132.

66 Walker's moose hides: Borque and Whitehead in Baker (1994), pp. 132–133, 142; Morison (1971), p. 468.

66 Maine Wabanaki in Tadoussac: Borque and Whitehead in Baker (1994), p. 136.

66 Gosnold encounters Micmacs: Quinn and Quinn (1983), p. 117.

66 Shallop-sailing Micmacs: Borque and Whitehead in Baker (1994), pp. 136–142.

66 Cartier's kidnappings: Morison (1971), p. 407 (four children) and p. 420 (ten natives).

67 Verrazano: James Axtell, "The Exploration of Norumbega," in Baker (1994), pp. 156–157; Morison (1971), pp. 303–308.

67 European treachery in New England: *On Gomez:* Axtell in Baker (1994), pp. 154–155. *On Pring:* Axtell in Baker (1994), p. 160; *Pring quotes:* Burrage (1932), p. 351; *On Champlain:* Calloway (1991), pp. 35–36; Prins in Judd (1995), p. 104.

68 Summary of Indian preconceptions: Calloway (1991), p. 34.

68 "Kill the menne of warre by famine": Thomas Churchyard (1579) as quoted in Nicholas P. Canny, "The Ideology of English Colonization: From Ireland to America," *William and Mary Quarterly*, Third Series, Vol. 30, No. 4 (October 1973), p. 582.

68 Christmas Day feast killings: Canny (1973), p. 581.

68 Edmund Spenser account of Munster: David Beers Quinn, *Elizabethans* *and the Irish* (Ithaca, N.Y.: Cornell University Press, 1966), pp. 132–133. Spenser's biography: The Edmund Spenser Homepage at Cambridge University: http://www.english.cam.ac.uk/spenser/biography.htm.

69 **Essex's atrocities:** Canny (1973), pp. 580–581; "Essex, Walter Devereux, 1st Earl of" in *The New Encyclopedia Britannica* (2002), Vol. 4, pp. 565–566; "Southampton," in *The New Encyclopedia Britannica* (2002), Vol. 11, p. 48.

69 **Gilbert's brutalities:** Extended to *"manne, woman, and children":* Canny (1973), p. 582, quoting Sidney's letter to Cecil of January 4, 1570; *"Kille the menne of warre by famine" and severed heads:* Canny, p. 582, quoting Thomas Churchyard (1579).

69 **Irish "wicked and faythless peopoll":** Sir Thomas Smith's letter to Fitzwilliam of 8 November 1572, as quoted in Canny (1973), p. 596.

69 **Irish prefer to "live like beastes":** Barnaby Rich (1578) as quoted in Canny (1973), p. 588.

69 **English view of Irish land practices:** Quinn (1966), pp. 8, 11.

69 **Tatar comparison and quote:** Joannes Boemus (1611) as quoted in Canny (1973), p. 587.

69 **Irish marriages:** Quinn (1966), pp. 80–81.

69 **Irish religion:** Canny, pp. 583–584.

70 **"Irish Dimmie trousers":** Quinn and Quinn (1983), p. 117.

70 **Bear skin as Irish mantle:** Burrage (1932), p. 348.

70 **Other Indian/Irish comparisons by Englishmen:** Quinn (1966), pp. 23–25.

70 **Indian encounters:** Quinn and Quinn (1983), pp. 267–304.

73 **Sheepscot dance account:** This is from Quinn and Quinn (1983), p. 278, quoting the original manuscript version of the Rosier relation, which was originally published in Samuel Purchas, *Pilgrimes,* 4th edition (1625).

74–75 **Anassou to Champlain:** W. L. Grant (ed.), *Voyages of Samuel de Champlain 1604–1618* (New York: Barnes and Noble, 1959), p. 77.

THREE: **The First Frontier**

76 **Gorges's early biography:** Richard Arthur Preston, *Gorges of Plymouth Fort* (Toronto: University of Toronto Press, 1953), pp. 25–55.

76 **Indians in England:** Henry S. Burrage, *Gorges and the Grant of the Province of Maine 1622* (Augusta: State of Maine, 1923), pp. 3–4; Preston (1953), pp. 25–55.

77 **Nature of royal charters:** Francis Jennings, *The Invasion of America: Indians, Colonialism and the Cant of Conquest* (New York: W. W. Norton, 1975), pp. 106–109.

77 **Popham "huge, heavie, ugly . . .":** Bernard Bailyn, *The New England*

Merchants in the Seventeenth Century (Cambridge, Mass.: Harvard University Press, 1955), p. 2.

77 The Virginia Charter (1606): Bailyn (1955), pp. 2–5; Bill Caldwell, *Islands of Maine* (Portland, Me.: Guy Gannett Publishing Co., 1981), p. 46; David B. Quinn and Alison M. Quinn, *The English New England Voyages 1602–1608* (London: Hakluyt Society, 1983), p. 72.

78 Indian population on eastern seaboard (c. 1606): Jennings (1975), p. 19, estimates 72,000 to 90,000 Indians were living in the New England states at this time, which would suggest that there were well over 100,000 living in the regions claimed by the 1606 charter.

78 Challons and Pring expeditions: Quinn and Quinn (1983), pp. 74–76; James P. Baxter, *Sir Ferdinando Gorges and His Province of Maine*, Vol. I (New York: Burt Franklin, 1967; originally published in 1890), pp. 70–73.

78 Scale of Popham undertaking: Caldwell (1981), p. 58; Henry S. Burrage, *Early English and French Voyages* (New York: Charles Scribner's, 1932), p. 397.

78 Popham as trading fort: Bailyn (1955), pp. 4–5.

79 Quotes from Popham colony accounts: Burrage (1932), pp. 406–408.

79 Quote from Jane Stevens: Ellen Barry, "Colony Lost and Found," *Boston Phoenix*, 27 October 1997.

79 Quotes on character of George Popham and Raleigh Gilbert: Sir Ferdinando Gorges letter to the Earl of Salisbury, 3 December 1607, reprinted in Quinn and Quinn (1983), p. 449–451.

80 Indian account of Popham colony to Jesuit: Lettre du Pierre Biard au R.P. Provincial à Paris, Port Royal, 31 January 1612, as published in Reuben Gold Thwaites (ed.), *The Jesuit Relations and Allied Documents*, Vol. 2 (New York: Pagent Book Co., 1959; originally published 1896), pp. 43–45.

80 Sources on the collapse of the Popham colony: Samuel Purchas, *Purchas his pilgrimage* (London: W. Stansby, 1614); Quinn and Quinn (1983), pp. 397–468; Sir Ferdinando Gorges, "A Briefe Narration (1608)," in *Collections of the Maine Historical Society*, Series I, Vol. 2 (Portland: Maine Historical Society, 1847), pp. 22–23.

80 "All of our former hopes . . .": Gorges in *Coll. Me. Hist. Soc.* (1847), p. 23.

81 Gilbert's men gaff lobsters: From Davies's journal as published in Quinn and Quinn (1983), p. 422. This particular incident occurred along the coast of Nova Scotia.

82 Francis Popham's fishing expeditions: Bailyn (1955), p. 5.

82 Jamestown involvement in early fishery: Faith Harrington, "We Tooke Great Store of Cod-fish," in Emerson W. Baker et al. (eds.), *American Beginnings: Exploration, Culture, and Cartography in the Land of Norumbega* (Lincoln: University of Nebraska Press, 1994), pp. 198–199.

82 **Three fishing crews near Monhegan (1614):** John Smith, "Description of New-England" (1616), in Burrage (1923), p. 104.

82 **John Smith's quotes:** John Smith, "Description of New-England" (1616), in Burrage (1923), p. 110–111, 120.

83 **John Smith's vision and further failures:** Charles E. Clark, *Maine: A Bicentennial History* (New York: W. W. Norton, 1976), pp. 23–26; Edwin A. Churchill, "The European Discovery of Maine," in Richard W. Judd et al., (eds.), *Maine: The Pine Tree State from Prehistory to the Present* (Orono: University of Maine Press, 1995), pp. 48–49.

83 **"Under color of fishing":** Gorges in *Coll. Me. Hist. Soc.* (1847), p. 24.

83 **Fishing operations in New World:** Nicolas Denys, *The Description and Natural History of the Coasts of North America (Acadia)* (Toronto: The Champlain Society, 1908), pp. 278–291.

84 **Christopher Levett's vision:** Clark (1976), p. 30.

84 **Damariscove station (1622):** Carl R. Griffin III and Alaric Faulkner, "Coming of Age on Damariscove Island, Maine," *Northeast Folklore* 21 (1980), p. 17, quoting John Pory, "Letter from John Pory to the Governor of Virginia (Sir Francis Wyatt), Autumn 1622, in Sidney V. James (ed.), *Three Visitors to Early Plymouth* (Plymouth, Mass.: Plimoth Plantation Inc., 1963), pp. 15–16; Edward Wilson, *Good News from New England* (1625), as published in *Collections of the Massachusetts Historical Society*, First Series, Vol. 7 (Boston: Little and Brown, 1800), pp. 245–246.

84 **Conditions at fishing stations:** Denys (1908), pp. 260–261, 281–282; Charles E. Clark, *The Eastern Frontier: The Settlement of Northern New England 1610–1763* (New York, Alfred A. Knopf, 1970), p. 23.

86 **Origins, character of fishermen:** Edwin A. Churchill, "Too Great the Challenge: The Birth and Death of Falmouth, Maine 1624–1676," doctoral dissertation, History Department, University of Maine (Orono), August 1979, pp. 89–90; Edwin A. Churchill, "The Founding of Maine, 1600–1640: A Revisionist Interpretation," *Maine Historical Society Quarterly*, Vol. 18, No. 1 (Summer 1978), pp. 27–29, 36.

86 **"Walking tavern" account (1645):** John Josselyn, "An Account of Two Voyages to New England" (1675), in *Collections of the Massachusetts Historical Society*, Series 3, Vol. 3 (Cambridge, Mass.: E. W. Metcalf & Co., 1833), p. 351.

86 **Accounts of Indian plagues (1616–19):** Prins in Judd (1995), p. 108–9; Jennings (1975), pp. 15–31; Thomas Dermer, "Dermer's Letter to Thomas Purchase, 1619," in Burrage (1932), p. 9; Thomas Morton, *New English Canaan* (London: 1632), ch. 3.

87 **Gorges quote on plagues:** Prins in Judd (1995), p. 108.

87 **The Council of New England:** Bailyn (1955), pp. 5–7; Samuel F. Haven, "History of Grants Under the Great Council of New England," in Mas-

sachusetts Historical Society, *Lectures delivered in a course before the Lowell Institute, in Boston* (Boston: The Massachusetts Historical Society, 1869), pp. 143–145; Preston (1953), p. 203.

89 Council and merchant monopoly: Bailyn (1955), pp. 7–9.

89 Thomas Weston biography: William Bradford, *Of Plymouth Plantation 1620–1647* (New York: Modern Library, 1967), p. 37n. (Samuel Eliot Morison, the editor of this volume, wrote the footnote in question.)

89 Weston and Pilgrim patent: Bradford (1967), pp. 37–39, 93n.; George F. Willison, *Saints and Strangers* (New York: Reynal & Hitchcock, 1945), pp. 111–115; Haven (1869), pp. 148, 152.

90 Character, behavior of Wessagusset settlers: Willison (1945), pp. 214–218.

90 Weston sells Gorges's cannons: Bradford (1967), p. 135.

90 Thomas Weston and Wessagusset: Willison (1945), pp. 207–208, 214–228.

90 Pilgrims slaughter Indians at Wessagusset: Jennings (1975), p. 186; Willison, pp. 223–229.

90 Robert Gorges episode: Willison (1945), pp. 234, 239; Bradford (1967), pp. 133n., 133–138; Preston (1953), pp. 226–228.

91 Massachusetts Bay patent and charter: E. J. Chandler, *Ancient Sagadahoc* (Thomaston, Me.: Conservatory of American Letters, 1997), pp. 69–70; Haven (1869), pp. 151, 155–156; "The Settlement of New England," *Littell's Living Age*, Vol. 6, No. 794, (13 August 1859), pp. 401–403.

92 New England population in 1630: These are my estimates based on the descriptions of settlements as laid out in Charles Knowles Bolton, *The Real Founders of New England* (Boston: F. W. Faxon, 1929), pp. 103–115, and in Willison (1945), pp. 261, 267–268.

I estimated a maximum of Pemaquid (150 people), Damariscove (20), Isle of Shoals (100), Pannaway (9), Newagen (20), Hilton/Dover (5), remaining Salem/Cape Ann Old Planters (40), Wessagusset diaspora (30), and maybe 50 others randomly scattered around Boston Bay and the trading posts. As for the Pilgrims' settlements, Willison says there were only 180 people there in 1625, but 30 more came in 1630 and at least 35 to 40 in 1629, plus births.

92 The 1629–31 patent mill: Chandler (1997), p. 70.

92 Origins of early Mainers: The sample is from Charles E. Banks, *Topographical Dictionary of 2885 English Emigrants to New England 1620–1650* (Baltimore: Southern Book Company, 1987). My tally, which excludes the Isle of Shoals, came to 124 emigrants to Maine. Of these the West Country accounted for 80 of the settlers (or 64.51 percent), Cornwall (9), Devonshire (55), Dorset (3), Gloucestershire (9), Somerset (1), and Wiltshire (3).

Of the remaining 44 emigrants, only 16 (12.9 percent) came from East Anglia: Essex (4), Kent (6), Suffolk (6).

Fifteen settlers (12.1 percent) came from the Midlands: Bedfordshire (3), Buckinghamshire (1), Cambridgeshire (1), Derbyshire (1), Lincolnshire (2), Nottinghamshire (1), Shropshire (1), Warwickshire (3), Worcestershire (1), Hertfordshire (1).

Seven (5.65 percent) came from the South of England: Hampshire (1), London (5), Middlesex (1).

Six (4.84 percent) came from the North: Durham (1), Lancashire (3), Yorkshire (2).

Not only did the vast majority come from the West Country, they were concentrated in Devonshire, which alone accounted for 44.4 percent of the emigrants. In fact, 33 of the settlers in the sample (or 26.6 percent) came from just one section of the Devon coast between Plymouth and Teignmouth, and that number jumps to 36 (29 percent) if adjacent interior villages are taken into account and 37 (29.8 percent) with the inclusion of the Plymouth harbor village of Sheviock, Cornwall.

94 Devon described: Carl Bridenbaugh, *Vexed and Troubled Englishmen 1590–1642* (New York: Oxford University Press, 1968), pp. 66, 69–70, 206.

94 Wage-earners "meanest": Bridenbaugh (1968), pp. 49–50.

94 People living in holes: Bridenbaugh (1968), p. 135. The quote is from John Taylor, 1629, traveling through Coventry, but Bridenbaugh says the situation was similar in Devon.

94 Puritans' counties of origin: My own calculations are based on the revised Banks tables compiled by Jonathan Schwartz and published in David Hackett Fischer, *Albion's Seed: Four British Folkways in America* (New York: Oxford University Press, 1989), pp. 34n.–35n.

These revised tables show the origins of 2,284 emigrants to Massachusetts, of which the seven eastern counties account for 972, or 42.6 percent of the total.

94 Origins of "Great Fleet" settlers: These calculations are based on Hadley Lewis's numbers as published in Fischer (1989), p. 35n.

95 Eastern counties described: Kevin Phillips, *Cousin's Wars* (New York: Basic Books, 1999), pp. 25–27; Fischer (1989), pp. 41–49; Bridenbaugh (1968), pp. 203–4.

96 Massachusetts Bay settlements and their goals: Fischer (1989), pp. 18–24, 64, 66, 181–188; Bridenbaugh (1968), p. 69.

96 Massachusetts Bay place names: Fischer (1989), p. 38n.

96 Maine settlements and their goals: Chandler (1997), pp. 97–99; Churchill in Judd (1996), pp. 56–57; Churchill, "Mid-Seventeenth Century Maine: A World on the Edge," in Baker et al. (1994), p. 243; Emerson Baker, "The World of Thomas Gorges: Life in the Province of Maine in the 1640s," in Baker et al. (1994), pp. 261–282; Charles E. Banks, *History of York, Maine, Volume I* (Portsmouth, N.H.: Peter E. Randall, 1990; first published 1931), p. 71.

96–97 Maine place names: Phillip R. Rutherford, *The Dictionary of Maine Place-Names* (Freeport, Me.: Bond Wheelright Co., 1970).

97 Farming two or three acres: Bridenbaugh (1968), pp. 48–50.

97 Gorges's new charter for Maine(1639): Henry S. Burrage, *The Beginnings of Colonial Maine* (Portland, Me., 1914), pp. 289–291; James P. Baxter, *Memoir of Sir Ferdinando Gorges* (Boston: Prince Society, 1890), pp. 180–182.

98 Banks quotes on Gorges's grant: Banks (1931), p. 59.

98 Thomas Gorges biography, descriptions of Gorgeana: Robert E. Moody (ed.), *The Letters of Thomas Gorges* (Portland: Maine Historical Society, 1978), pp. ix, 1, 7–17; Baker in Baker et al. (1994), pp. 244, 247.

99 Mainers suspicious of Thomas Gorges: Churchill in *MEHSQ*, p. 33; Moody (1978), p. xi.

99 Thomas Gorges on character of Indians: Moody (1978), p. 2.

99 Religious tolerance under Thomas Gorges: Baker in Baker et al. (1994), p. 276; Moody (1978), p. 57.

99 "The winter was very tedious . . .": Moody (1978), p. 58.

99 Agamenticus becomes Gorgeana: Baxter (1890), pp. 185–188.

99 Thomas Gorges protests he can't fill offices: Baker in Baker et al. (1994), p. 281; Moody (1978), pp. 89, 115.

100 Puritan intolerance: Daniel J. Boorstin, *The Americans: The Colonial Experience* (New York: Vintage Books, 1958), pp. 1–9.

101 Puritan justice, punishments: William D. Williamson, *The History of the State of Maine*, Vol. 1 (Hallowell, Me.: Glazier, Masters & Co., 1832), pp. 380–381; Fischer (1989), p. 194.

101 Thomas Gorges on Puritan justice: Thomas Gorges's letter of September 1641 to Sir Ferdinando Gorges, in Moody (1978), p. 55.

101 Puritans' atrocities to Indians: Jennings (1975), pp. 212, 221–227; Charles M. Segal and David C. Stineback, *Puritans, Indians, and Manifest Destiny* (New York: Putnam, 1977), pp. 108–112.

102 Puritans covet Maine, disparage Mainers (1650): Clark (1976), pp. 39–41; Churchill in *MEHSQ*, pp. 34–35; Clark (1970), p. 31.

102 Maine governing itself: Clark (1970), p. 48; Churchill in *MEHSQ*, pp. 32–33.

102 Puritan takeover: Williamson (1832), Vol. 1, pp. 344–345, 350–355, 387–393; Burrage (1914), pp. 370–382.

104 Puritan court dockets clogged with unruly Mainers: For examples see *Province and Court Records of Maine*, Vol. 1 (Portland: Maine Historical Society, 1928), pp. 5, 12, 24, 41–42, 52–53, 56–57, 81, 91–92, 103–7, 139–143, p. 151, 153, 162, 169, 182, 185, 192, 210–212, 216–217.

104 Boston merchants exploitative: John Josselyn, *An Account of Two Voyages to New-England* (1675), in *Collections of the Massachusetts Historical*

Society, 3rd Series, Vol. 3 (Cambridge, Mass.: E. W. Metcalf and Co., 1833), pp. 249, 352.

104 Not all Maine's population was English—footnote sources: Charles E. Banks, "Scotch Prisoners Deported to New England by Cromwell, 1651–2," in *Proceedings of the Massachusetts Historical Society*, Vol. 61 (Oct. 1927–June 1928), Boston: Massachusetts Historical Society, 1928, pp. 15–16; Baker in Baker et al. (1994), pp. 277–278; Joseph Williamson, "Slavery in Maine," *Collections of the Maine Historical Society*, Vol. 2 (Bath: MEHS, 1876), pp. 207–216; Josselyn (1675), p. 249.

104 Indians outnumber English: The population of Maine's Indians after the 1616–17 plague was estimated at 5,000 by Howard S. Russell, *Indian New England Before the Mayflower* (Hanover, N.H.: University Press of New England, 1980), p. 28. An estimate of 7,000 seems fair given that a second epidemic struck in the 1630s, and dispersed survivors would have been more resistant to disease over the following two generations.

105 Massachusetts, Maine, and Ferdinando Gorges the younger: Churchill in Judd (1996), pp. 64–65; Josselyn (1675), pp. 342–343.

105 Maine sold to Massachusetts by Gorges the younger: Clark (1970), p. 64.

106 Acadia's 1670 population: Aline S. Taylor, *The French Baron of Pentagouet: Baron St. Castin and the Struggle for Empire in Early New England* (Camden, Me.: Picton Press, 1998), p. 11.

106 Acadians and Micmacs (and Quinn quote): Arthur Quinn, *A New World: An Epic of Colonial America from the Founding of Jamestown to the Fall of Quebec* (New York: Faber and Faber, 1994), pp. 386–387.

106 French gunsmiths: Alaric Faulkner and Gretchen Faulkner, "Acadian Settlement: 1607–1700," in Baker et al. (1994), pp. 91–92.

107 Significance of King Philip's War: Stephen Saunders Webb, *1676: The End of American Independence* (New York: Alfred A. Knopf, 1984), pp. xv–xvi, 411; Russell Bourne, *Red King's Rebellion: Racial Politics in New England 1675–1678* (New York: Atheneum, 1990), p. 242.

107 Proportional losses in Maine: My calculations based on approximately 500 dead and the proportional destruction of homes in the province. Williamson (1832), Vol. 1, p. 253, said there were 260 confirmed deaths in Maine, but adds "there were probably many others, the accounts of whose deaths have never been recorded."

108 Thomas Gardiner's protest: quoted from Faulkner and Faulkner in Judd (1996), p. 92; Bourne (1990), p. 225.

108 Reduction of French fort: Faulkner and Faulkner in Judd (1996), pp. 91–92.

108 Indians would starve without firearms: Williamson (1832), Vol. 1, pp. 517–518.

108 Saco drowning incident: Williamson (1832), Vol. 1, p. 519.

108 1675 attacks in western Maine: Bourne (1990), pp. 210–211, 217–220.

109 Abenakis' letter about starving: Taylor (1998), p. 36.

109 Starvation prompts maggot collecting, exodus: Taylor (1998), p. 34; Bourne (1990), p. 235.

109 Great raid of August 1676: Ida Sedgwick Proper, *Monhegan: The Cradle of New England* (Portland, Me.: The Southworth Press, 1930), pp. 204–210; Francis B. Greene, *History of Boothbay, Southport and Boothbay Harbor, Maine 1623–1905* (Portland, Me.: Loring, Short & Harmon, 1906), pp. 87–89; Bourne (1990), p. 227; Charles B. McLane, *Islands of the Mid-Maine Coast, Volume IV: Pemaquid Point to the Kennebec River* (Rockland, Me.: Island Institute, 1994), pp. 64, 75; Griffin and Faulkner (1980), p. 20.

110 Henry Champnois and Mugg Hegone: Barbara Skinner Rumsey, *Colonial Boothbay: Mid-1600s to 1775* (East Boothbay, Me.: Winnegance House, 2000), pp. 42, 43, 80; Bourne (1990), p. 233.

110 Monhegan and refugees: Proper (1930), pp. 205–206; Charles McLane, *Islands of the Mid-Maine Coast, Volume III: Muscongus Bay and Monhegan Island* (Rockland, Me.: Island Istitute, c. 1977), pp. 217–219.

111 Waldron biography: Bourne (1990), p. 229.

111 Waldron's cruel deception: Bourne (1990), 232; Taylor (1998), pp. 40–41.

112 St. Castin and Penobscots: Taylor (1998), pp. 40–41.

112 Indian campaigns of fall 1676 and spring 1677: Ibid., pp. 41–49; Bourne (1990), pp. 233–240.

112 Duke of York's intervention: Bourne (1990), p. 241.

112 Terms of the Peace of Casco: Taylor (1998), p. 50; Bourne (1990), p. 241.

112 Royal commission's findings: Charles B. McLane, *Islands of the Mid-Maine Coast, Volume IV: Pemaquid Point to the Kennebec River* (Rockland, Me.: Island Institute, 1994), pp. 15–16. These were the findings of Edward Randolph, agent of the Lords of the Committee on Plantations in London.

112 County of Cornwall laws: McLane (1994), pp. 16–18; Bourne (1990), p. 241.

112 Causes of later Indian wars: David L. Ghere, "Diplomacy and War on the Maine Frontier, 1678–1759," in Judd et al. (1995), pp. 124–130.

113 Early engagements and Waldron's execution (1688–89): Greene (1906), pp. 94–96.

113 Population estimate for 1689: This is my estimate, based on the following information. Clark (1970), pp. 170, 226, estimates that in 1690—after the evacuation—Maine had a population of about 2,000 people. In 1689, another 500 fled to the islands and the area east of the Kennebec and perhaps 500 more

were killed throughout Maine. This leaves the area between Wells and the Kennebec, including the substantial settlements of Falmouth, Casco Bay, Saco, and Black Point (Scarborough), which probably accounted for another 3,000 people. This would make at least 6,000 residents in 1689, roughly the same number as in 1675, just before King Philip's War.

114 Indian atrocities in later wars: Samuel Penhallow, *The History of the Wars of New-England With the Eastern Indians* (Boston: T. Fleet, 1726), pp. 4, 6, 32; Cotton Mather, "Decennium Luctuosum" (1699), in Charles H. Lincoln, *Narratives of the Indian Wars 1675–1699* (New York: Barnes and Noble, 1913), pp. 238–239, 202, 210, 212–213.

114 English atrocities in later wars: Penhallow (1726), pp. 104–106; Ghere in Judd (1995), p. 127.

114 £100 per scalp: Penhallow (1726), p. 107.

114 Effects of wars on Mainers: Clark (1970), pp. 69–76.

115 Effects of wars on Indians: Ghere in Judd (1995), pp. 129–134.

115 Starvation quotes, winter 1698–99: Mather in Lincoln (1913), p. 273.

FOUR: **Insurrection**

117 Dunbar's Sagadahoc scheme: Francis B. Greene, *History of Boothbay, Southport and Boothbay Harbor, Maine 1623–1905* (Portland, Me.: Loring, Short & Harmon, 1906), pp. 109–110; Charles B. McLane, *Islands of the Mid-Maine Coast, Volume IV: Pemaquid Point to the Kennebec River* (Rockland, Me.: Island Institute, 1994), p. 27.

117 Belcher's description of Dunbar: Belcher to Jonathan Belcher Jr., letter of June 2, 1737, as quoted in John A. Schutz, "Succession Politics in Massachusetts, 1730–1741," *William and Mary Quarterly*, Third Series, Vol. 15, No. 4 (October 1958), p. 517.

117 Dunbar's "impossibly bad temper": Schutz (1958), p. 514.

117 Dunbar's connections with the Board of Trade: Greene (1906), p. 109.

118 Conditions in Scotland: David Hackett Fischer, *Albion's Seed: Four British Folkways in America* (New York: Oxford University Press, 1989), pp. 626–629.

118 William Wallace, Robert the Bruce: Ibid., p. 624.

118 Conditions in Northern Ireland: James G. Layburn, *The Scotch-Irish: A Social History* (Chapel Hill: University of North Carolina Press, 1962), pp. 113–114, 122–127; Jonathan Bardon, *A History of Ulster* (Belfast, U.K.: The Blackstaff Press, 1992), pp. 128, 170–178.

119 Early Scotch-Irish immigrants to New England: Barbara Skinner Rumsey, *Colonial Boothbay: Mid-1600s to 1775* (East Boothbay, Me.: Winnegance House, 2000), pp. 100–102; Layburn (1962), pp. 238–239; William Willis, "The Scotch-Irish Immigration to Maine," *Collections of the Maine*

Historical Society, Series 1, Vol. 6 (Portland: Maine Historical Society, 1859), pp. 10–17.

120 Difficult conditions of early Boothbay area settlers: "Petition of the Inhabitants of Boothbay (1772)," in James Phinney Baxter (ed.), *Documentary History of the State of Maine*, Vol. 14 (Portland, Me.: Lefavor-Tower Company, 1910), pp. 166–170; "Deposition of Samuel McCobb," 23 October 1772, in Greene (1906), pp. 117–119; "Deposition of John Beath," 23 October 1772, in Greene, pp. 119–121.

121 King George II forbids Massachusetts attack on Dunbar: Rumsey (2000), p. 95.

122 Stephen Lazabe incident: "Deposition of Joseph Johnson," *York County Court of Common Pleas*, North Yarmouth, 4 October 1736.

122 Sloop and sheriff incident: "Deposition of Thomas Pickenden," London, 19 January 1730, in James Phinney Baxter (ed.), *Documentary History of the State of Maine*, Vol. 11 (Portland, Me.: Lefavor-Tower Company, 1908), pp. 21–23.

122 Josiah Glover incident: "Complaint of Josiah Glover to His Excellency Jonathan Belcher," Cambridge, 6 September 1730, in Baxter (1908), Vol. 11, pp. 44–47.

122 Leading Boston families of the 1730s: Bernard Bailyn, *The New England Merchants in the Seventeenth Century* (Cambridge, Mass.: Harvard University Press, 1955), pp. 197–198; John J. Waters and John A. Schutz, "Patterns of Massachusetts Colonial Politics: The Writs of Assistance and the Rivalry between the Otis and Hutchinson Families," *William and Mary Quarterly*, Third Series, Vol. 24, No. 4 (October 1967), p. 548.

123 Three great proprietary claims described: Alan Taylor, *Liberty Men and Great Proprietors: The Revolutionary Settlement on the Maine Frontier, 1760–1820* (Chapel Hill: University of North Carolina Press, 1990), pp. 12–13; Samuel F. Haven, "History of Grants Under the Great Council of New England," in Massachusetts Historical Society, *Lectures delivered in a course before the Lowell institute, in Boston* (Boston: Massachusetts Historical Society, 1869), pp. 156–160.

123 Great Proprietors fight Dunbar: Greene (1906), p. 123; McLane (1994), Vol. 3, p. 28.

124 "There will be a kind of warr . . .": "Colonel Dunbar to Mr. Secretary Popple," letter of 15 September 1730, in Baxter (1908), Vol. 11, p. 50.

124 Waldo gains control of Muscongus Patent: McLane (1994), Vol. 3, p. 28 (110 of 120 shares is 92 percent); Thomas Morgan Griffiths, *Maine Sources in* The House of Seven Gables (Waterville, Me: 1945), pp. 26–27.

124 Waldo's biography and business interests: Amelia C. Ford, "Samuel Waldo," in *Dictionary of American Biography* (Washington, D.C.: American Council of Learned Societies, 1928–1936), reproduced in History Resource

Center (Farmington Hills, Mich.: Gale Group); "Background notes to the Richard Fry Papers," Ann Arbor, Mich.: University of Michigan, www.clements. umich.edu/Webguides/S/SmFry.html (accessed 15 April 2002).

124 Waldo according to Thomas Griffiths: Griffiths (1945), p. 28.

125 Dunbar settlers not to leave until "his majesty" says so: "Deposition of John Beath," 23 October 1772, in Greene (1906), p. 120.

125 Dunbar settlers loyal to king before Revolution: "Deposition of William Fullerton," 23 October 1772, in Greene (1906), p. 121.

126 Dunbar settlers lose court cases, retain land: Rumsey (2000), pp. 118–125.

126 Georgetown Island incident (1722): Ibid., pp. 99, 135.

126 Waldo inspired by Dunbar settlers: Henry Jones Ford, *The Scotch-Irish in America* (Princeton, N.J.: Princeton University Press, 1915), pp. 246–247.

126 Scotch-Irish settlers to Warren and St. George: Willis (1859), p. 21; Ford (1915), p. 247; Cyrus Eaton, *History of Thomaston, Rockland, and South Thomaston, Maine* (Hallowell, Me.: Masters, Smith & Co., 1865), p. 44; McLane (1994), Vol. 3, pp. 28–29.

126 Other Scotch-Irish trickle into Midcoast: Eaton (1865), p. 43, 164; Greene (1906), p. 465; Willis (1859), p. 22.

127 Waldo's advertisements in Germany: *Imperial Post*, 23 March 1753, reprinted as "Gen. Waldo's Circular" in *Collections of the Maine Historical Society*, Series 1, Vol. 6 (Portland, Me.: MHS, 1859), pp. 325–332.

127 Waldo's German settlers: John L. Locke, "Introduction to the Translation of Gen. Waldo's Circular—1753," *Collections of the Maine Historical Society*, Series 1, Vol. 6 (Portland, Me.: MHS, 1859), p. 322; Wilford W. Whitaker and Gary T. Horlacher, *Broad Bay Pioneers* (Rockport, Me.: Picton Press, 1998), pp. xv–xvi, 40, 49.

127 Waldo's lowland Scots: Willis (1859), p. 23; Bernard Bailyn, *The Peopling of British North America* (New York: Random House, 1988), p. 72.

128 Treatment of German immigrants: Erna Risch, "Joseph Crellius, Immigrant Broker," *New England Quarterly*, Vol. 12, No. 2 (June 1939), pp. 241–267; Cyrus Eaton, *Annals of the Town of Warren* (Hallowell, Me.: 1851), pp. 80–87.

129 Waldo lobbies for fort, dies: Joseph Williamson, "Brigadier General Samuel Waldo," *Collections of the Maine Historical Society*, Series 1, Vol. 9 (Portland: Maine Historical Society, 1887), pp. 13–14.

129 Descriptions of suffering in the late French and Indian Wars: "Petition of the Inhabitants of Boothbay (1772)," pp. 167–168; "Deposition of Samuel McCobb," 23 October 1772, in Greene (1906), p. 118.

129 German settlers in Wiscasset in 1760: Parson Jacob Bailey's account from William S. Bartlet, *The Frontier Missionary: A Memoir of the Life of Rev. Jacob Bailey* (Boston: Ide & Dutton, 1853), p. 88.

130 **Indians after 1763:** McLane (1994), Vol. 4, p. 30; David L. Ghere, "Diplomacy and War, 1678–1759," in Richard W. Judd et al. (eds.), *Maine: The Pine Tree State from Prehistory to the Present* (Orono: University of Maine Press, 1995), p. 139.

130 **Options for northeast settlers in 1760s and 1770s:** Taylor (1990), pp. 61, 63; John Bartlett Brebner, *The Neutral Yankees of Nova Scotia: A Marginal Colony During the Revolutionary Years* (New York: Columbia University Press, 1937), pp. 25, 26, 28.

130 **Maine "an assalum":** "Nathaniel Dudley to Charles Vaughan," 7 March 1792, Kennebeck Proprietors' Papers, Box 3, Maine Historical Society, quoted in Taylor (1990), p. 63.

131 **Maine's population doubles:** James S. Leamon, *Revolution Downeast: The War for American Independence in Maine* (Amherst: University of Massachusetts Press, 1993), p. 6.

131 **Geographical spread in Maine 1760–1780:** Charles B. Fobes, "Path of the Settlement and Distribution of the Population of Maine," *Economic Geography*, Vol. 20, No.1 (January 1944), p. 66.

131 **Effect on Nova Scotia and New Brunswick:** Brebner (1937), pp. 24, 315; Ann Gorman Condon, *The Envy of the American States: The Loyalist Dream for New Brunswick* (Fredricton, N.B.: New Ireland Press, 1984), pp. 73–38.

131 **Composition of the 1765–1775 settlers:** Brebner (1937), p. 56; Taylor (1990), p. 62; Greene (1906), pp. 486–647; Muriel Sampson Johnson, *Early Families of Gouldsborough, Maine* (Camden, Me.: Picton Press, 1990), p. 6; John Pendleton Farrow, *History of Islesborough, Maine* (Bangor: Thomas W. Burr, 1893), pp. 9–15, 122, 228–293; George L. Hosmer, *An Historical Sketch of the Town of Deer Isle, Maine* (Boston: The Fort Hill Press, 1905); Charles A. E. Long, *Matinicus Isle: Its Story and Its People* (Lewiston, Me.: Lewiston Journal Printshop, 1926), pp. 132–196; George W. Drisko, *History of Machias, Maine* (Machias, Me.: Press of the Republican, 1904), pp. 10–11, 342–578.

131 **Lament of Brunswick area settlers:** Quoted from Taylor (1990), p. 13.

132 **John Hancock:** www.unitedstates-on-line.com/massachusetts/hancock.html, viewed 21 April 2002; Donald J. Proctor, "John Hancock: New Soundings on an Old Barrel," *Journal of American History*, Vol. 64, No. 3 (December 1977), pp. 652–677.

132 **James Bowdoin:** George Thomas Packard, "Bowdoin College," *Scribner's Monthly*, Vol. 12, No. 1 (May 1876), p. 47; "James Bowdoin" at http://www.virtualology.com/jamesbowdoin/.

132 **James Pitts:** Justin Winsor (ed.), *The Memorial History of Boston, Volume II: The Provincial Period* (Boston: James R. Osgood & Co., 1881), pp. 553, 545.

132 **Charles Apthorp:** Teacher's Guide to American Art: www.thinker.org/fam/education/publications/guide-american/slide-4.html. Viewed 21 April 2002.

132 Benjamin Hallowell: Coolidge (1999), pp. 61–63.

132 Silvester Gardiner: Olivia Coolidge, *Colonial Entrepreneur: Dr. Silvester Gardiner and the Settlement of Maine's Kennebec Valley* (Gardiner, Me.: Tilbury House, 1999), pp. 28–33; Robert Hallowell Gardiner, *Early Reflections of Robert Hallowell Gardiner 1782–1864* (Hallowell, Me.: White & Horne Co., 1936), pp. 14–16.

132 William and Florentius Vassall: "William Vassall" in *Biographical Sketches of Those who Attended Harvard College in the Classes 1731–1735*, Volume 9 (Boston: Massachusetts Historical Society, 1956); Gordon E. Kershaw, *The Kennebeck Proprietors: The Revolutionary Settlement on the Maine Frontier, 1760–1820* (Chapel Hill: University of North Carolina Press, 1975), pp. 36, 88–89.

132 Kennebeck Proprietors buy off Shirley: Alan Taylor, "A King of Warr: The Contest for Land on the Northeastern Frontier, 1750–1820," *William and Mary Quarterly*, Third Series, No. 1 (January 1989), p. 14.

132 Kennebeck Proprietors get forts built: Robert H. Gardiner, "History of the Kennebec Purchase," *Collections of the Maine Historical Society*, Vol. 2 (Portland, Me.: MHS, 1847), pp. 279, 282. The three were Fort Richmond, Fort Western (Augusta), and Fort Halifax (Winslow).

132 Kennebeck Proprietors and Lincoln County courts: Kershaw (1975), pp. 163–165.

132 Kennebeck Proprietors and Kennebec County courts: Taylor (1990), p. 11.

133 Thomas Flucker: Griffiths (1945), p. 29; Benson J. Lossing, *Pictorial Field Book of the Revolution*, Vol. 1 (New York: Harper and Brothers, 1850), chapter 22.

133 Thomas Hutchinson: http://www.virtualology.com/annemarburyhutchinson/. Viewed 24 April 2002.

133 Scotch-Irish pridefulness: Fischer (1989), pp. 613–615.

133 "I am worried day and night . . .": "Samuel Goodwin to the Kennebeck Proprietors," 16 November 1761, quoted in Kershaw (1975), p. 150.

134 Linekin/Montgomery incident (1755): Rumsey (2000), pp. 136–138, 146, 148, 153.

134 Newcastle incident (1761): Taylor (1989), p. 19.

134 Woolwich incident (1768): *Boston Evening Post*, 26 December 1768, as quoted in Taylor (1990), p. 264.

134 McFarland incident (1761): Taylor (1989), p. 10.

134 Damariscotta incident (1765): Ibid., p. 9.

134 Gardiner/howling "Indians" incident (1761): Taylor (1989), pp. 18–19.

134 1772 petition to the king: "Petition of the Inhabitants of Boothbay (1772)," in Baxter, Vol. 14 (1910), pp. 168–170.

135 Mainers' disillusionment with crown policies (1763–1773): Leamon (1993), pp. 33–35.

136 Content of the Coercive Acts (1774): Danby Pickering (ed.), *Statutes at Large* (Cambridge, U.K.: J. Bentham, 1762), Vol. 30, pp. 336–340, 381–384.

136 Thompson's War and Mowatt's capture (1775): Leamon (1993), pp. 60–67.

137 Machias conditions and "clam years": M. E. C. Smith, "Machias in the Revolution and Afterward," *New England Magazine*, Vol. 18, No. 6 (August 1895), p. 675.

137 *Margaretta* incident (1775): Smith (1895), pp. 674–681; Leamon (1993), pp. 67–69.

138 O'Brien described: Smith (1895), p. 677.

138 Portland bombarded (1775): Leamon (1993), pp. 69–73.

138 Bombardment of Portland described: Rev. Jacob Bailey's account as quoted in James P. Baxter, "The Story of Portland," *New England Magazine*, Vol. 19, No. 3 (November 1895), pp. 359–360; Louis C. Hatch, *Maine: A History* (New York: The American Historical Society, 1919), pp. 31–32.

139 Brebner quote on Nova Scotians: Brebner (1937), p. 314.

139 New Brunswickers declare support for Revolution: Brebner (1937), p. 319; Condon (1984), p. 78.

139 Nova Scotian smuggling and privateering ports: Brebner (1937), pp. 316–317.

139 Eddy's and Allan's biographies and invasions (1776–77): Brebner (1937), pp. 317–321.

139 New Ireland project: Leamon in Judd (1996), pp. 156–157, 161; Joseph Wiliamson, "The Proposed Province of New Ireland," *Collections of the Maine Historical Society*, Series 1, Vol. 7 (Bath, Me.: Maine Historical Society, 1876), p. 26.

140 St. Andrews population: Condon (1984), p. 85.

140 James Shurtleff quote: Taylor (1990), p. 114.

141 Proprietors' post-Revolutionary successors: Taylor (1990), pp. 34–35; Coolidge (1999); Hallowell, pp. 120–121.

141 Henry Knox: Noah Brooks, *Henry Knox: A Soldier of the Revolution* (New York: G. P. Putnam and Sons, 1900), pp. 4–6, 26; Taylor (1990), pp. 38–39; Griffiths (1945), p. 31; James Parton, "The Cabinet of President Washington," *Atlantic Monthly*, Vol. 31, No. 183 (January 1873), p. 30; "Biographical sketches of Major-General Henry Knox," *The Port Folio* (Philadelphia), Vol. 9, No. 2 (August 1811), pp. 100–104.

141 Society of the Cincinnati: Sidney Kaplan, "Veteran Officers and Politics in Massachusetts, 1783–1787," *William and Mary Quarterly*, Third Series, Vol. 9, No. 1 (January 1952), pp. 31, 35–40.

142 Knox re-creates Waldo Patent: Taylor (1990), pp. 39–40.

142 Knox and the Bingham Purchase: Ibid., pp. 40–41.

142 Geographical bounds of the Bingham Purchase: Judd (1995), p. 55; *The Maine Atlas and Gazetteer* (Yarmouth, Me.: DeLorme, 1997), p. 4.

142 Knox mansion: Griffiths (1945), pp. 4–21; Taylor (1990), p. 43.

143 Taylor quotes: Taylor (1990), pp. 33–34.

143 Talleyrand's quote (1794): Frederick S. Allis Jr., "William Bingham's Maine Lands 1790–1820," in *Collections of the Colonial Society of Massachusetts*, Vols. 36–37 (Boston: Colonial Society of Massachusetts, 1954), p. 20.

143 Bingham's quote (1800): Letter of William Bingham to David Cobb, 26 June 1800, in Allis (1954), Vol. 37, p. 1056.

144 Maine's post-Revolutionary population explosion: Leamon in Judd (1995), p. 170; Fobes (1944), pp. 66–67.

144 Settlement of the Downeast coast: Wayne M. O'Leary, *Maine Sea Fisheries: The Rise and Fall of a Native Industry, 1830–1890* (Boston: Northeastern University Press, 1996), pp. 16–20.

144 Difficulties of farming the frontier: Taylor (1990), pp. 66–70.

144 Poverty of settlers: Ibid., pp. 72–73.

145 Liancourt quote (1799): Allis (1954), Vol. 36, p. 3.

145 Resistance (1789–1800): Taylor (1990): surveyors confronted, p. 265; killing of surveyor's horse, house burnings, pp. 270–271; George Ulmer incidents, pp. 155–159; other supporters assaulted, p. 265; Brigadier Island mutiny, p. 192; threat to Montpelier, p. 159; Pittston sheriff assaulted, p. 266; Trueman incident and jailbreak, pp. 115–116; quote from Knox agents about settlers, p. 95.

146 Scotch-Irish dominance of Midcoast backcountry: Elizabeth Freeman Reed, "Liberty, Montville, and Palermo, Waldo County, Maine," genealogical manuscript notes, Boothbay Historical Society.

146 Renewed resistance (1800–1810): Taylor (1990): white Indians eat horses, pp. 192–193; rumors of an attack on Augusta, p. 184; sheriffs detained, beaten, pp. 274–275; prisoners liberated in Castine, p. 271; settlers' restraint, p. 199; killing, release of murderers, pp. 203–204.

147 Federalist establishment: Ronald F. Banks, *Maine Becomes a State: The Movement to Separate Maine from Massachusetts, 1785–1820* (Middletown, Conn.: Wesleyan University Press, 1970), p. 49; James S. Leamon, Richard B. Wescott, and Edward O. Schriver, "Separation and Statehood, 1783–1820," in Judd (1995), p. 171.

147 Knox's political connections: Taylor (1990), pp. 209–211, 219.

148 Knox on the Massachusetts settlers' rebellion (1786): Henry Knox to George Washington, letter of 23 October 1786.

148 Rise of the Jeffersonians: Charles E. Clark, James S. Leamon, and Karen Bowden (eds.), *Maine in the Early Republic: From Revolution to State-*

hood (Hanover, N.H.: University Press of New England, 1988), pp. 6–7; Taylor (1990), pp. 212–213; Leamon et al. in Judd (1995), p. 179.

148 *Columbian Centinel* quote: Louis C. Hatch, *Maine: A History* (New York: The American Historical Society, 1919), p. 71.

149 Moses Greenleaf quote: Banks (1970), p. 52.

149 Knox's death (1806): Cyrus Eaton, *History of Thomaston, Rockland, and South Thomaston, Maine*, Volume I (Hallowell, Me.: Masters, Smith & Co., 1865), p. 267.

149 Bingham's death, lands disposed of: Robert Alberts, *The Golden Voyage: The Life and Times of William Bingham* (Boston: Houghton Mifflin, 1969), pp. 428, 431, 528n.

149 Jeffersonians in power: Taylor (1990), pp. 215–217, 222–231, 239; Banks (1970), pp. 55–56.

150 *Eastern Argus* on Ohio Fever: "The District of Maine No. IV," *Eastern Argus*, 22 November 1815, p. 3.

151 Federalists resist War of 1812: Clark et al. (1988), p. 6; Banks (1970), p. 58; Leamon et al. in Judd (1995), p. 183.

151 Federal withdrawal from Maine, King's reaction: Banks (1970), pp. 58–59.

151 Maine occupied in War of 1812: Hatch (1919), pp. 75–79; Greene (1906), p. 257; Clark et al. (1988), p. 6; William Henry Kilby, "A New England Town Under Foreign Martial Law," pp. 688–691; *The Weekly Recorder* (Chillicothe), Vol. 1, No. 15 (11 October 1814), p. 118.

152 Massachusetts's treasonous behavior in 1814: Banks (1970), pp. 60–64; Leamon et al. in Judd (1995), p. 183.

152 Whiting's letter (1814): Banks (1970), p. 66.

153 *Eastern Argus*, Sam Whiting writings on succession: "To non-resident Proprietors," *Eastern Argus*, 24 July 1816, p. 1; "Defend the tenants from the lords," *Eastern Argus*, 14 August 1816, p. 1; *Eastern Argus*, 22 November 1815, p. 3.

153 Federalists back down, *Advertiser* comments: Hatch (1919), p. 124; Leamon et al. in Judd (1995), pp. 183–184.

154 Maine's constitution: Leamon et al. in Judd (1995), pp. 187–189.

FIVE: **Boom to Bust**

157 Vinalhaven soils: George Brown Goode, *The Fisheries and Fishery Industries of the United States*, Section 2: *A Geographical Review of the Fisheries Industries and Fishing Communities for the Year 1880* (Washington, D.C.: United States Commission of Fish and Fisheries, 1887), p. 50.

157 Freezes of 1816: James B. Vickery, Richard W. Judd, and Sheila McDonald, "Maine Agriculture, 1783–1861," in Richard W. Judd et al. (eds.),

Maine: The Pine Tree State from Prehistory to the Present (Orono: University of Maine Press, 1995), p. 249.

158 Maine's fleet in 1800: Wayne M. O'Leary, *Maine Sea Fisheries: The Rise and Fall of a Native Industry, 1830–1890* (Boston: Northeastern University Press, 1996), p. 344.

158 Relative tonnage comparisons: Lincoln P. Paine, *Down East: A Maritime History of Maine* (Gardiner, Me.: Tilbury House, 2000), pp. 66, 89.

158 Boothbay fishing fleet in early 1800s: Francis B. Greene, *History of Boothbay, Southport and Boothbay Harbor, Maine 1623–1905* (Portland, Me.: Loring, Short & Harmon, 1906), p. 368.

158 Vinalhaven fishermen to Labrador (1804): Goode (1887), Sec. 2, p. 50; Chebacco boats: http://www.essexshipbuildingmuseum.org/lewstory.html.

158 Maine offshore vessels 11 percent of U.S. fleet: O'Leary (1996), p. 344.

158 O'Leary on Downeast Maine settlement: Ibid., pp. 18–20.

159 Fishing bounty's role in expansion: Ibid., p. 42.

159 Reasons for emphasis on cod: O'Leary in Judd (1995), pp. 290–292.

160 Eastern Penobscot ownership stats: O'Leary (1996), p. 367.

160 Matinicus families and ownership stats: Charles A. E. Long, *Matinicus Isle: Its Story and Its People* (Lewiston, Me.: Lewiston Journal Printshop, 1926), pp. 35, 54.

160 Monhegan families and ownership stats: Charles McLane, *Islands of the Mid-Maine Coast, Volume III: Muscongus Bay and Monhegan Island* (Rockland, Me.: Island Institute, c. 1997), pp. 227, 246.

160 Boothbay families and ownership stats: Greene (1906), pp. 362–365, 569.

160 Role of bounty law in democratic ownership: Paine (2000), pp. 121–122.

161 Boothbay and Eastport's mackerel fleet: Goode (1887), Sec. 2, pp. 16, 68.

161 Three hundred mackerel vessels in sight of each other: John Davis, "Speech delivered in the Senate of the United States, Jan. 24, 1839, on the Bill to Abolish the Duty on Salt," *North American Review*, Vol. 57, No. 120 (July 1843), p. 74.

161 Quote on mackerel abundance around 1830: S. B. Hume quoted in Goode (1887), Sec. 2, p. 16.

161 Account of mackerel fishing: Ibid., p. 73.

161 Discovery, witnessing of herring torching: Ibid., pp. 65–66.

162 Lubec's smokehouses: Goode (1887), Sec. 2, pp. 19, 474.

162 Herring trips to Magdalens: Ibid., pp. 16, 50, 56, 65, 69.

162 Dominance of Maine fisheries in 1860: O'Leary (1996), pp. 7–11, 84,

110; William Hutchinson Rowe, *Maritime History of Maine* (New York: W. W. Norton, 1948), p. 276.

162 **Importance to local communities:** O'Leary (1996), pp. 6, 8–9; Rowe (1948), p. 277.

163 **The triangular fish trade:** Paine (2000), pp. 67–69; Lawrence C. Allin, "Shipbuilding and Shipping in the Period of Ascendency," in Judd (1995), pp. 303–304.

164 **Lumbering:** Richard W. Judd, "Maine's Lumber Industry," in Judd (1995), pp. 265–268, 270–271.

164 **Granite industry:** Lawrence C. Allin, "Maine's Granite Industry," in Judd (1995), pp. 275, 277; Bill Caldwell, *Islands of Maine* (Portland, Me.: Guy Gannett Publishing Co., 1981), pp. 181–184; Philip W. Conkling, *Islands in Time* (Rockland, Me.: Island Institute, 1999), pp. 123–127.

165 **Tudor and the ice industry:** Daniel J. Boorstin, *The Americans: The National Experience* (New York: Random House, 1965), pp. 10–16.

166 **Maine's ice industry:** Richard W. Judd, "Maine's Ice Industry," in Judd (1995), pp. 284, 285.

166 **Mid-nineteenth-century immigration:** James H. Mundy, *Hard Times, Hard Men: Maine and the Irish, 1830–1860* (Scarborough, Me.: Harp Publications, 1990), pp. 7–16, 21; Charles E. Clark, *Maine: A Bicentennial History* (New York: W. W. Norton, 1976), pp. 141–143; Grant E. Finch and Gordon F. Howe, "The Lime Industry at Rockland, Maine," *Economic Geography*, Vol. 6, No. 4 (October 1930), pp. 393–394.

166 **Civil War casualties, veterans:** Jerry Desmond, "Maine in the Civil War," in Judd (1995), p. 358.

167 **Moves by the Republican Congress:** Wayne M. O'Leary, "Crisis and Decline in the Deep-Sea-Fishing Industry," in Judd (1995), p. 392.

167 **Relative merits, expenses of tub trawling:** O'Leary (1996), pp. 160–169.

168 **Relative merits, expenses of purse seining:** Ibid., p. 163.

168 **Size of purse seines:** Rowe (1948), p. 279.

168 **Contraction and consolidation of Maine fleet:** O'Leary (1996), pp. 344–345, 181–190.

168 **Effect of loss of bounty on fishermen:** Ibid., pp. 197–214.

169 **N. V. Tibbetts quote:** N. V. Tibbetts, "Scarcity of Cod and Haddock on the Coast of Maine," letter to S. F. Baird of 27 February 1886, *The Bulletin of the United States Fish Commission*, Vol. 6 (1886) (Washington, D.C.: Government Printing Office, 1887), p. 75.

169 **Inshore's advantages over offshore:** Nathan R. Lipfert, "The Shore Fisheries, 1865–1930," in Judd (1995), pp. 421–422.

169 **Seasonal rotation of inshoremen:** *Eastern Maine:* Goode (1887), Sec. 5, p. 679; Goode, Sec. 2, p. 25. *North Haven:* Goode, Sec. 5, pp. 679,

756–757; Goode, Sec. 2, p. 51. *Bristol:* Goode, Sec. 5, p. 679; Goode, Sec. 2, pp. 59, 61.

170 **Lobster easily available in colonial period:** Goode (1887), Sec. 5, p. 659; John N. Cobb, "The Lobster Fishery of Maine," *Bulletin of the United States Fish Commission,* Vol. 19 for 1899 (Washington, D.C.: Government Printing Office, 1901), p. 243.

170 **Indentured servants protest:** Bill Caldwell, *Islands of Maine: Where America Really Began* (Portland, Me.: Guy Gannett Publishing Co., 1981), p. 195.

171 **Lobster as mackerel chum:** Goode (1887), Sec. 5, p. 660.

171 **Hoop traps described:** Ibid., p. 665, 699; Cobb (1901), pp. 246–247.

171 **New York City fishery and market:** Goode (1887), Sec. 5, pp. 681, 705, 711.

171 **Invention of smack, use in Provincetown by 1802:** "A description of Provincetown, in the county of Barnstable, September 1802," *Collections of the Massachusetts Historical Society,* Vol. 8 (1802), pp. 198–200; Goode (1887), Sec. 5, pp. 702, 705; David Littleton-Taylor, "Lobster Smacks in Maine," unpublished term paper, University of Maine at Orono, 1 May 1973, pp. 7–8.

172 **Provincetown's concerns in 1812:** Goode (1887), Sec. 5, pp. 697, 702–704.

172 **Advent of Boston lobster market:** Ibid., p. 704; Goode, Sec. 2, p. 198.

172 **Harpswell visited in 1830s:** Goode (1887), Sec. 2, p. 79; Cobb (1901), p. 243.

172 **Elisha Oakes accounts:** Goode (1887), Sec. 5, pp. 700–701.

174 **Early lobster canneries:** Ibid., pp. 687–689; Charles H. Stevenson, "The Preservation of Fishery Products for Food," *Bulletin of the United States Fish Commission,* Vol. 18 for 1898 (Washington, D.C.: Government Printing Office, 1899), p. 521; Earl Chapin May, *The Canning Clan* (New York: MacMillan Co., 1937), pp. 10–13, 434–435.

175 **Lobsters not present in Eastport:** Goode (1887), Sec. 5, p. 702.

175 **Smackmen introduce fishermen to lobstering:** Goode (1887), Sec. 2, pp. 39 (Swan's Isle), 41 (Deer Isle).

176 **William Bishop account (1880):** William H. Bishop, "Lobster at Home," *Scribner's Monthly,* Vol. 22, No. 2 (June 1881), pp. 215–216.

176 **Lath traps described:** Goode (1887), Sec. 5, pp. 666–668; Bishop (1881), p. 211.

176 **Fishermen tended twenty-five to fifty pots (1860):** Goode (1887), Sec. 5, p. 699; from open dories until 1860s: Paine (2000), pp. 126–127; Bishop (1881), p. 212.

176 **Buoys and lines (1855–60):** Goode (1887), Sec. 5, p. 667.

177 **Portland average lobster catch (1855–60):** Robert Earrll's estimates as related in Goode (1887), Sec. 5, p. 708.

177 Harpswell average catch/two-pounders thrown: Goode (1887), Sec. 5, p. 701.

177 Cobb on large lobsters: Cobb (1901), p. 260.

177 Bishop lobster claw: Bishop (1881), p. 212.

177 Flounder as bait: Goode (1887), Sec. 5, p. 675.

177 Lobster cars: Ibid., p. 673.

178 Arrival of smacks: Bishop (1881), p. 215; Cobb (1901), p. 251.

178 Lobstermen's income: (c. 1855): Goode (1887), Sec. 5, p. 701; price is for 130-ton schooner *Eothen*, built in Castine in April 1860, as cited in O'Leary (1996), p. 369; dories cost $25 in 1875 (O'Leary, p. 169), but much less before Civil War inflation.

178 Canneries described: Bishop (1881), pp. 216–218; Goode (1887), Sec. 5, pp. 692–695.

179 Refuse, Boothbay pigs: Goode (1887), Sec. 5, pp. 693–695.

179 Canneries circa 1879: Ibid., pp. 689, 695; Bishop (1881), p. 216.

179 *Harper's* on canneries: "Mount Desert," *Harper's New Monthly Magazine*, Vol. 45, No. 267 (August 1872), p. 325.

180 Early Boothbay resorters (1830s): Greene (1906), pp. 411–412 (first quote is of state geologist "Dr. Jackson").

180 Early MDI artists (1830s–40s): Pamela J. Belanger, *Inventing Acadia: Artists and Tourists at Mount Desert* (Rockland, Me.: The Farnsworth Art Museum, 1999), pp. 29, 109.

181 Isles of Shoals as first resort: Caldwell (1981), pp. 69–70.

181 Bar Harbor hotels and Rodick House: Belanger (1999), p. 116; Cleveland Amory, *The Last Resorts* (New York: Harper & Brothers, 1948), p. 282.

181 Waite's accounts of southern resorts (1871): Otis F. R. Waite, *Guidebook for the Eastern Coast of New England* (Concord, N.H.: Edson C. Eastman and Company, 1871), pp.142–145.

182 Boothbay summer developments: Greene (1906), pp. 412–420.

182 Monhegan development: McLane (1997), Vol. 3, pp. 240, 242.

183 Pulitzer's "cottage": Amory (1948), pp. 288–289.

183 Kennedy mansion: Belanger (1999), pp. 119–120.

183 Rockefeller's mansion: *Bangor Daily News*, 13 October 2000.

183 Godkin quotes: Edwin Lawrence Godkin, *Reflections and Comments: 1865–1895* (New York: Charles Scribner's Sons, 1896), pp. 295–308 (as quoted in Belanger [1999], pp. 118–119).

183–184 Drake quotes: Samuel Adams Drake, *Nooks and Corners of the New England Coast* (New York: Harper & Brothers, 1876), p. 54.

184 Vanderbilt purchase: Amory (1948), p. 287.

184 Monhegan tax assessments (1894): McLane (1997), Vol. 3, p. 242.

184 Foley and Sprague anecdotes: Amory (1948), pp. 324–326.

184–185 J. P. Morgan and Rockefeller anecdotes: Art Harris, "Maine's Keepers of the Very Rich," *The Washington Post*, 2 July 1978, p. B1.

185 Employment at Bar Harbor: Louise Dickinson Rich, *The Peninsula* (Riverside, Conn.: The Chatham Press, 1958), p. 61.

185 MDI Prayer (1884): G. W. Helfrich and Gladys O'Neil, *Lost Bar Harbor* (Camden, Me.: Down East Books, 1982), p. 9.

185 100,000 hotel visitors: Richard W. Judd, "Saving the fishermen as well as the fish: conservation and commercial rivalry in Maine's lobster industry, 1872–1933," *Business History Review*, Vol. 62, No. 4 (December 1988).

185 Clams in demand: Lipfert in Judd (1995), pp. 424–425.

186 Fresh fish preferred over salted/icebox use: O'Leary (1996), pp. 265–266.

186 Davis on hake and haddock (1839): Davis (1843), p. 64.

186 Prices paid for lobsters in 1880: Goode (1887), Sec. 5, p. 686.

186 Shipping of Eastport lobsters in barrels: Ibid., p. 745.

186 Size of cannery lobsters in 1880s: Cobb (1901), p. 256; term "snappers" from George Burnham Jr. in Goode (1887), Sec. 5, p. 731.

186 Employment, value, importance of lobsters in 1880: Goode (1887), Sec. 5, pp. 770–771; O'Leary (1996), p. 258.

187 Lobsters transplanted to California: Goode (1887), Sec. 5, pp. 740–745; Richard Rathbun, "The Transplanting of Lobsters to the Pacific Coast of the United States," *Bulletin of the United States Fish Commission*, Vol. 8 for 1888 (Washington, D.C.: Government Printing Office, 1890), pp. 453–473.

187 Lobsters transplanted to Chesapeake: Lieut. W. M. Wood, "Transplanting lobsters to the Chesapeake—Experiments upon the temperature they can endure," *Bulletin of the United States Fish Commission*, Vol. 5 for 1885 (Washington, D.C.: Government Printing Office, 1885), pp. 31–32.

187 Lobsters shipped to England (1877): Cobb (1901), p. 253.

187 Lobster pound created (1875): Lipfert in Judd (1995), p. 424.

188 Signs of trouble in fishery (c. 1880): Goode (1887), Sec. 5, pp. 701, 706–708; Cobb (1901), p. 256.

188 Canners' "conservation" laws: James M. Acheson, "The Politics of Managing the Maine Lobster Industry: 1860 to the Present," *Human Ecology*, Vol. 25, No. 1 (1997), pp. 6–7.

189 Dealers'/lobstermen's objections to canners' laws: Goode (1887), Sec. 5, pp. 726, 729.

189 Fisheries petitions: Ibid., p. 730.

189 1879 law/canners fight back: Richard W. Judd, "Saving the Fishermen as Well as the Fish: Conservation and Commercial Rivalry in Maine's Lobster Industry 1872–1933," *Business History Review*, Vol. 62, No. 4 (1988), pp. 596–625.

189 J. Wilson Jones proposal: Goode (1887), Sec. 5, p. 731.

189 **Further conservation laws to 1895:** Acheson (1997), p. 8.

189 **Cannery production shrinks:** Cobb (1901), p. 257.

189 **George Burnham Jr.'s quote:** Goode (1887), Sec. 5, p. 731.

190 **Flouting of conservation laws:** Judd (1988), pp. 612–613; N. J. Hanna, "Reply to *Boston Globe* Article on 'Do Our Laws Protect Wrong Size?,' " undated newspaper clipping on file at the Monhegan Museum, Monhegan, Me.

190 **Herrick's work:** Francis H. Herrick, "The Protection of the Lobster Fishery," *Bulletin of the United States Fish Commission*, Vol. 17 for 1897 (Washington, D.C.: Government Printing Office, 1898), pp. 217–224; Francis H. Herrick, "Natural History of the American Lobster," *Bulletin of the United States Fish Commission*, Vol. 29 for 1909 (Washington, D.C.: Government Printing Office, 1911).

191 **Prices:** Cobb (1901), p. 257; Judd (1988).

191 **Gear/landings 1905–1929:** U.S. fisheries commissioner Henry O'Malley as quoted in Alfred Eden, "New England Lobster Industry Has Support of Commissioner O'Malley," *Atlantic Fisherman*, Vol. 13, No. 1 (February 1932), p. 1.

191 **Lobster fishery in the Great Depression:** Judd (1988); Acheson (1997), pp. 10–14.

191 **Depletions of other fisheries in 1930s:** Edward A. Ackerman, "Depletion in New England Fisheries," *Economic Geography*, Vol. 14, No. 3 (July 1938), pp. 233–238.

SIX: **Down and East**

194 **Census data for Maine counties, 1860–1910:** Official census data as accessed at the University of Southern Maine's Folger Library, http://www.library.umaine.edu/census/countysearch.asp. Viewed 8 February 2003.

194 **Abandoned farms:** James B. Vickery and Richard W. Judd, "Agricultural Crisis and Adaptation, 1861–1900," in Richard W. Judd, *Maine: The Pine Tree State from Prehistory to the Present* (Orono: University of Maine Press, 1995), pp. 405–406; Leonard O. Packard, "The Decrease of Population along the Maine Coast," *Geographical Review*, Vol. 2, Issue 5 (November 1916), pp. 340–341.

194 **Abandoned ships:** During my childhood in the 1970s, three- and four-masted schooners were still rotting in the mudflats of Boothbay Harbor, Wiscasset, and other coastal towns. Most had been there since they were abandoned by their owners at the turn of the century, or at the start of the Great Depression.

194 **Charles Dodge interview:** David Littleton-Taylor, interview with Charles P. Dodge, recorded Friendship, Me., 7 October 1972, Maine Folklife Center, University of Maine, Tape 727, NA727.

194 Holman Day quotes: Holman Day, "The Queer Folk of the Maine Coast," *Harper's Monthly Magazine*, Vol. 119, No. 712 (1909), p. 521.

194 E. P Morris account: E. P. Morris, "Along the Maine Coast," *Geographical Review*, Vol. 2, No. 5 (November 1916), p. 333.

195 Bush Island, water tramps: Day (1909), pp. 525–528.

195 Malaga Island: Deborah DuBrule, "Evicted: How the state of Maine destroyed a 'different' island community," *Island Journal*, No. 16 (1999), pp. 48–52, 90–91.

195 Maine seen as idyllic rural past: See George H. Lewis, "The Maine That Never Was: The Construction of Popular Myth in Regional Culture," *Journal of American Culture*, Vol. 16, No. 2 (Summer 1993).

196 Robert Herrick quote: Robert Herrick, "The State of Maine—'Down East,'" *The Nation*, 23 August 1922, p. 182.

196 Rhodes quote: Harrison Rhodes, "Maine and the Summer Sea," *Harper's Magazine*, Vol. 135 (August 1917), p. 306.

196 "Vacationland": Lewis (1993).

196 Mitchell quote: Edwin Valentine Mitchell, *Maine Summer* (New York: Coward-McCann, 1939), p. 20.

197 Bar Harbor resistance: Stephen J. Hornsby, "The Gilded Age and the Making of Bar Harbor," *Geographical Review*, Vol. 83, No. 4 (October 1993), pp. 462–463.

197 Islesboro resists car: Darrell A. Rolerson, "When Islesboro Said 'Whoa' to the Horseless Carriage," *Down East*, April 1968, pp. 44–46.

197 Resistance to bridges: Mitchell (1939), pp. 27–28.

197 Activities of Mount Desert land trust: Hornsby (1993), pp. 463–464; Pamela J. Belanger, *Inventing Acadia: Artists and Tourists at Mount Desert* (Rockland, Me.: The Farnsworth Art Museum, 1999), pp. 123–125.

198 "Aborigines": Rhodes (1917), p. 312.

198 1914 newspaper article: L.P., "Monhegan's Three Hundred Years," 27 June 1914 (newspaper clip on file at the Monhegan Museum, Monhegan, Me.).

199 Depression-era cottage cutbacks: Hornsby (1993), p. 466.

199 Walter Trundy interview: David Littleton-Taylor, interview with Walter F. Trundy, recorded at Stockton Springs, Me., 27 June 1973, Maine Folklife Center, University of Maine, Tape 767, NA767.

199 *Bangor Daily News* quote: Henry Buxton, *Assignment Down East* (Brattleboro, Vt.: Stephen Daye, 1938), p. 79.

199 DeVoto article: Bernard DeVoto, "New England—There She Stands," *Harper's Monthly Magazine*, Vol. 164 (March 1932), pp. 404–415.

200 Couple living on small Kennebec island: Dorothy Hay Jensen, "Art and the WPA," *Down East*, June 1987, p. 79.

200 Ray Phillips: Robert Uzzell, "Ray Phillips, Hermit of Manana Island,

Likes His Way of Life," *Maine Coast Fisherman*, October 1954, p. 10; Raymond Morin, "He's Lived 23 Years Alone on a Lonely Island Off the Coast of Maine," *Worcester Sunday Telegram*, 22 August 1954, p. 7.

200 Scott and Helen Nearing: Helen and Scott Nearing, *Living the Good Life: How to Live Sanely and Simply in a Troubled World* (New York: Schocken Books, 1954), pp. 4–12; Helen Nearing, *Loving and Leaving the Good Life* (Post Mills, Vt.: Chelsea Green Publishing, 1992), pp. 95–102, 116–120.

201 Mobile gear's history in Europe: Andrew W. German, "Otter Trawling Comes to America: The Bay State Fishing Company, 1905–1938," *American Neptune*, Vol. 44, No. 2 (Spring 1984), pp. 115–115.

201 Beam trawling mocked in Rhode Island: Ibid., p. 114.

202 Introduction of otter trawling in U.S., size of early trawlers: A. B. Alexander, H. F. Moore, and W. C. Kendall, *Otter Trawl Fishery*, Bureau of Fisheries Document No. 816 (Washington, D.C.: Government Printing Office, 1915), pp. 13–14, 19–21; German (1984), pp. 116–119.

202 Opposition to early trawlers: Alexander et al. (1915), pp. 6–7, 94–97; German (1984), pp. 120–123.

203 Technological innovations: German (1984), pp. 127–131.

203 Advent of Maine shrimp fishery: *Portland Press Herald*, 12 February 1936, pp. 1, 12; *Portland Press Herald*, 8 February 1936, p. 12; David D. Platt, *Penobscot: The Forest, River, and Bay* (Rockland, Me.: Island Institute, 1996), p. 59 (quoting a 1934 assessment of the new shrimp banks by Maine's Department of Sea and Shore Fisheries).

203 Halibut decline: Edward A. Ackerman, "Depletion in New England Fisheries," *Economic Geography*, Vol. 14, No. 3 (July 1938), p. 235; Henry B. Bigelow and William C. Schroeder, *Fishes of the Gulf of Maine*, Fishery Bulletin of the Fish and Wildlife Service Vol. 53 (Washington, D.C.: Government Printing Office, 1953), pp. 255–257.

204 Haddock decline: Ackerman (1938), pp. 235–237.

204 Winter, yellowtail flounder decline: William F. Royce, Raymond J. Buller, and Ernest D. Premetz, "Decline of the Yellowtail Flounder (Limanda Ferruginea) Off New England," *Fishery Bulletin*, Vol. 59, No. 146 (Washington, D.C.: Government Printing Office, 1959), p. 169; Ackerman (1938), p. 237.

204 Clam decline: Platt (1996), pp. 48–49.

204 Salmon and shad decline: Ackerman (1938), pp. 234–235.

204 Inshore and offshore cod: David Dobbs, *The Great Gulf: Fishermen, Scientists, and the Struggle to Revive the World's Greatest Fishery* (Washington, D.C.: Island Press, 2000), pp. 125–128.

205 Why inshore cod weren't targeted: Author's interview, James Wilson, Professor of Marine Policy, University of Maine, Orono, Me., 5 December

2002; Philip W. Conkling, *Islands in Time: A Natural and Cultural History of the Islands of the Gulf of Maine* (Camden, Me.: Down East Books, 1999), p. 235.

206 Number of inshore spawning grounds: Edward P. Ames, *Cod and Haddock Spawning Grounds in the Gulf of Maine* (Rockland, Me.: Island Institute, 1997), p. 10.

206 Inshore cod vanish in Penobscot Bay: Platt (1997), pp. 57, 59.

206 On the role of Maine's paper industry: See Jerome G. Daviau, *Maine's Life Blood* (Portland, Me.: House of Falmouth, 1958); William C. Osborn, *The Paper Plantation* (New York: Viking, 1974); Douglas M. Johns, "The Purging of the Androscoggin," *Habitat*, June/July 1985, p. 27.

206 Ames study and quotes: Ames (1997), pp. 12–16.

208 *Fairtry* and buildup of factory-trawler fleet: William W. Warner, *Distant Water: The Fate of the North Atlantic Fisherman* (Boston: Little, Brown and Co., 1977), pp. 32–54.

209 Poor condition of Maine fisheries circa 1958: Steve Riley, "Fishing Industry of Maine in Peril, Statistics Indicate," *Portland Sunday Telegram*, 22 June 1958, pp. 1A, 10A; T. M. Prudden, *About Lobsters* (Freeport, Me.: The Bond Wheelright Company, 1962), p. 10; "Commissioner Crie Pleads for White-Nelson Bill at Meeting of Lobster Fishermen," *Atlantic Fisherman*, Vol. 12, No. 10 (November 1932), p. 1.

210 Soviets arrive, fish Georges like "harrows": Warner (1977), p. 6.

210 Number of foreign vessels in 1970, fishing at Jeffrey's Bank: Douglas C. Wilson, "Soviet Inroads Could Mean Quota on Flounder," an article from the *Providence Journal-Bulletin* reprinted in the *Maine Sunday Telegram*, 27 December 1970, p. 16A; Sean Beeny, "State's Fishing Industry Seen Growing Worse," *Maine Sunday Telegram*, 27 December 1970, p. 16A.

210 O'Hara quotes, foreign fishing on Cashes: Author's interview, Frank O'Hara Sr., owner, O'Hara Seafoods, Rockland, Me., 16 December 2002.

210 Boeri and Gibson quote: David Boeri and James Gibson, *Tell It Goodbye, Kiddo: The Decline of the New England Offshore Fishery* (Camden, Me.: International Marine Publishing, 1976), p. 123.

211 Fishing pressure, overfishing, landings assessments: Stephen H. Clark and Bradford E. Brown, "Changes in Biomass of Finfishes and Squids from the Gulf of Maine to Cape Hatteras, 1963–74," *Fishery Bulletin*, Vol. 75, No. 1 (January 1977), pp. 1–2.

211 1968 landings figures: Sidney Shapiro, ed., *Our Changing Fisheries*, Washington, D.C.: National Marine Fisheries Service, 1971), p. 173.

211 United Nations by-catch estimates: The State of World Fisheries and Aquaculture 1998 (Rome: UN Food and Agriculture Organization, 1999).

211 Lobster tagged by Soviets: Shapiro (1971), p. 164 (photo caption).

212 Effect on Maine: Beeny (1970), p. 16A.

212 Landings figures: All are official figures from Maine's Department of Marine Resources. Historical landings information for each species is available via www.maine.gov/dmr/commercialfishing/.

212 Tim Asbury quote: Beeny (1970), p. 16A.

212 Iceland's cod wars: Mark Kurlansky, *Cod: A Biography of a Fish That Changed the World* (New York: Penguin, 1997), pp. 158–169.

213 *National Fisherman* quotes: Burton T. Coffey, "Effects of 200-Mile Limit Will Be Slow in Coming," *National Fisherman*, Vol. 56, No. 13 (1976 Yearbook issue), pp. 6–7.

213 John Gould: Author's interview, John Gould, writer and humorist, Rockland, Me., 22 November 2002.

214 Maine Turnpike: *The Maine Trail: The Maine Turnpike, 1947–1997* (pamphlet) (Portland, Me.: Maine Turnpike Authority, 1997), pp. 1–3.

214 Tourism revenue statistics: *The Maine Handbook: A Statistical Abstract* (Augusta, Me.: Maine Department of Economic Development, 1968), p. 154.

214 José Yglesias quote: José Yglesias, "Down East Almanac," *New York Times Magazine*, 6 October 1985, p. 90.

214 Maine underemployment problems as poverty cause: Joyce Benson et al., *Poverty in Maine, 1970–1980*, Vol. 1 (Augusta, Me.: Maine State Planning Office, March 1985), p. 17.

215 1960 poor statistics: Maine Agricultural Experiment Station, *Poverty in Maine*, Miscellaneous Report No. 116 (Orono: University of Maine, October 1964), p. 2; Associated Press, "22 Percent of Maine Families Are Classified as Poor," *Portland Press Herald*, 11 November 1964.

215 Late-sixties poverty statistics: Benson et al. (1985), pp. 3, 17–18; Pamela Holley Wood, "Being Poor in Rural Maine," *Salt Magazine*, December 1988, pp. 8–9.

215 Maine's poverty rank in U.S.: *Maine Handbook* (1968), p. 33; Joel Garreau, *The Nine Nations of North America* (New York: Avon Books, 1981), pp. 15–16; Clark T. Irwin, "Family Income Study Puts Maine in Cellar," *Portland Press Herald*, 2 July 1979, pp. 1, 8 (Maine ranked fiftieth with adjustments); Warren Talbot, "Maine Ranked Low In Personal Income," United Press International report in *Portland Evening Express*, 8 September 1980, p. 2 (Maine ranked forty-seventh *without* adjustments).

215 Happy Valley: William Langley, "A Slum Can Be Surrounded by Scenery," *Portland Press Herald*, 19 December 1967, p. 1A.

216 Malaga islanders still stigmatized: Deborah DuBrule, " 'You Must Be from Malago.' " *Island Journal*, No. 16 (1999), p. 53.

216 Poverty in Waldo County, 1967: William Langley, "Waldo County Close Second as Poorest," *Portland Press Herald*, 18 December 1967, p. 1A.

216 Ervins Bubier's junk pile: Mark Childs, "Piecing Together a Year," *Salt Magazine*, December 1988, pp. 17–32.

216 Phippen's descriptions of Maine, biography: Sanford Phippen, *The Messiah in the Memorial Gym and Other Writings 1973–1998* (Nobleboro, Me.: Blackberry Books, 1998), pp. 77–78.

216 Phippen quotes: Author's interview, Sanford Phippen, writer, Orono, Me., 5 December 2002.

218 Transformation of Boothbay Harbor: See "Saving Boothbay Harbor," *Maine Times*, 13 May 1977, pp. 16–17.

218 Tim Sample quotes: Jeff Clark et al., "Voices of Maine," *Down East*, 1989 Annual, p. 52.

219 Maine in-migration and Ploch's studies: Peggy Fisher, "Learning Who They Are," *Maine Times*, 27 August 1976, p. 12; *Maine Sunday Telegram*, 23 January 1977, p. 20; Jeff Clark, "Why the In-Migration Continues," *Maine Times*, 25 September 1981, p. 18.

220 Waldoboro study by Bates students: Alice Sproul, Carl Flora, and James McKusick, "The Impact on a Sample Community," *Maine Times*, 27 August 1976, pp. 14–16.

220 Walter Trundy's comments: David Littleton-Taylor, interview with Walter F. Trundy, recorded at Stockton Springs, Me., 27 June 1973, Maine Folklife Center, University of Maine, Tape 767 NA767.

221 Joyce Benson's quote: Author's telephone interview, Joyce Benson, State Planning Office, Portland/Augusta, Me., 22 January 2003.

221 *Farmstead* editor: Alumni notes article on Terrence Day, *Colby Magazine*, Fall 2000.

221 In-migration, 1970–80: "Migration Detailed," *Maine Times*, 13 August 1982, p. 9; Jeff Clark, "Why the In-Migration Continues," *Maine Times*, 25 September 1981, p. 18.

221 Condominium boom: Dennis Bailey, "The Recession Proof Gold Coast," *Maine Times*, 13 August 1982, pp. 3–5.

222 Tourism statistics (1985): Maine State Development Office, *Maine Tourism Study 1984–85*, Vol. 2 (Kenosha, Wis.: Center for Survey and Marketing Research, University of Wisconsin–Parkside, February 1986), p. 1; "The Saturated South," *Salt Magazine*, August 1987, p. 9.

222 Ann Little quote: Sherine Adeli, "Seaside Tourism: Where Millions Meet on the Street," *Salt Magazine*, August 1987, p. 17.

222 Maine Tourism Bureau campaigns: *Maine: The Way Life Should Be* (Augusta, Me.: Maine Office of Business Development, 1988), p. 11.

223 Growth of catches, fleet 1976–79: Peter B. Doeringer, Philip I. Moss, and David G. Terkla, *The New England Fishing Economy: Jobs, Income, and Kinship* (Amherst: University of Massachusetts Press, 1986), pp. 26–29.

224 James Wilson quotes: Author's interview, James Wilson, Professor of Marine Policy, University of Maine, Orono, Me., 5 December 2002.

225 NEFMC backs down to groundfishermen: Doeringer et al. (1986), pp. 27–28.

225 Widespread cheating circa 1977: "Illegal Catches Swell N.E. Market, Making Hard Times Even Harder," *National Fisherman*, July 1980, p. 4; author's telephone interview, Peter Shelley, Conservation Law Foundation, Portland/Rockland, Me., 23 January 2003.

226 U.S. and Canadian claims: International Court of Justice, *Case Concerning Delimitation of the Maritime Boundary in the Gulf of Maine Area: Memorial Submitted by the U.S.A.*, Court Brief, The Hague: 22 September 1982, pp. 86–94; Note from the Department of State to the Embassy of Canada, 20 September 1978, reproduced in ICJ, *Case Concerning . . . : Documentary Annexes: USA, Volume 4*, Court Brief, The Hague: 1984, Annex 66. The entire thirty-volume case file can be found at the University of Southern Maine Law Library in Portland.

226 Machias Seal Island dispute: Note No. 126 from the Embassy of Canada to the Department of State, 22 December 1976; Note No. 221 from the Embassy of Canada to the Department of State, 26 May 1977; both reproduced in ICJ, *Documentary Annexes: USA, Volume 4*, Annex 66.

227 Canadian complaints about U.S. management, Johnston quote: Mike Flemming, " 'All Out Fishing' Expected," *Halifax Chronicle-Herald*, 3 June 1978, p. 1.

227 U.S. tactics, Senate opinion in negotiations: Lovell (1980), quoting Library of Congress assessment of fisheries treaty, p. 8A; author's telephone interview, Peter Shelley, Conservation Law Foundation, Portland/Rockland, Me., 23 January 2003.

227 Mid-1980s on Georges Bank: Dobbs (2000), pp. 58–59, 104–111.

228 Congressional letters to Commerce: Letter from Gerry Studds and Don Young to Commerce Secretary Malcolm Baldrige, 19 May 1987; letter from William Cohen, George Mitchell, Edward Kennedy, John Kerry, John Chafee, and Claiborne Pell to Acting Commerce Secretary Clarence Brown, 6 August 1987.

229 Fishermen catching 70 percent of groundfish: Scott Allen, "Georges Bank: Comeback Is No Sure Thing," *Boston Globe*, 19 December 1994, p. 29; Dobbs (2000), p. 67 (quoting Steve Murawski of NMFS).

229 Ecological damage by trawlers: Janet Raloff, "Fishing for Answers: Deep Trawls Leave Destruction in Their Wake, But for How Long?," *Science News*, 26 October 1996, pp. 268–269, 271; Jeremy Collie, "Studies in New England of Fishing Gear Impacts on the Sea Floor," in Eleanor Dorsey and Judith Pederson (eds.), *Effects of Fishing Gear on the Sea Floor of New England* (Boston: Conservation Law Foundation, 1998), pp. 53–61; Bigelow (1953), pp. 48–49; Lance Garrison and Jason Link, "Fishing Effects on Spatial Distribution and Trophic Guild Structure of the Fish Community in the Georges

Bank Region," *Journal of Marine Science*, Vol. 57 (2000), pp. 723–730; author's interview, Les Watling, oceanographer, Walpole, Me., 27 May 1997.

229 CLF intervention: Author's interview, Shelley; Dobbs (2000), p. 59.

230 Maine vessels on Georges Bank (1977–1991): ICJ, *Case Concerning . . . Counter-Memorial Submitted by the U.S.A.*, Court Brief, The Hague: 28 June 1983, pp. 73–74.

230 Gulf of Maine cod collapse, closures: Allen (1994), p. 29; Andrew Weegar, "New Regulations on Cod Likely Too Little, Too Late," *Maine Times*, 18 December 1997, p. 12; John Richardson, "Gulf of Maine Cod at 'Lowest Level Ever,' " *Portland Press Herald*, 4 December 1998, p. 1A; Scott Allen, "A Top N.E. Fishing Ground Collapses," *Boston Globe*, 4 December 1998, p. 1A; John Richardson, "Gulf of Maine Cod Collapses Threaten All-Out Ban," *Portland Press Herald*, 6 December 1998, p. 1A; Dobbs (2000), pp. 59–60.

230 Regulations in Gulf, 1997–99: NMFS Northeast Fisheries Science Center Press Release No. NR99-05, "Fishing Restrictions to Protect Gulf of Maine Cod Go into Effect May 1," 30 April 1999; NMFS Northeast Fisheries Science Center Press Release No. NR00-19, "Federal Court Upholds Rules Intended to Rebuild Depleted Dogfish Stock," 3 August 2000.

SEVEN: **Triumph of the Commons**

235 Importance of marine snow: Robert S. Steneck, e-mail to author, 16 August 2001, 0842 EST; Robert S. Steneck, e-mail to author, 10 September 2001, 1111 EST.

237 Horse mussels, other ecological features at Thread of Life: Ibid.; Kenneth L. Gosner, *A Field Guide to the Atlantic Seashore from the Bay of Fundy to Cape Hatteras* (Boston: Houghton Mifflin, 1978), pp. 96–97, 146–147, 246, 266–270.

239 Lobster densities: Robert S. Steneck and Carl J. Wilson, "Large-Scale and Long-Term Spatial and Temporal Patterns in Demography and Landings of the American Lobster, Homarus Americanus, in Maine," *Marine and Freshwater Research*, No. 52 (2001), pp. 1309–1319.

239 Steneck quotes: Author's telephone interview, Robert S. Steneck, Walpole, Me., 11 December 2002; author's telephone interview, Robert S. Steneck, Washington, D.C./Townsend, Australia, 20 November 2000.

240 Concerns about stock in 1965: Bill Caldwell, "Whither the Lobster," *Portland Sunday Telegram*, 30 May 1965, p. 1D.

240 Concerns about stock in 1978: Tom Bradley, "Maine Lobster-Fishing Collapse Forecast," *Portland Press Herald*, 28 March 1978, pp. 1, 8.

240 1979 landings, 1980 concerns about stock: Sheila Wellehan, "Lobster Industry Snaps Back," *Portland Press Herald*, 30 June 1980, p. 1.

240 Increase in full-time lobstermen, 1973–1998: James M. Acheson, "Confounding the Goals of Management: Response of the Maine Lobster Industry to a Trap Limit," *North American Journal of Fisheries Management*, Vol. 21, No. 2 (May 2001), pp. 409–412; A. M. Huq and H. I. Hasey, *Socio-Economic Impact of Changes in the Harvesting Labor Force in the Maine Lobster Fishery* (Washington, D.C.: National Marine Fisheries Service, Economic Research Division, 1973), p. 1.

241 Increase in traps, 1980–1999: Acheson (2001), p. 407.

241 Official landings statistics, 1965–2002: www.state.me.us/dmr/commercialfishing/lobster.htm.

241 Importance of lobster to Maine economy: Trevor Corson, "Stalking the American Lobster," *The Atlantic Monthly*, April 2002, p. 62.

242 Maine laws to protect lobsters from competition: Jim Brunelle, "Expensive Lobster Under Attack in Legislature," *Portland Press Herald*, 15 February 1973, pp. 1, 12; Emery Stevens, "Lobster Meat Laws Ruled Illegal," *Maine Sunday Telegram*, 31 March 1968, p. 15A.

242 Lobster anatomy, sensory, feeding, burrowing habits: Francis H. Herrick, "Natural History of the American Lobster," *Bulletin of the United States Fish Commission*, Vol. 29 for 1909 (Washington, D.C.: Government Printing Office, 1911), pp. 177–189, 219–237.

244 Winsor Watson quotes: Author's interview, Winsor Watson, University of New Hampshire zoologist, Durham, N.H., 26 November 2002.

245 Long-distance migrations: Peter Lawton and Katie Lavalli, "Postlarval, Juvenile, Adolescent, and Adult Ecology," in J. R. Factor, *Biology of the Lobster Homarus americanus* (San Diego: Academic Press, 1995), pp. 47–88; Herrick (1911), pp. 180–181.

245 Diane Cowan biography and quotes: Author's interview, Diane Cowan, Lobster Conservancy, Friendship Long Island, Me., 26 October 2000.

245 Cowan's work on lobster courtship: Diane F. Cowan and Jelle Atema, "Moult Staggering and Serial Monogamy in American Lobsters, *Homarus Americanus*," *Animal Behavior*, No. 39 (1990), pp. 199–206; Diane F. Cowan, "The Role of Olfaction in Courtship Behavior of the American Lobster *Homarus Americanus*," *Biological Bulletin*, No. 181 (December 1991), pp. 402–7; Diane Cowan, "Serial Monogamy in *Homarus Americanus*," *The Lobster Newsletter*, Lobster Conservancy, July 1990; Paul J. Bushmann and Jelle Atema, "Chemically Mediated Mate Location and Evaluation in the Lobster, *Homarus Americanus*," *Journal of Chemical Ecology*, Vol. 26, No. 4 (2000), pp. 883–899.

246 Molting process: Herrick (1911), pp. 200–212.

247 Copulation: Cowan (1990); Cowan and Atema (1990), p. 199; author's interview with Cowan.

247 **Sperm and egg storage, development, release:** Corson (2002), p. 75; Herrick (1911), pp. 213, 298–299; T. M. Prudden, *About Lobsters* (Freeport, Me.: Bond Wheelright Company, 1962), pp. 25–26.

248 **Egg-supply theories:** "Are Lobsters Overfished?," *Maine Times*, 8 June 2000; Jean Marbella, "Boiling Over Lobsters," *Baltimore Sun*, 30 August 1998.

248–250 **Steneck's and Wahle's work:** Author's telephone interview, Robert S. Steneck, Portland/Walpole, Me., 11 December 2002; author's telephone interview, Robert S. Steneck, Washington, D.C./Townsend, Australia, 20 November 2000; author's telephone interview, Richard A. Wahle, Washington, D.C./ Boothbay Harbor, Me., 29 November 2000; Author's telephone interview, Richard A. Wahle, Portland/Boothbay Harbor, Me., 20 December 2002; Richard A. Wahle, "Recruitment, Habitat Selection, and the Impact of Predators on the Early Benthic Phase of the American Lobster," doctoral dissertation, Orono, Me.: University of Maine, 1990; Lewis S. Incze, Richard A. Wahle, and Alvaro T. Palma, "Advection and Settlement Rates in a Benthic Invertebrate: Recruitment to First Benthic Stage in *Homarus Americanus*," *Journal of Marine Science*, No. 57 (2000), pp. 430–437; Steneck and Wilson (2001).

250 **Cowan's work on Friendship Long Island:** My visit with Diane Cowan took place on 26 October 2000. See also Colin Woodard, "Maine's Catch," *The Chronicle of Higher Education*, 5 January 2001, p. 19. The results of Cowan's expanded fieldwork are found in Sara L. Ellis and Diane F. Cowan, *Intertidal Lobster Monitoring Program: Penobscot Bay Lobster Collaborative 1998–1999* (Friendship, Me.: Lobster Conservancy, October 1999).

252 **Incze's work:** Author's telephone interview, Lewis S. Incze, Wiscasset/ Walpole, Me., 27 October 2000.

252 **Rosenberg footnote:** Author's interview, Andrew Rosenberg, San Diego, 17 November 2003.

253 **Pettigrew quote:** Author's telephone interview, Neal R. Pettigrew, Washington, D.C./Walpole, Me., 15 November 2000.

254 **Elderkin quotes:** Author's interview, Jennifer Elderkin, lobsterman, Southport, Me., 22 July 2002.

254 **Lobster boat design evolution:** C. Richard Lunt, "Lobsterboat Building on the Eastern Coast of Maine," Ph.D. dissertation, Bloomington, Ind.: Indiana University, December 1975; Lincoln P. Paine, *Down East: A Maritime History of Maine* (Gardiner, Me.: Tilbury House, 2000), pp. 127–131.

257 **V-notch surveys, Wilson quote:** Author's telephone interview, Carl Wilson, Department of Marine Resources, Portland/Boothbay Harbor, Me., 10 December 2002.

259 **Lobster trap video:** Author's interview, Winsor Watson, University of New Hampshire zoologist, Durham, N.H., 26 November 2002; Steven H. Jury, Hunt Howell, Daniel F. O'Grady, and Winsor H. Watson, "Lobster Trap

Video: *In Situ* Video Surveillance of the Behaviour of *Homarus americanus* in and around Traps," *Marine and Freshwater Research*, Vol. 52 (2001), pp. 1125–32; author's telephone interview, Pat White, Maine Lobstermen's Association, Portland/York, Me., 18 December 2002.

262 **William Atwood:** Author's interview, William Atwood, Atwood Lobster Company, Sprucehead Island, Me., 26 July 2002.

263 **French Christmas lobster:** "Vive le Homard!," *Down East*, December 1990, p. 32.

264 **Corroding lobster aircraft:** Mike Brown, "Playing the Lobster Game," *Down East*, November 1984, pp. 64, 66.

265 **Air traffic strike:** "Lobster Crisis," *Down East*, November 1981, p. 28.

265 **Growth of Maine, U.S. exports 1995–2000:** W. William Anderson, former chairman of the Maine Lobster Promotion Council, Letter to the Editor, *Boothbay Register*, 15 March 2001; Joel Chetrick, "U.S. Lobster Lands a Big Success in the EU," *Fishery Products Market News*, January 2003, p. 9.

266 **Nova Scotian exports to Asia:** Communications Nova Scotia, "Fisheries—Lobster Breaking into New Markets," Press Release CNS 822 (Halifax, N.S.: Government of Nova Scotia, 20 November 1996).

266 **Lobster value ranking in U.S., Canada:** Canadian Department of Agriculture, "All About Canada's Fish and Seafood Industry," atn-riae.agr.ca/seafood/industry-e.htm. Viewed 8 January 2003; National Marine Fisheries Service, *Fisheries of the United States 2001* (Washington, D.C.: GPO, September 2002), p. viii.

266 **Hardin's article:** Garrett Hardin, "The Tragedy of the Commons," *Science*, Vol. 162 (1968), pp. 1243–1248.

267 **Thomas Hobbes:** Thomas Hobbes, *Leviathan* (London: 1651); "Thomas Hobbes" in *Encyclopedia Britannica*; David Ralph Matthews, *Controlling Common Property* (Toronto: University of Toronto Press, 1993), pp. 71–73; Elinor Ostrom, *Governing the Commons* (New York: Cambridge University Press, 1990), pp. 8–9, 23. The effects of the enclosure movement on Devon are discussed in chapter four of this book.

267 **Success of English commons:** Jeremy Rifkin, *Biosphere Politics* (New York: Crown Publishers, 1991), pp. 38–39.

268 **Examples of other successful commons:** Ward H. Goodenough, "Property, Kind, and Community on Truk," *Yale University Publications in Anthropology No. 46* (New Haven, Conn.: Yale University Press, 1951), p. 41; Edvard Hviding and Eyolf Jul-Larsen, *Community-Based Resource Management in Tropical Fisheries* (Windhoek: University of Namibia, 1995), pp. 44–46; R. E. Johannes, "Traditional Law of the Sea in Micronesia," *Micronesica*, Vol. 13 (December 1977), pp. 121–126; Ostrom (1990), pp. 61–65.

268 **James Acheson and lobster territories:** Author's interview, James M.

Acheson, University of Maine, Orono, Me., 5 December 2002; James M. Acheson, *The Lobster Gangs of Maine* (Hanover, N.H.: University Press of New England, 1988), pp. xi–xii.

269 Territories and harbor gangs: Acheson (1988), pp. 48–83.

270 Jean Symonds example: Author's interview, Jean Symonds, lobsterman, Corea, Me., 29 July 2002; author's interview, Colby Young, lobsterman and boatyard owner, Corea, Me., 29 July 2002; Muriel L. Hendrix, "Washing Ashore and Finding a Niche in Corea," *Island Journal*, Vol. 19 (2002), pp. 64–67.

271 Harvey Crowley quote: Author's interview, Harvey Crowley, retired lobsterman, Corea, Me., 29 July 2002.

271 Shafmaster incident: Christine Kukka, "Gear Towed to Canada in Latest Lobster War," *Portland Press Herald*, 7 December 1988, pp. 1, 12.

271 Matinicus cedes Seal Island: Francis P. Bowles and Margaret C. Bowles, "Holding the Line: Property Rights in the Lobster and Herring Fisheries of Matinicus Island, Maine," in John Cordell (ed.), *A Sea of Small Boats* (Cambridge, Mass.: Cultural Survival Inc., 1989), p. 237.

271 Lobster wars: Bowles and Bowles (1989), p. 237; Acheson (1988), p. 74; author's interview, Stanley Tupper, attorney, Boothbay Harbor, Me., 9 October 2001; Kim Clark, "Fraction Fuels Lobster War," *Portland Press Herald*, 22 November 1982, p. 1, 16.

272 Lobstermen vs. scientists: Author's interview, Colby Young, lobsterman, Corea, Me., 29 July 2002; author's interview, James Wilson, Professor of Marine Policy, University of Maine, Orono, Me., 5 December 2002.

273 David Norton: Author's interview, David Norton, lobsterman, Boothbay, Me., 15 December 2002.

276 Lobster zones established: James M. Acheson and Laura Taylor, "The Anatomy of the Maine Lobster Comanagement Law," *Society and Natural Resources*, Vol. 14 (2001), pp. 425–441; James M. Acheson, "Confounding the Goals of Management: Response of the Maine Lobster Industry to a Trap Limit," *North American Journal of Fisheries Management*, Vol. 21, No. 2 (May 2001), pp. 404–416.

277 Lobster zone feedback, problems: Author's interviews with Harvey Crowley (2002), Pat White (2002), and David Norton (2002); Acheson (2001).

EIGHT: **Brave Old World**

279 Warren widening: Author's telephone interview, Bruce Van Note, Maine Department of Transportation, Port Isabel, Tex./Winthrop, Me., 23 October 2002; author's telephone interview, Stephen Burke, Route One Advocacy Group, Wiscasset/Warren, Me., 24 July 2002; author's telephone interview, Susan Beebe, artist, Wiscasset/Camden, Me., 10 October 2002; Alice McFadden,

"Bad Day in the 'Hood," *The Free Press* (Rockland, Me.), 20 June 2002, pp. 1, 26–27; Dennis Hoey, "Where Trees Stood, Controversy Simmers," *Maine Sunday Telegram*, 23 June 2002, p. 1B; Tom Groening, "Route 90, Coastal Travel Alternative?," *Bangor Daily News*, 25 June 2002, p. B1.

281 Support for widening: Author's interview, James Raye, former mayor, Rockland, Me., 22 November 2002; author's telephone interview, Bob Hastings, Rockland Area Chamber of Commerce, Wiscasset/Rockland, Me., 9 October 2002.

282 Beebe quote: Author's telephone interview, Susan Beebe, artist, Port Isabel, Tex./Camden, Me., 10 October 2002.

282 Colgan quote: Author's telephone interview, Charles S. Colgan, University of Southern Maine, Wiscasset/Portland, Me., 9 October 2002.

282 Population growth in 1990s: All statistics are from the 2000 United States Census as posted by the *Portland Press Herald* at http://www.mainetoday.com/census2000/data/index.shtml.

283 Sherwood quotes, in-migration data: Author's telephone interview, Richard Sherwood, State Planning Office, Port Isabel, Tex./Augusta, Me., 22 October 2003; Joyce Benson and Louis A. Ploch, *In-migration to Maine: A Twenty-Year Perspective, Parts I and II*, Staff Papers REP 465, 467 (Orono: Maine Agricultural and Forest Experiment Station, August, September 1995).

283 Greater Portland sprawl: "Sprawl Rate Among Worst in US," *Portland Press Herald*, 24 July 2001, p. 1A; "Southern Maine Sprawl Among Worst in the Nation," editorial, *Maine Sunday Telegram*, 29 July 2001, p. 4C.

284 Evan Richert's predictions, analysis: Shawn O'Leary, "State Foresees Major Sprawl by 2050," *Bangor Daily News*, 16 March 2001, p. A6; Evan Richert, "A Talk on Sprawl and the Techniques to Retain the Character of a Rural Town," transcript of talk given at Edgecomb Town Hall, Edgecomb, Me., 5 March 2002; author's interview, Evan Richert, University of Southern Maine, Portland, Me., 12 April 2003.

285 Land fragmentation and wildlife: Frank O'Hara et al., *The Cost of Sprawl* (Augusta, Me.: Maine State Planning Office, May 1997), pp. 11–12; Richert interview (2002); author's interview, Amanda Russell, planner, Edgecomb, Me., 24 July 2002.

285–286 Roads, schools, police, other sprawl costs: O'Hara et al. (1997), pp. 8–10; Richert interview (2002); Evan Richert, "Edited Opening Remarks of Evan Richert, Director, State Planning Office," in *Paradox of Sprawl*, transcript of Eco/Eco Civic Forum held in Bar Harbor, Me., 30–31 October 1997, pp. 5–13.

287 Barringer quotes: Author's interview, Richard E. Barringer, University of Southern Maine, Portland, Me., 12 March 2003.

287 Changes to Maine's economy, job structure: Anthony P. Carnevale and Donna M. Desrochers, "Learning and Earning in Vacationland: Promoting Education and Economic Opportunity in Maine," *Maine Policy Review*, Winter 2002, pp. 1–8.

289 Charles Butt's apple tree: Associated Press, "Apple Tree's 20-Mile Move Makes Memorable Jam on Mount Desert," *Portland Press Herald*, 21 June 2003, p. 2B.

289 Mary Brewer's quotes, editorial: Author's interview, Mary Brewer, managing editor, *Boothbay Register*, Boothbay Harbor, Me., 9 October 2002; Mary Brewer, "The Death of the Maine Coast Native—No Exaggeration," *Boothbay Register*, 8 August 2002, p. 2.

291 Ralph W. Stanley background: Heather Wilkinson, "Boatbuilder Ralph Stanley Chosen for NEA Fellowship," *Ellsworth American*, 27 May 1999; Sandra Dismore, " 'I Need the Water, I Need the Inspiration,' " *Working Waterfront* (Rockland, Me.), November 1999.

292 Richard Stanley quotes: Author's interview, Richard Stanley, Ralph W. Stanley Boatyard, Southwest Harbor, Me., 19 May 2003.

292 Property boom and taxes in Southwest Harbor: Sara Kehaulani Goo, "Locals Are Ousted as Maine Town Gentrifies," *Wall Street Journal*, 17 October 2000.

294 David Rockefeller quotes: Author's telephone interview, David Rockefeller Jr., vice chair, National Park Foundation, Portland, Me./Cambridge, Mass., 13 May 2003.

294 Linda Sicotte story: Author's telephone interview, Linda Sicotte, Portland/Bristol, Me., 13 December 2002.

297 Charles Cawley biography, behavior: Rob Wherry, "The Green-and-Gray Monster," *Forbes*, 13 November 2000; Nicholas Varchaver, "Who's the King of Delaware," *Fortune*, 13 May 2000, pp. 124–130; Kenneth Chutchiam, "Charles Talks," *Maine Times*, 3 September 1998, p. 4; Tom Groening, "County Responds to MBNA on Airport Issue," *Bangor Daily News*, 25 September 2001, p. 3.

298 Cawley's politics: Steve Campbell, "Bush Comes to Maine This Week to Raise Money for GOP," *Portland Press Herald*, 11 June 2000, p. 2C; Robert Long et al., "MBNA's Campaign Clout Grows," *News Journal* (Wilmington, Del.), 12 March 2000, p. 1A; Paula Dwyer, "Tougher Bankruptcy Laws—Comliments of MBNA?," *Business Week*, 26 February 2001, p. 43; "MBNA Big Donor Behind Debtor Bill," *Maine Sunday Telegram*, 22 July 2001, p. 1A. Detailed information on campaign contributions is available from the Center for Responsive Politics at www.opensecrets.org.

298 MBNA expansion, philanthropy: Lynn Blumenstein, "$1 Million Gift to Rockland Public Library," *Library Journal*, 1 January 2000, p. 25; Kimberly Blanton, "Culture Clash in Maine Town," *Boston Globe*, 20 February 1996; Clarke Canfield, "As MBNA Grows Strong, So Does Presence Here," *Port-*

land Press Herald, 14 March 1999, p. 1B; Andy Kekacs, "An Issuer of Credit Cards . . . and Good Will to Many Maine Communities," *Waterville Morning Sentinel*, 19 August 2001, p. A1; Edgar Allen Beem, "The Wyeths' World," *Boston Globe*, 26 July 1998.

299 Paul Cartwright quotes: Author's interview, Paul Cartwright, carpenter and selectman, Camden, Me., 22 November 2002.

299 Criticisms of MBNA: Edgar Allen Beem, "Painting the Town Green," *Maine Times*, 13 May 1994, p. 2; Blanton (1996).

300 James Raye quotes: Author's interview, James Raye, former Rockland mayor, Rockland, Me., 22 November 2002.

301 Laurie LaChance quotes: Author's telephone interview, Laurie LaChance, State Planning Office, Portland/Augusta, Me., 10 April 2003.

301 Two Maines phenomenon: "Two Maines," editorial, *Bangor Daily News*, 19 September 1998; Wayne E. Reilly and Michael McDonald, "The Gulf Between the Two Maines Is Widening," *Bangor Daily News*, 12 September 1998, p. 1.

302 Northern Maine secessionists: Mary Ann Lagasse, "Statehood the Goal for Group in Kingman," *Bangor Daily News*, 23 October 1997; Bill Nemitz, "Breaking Up Maine Is Hard to Do," *Portland Press Herald*, 18 October 1997; Jeffrey K. Jacob, "North Massachusetts," letter to the editor, *Bangor Daily News*, 17 November 1998; Ray Leighton, "Two Maines Solution," *Bangor Daily News*, 17 September 1998.

303 Ed Suslovic quotes: Author's telephone interview, Ed Suslovic, realtor, Port Isabel, Tex./Portland, Me., 22 October 2002.

303 Chamberlains, Dunstan Crossing development: Author's interview, John Chamberlain, Saco and Scarborough, Me., 11 April 2003; Ryan Blethen, "Councilors Endorse Dunstan Corner Plan," *Portland Press Herald*, 22 August 2002; Tom Bell, "Great American Neighborhood May Come to Scarborough," *Portland Press Herald*, 24 June 2001.

304 New Urbanist solutions: Author's interview, Andres Duany, town planner, Portland, Me./Miami, Fla., 10 April 2002; see also Andres Duany, Elizabeth Plater-Zyberk, and Jeff Speck, *Suburban Nation: The Rise of Sprawl and the Decline of the American Dream* (New York: North Point Press, 2000); Colin Woodard, "Sprawling 'Burbs Tighten Up," *Christian Science Monitor*, 22 May 2003, p. 16.

304 SPO's homebuyer survey: Evan D. Richert, *Markets for Traditional Neighborhoods* (Augusta, Me.: Maine State Planning Office, August 1999), pp. 5, 28.

304–305 John DelVecchio quotes: Author's telephone interview, John DelVecchio, State Planning Office, Port Isabel, Tex./Augusta, Me., 12 July 2002.

305 Dunstan Crossing voted down: Mark Peters, "Voters Reject 'Great Neighborhood,' " *Portland Press Herald*, 30 July 2003, p. 1A.

306 Nigel Calder quotes: Author's interview, Nigel Calder, writer, Alna, Me., 8 October 2002.

308 GoMoos: Author's interview, Philip Bogden, GoMoos CEO, Portland, Me., 7 April 2003; Hauke L. Kite-Powell and Charles Colgan, *The Potential Economic Benefits of Coastal Ocean Observing Systems: The Gulf of Maine* (Washington, D.C.: NOAA, Office of Naval Research, and the Woods Hole Oceanographic Institution, December 2001), p. 11; author's telephone interview, Lew Incze, University of Southern Maine, Portland/Portland, Me., 6 March 2003.

309 David Norton quotes: Author's interview, David Norton, lobsterman, Boothbay, Me., 15 December 2002.

309 National ocean observing plans: Meredith Goad, "Scientists Studying Ocean Data Network," *Portland Press Herald*, 12 June 2003, p. 1B; National Office for Integrated and Sustained Ocean Observations, *An Integrated and Sustained Ocean Observing System for the United States* (Arlington, Va.: Oceans.US, 23 May 2002).

310 Multibeam sonar: Author's interview, Larry A. Mayer, University of New Hampshire, Durham, N.H., 9 April 2003; author's interview, Randy Cutter, University of New Hampshire, Durham, N.H., 9 April 2003; author's telephone interview, John Hughes Clarke, University of New Brunswick, Portland, Me./Fredericton, N.B., 15 April 2003. In the summer of 2003, much of UNH's imagery was available on its website at www.ccomm.unh.edu.

312 Les Watling quotes: Author's telephone interview, Les Watling, Darling Marine Center, Portland/Walpole, Me., 21 May 2003.

313 Marine protected areas: Author's telephone interview, Bill Ballantine, Leigh Marine Laboratory, Washington, D.C./Leigh, New Zealand, 1 August 2001. See also Colin Woodard, *Ocean's End: Travels Through Endangered Seas* (New York: Basic Books, 2000), pp. 234–235, 140–142; Colin Woodard, "A Beacon of Hope for an Ocean Birthright," *Conservation Matters*, Fall 2001.

313 Jane Lubchenco quotes: Author's telephone interview, Jane Lubchenco, Oregon State University, Portland, Me./Corvallis, Ore., 29 April 2003.

314 Gulf of Maine Research Institute: Author's interview, Don Perkins, Gulf of Maine Research Institute, Portland, Me., 7 March 2003; "Research Programs," white paper, Gulf of Maine Aquarium, 2003.

316 Bangor Wal-Mart protests: Mark Peters, "Battle Over Proposed Bangor Wal-Mart Polarizes Community," *Portland Press Herald*, 29 June 2003, pp. 1A, 8A.

318 Bill and Doug Boynton quotes: Author's interview, Douglas Boynton, lobsterman, Monhegan, Me., 19 July 2000; author's interview, Bill Boynton, art gallery owner, Monhegan, Me., 18 July 2001.

For Further Reading

For those wishing to learn more about the topics raised in the book, I highly recommend the following titles, some of which can still be found in bookstores, others in the library.

The journal of James Rosier and those of other explorers from **the early contact period** have been published numerous times over the past two centuries, and provide a fascinating window on the lost world of Wabanaki New England. The best source, if you can obtain it, is David and Alison Quinn's *The English New England Voyages 1602–1608* (1983), which includes invaluable annotation on the meaning of the sometimes mysterious passages. Emerson Baker and several fellow historians banded together to assemble *American Beginnings: Exploration, Culture, and Cartography in the Land of Norumbega* (1994), an edited volume of scholarly articles that provides a fascinating introduction to early-seventeenth-century Maine.

Readers interested in the **Puritans** and their relations with the Indians of New England will find Francis Jennings's *The Invasion of America: Indians, Colonialism, and the Cant of Conquest* (1975) particularly sobering. The **cultural origins** of the Puritans and **Scotch-Irish** are exhaustively detailed in David Hackett Fischer's fascinating *Albion's Seed: Four British Folkways in America* (1989). On the backcountry **rebellion against the Great Proprietors** I highly recommend *Liberty Men and Great Proprietors* (1990), a detailed scholarly study of resistance in the Midcoast region by historian Alan Taylor.

The finest source for information on **nineteenth-century fisheries** in Maine and, in fact, the entire United States is George Brown Goode's epic multivolume *The Fisheries and Fishery Industries of the United States* (1887), a monumental harbor-by-harbor, species-by-species survey of the industry that, sadly, has never been repeated. It can be found in many repository libraries, though I hope somebody sees fit to republish it so that it is more widely available to scholars and scientists. Also valuable—and far more easy to obtain—is Wayne O'Leary's *Maine Sea Fisheries: The Rise and Fall of a Native Industry, 1830–1930*, published in 1996.

On **lobsters and lobstering,** James Acheson's anthropological study *The Lobster Gangs of Maine* (1988) remains the seminal scholarly account. Mike Brown's funny and readable *The Great Lobster Chase* (1987) makes an excellent complement. For an introduction to current lobster research see Philip Conkling and Anne Hayden's *Lobsters Great and Small*, published by the Island Institute in 2002.

Finally, for those wishing to gain further insight into the complex relationship between **natives and summer people,** there's Sanford Phippen's 1997 novel *Kitchen Boy* (available from Maine's own Blackberry Books), Pamela Belanger's scholarly *Inventing Acadia: Artists and Tourists at Mount Desert* (1999), and Louise Dickinson Rich's *The Peninsula* (1958), a personal account of her time living in Corea, just across the road from Harvey Crowley's windswept home.

Index